D1362219

Massacre in Shansi

Massacre in Shansi

Nat Brandt

Syracuse University Press

First Edition 1994

94 95 96 97 98 99 6 5 4 3 2 1

The paper used in this publication meets the minimum requirements of American Standard for Information Sciences—Performances of Paper for Printed Library Materials, ANSI Z39.48-1984. ∞

Library of Congress Cataloging-in-Publication Data

Brandt, Nat.
Massacre in Shansi / Nat Brandt.
p. cm.
Includes bibliographical references and index.
ISBN 0-8156-0282-0 — ISBN 0-8156-0283-9 (pbk.)
1. Missions, American—China—Shansi Province. 2. Missionaries—China—Shansi Province. 3. China—HIstory—Boxer Rebellion, 1899–1901—Casualties. I. Title.
BV3420.S43B73 1994
266'.0237305117—dc20 93-41314

Manufactured in the United States of America

To my wife Yanna, without whose encouragement and editorial acumen none of my books would have been published

❁ *"The work is* slow. *Do you know what that word means? I did not before coming to China. We can freely go into any village of this great plain I suppose, but that does not mean that the people are reaching out* their *arms to receive us and the Gospel we bring. We are treated with much contempt and great indifference by the people, and from a human point of view the work seems hopeless. But the work is the Lord's and not our own."*

—*George Williams*

"When I look upon the school boys in the Chapel, and see them intently listening and taking in the subject of the meeting, and hear all their voices, in harmony, and hearty Church prayer meeting—I feel in my heart, 'It pays.'"

—*Jennie Clapp*

"The Gods assist the Boxers . . .
It is because the Foreign Devils disturb the 'Middle
Kingdom,' urging the people to join their religion . . .
No rain falls,
The earth is getting dry.
This is because the Churches stop Heaven.
The Gods are angry,
The Genii are vexed. . . .
Push aside the railroad tracks,
Pull out the telegraph poles. . . .
Let the various Foreign Devils all be killed.
May the whole elegant Empire of the Great Ching
Dynasty be ever prosperous."

—Boxer placard

A journalist by profession, Nat Brandt has been a newswriter for CBS News, a reporter on a number of newspapers, an editor on the *New York Times,* managing editor of *American Heritage,* and editor-in-chief of *Publishers Weekly.* Since 1980, Mr. Brandt has been a free-lance writer, chiefly in the area of American history. He is the author of *The Man Who Tried to Burn New York,* which won the 1987 Douglas Southall Freeman History Award; *The Town That Started the Civil War,* a Book-of-the-Month Club selection; *The Congressman Who Got Away With Murder; Con Brio: Four Russians Called the Budapest String Quartet;* and with John Sexton, *How Free Are We? What the Constitution Says We Can and Cannot Do.*

❁ Contents

Illustrations

ILLUSTRATIONS

MAPS

❁ *Preface*

The nineteenth century witnessed a constant, continuing clash between European rivals that would lead, eventually, to their meeting on the battlegrounds of World War I. Outside of the Continent, their competition for colonial domination fastened first on Africa, then on China. The huge "dark" continent of the former—a composite of scattered, mostly unrelated small kingdoms—fell easily to Western powers. In China, however, the Europeans encountered a more determined people, and a civilization that had once been a leader in the arts, industry, and commerce. The European encroachments were successful chiefly because they coincided with the decline of the Ching dynasty of the Manchus. But whatever the falterings of the Manchus were, they did not diminish the pride of the Chinese people in their history and culture. They had given the world the printing press, paper, the compass, gunpowder.

The Europeans who went to China pressed on them opium, manufactured cotton goods, and other wares and wanted to build for them and operate railroad lines, string telegraph poles, dig coal and ore mines, and, in the process, convert them to Christianity. The two civilizations—Chinese and Western European—represented, respectively, the past and the future. They were on a collision course, one that still resonates.

Chinese opposition to the foreign incursions led to several wars in the nineteenth century, and finally to the most publicized eruption of them all, the Boxer Rebellion of 1900. During the brief four months at the height of the uprising, the death toll was staggering among missionaries and their converts: An estimated total of at least 32,000 Chinese Christians were slain. More than 185 Protestant missionaries and members of their families, and 47 Roman Catholic clerics and nuns were killed, as well. It was the greatest single tragedy in the history of Christian evangelicalism. Like their counterparts who have been killed in recent times in Latin America and Africa, the missionaries had no overt political agenda, but they represented ideas repugnant to the very people they were trying to help or convert.

A microcosm of this clash of cultures is reflected in the lives of a small group of Protestant missionaries who were trapped in the craze of the Boxer Rebellion. Their names appear on bronze tablets on the only monument in America ever erected to individuals who died in that uprising, the Memorial Arch on the campus of Oberlin College in Oberlin, Ohio. There were eighteen of them—six men, seven women, and five children—all associated with the American Board of Commissioners for Foreign Missions—the ABCFM, or American Board, for short. Fifteen of them were connected by birth, schooling, or marriage to Oberlin College and attached to the American Board's "Oberlin-in-China" Shansi Mission. The remaining three missionaries were members of the American Board's neighboring North China Mission.

This book is their story, told from their perspective and through their eyes—a Western, American viewpoint, flawed by the missionaries' lack of knowledge about China and the Chinese. In many ways, sympathizers who witnessed their tribulations and deaths, as well as missionaries who survived, glorified these "martyrs" at the expense of consideration of any Chinese who perished with them or because of them during the Boxer Rebellion.

This book, then, is also the story of the Chinese who were their friends and associates—who worked with them, prayed with them, and died with them.

It is easy to find the words to describe, in general terms, the missionaries whose story is told in these pages. They were dedicated, devoted, persistent, idealistic, hard-working, well-meaning, spiritually motivated. In this sense, they represented a multitude of young men and women in the latter half of the nineteenth century—particularly in England and the United States—who burned with a passion to bring the Gospel to the peoples of the world that were not Christian. Spurred by the fever of a great religious revival, they were eager to teach the great mass of unbelievers the Truth lest they die in ignorance and without hope of salvation.

These same missionaries can also be described as self-righteous, arrogant, bigoted, narrow-minded, and uncompromising. It is easy to condemn them in such terms. But they mirrored all the flaws, prejudices, and viewpoints of their heritage, an attitude of superiority fostered in great part by the astounding advances of western civilization as a result of the Industrial Revolution. The missionaries believed unquestioningly that such advances could not have taken place anywhere but in a Christian world. "Now we realize the great vision of Columbus, and reach the Indies by the West," a special committee of the American Board reported in 1852. "The barrier of ages is broken; and the heart of China is now open to the direct influence of Protestant America."[1]

The missionaries were who they were—creatures of their time and place. But they were something else, too. Like most Americans in the nineteenth century, most missionaries were, by and large, unsophisticated in the ways of the world. Incredibly naïve, their views of international politics were simplistic. Few of them understood the ramifications of the actions of the so-called Powers that had already fought over huge sections of Africa and were in the process of *gua-fen*, "carving up the melon," China. Most of them did not or could not comprehend what the impact of the two great cultures—Chinese and Western—careening head-on, about to crash, would be. They did not seem to realize that they, as missionaries, were the carriers and spreaders of Western ideas and mores and might be caught in the middle when the collision came.

Most missionaries in China tried to remain aloof from other foreigners and to avoid political entanglements. They frowned on the greed and licentiousness of the European merchants who lived in great wealth and ease in enclaves in cities such as Canton and Tientsin. They also shied from contact with diplomats whose conduct of living bordered on the hedonistic.

In turn, they—the missionaries—were looked on as outcasts by those other foreigners. They were ridiculed as pompous and rigid moralists, disdained as social equals, and considered chronic complainers. Which is ironic, because, to the Chinese, who made no subtle distinctions, the missionary became the embodiment of all despised foreigners, and symbolic of the political intimidation known as gunboat diplomacy. In an empire of some four hundred million people, relatively few Chinese ever saw, much less met, a foreigner. In the interior, away from the coastal trade cities or Peking, the foreigner with whom the Chinese did have contact was never a diplomat or a merchant. It was a missionary. And it was on the missionary that they vented most of their hostility during the Boxer Rebellion. No diplomat or merchant was ever reported slain in the provinces of Shansi or Shantung in the summer of 1900, but those provinces were where several hundred Protestant and Catholic missionaries were killed—as were thousands upon thousands of their converts.

The schism that developed between the Chinese, on the one hand, and the missionaries and other foreigners, on the other, is best illustrated by the terms they applied to one another. To the Chinese, all foreigners were barbarians or *yang kuei-tzu*—"foreign devils." Chinese converts were *erh mao tzu*—"secondary devils" or "second hairy ones." The term for Catholicism—*T'ien-chu chiao*—could be written in Chinese characters that had the same sound but which meant "the squeal of the celestial hog."

To the missionaries, all Chinese were "heathens," a word they used over and over again without regard to four thousand years of Chinese history or any sensitivity to the combination of religious thought that permeated Chinese life—Confucianism, Taoism, and Buddhism. Only their converts deserved better; the missionaries called them "Christians." They added a "Mr." or "Mrs." when the Chinese person was an adult who worked for them in a teaching or preaching capacity, or they gave them a western name such as Lois or Ruth.

The missionaries were unaware that they were witness to, and would become victims of, the great upheaval taking place in China. They have would been shocked to learn that a generation afterwards the Boxers were already being regarded as anti-imperialist patriots, or that later, under the Communists, they and their female counterparts, the Red Lanterns, who played a minor role in the movement, would be lionized as heroes of a new order.

NAT BRANDT
New York City
January 1994

❁ *Acknowledgments*

This is the second book I have written that entailed doing the major portion of the research in the Archives of Oberlin College. As with the first book, I am in particular debt to the college archivist, Roland Baumann, for his unstinting assistance and support. He and his staff graciously provided every means available to them to make my visit productive. And they offered research leads and insights that were particularly helpful to me. I am grateful to all of them—Brian Williams, assistant archivist; Valerie S. Komor, project archivist, and Patricia K. Delewski, departmental assistant.

Others at Oberlin deserve my thanks, too: Ray English, director of libraries, who made available to me the services of the Oberlin College Library, and all the members of his staff; Dina Schoonmaker, the library's curator of special collections and preservation officer, who scoured her collections for material for me; and Carl W. Jacobson, executive director of the Oberlin Shansi Memorial Association, and his assistant, Debbie Jenkins, who made my research visit to Oberlin possibly. Dr. Jacobson was especially helpful in vetting several chapters that relate to Shansi, secret societies, and OSMA. Also, Professor James Geiss of Princeton University made a number of helpful suggestions, for which I am grateful. (Any mistakes, errors of judgment, or misrepresentations are, of course, mine.)

I owe thanks as well to a number of librarians and archivists at other institutions who went out of their way to make my task easier. They include Alan C. Aimone, chief, Special Collections, United States Military Academy, West Point; Dr. Harold Field Worthley, librarian, The Congregational Library, Boston; Martha Lund Smalley, archivist, and her assistant, Joan Duffy, of the Yale Divinity School Library, New Haven; and Kermit J. Pike, director of the Western Reserve Historical Society, with whose kind permission I have quoted from the letters, in the society's possession, written by Charles and Eva Price to Charles Oviatt Hale.

David Liu gave kindly of his time to help with the transliteration of Chinese words and expressions transliterated in letters written by missionaries.

As usual, I could not have written this book without the encouragement, patience, and advice of my wife, Yanna.

The book epigraphs are from the following sources: George Williams to Judson Smith, February 14, 1893, Papers, American Board of Commissioners for Foreign Missions to Asia, 1827–1919, Shansi Mission (ABC 16.3.15), reel 321, Houghton Library, Harvard University; Jennie Clapp to "My dearest Mary Ella," November 10, 1899, Papers of Chauncy N. Pond, 1892–1919, Oberlin College Archives; Robert E. Speer, *A Memorial of Horace Tracy Pitkin* (New York: Fleming H. Revell, 1903), 267–69.

The chapter epigraphs are from the following sources: Those from Confucius are from Chester C. Tan, *The Boxer Catastrophe* (New York: Octagon, 1976), and James Legge, *Confucius: Confucian Analects, The Great Learning and the Doctrine of the Mean* (New York: Dover, 1971); for chapter 16, Isaac Ketler, *The Tragedy at Paotingfu* (New York: Fleming H. Revell, 1902), 377; for chapter 17, sermon by Rev. Thomas Wellesley Pigott on June 24, 1900, Papers of Lydia Lord Davis, 1862–1944, Oberlin College Archives; for chapter 19, *Oxford Dictionary of Quotations* (New York: Oxford Univ. Press, 1955), 542; for chapter 20, Lizzie Atwater to "Dear, dear Ones," August 3, 1900 (reprint, *Oberlin News*, December 25, 1900).

The biblical passages quoted in the text are from a King James version of the Bible published in 1844 by the American Bible Society that is in the Special Collections division of the Oberlin College Library.

❁ A Note on Transliteration

The reader will encounter a particular difficulty should he/she glance at a modern-day map of China or read a history of China written within the last decade or so and try to locate cities mentioned in this text or the individuals who were involved in the events it covers. In the latter part of the twentieth century, the People's Republic of China introduced a system of transliteration of Chinese into English called *pin-yin* in an attempt to correct the old methods of romanization of Chinese names and words, which were arbitraty and often misleading as to pronunciation. *J*'s became mixed with *r*'s, and *p*'s with *b*'s. But *pin-yin* often leads to further confusion because it is based on the sounds of the letters of the Cyrillic alphabet. (Thus *x*, for example, is pronounced as if it were *sh.*) In addition, *pin-yin* presumably follows the old court pronunciation of Peking dialect, which is quite unlike other dialects, as the missionaries who served in Shansi Province in the nineteenth century discovered.

In *pin-yin*, Peking—or Peiching, as it was sometimes referred to—is now Beijing. Paoting is Baoding; Tientsin has become Tianjin; the province of Shansi is Shanxi. The Dowager Empress Tz'u Hsi is now known as Cixi; the Emperor Kuang Hsü is Guangxi, and the villainous governor Yü Hsien as Yu Xian or Yuxian. Other changes have been more dramatic. Canton is now Guangzhou; the province of Chih-li is Hebei.

I have adhered to the way the missionaries referred to places and people, and to the spellings they employed—Fenchow-fu, Jen Tsun, Paotingfu, Taiku, Tai Yuan—as opposed to the forms Sinologists prefer—Fen-chou fu, Jen-ts'un, Pao-ting fu, T'ai-ku, T'ai-yüan. In truth, the missionaries sometimes spelled a number of names and locations in different ways. For example, as least one spelled the outstation Jen Tsun, pronounced "ren-tsoon," as Ren Tsun, and yet another spelled it with an aspirate mark—Jen T'sun—in an attempt to convey the proper sound. I found similar variations with regard to the spelling of cities and villages—for example, Taiku, which is pronounced "ty-goo," might be spelled Tai'ku or Tai-Ku. When the missionaries I quote wrote about the young Chinese teacher embroiled in the controversy in Taiku, most spelled his name Fei Chi Hao, but he is also referred to by the way his name was spoken—Fay Chee How. The Manchu dynasty was spelled either Ching or Ch'ing. (It is now, in *pin-yin,* spelled Qing.)

Where necessary, I have made deliberate choices as to spellings to make them consistent for the English reader not used to Sinological conventions. Thus, the Ching rather than the Ch'ing dynasty, because otherwise the Taiping in Taiping Rebellion should logically be spelled T'ai-p'ing. In addition, frequently, when the letter in question is a copy made by hand or on a typewriter, the person doing the transcript made typographical mistakes. I have corrected such errors when they were obvious; otherwise, I have adhered to the original text of the letters and journals.

❁ *Cast of Characters*

The Oberlin Band, Shansi Mission

Ernest Richmond Atwater—*missionary stationed in Fenchow-fu*
Jennie Pond Atwater—*his first wife*
Elizabeth (Lizzie) Graham Atwater—*his second wife*
Bertha, Celia, Ernestine and Mary Atwater—*his daughters*
Susan Rowena Bird—*associate missionary stationed in Taiku*
Dwight Howard Clapp—*missionary stationed in Taiku*
Mary Jane (Jennie) Clapp—*his wife*
Francis Ward Davis—*missionary stationed in Jen Tsun*
Lydia Lord Davis—*his wife*
Mary Louise Partridge—*associate missionary stationed in Li Man*
Charles Wesley Price—*missionary stationed in Fenchow-fu*
Eva Jane Price—*his wife*
Florence Price—*their daughter*
George Louis Williams—*missionary stationed in Taiku*
Alice Moon Williams—*his wife*

Original Members, Oberlin Band

Iranaeus J. Atwood—*missionary and station doctor*
Chauncey Cady—*missionary*
Martin Luther Stimson—*missionary*
Charles D. Tenney—*missionary*

Chinese Friends

Chang Cheng Fu—*Mission student, known as Er Wu*
Chang Ch'iang Hsiang—*college student, son of Bible woman Mrs. Chang*

Fei Chi Hao—*teacher, Shansi Mission*
K'ung Hsiang Hsi—*college student*
Li Yu—*medical helper, known as both Hei Kou and Black Dog*
Liu Chang Lao—*Mission teacher, known as Teacher Liu*
Liu Feng Chih—*Mission pastor, known as Deacon Liu*
Sang, Dr. and Mr. Ai Ch'ing—*wife and husband medical team*

American Board Colleagues, North China Mission

Annie Allender Gould—*associate missionary stationed in Paotingfu*
Mary Susan Morrill—*associate missionary stationed in Paotingfu*
Horace Tracy Pitkin—*missionary stationed in Paotingfu*
Letitia Thomas Pitkin—*his wife*
Meng Chang-chun—*pastor, known as Meng I*

Missionary Friends

George B. Farthing—*senior member, English Baptist Mission, Tai Yuan*
Tinnie D'Etta Hewett—*Oberlin missionary, wife of James B. Thompson*
Li-pai—*shepherd, helper, Shou Yang*
Thomas Wellesley Pigott—*independent missionary, Shou Yang*
Jessie Pigott—*his wife*
Wellesley William Pigott—*their son*
Timothy Richard—*founder, English Baptist Missionary Society*
Judson Smith—*former Oberlin professor, American Board executive*
Yung Cheng—*member, English Baptist Mission, Tai Yuan*

Imperial China Officials

Tz'u Hsi—*Dowager Empress of China*
Yü Hsien—*governor, Shansi Province*

And sundry and various missionaries and Chinese in the provinces of Shansi, Chih-li, and Shantung

❁ *Massacre in Shansi*

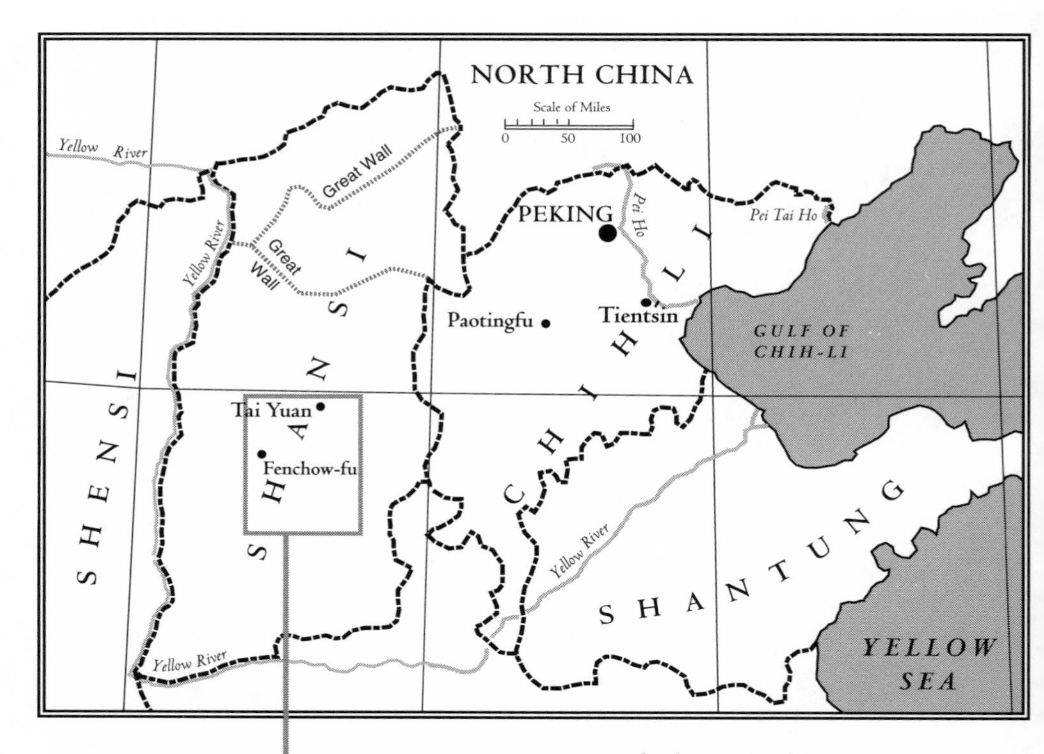

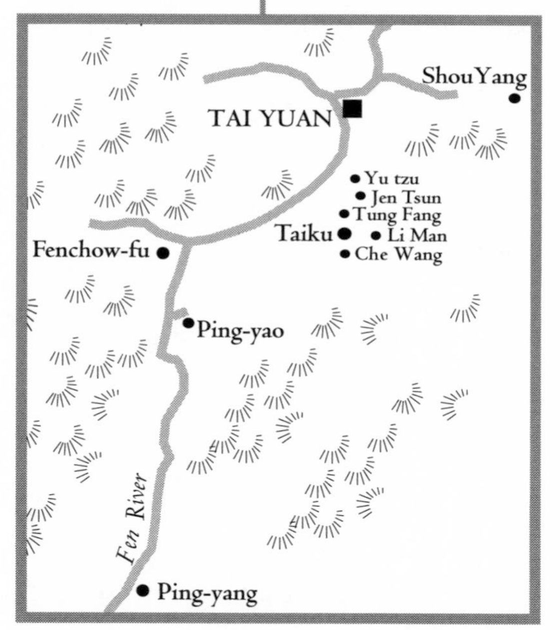

North China with a detail of Shansi Province

❁ *Prologue*

It was early in the morning of what was going to be another parched, scorching mid-August day. Hundreds of Chinese jammed the narrow street outside the American missionary compound, waiting.

The gate swung open, and two mule-drawn carts rumbled out. The missionaries were wedged into the carts, surrounded by their baggage. Twenty soldiers walked beside the carts, ten men on each side. They jostled their way through the growing throng—curious shopkeepers and clerks, women who minced along on bound feet, beggars in filthy rags, and glowering youths who wore the red headband and badges of the Boxers. The crowd was muted, silent. The only sound was the creakings of the crude carts as the mules pulled them through the cramped streets of Fenchow-fu, beyond the towering city gates and down the dusty road.

The missionaries and their families were finally on their way to the coast—and safety. The past three months they had lived a constant state of anxiety fueled by contradictory rumors. They had been so isolated, so cut off from the rest of China and the world, that they had no idea of what had transpired in Peking and Tientsin. Were they still under siege? Were all the foreigners in Peking—diplomats and missionaries—alive or dead? Was it true that foreign troops had landed? Were the troops on their way to rescue them, or had they been routed?

The missionaries' hopes had risen and fallen with each succeeding rumor. There was only one constant: the despair they felt every time they learned cruel reality. The rebellious peasants and villagers known as Boxers had first flooded the province with hate-inspired posters, then robbed and murdered Chinese converts, and finally attacked missionaries and looted and burned their stations. Eleven of their compatriots in other outposts were already dead.

But somehow they had survived, and their hopes were now fueled by the promise of a protective escort across the mountains and all the way to the coast, hundreds of miles away.

Three of the missionaries sat in the first cart. One of them was a woman nine months pregnant. Her husband had appealed to the district magistrate to delay the missionaries' departure, but the official was adamant: There would be no delay, the foreigners had to leave this day.

The woman's two little stepdaughters sat behind her, along with a young Chinese teacher. The teacher was playing with the two little girls, prattling on and on about where they were going and how they would soon be back among friends. There were four missionaries and a child in the second cart, as well as two Chinese members of the Fenchow-fu church.

The missionaries attached no significance to the fact that the man in charge of the troops, a supposed friend of theirs, had proceeded down the road with another unit of soldiers well before the missionary caravan left the compound. And once underway, they seemed to pay no attention when several soldiers exchanged words with the Chinese teacher in the first cart, or when the teacher suddenly slipped off the back of the cart and hastily disappeared down a pathway through a field that bordered the road.

Oblivious, the missionaries chatted happily as the carts rumbled along. One of the men was conversing amiably with the carter he sat beside. The women were commenting on the new uniforms the soldiers wore. All of them were pleased by the number of Chinese who had lined the streets to see them off.

The carts slowly wound their way in the already-burning summer sun, until, about seven miles from Fenchow-fu, the tiny village of Nan Kai Shih came into view.

ONE ❁ *The Newlyweds*

To have friends coming to one from distant parts—
is not this a great pleasure?
—Confucius

Lydia Lord Davis boarded the steamship *Oceanic* in San Francisco with trepidation. "I am afraid of any body of water larger than a bath tub," she confessed.[1]

The Oriental and Occidental liner was scheduled to sail September 11, 1889, for Yokohama, Japan, with a stopover enroute in Honolulu. In its steerage were five hundred passengers, mostly Chinese workers returning home. Four hundred more Chinese were expected to embark at Honolulu. Like the Chinese in steerage, Lydia and her husband, Francis Ward Davis, planned to transfer in Japan to a ship to take them to China.

They were an odd couple, in a way. Lydia's fear of water was in sharp contrast to the experience of Francis, ten years her senior. She had apparently never ventured outside of northern Ohio. He was a man of the world, a seasoned traveler who had sailed aboard whalers on several voyages.

Then, too, Lydia came from a family dedicated to serving Christ; she and Francis, in fact, had been married only four weeks earlier by her great-uncle, a minister "who was no doubt glad to send out another member of the family to missionary service."[2] Francis's background was far removed from such ties. He was the product of a mixed marriage; his mother was a Roman Catholic, though she did convert and became a Methodist. Moreover, not too many years earlier, when Francis was in his late twenties, he had a reputation of being an outspoken religious skeptic and a *"free love advocate."*[3]

The only thing that Lydia and Francis seemed to share was the fact that both of them were the products of small towns, as were most Americans in the nineteenth century. Lydia was born on August 31, 1867, in Ravenna, Ohio. Though she was not a college graduate, she did have some advanced training and, always interested in the education of youngsters, was able to obtain a position as a kindergarten teacher in her hometown. In the fall of 1888, when she was twenty-one years old, she decided that, like many of her relatives, she, too, wanted to be a missionary. She applied to the American Board of Commissioners for Foreign Missions, headquartered in Boston, but was turned down. Her age, she was informed, was "a little less than we desire on the part of those whom we send abroad," especially so "for obvious reasons": An unmarried woman "needs the advantage of longer experience and more mature years than similar work might require here at home."[4]

Francis, who was born September 8, 1857, grew up in Princeton, Massachusetts. His ancestors on the Davis side had emigrated from England to the Massachusetts Bay Colony in the late 1630s. They were chiefly farmers, and a goodly number of them—sons, wives, daughters, and other relatives—were slain by Indians. Francis's father was a blacksmith and, like him, Francis became a smithy. He was adept with his hands and held a variety of jobs. He not only worked aboard a whaler but also at one time was a handyman in a boarding house and at another time set type in a printing shop. As one of those who knew him later as a missionary said, Francis's "gifts lay in the line of practical effort rather than scholastic attainment."[5]

Francis was not a religious man, but he nevertheless attended evening services in the Congregational Church in Princeton and apparently took some pleasure in challenging authority. He was known as the best debater in town—"clear headed, deliberate and composed in his utterance."

In 1883 a new minister, Rev. Archibald L. Love, took over the pastorship of the church and quickly discovered Francis's penchant for questioning accepted beliefs. At an evening service Francis attended, Love urged the audience to ask him whatever they wanted to know about the Congregational credo. Francis was "quite active in pushing in his fire of question," but nonetheless interested. Afterward, he asked Love if he could take the pastor's written statements of belief home with him.

Hoping to engage him in further talk, Love agreed to do so if Francis would return the papers in person.

Francis began attending church services frequently, "but generally with a sneer upon his face." Christians, he cynically told Love, "felt like children & wanted the comfort of a strong helper & so were led to believe in God." For his part, Francis said, "he had no such need and looked down with contempt upon our childish faith."

Love persisted, encouraged in part by the fact that Francis was at least coming to church. One wintry night in February 1885, they were walking home together after prayer meeting when Love urged Francis to go as far as he could to believe and not wait "for the whole path to be illumined." Francis confided that he was trying his best to believe, but without success. Love pressed him. Hadn't Francis admitted that smoking was both profitless and harmful? Yet he hadn't given up tobacco. Wasn't that hypocritical? Francis granted Love's point and promised to stop smoking. As the two men parted, Love had no idea that he had made any great impression on Francis.

But the following Sunday at evening prayer meeting, to the amazement and disbelief of most people in the congregation, Francis rose and professed his faith: "I am now ready to stand on the Lord's side and am determined to do my best to serve him." Love himself thought that "it was too good to be true," but the minister had to admit that he had "never heard one more simple & earnest & childlike in his faith & prayer."[6]

Within a matter of months, Francis also decided he wanted to become a minister, and that fall he applied to the Oberlin Theological Seminary in Oberlin, Ohio. He was twenty-eight years old—older than most men in his class, but not unusually so; a classmate was thirty-nine when he entered the seminary.[7]

Davis went off to Oberlin with $50 in his pocket that Mrs. Love lent him, but it wasn't enough to cover his tuition and expenses, so he worked in his spare time as janitor of Council Hall, the seminary building. A fellow "theolog" recognized that Francis lacked the proper preparation for ministerial studies but he was "faithful, rather than brilliant, and more lovable as one knew him better." Francis's religion, he said, "was of the undemonstrative kind."[8]

Early on, Francis became interested in foreign missions and thought of going to Africa. But before he graduated in the spring of 1889, he met Martin Luther Stimson, a missionary who had recently returned from China. Stimson persuaded Davis to ask the American Board for assignment to join a group of zealous Oberlin graduates who were working in the remote province of Shansi, far from the coast of China and the foreign enclaves in the seaports along it. Davis eagerly sent his application to the Board, requesting that he be assigned to China. The Board accepted him as a missionary candidate and urged upon him "the advisability of marriage." But Francis wrote back that he did not have "any definite prospects in that direction."[9]

Francis graduated from the seminary on May 31, 1889; a little more than three weeks later he was ordained as a minister in Oberlin. He was now the Reverend Francis W. Davis. He was some two months shy of his thirty-second birthday.

After his graduation, but before his ordination, Francis traveled some fifty miles from Oberlin to Ravenna to attend a meeting of the Christian Endeavour Society and to serve as preacher of the Congregational Church as a summer substitute for the regular minister. Lydia was a member of the church. The two met and evidently spoke about their mutual desire to serve as missionaries. Francis was immediately smitten by the comely, petite young woman. It is clear that he was strongly attracted to her. Their courtship was whirlwind, carried on through the mail, a model of Victorian propriety.

Although he had informed the American Board that he had no prospects for marriage, Francis quickly changed his mind after meeting Lydia, and, with the prospect of leaving for China looming, he lost no time in wooing her. Without mincing words, Francis, in his first letter to her on June 20—addressed to "Dear Miss Lord"—immediately suggested that they

> look at 5 points of contact 1 Physical, 2 Social, 3 Mental, 4 Moral, 5 Spiritual and 5 causes of agreement and disagreement 1 Religious and other beliefs 2 Employment, 3 Environment, 4 Family Government, 5 Social Relations. Each of these admits of many subdivisions and I shall be only to[o] glad to express my opinion and to hear and defer to your own on these subjects.

Francis signed the letter, "Yours in the Lord, F. W. Davis."

Four days later, following his ordination, Francis again wrote "Dear Miss Lord," asking, "How do you do?" He hadn't received a response from her and wondered if she had written. If she hadn't written, he boldly said, "I shall come and see for myself." This time, he signed the letter, "With my best love, F. W. Davis."

Lydia wrote "Mr. Davis" back the next day, in response to his first letter. She was both proper and coy:

> I think the plan of considering the points you wrote of, is good and comprehensive.
>
> I must confess I never thought of them in any such systematic manner, if indeed I did at all. Your first point of contact Physical, I scarcely understand what you mean. . . .

Francis was quick to explain:

> I began with the Physical because we are men and women because we are physical. You remember that Christ says in Matt XIX 5 "For this cause shall a man leave father and mother and shall cleave to his wife." Physical contact covers a wide field of intercourse the whole of which I s[h]all not attempt to cover in the following summary.
>
> 1 Bodily touch, hand clasp &c
> 2 Talking with the eyes
> 3 Influence of the inflections of the voice which words cannot translate.

This time, Francis ended the letter, "Wish you every joy with love."

Francis and Lydia must have spent some time together between July 1 and July 6 because by the latter date they were engaged and he was writing the American Board to announce their pending marriage and to apply for her appointment as an associate missionary—which was the title given to female missionaries. He told Lydia not to worry about filling out the Board's application form; if she had any problem with questions about the Scriptures, he would help her answer them. And she didn't have to take a medical examination if she didn't want to; he hadn't, because his family doctor had died and everyone who knew Francis could testify as to his "health and vigor." He suggested that her physician fill out the blanks "from your testimony which will be just as good as a physical examination which I know would be embarrassing."

She was now "My dear Lydia," and he was gushing, "With love unceasing and joy increasing at my glorious prospects of you and with you, I remain with love and kisses Your Francis." Enroute to Boston, to visit the American Board's offices and to select the provisions they would be sending on ahead to China, he wrote with a flourish, "With love and joy and hugs and kisses innumerable from your loving lover Francis."[10]

On August 14, 1889, some two months after they first met, Francis and Lydia were married. Twelve days later, the newlyweds started by railroad for San Francisco, where they spent several days before embarking for China. Their brief visit there almost caused Lydia to back out of the trip. The streets were overflowing with Chinese. Thousands of them, recruited chiefly from the area around Canton in South China, had flocked to the West Coast, first as laborers in the gold mines of California in the late 1840s, then to work on the building of railroads in the West. It was Lyda's first glimpse of what many Americans considered the strange habits of the Chinese people—the queues they wore, their way of dressing, the food they ate, their high-pitch chatter, and their propensity for gambling and smoking opium. Lydia was aghast at "how repulsive they seemed to me when I saw them in large numbers. If I could honorably have turned back and resumed my school teaching in Ravenna, I would gladly have done so."[11]

Lydia's reaction was due in large part to complete ignorance. She and Francis were going to a country about which they knew little, if anything; they knew nothing of its history, its customs or its religious life. Moreover, they had not even tried to learn to speak or to read the language. They were totally unprepared for living in China.

The voyage to Honolulu took a week. Going with them to Shansi on the *Oceanic* was a classmate of Francis's from Oberlin, Charles Wesley Price, his wife, Eva, and two sons. After a brief stay in Honolulu to take on the additional steerage passengers, the *Oceanic* continued on to Yokohama, which the two missionary families reached nearly two more weeks later. They spent a bit of time sightseeing in Japan before boarding a coastal vessel headed for the Asian mainland.

Huddled together on the ship's deck, the Davises first glimpsed China in the midst of a torrential rainstorm on a Sunday afternoon during the latter part of October. Lydia grew contemplative at the sight of the land shrouded in gray. She quickly jotted down her impressions in a diary. They were prescient:

> We saw the land of China for the first time through the rain and through the mist which gathered in our eyes. This strange land before us to be our future for health or for sickness for prosperity or adversity for good or for ill for life or for death[,] all this comes over us and the feeling is one of awe now of hesitancy, as if we were in a strange place feeling our way in the dark, and it would be so if we [were] going in our own strength but the dear Lord has said, "I will guide thee with mine eye, I will never leave thee no[r] forsake thee." [A]nd so the fear is all taken away.[12]

A day later, on October 23, the Davises and the Prices took a train to Tientsin,[13] sixty miles inland from the coast. Once there, they had to transfer to water transportation. There was no railway service from Tientsin to their first destination, Paotingfu, the capital of Chih-li Province, where there was an American Board station. Nor was there any rail service from Paotingfu across the mountains into Shansi Province, where the couple were to be posted in one of the two main stations of the Shansi Mission, Taiku and Fenchow-fu. To reach Paotingfu they would have to travel by boat; to cross into Shansi, they would have to ride in mule litters.

Devello Z. Sheffield, who had just founded the North China College at Tung Chow, just outside Peking, was in Tientsin to escort the Davises and the Prices to Paotingfu. On October 26 the missionary party started out. Their final destination—where they would join a mission started seven years earlier by other graduates of the Oberlin Theological Seminary—was some five hundred miles away in the bleak interior of China.

On a Sunday that same fall, a conversion as remarkable as Francis Davis's was taking place in the Shansi Mission's chapel in Taiku. Dwight Howard Clapp, an Oberlin Theological graduate who had joined the mission five years earlier, was preaching to fellow missionaries and a small group of Chinese men and women. He used as his lesson that day Luke 8:26–39, about "the man out of whom the devils were departed, sitting at the feet of Jesus, clothed, and in his right mind: of the devils . . . healed."

One of the Chinese in Clapp's audience listened with particular intensity to the preacher's words. His name was Liu Feng Chih. He was an unusually tall, robust Chinese man in his late forties who sported a moustache that grew down from his upper lip in oriental fashion. Liu's given name translated as Loving Cat, but he was anything but that. He was a man known for his violent temper. At one time, Liu had been a wealthy man who owned numerous trains of camels that carried tea, cotton and sugar to Manchuria and Mongolia. He was a man of influence, a member of the literati. But Liu became addicted to opium when he was only twenty years old, and despite an attempt to reform himself in his mid-twenties, had been unable to break the habit. He smoked as much as three ounces of opium a day. He also took to gambling, sometimes losing hundreds of dollars at one sitting. Over the years, he had increasingly neglected his business until it had finally failed.

Liu had heard of the opium refuge that American missionaries ran at Taiku. Persuaded that his large family faced poverty and starvation if he didn't reform, he asked to be admitted to it. He was accepted and left his home in the nearby village of Che Wang to enter the refuge. Liu stayed in it for forty days, never leaving the courtyard and under surveillance virtually all the time. The missionaries injected him with a weak solution of morphine. They gave him further injections every day, but they reduced the strength until they were administering only clear water. Meanwhile, they read to him and other addicts in the refuge from the Scriptures, hoping to instill some sense of sacrifice and conviction into their lives. Liu himself studied a translation of the Bible into Chinese, comparing it to Confucian teachings, and was seemingly much interested in what it said. But despite the missionaries' prayers and ministrations, he continued to suffer terribly. One night, unable to sleep for two days, he was pacing his room about midnight, when his nephew suggested that he take a little opium "to relieve" his distress.

The nephew, whose name was Fu T'ang, was a ne'er-do-well, an addict himself who had absconded from a bank with a large sum of money and was accused of killing his wife with a stiletto because she chided him for using opium. Fu had fled, been caught, fled again, and was finally persuaded to join his uncle at the opium refuge. But he arrived there prepared. He now showed Liu where he had hidden some opium pills in a chink in the wall.

Liu took a few of the pills in his hand and was about to raise them to his mouth, when he suddenly stopped himself. "What did I come here for!" He threw the pills on the floor, crushed them with his shoe, and resumed his pacing until dawn. As daylight approached, Liu found he had lost his craving for opium, and he fell asleep for a long time. When he awoke, he felt transformed.

Liu stayed on with the missionaries at Taiku for several months after breaking off the opium habit. When he finally returned home, he carried with him copies of the Old and New Testaments and spent his time reading. Although he said that he did not completely comprehend them, "my heart was strengthened and I was kept from returning to opium."

Liu was subsequently asked to return to Taiku to teach in the boys' boarding school that the missionaries were establishing. He agreed and began to attend the daily morning prayers at the Mission as well as Sunday services. He threw out the idols in his home and ripped down the usual slogans and mottoes that Chinese people pasted on their gateways as part of their New Year celebrations. He replaced them with new ones: "Plenty of food, wine, & good clothes is not happiness," "Penury, hunger and rags is not misery," "Rejoice in the heavenly way." Liu realized, he wrote, "that man's life is as a cloud, that appears but for a little time, and then passes away." Similarly, he continued, "Man's sorrow & joy, prosperity & poverty, are alike transient. The only place of joy is Heaven, and we know that all alike may go there, whether man or woman, young or old. By faith and works we may attain to salvation."

That Sunday in the fall of 1889, as Clapp preached, Liu thought back on his life: "From my youth, I was a spendthrift. I smoked opium, was lazy and careless in business, being continually led astray by others. When others praised me I liked them. When others rebuked me I was angry." It was only while he was in the opium refuge, hearing for the first time about Christianity, that he learned that "all other gods are altogether false." Now, hearing Clapp, he "knew that although my sins were many Jesus could forgive them. All depend upon repentance and faith in Him. . . . This is the true way I have found. Is it not ten thousand times better than the joys of earth[?]"

Liu was especially moved one Sunday not long afterwards when Clapp read from the Bible, "The summer is over, the harvest is ended and ye are not saved." [Jeremiah 8:20] In some way that Liu said he could not explain, he was "overcome" by a sense of his sins. Liu abruptly stood up before the congregation, acknowledged his repentance, and declared himself for Christ. Overcome by the unexpected declaration, Clapp dropped to the floor and, kneeling, prayed for him. Liu was ecstatic. "This repentance of mine," he said, "gave me true peace of mind. I knew that the truth in Christ leads to the right way, saves men's souls, ensures Heaven and eternal life. This is true joy, and from this time I had true peace of heart."[14]

Two years later, in the winter of 1891, Liu was formally baptized as a Christian. He was still being paid to teach, but he often let one of his older students take over his duties. An eloquent speaker, he preferred to preach before other Chinese both in the street chapel that the Mission operated or in the small meeting rooms rented in neighboring villages. He soon earned the sobriquet Deacon Liu and became a mainstay of the Mission—"a Paul in the heart of China,"[15] as one of the missionaries put it. They considered him "our good Bro. Liu,"[16] or "our noble Mr. Liu" about whom "we exclaim, What hath God wrought and take courage."[17]

Liu was not the first Chinese person to be accepted as a communicant by the Shansi Mission. A Mission helper named Lao Wang was baptized in 1887, and later a woman, Mrs. Tsui, also became a communicant. But they evidently had backslid and were no longer considered true Christians. There were a number of grounds for excommunication, most of them customs or habits long engrained in the lives of many Chinese—drinking intoxicants, for example, or smoking opium, gambling, selling children, keeping concubines, foot binding, and participating in ancestor worship and in other Chinese religious customs. That Lao and Mrs. Tsui were no longer considered Christians was not unusual; a number of converts succumbed to their former ways. So Liu has always been hailed as the first convert of the Shansi Mission—the first genuine one after nearly ten years of evangelizing.

The difficulty in converting the Chinese, as the newcomers to the field who were on their way to Shansi—the Davises and the Prices—would soon discover, was not just a matter of language. Christian values and Chinese tradition did not readily mix.

TWO ❁ *Shansi*

The scholar who cherishes the love of comfort is not fit to be deemed a scholar.
—Confucius

The Davises and the Prices made the first leg of the trip to Paotingfu along the Clear River, one of many inland waterways that were the chief means of transportation in the empire. They each hired a "little native houseboat." The boats, which were some fifty feet long and ten feet wide, contained three cabins and were manned by four Chinese—one to steer, the other three to do the heavy work of raising the sail, "tracking," and "poling." When the wind was up, the crew raised an "old, tattered sail." When the wind died, they tracked—walking along a plank-laden towpath pulling the boat along with ropes. When there was no towpath, they resorted to poles to propel the boats.[1]

The trip went slowly, mainly because the wind was contrary and the crew had to pole most of the way. To add to their difficulty, the river was shallow and narrow, its bottom filled with silt. At night, the boats tied up along a bank. The trip to Paotingfu—150 miles from Tientsin—took six days. "One living in China," commented Charles Price, "is liable to forget that time is important, or at least lose some of the push and rush which in America we seem to think so important."[2]

At Paotingfu, where the river was too narrow even for the small houseboats, the missionaries were compelled to wait a week until they could hire mule litters for themselves and pack mules to carry their baggage across the mountains into Shansi, whose name means "west of the hills." Lydia Davis looked at the litters with skepticism. They consisted

A typical mule-drawn Chinese cart. Courtesy Special Collections, U.S. Military Academy, West Point.

of "a queer basket with sides and top, just large enough for two people, and there are poles at the sides and these poles extend out in front and back and fastened upon the backs of mules."[3] The missionaries, however, made good time in the litters, about thirty miles a day, not bad considering the rough, winding, rock-strewn road. But going around bends high on the side of a mountain, the litters would sometimes tilt precariously over open space, and it was not unusual for a pack mule to fall down the mountainside. No wonder that Eva Price was terrified. They had to "climb, crawl, slip, tumble and jerk" over the mountains while the litter "teeters and totters, quivers, quavers, jostles, and jerks."[4] If the mules were out of step, it was "jerkity jerk" all the way.[5]

Along the way, the travelers stopped off at night at depressing Chinese inns—"grand palaces," mocked one missionary, that bore names such as "Everything Runs Smooth," "Harmony and Abundance," and

"Lofty and Aspiring."[6] Some of them "a man in the United States wouldn't put his horse in."[7] The amenities in the inns were few. Usually there was only one ironware or tin bowl of water for all to share for washing. The families slept on the long brick *kangs* the Chinese used for communal beds. Lydia Davis was not put off by the discomfort as much as she was by having to share her *kang* with "smaller animal life."[8] But the accommodations were better than a previous missionary party encountered; they had to spend two nights as "troglodytes, living in a 'hole in the ground' in caves dug out of the side of a hill."[9]

Charles Price found eating in the inns "a trial." The menus were monotonous: *kua mien*, a kind of macaroni, boiled with cabbage in soup stock; boiled millet served without sugar or salt (rice, grown in faraway southern China, was a luxury); flapjacks made of sodden buckwheat flour strings, which were boiled in weak soup and served with curds made of fermented beans; or *bo-bos*, steamed dumplings filled with chopped pork and vegetables that were dipped in bitter vinegar before eating. "One can get used to most anything," Price added stoically.[10]

Some foreigners also found the Chinese custom of not taking their breakfast until eleven o'clock "very trying on the stomach."[11] Experienced travelers who didn't like the Chinese edibles often brought their own victuals with them in a food box—usually stewed chipped beef or some canned salmon, a jar or two of beef extract, some crackers, and cocoa.

The road the missionaries were following climbed over high mountains, through peaks known as the "Heavenly Gates" at the pass called Niang-tzu, and down to the plateau of central Shansi, several thousand feet above sea level.

History permeates Shansi. Two sections of the Great Wall rise in the north. The flood-prone Yellow River—China's "sorrow"—is its western border, next to the neighboring province whose name, Shensi, often caused confusion. Shansi is a province filled with ancient pagodas, monasteries, and cave temples, a reminder that the plateau is considered the cradle of the Chinese nation. One mountain peak on the edge of the plateau is called Red Tsu Shan—the Mountain of the Ancient Man, China's Ararat. The Chinese believed that the man and the woman who became the parents of the whole human race were saved during a great

A sedan chair presented to the missionary wives at Taiku. Courtesy Oberlin College Archives.

flood by jumping on the back of two lions who bore them to the topmost ledge of Red Tsu Shan. It was also in Shansi that the Han dynasty is said to have originated two hundred years before Christ, and its people thus claim that they are descended directly from the forebears of the Chinese people. Marco Polo was impressed by Shansi's prosperity back in the late thirteenth century, especially in Tai Yuan, the provincial capital—a "great centre of trade and industry, which supplies great quantities of the equipment needed for the Great Khan's armies."[12]

In Marco Polo's time, the region was full of vineyards and silk farms, with thriving towns and villages, and roads thronged with merchants and their wares. By the early nineteenth century the cities of Taiku, Ping-yao and Ch'i Hsien had developed into banking centers, with so much gold and silver buried in their financiers' backyards that the entire province was said to be a "solid mountain of precious metal."[13] The banks innovated in handling long-distance remittances, specializing in particular in drafts and credit accounts for traders and merchants all through the empire. Shansi men worked as bankers and traders not only throughout China but also in Japan.

Actually, beneath Shansi's surface was a gold mine of sorts, several in fact—deposits of coal, iron, sulphur, and copper. The coal deposits were so extensive that they alone covered an area greater than the state of Pennsylvania and would one day account for a third of the country's fuel production. In the nineteenth century, however, the Chinese gathered and sold only the pieces that lay on or near the surface of the ground.

By the latter part of the century, the Manchus' neglect of the province had made it an almost-forgotten backwater of the Empire. The province's prosperity had dwindled into near poverty. Its farmers grew barely enough grain and vegetables to feed the people of the province. The cultivation and smoking of opium—instead of growing the millet that was urgently needed—was so widespread that many if not most of its citizens were addicted. The lack of navigable rivers and the cost of overland transportation made the importation of grain into the province prohibitive. Its roads, never adequate, fell into disrepair. A myriad of small villages clustered around numerous central market towns, all within a day's walk.

Despite its earlier renown, the Shansi plateau—175 miles wide and 350 miles long—was effectively cut off from its neighbors. It was so isolated, and insulated, that matters that occurred in Peking, in Tientsin or even in Paotingfu in neighboring Chih-li Province seemed too distant to affect the daily routine in Shansi. This was especially true because the people of Shansi were traditionally peace-loving, fonder, so it was said, of money than of fighting.

No matter what the hardships of journeying into this vast, almost barren area were, the Davises and the Prices were enchanted by the vistas along the way. Charles Price once found himself on "a rather dim path" on a ledge hundreds of feet above the plain. Looking to the east he saw cities and villages more than a score of miles away. To the south he could see, forty miles in the distance, mountains whose tops were covered with snow glistening in the sunshine. "America," Price wrote a friend, "may have some views more awe inspiring but certainly nothing more beautiful than this. How wonderfully God has blessed this people if their eyes were only opened to see the good things He has given them."[14] "Some of the views," another missionary said, "*burst* upon the traveler" and "are sublime and beautiful indeed."[15]

As the missionaries descended onto the Shansi plateau, however, the views became forbidding. The central plateau, which slopes gently southward, is a jumble of precipices, canyons, and rocky land.

Light-brown loess is the chief characteristic of Shansi. Over thousands of years, winds from the Gobi Desert in the north have deposited a thick layer of this fertile, productive alluvium in its valleys, especially in the basin region around Tai Yuan and beside the largest of Shansi's rivers, the Fen, on opposite sides of which the two main stations of the Shansi Mission, Taiku and Fenchow-fu, were situated. In some places the loess is hundreds of feet deep; in other places it is as much as two thousand feet deep.

The loess lends itself to being carved up for terrace farming, as well as for being tunneled into for cave dwellings called *yaos.* It is so porous and crumbly that over the years the traffic of carts, camel caravans, and mules gradually sank rural roads as much as fifty or a hundred feet deep. Traveling along them was like riding in a deep trench. These man-created ravines readily became irrigating canals for farmers when a river such as the Fen overflowed.

"Everywhere," Francis Davis said, "the loess breaks down like rock when undermined and a great slice a few feet thick but a hundred feet long and 50 to 60 feet high will topple over like a falling tree. It stands sometimes for years in solitary mounds or pencils ready to fall at any time but *waiting,* like everything in China until something too strong to be resisted strikes it and then it falls because it was 'fate.'"[16]

The missionaries never ceased to complain about the huge clouds of dust from the loess that got into everything when windstorms occurred. One complained of the "high winds which raise the dust in clouds from the bare lead-colored ground, until you and your possessions are of the 'earth, earthy,' and you long for a swim or a snow-drift."[17] After she was settled in her new home, Eva Price fretted, "Oh! how the wind is whirling and swirling this fine dust into every crack and crevice of our not over tight doors and windows, until a thick coating of dust lies over every thing in the house even to our teeth!"[18] On another occasion—"a queer day," she said—"Wind blew a gale which, of course raised clouds of dust, and mixed with the dust came a little dash of rain, which by the time it reached our windows was literally *mud* so we can truly say it rained mud. . . We could scarcely see out."[19]

The dust was particularly pervasive in times of drought. The rivers in Shansi ordinarily flow swiftly when there is rain, but they become dry beds when there is no rain, and that happens frequently. When a drought occurs, famine often follows in its wake.

THREE ❁ *The Great Famine*

To see what is right and not to do it is want of courage.
—*Confucius*

The Davises and the Prices were the latest missionaries in a steady stream of evangelical Christians from America and England who had worked in Shansi ever since a famine struck North China in the late 1870s. It was one of the worst natural catastrophes in world history.

The climate of Shansi resembles that of the northern part of the United States, but its average annual rainfall is comparable to that of the Dust Bowl in the Southwest, barely sufficient to maintain cultivation in the best of times. Rainfall is so uncertain that at times the area's staple, millet, as well as wheat, beans, barley, and oats cannot be sown. Nor can potatoes, cabbages, lettuce, onions, and leeks be grown. Peach, pear, apricot, and apple trees wither. When that happens, the people of the province suffer famines.

In a normal year the rainy season begins in July and often continues into August. It is the time for sowing. In 1877 there was no rain, and no crops were grown anywhere in Shansi, or four other provinces of North China—Chih-li, Shantung, Shensi and Honan. There was no rain in 1878 either, and again no crops. It was the same the following year. And then came a swarm of locusts that devoured what little grain had managed to sprout beside the riverbeds. The fragile balance between survival and starvation tilted.

In the past, an elaborate network of emergency granaries set up by the Imperial government successfully forestalled food shortages. But an enormous increase in population in the past hundred years had outstripped the capacity of the warehouses, and inefficiency and corruption impeded the distribution of what stocks of grain were on hand. Few supplies were transported in slow-moving caravans over the mountains into the province. The cost of food became exorbitant.

People resorted to eating dried leaves, tree roots, bark, sawdust, dried mud, and even baked pellets of finely ground stone mixed with soil or millet husks—which caused terrible stomach cramps and eventual death. An epidemic of typhoid fever broke out. Pillaging was widespread. Starving men and women languished helpless on roadsides, prey to hungry dogs and magpies. A Westerner who visited the area saw "hundreds of corpses" along the roads.[1] Wolves became so bold that they sprang into villages, snatched infants in their jaws and raced off to eat them. There were stories of cannibalism, of human flesh being peddled in markets, of children being boiled and devoured.

An estimated nine and a half million people died of starvation in the Great Famine.[2] Nearly five and a half million of them, or more than one out of every three persons who lived in Shansi, died in that province alone.[3]

Protestant missionaries saw the Great Famine as a rare opportunity not only to help the Chinese people with food and medicines but also to introduce them to the Christian faith. Roman Catholics had established missions in Shansi as early as the seventeenth century, but by the end of the widespread starvation only a dozen or so priests were left, scattered throughout the area. The region was wide open for Protestant penetration.

Missionary leaders such as J. Hudson Taylor of England, founder of the China Inland Mission, said that famine relief "synchronizes with the wider opening up of China to missionary effort, thus giving us the call to help, and affording us the opportunity of showing practically that Christianity teaches men to 'love this neighbor as himself.'"[4] Timothy Richard, who founded the English Baptist Missionary Society, saw the disaster as a chance to establish goodwill that would lead to sympathy for and support of Christian evangelical efforts.

Taylor's CIM, as it was called, was made up mostly of Church of England adherents, but its policy was "undenominational"—that is, Taylor was anxious to help, not compete, with other Protestant societies. In his eyes, the CIM's main purpose was not the winning of converts or the education of a Christian community but the diffusion of a knowledge of the Gospel throughout the Chinese Empire as quickly as possible.

On the other hand, although Timothy Richard also believed that the famine gave missionaries "unprecedented opportunities for the preaching of the Gospel,"[5] he took a more sweeping view. He believed in introducing in China every positive feature of Western civilization. He wanted to transform China's culture into an abundant economic life that was both intellectual and spiritual. Richard was appalled a year or so after the Great Famine by a talk he had with farmers in northern Shansi. Heavy rainfalls had drenched the countryside that year. Richard asked the farmers what kind of harvest they had just reaped. "Very bad," came the answer, "it is too good. Everybody has plenty and there is no market. The expense of carting the grain to a district that needs it is so great, and labourers are so few and wages so high, that we farmers have no alternative but to leave the crops rotting in the fields." To Richard, "This lamentable state of affairs was one of the strong arguments that I used when urging the authorities to build railways, so as to secure cheap transport for grain both in time of need and in time of plenty."[6] He went on:

> In pondering Western civilization, I felt that its advantage over Chinese civilization was due to the fact that it sought to discover the workings of God in Nature, and to apply the laws of Nature for the service of mankind. . . . I was convinced that if I could lecture to the officials and scholars and interest them in these miracles of science, I would be able to point out to them ways in which they could utilize the forces of God in Nature for the benefit of their fellow country-men. In this way I could influence them to build railways, to open mines, to avert recurrences of famine, and save the people from their grinding poverty.[7]

Taylor's China Inland Mission was the first to begin famine-relief operations in Shansi in 1877, but it was soon followed by Richard's English Baptists. Before the last year of the century, more than one hundred and fifty Protestant missionaries would be working in Shansi, most of them members of the CIM or English Baptists.

The call to go to China was especially vocal in the United States. "Three hundred to four hundred millions of souls are here crowded together within the limits of these eighteen provinces," read an appeal for missionaries by the American Board of Commissioners for Foreign Missions. "Nine tenths of this field are still unoccupied—nine tenths of these multitudes are still unreached by the gospel." Although the Board cited no figures, it claimed that the number of church members in China doubled about every seven years, and that with the exception of Japan, Madagascar, and the Polynesian Islands, "perhaps in no other part of the heathen world has more fruit been gathered in proportion to the seed sown." Moreover, the prospects for the future were unlimited:

> Work done for China will certainly tell on the future of the world's history. . . . Christianized, China has a noble history before her, and must become a mighty factor in the great political, social, and religious movements of coming generations. Whoever is permitted to bear the humblest part in securing her conversion, though his name and work may find no place on the historic page, yet will surely send his influence down through the channels of human life, and do much to shape the destiny of the whole human family. Was ever such a tempting prize held up to animate the messenger of good tidings longing to do all he can for the salvation of souls, for the elevation of his race, and for the glory of God?[8]

This was heady stuff, and it came at a time when religious fervor was sweeping America, in particular in New England, Ohio, and upper New York State, where fire-and-brimstone revivals were once so intense that the region became known as the Burned-over District. The American Board dated its beginnings to 1808, when five young Congregationalists from the Phillips Academy and Theological Seminary in Andover, Massachusetts, were ordained as "Missionaries to the heathen in Asia," determined to preach the Gospel "to every creature" and bring about "no less than the moral renovation of a world."[9] As the nineteenth century progressed, evangelists felt a particular urgency to go out and spread the Word: the expectation of the coming advent of the millenium, the thousand-year reign of Christ. That meant it was imperative to convert the world in a single generation. The idea, the ambition of it, seems unbelievable today—and, in truth, the foreign missionary movement quickly outgrew millenarianism—but the unrealistic goals that were set endured in many cases, and the nineteenth century became, for Protestants, the missionary century.

The call to China was felt with particular urgency in a small college town in Ohio, Oberlin.

FOUR *The Oberlin Band*

The Founding Members

If a man in the morning hear the right way,
he may die in the evening without regret.
—*Confucius*

One of those who heard the call was Martin Luther Stimson. Writing in his room at Oberlin Theological Seminary an hour after midnight, on January 5, 1881, Stimson insisted—for some unknown reason—that what he was about to relate was *"confidential."* His letter was addressed to the headquarters of the American Board of Commissioners for Foreign Missions in Boston. The Board had already accepted Stimson and his fiancée, Emily Brooks Hall, for missionary work and had proposed that they go to Natal, Africa. But Stimson suggested an alternative, an unusual scheme:

> A band of 12 graduates of Oberlin Seminary (except one, an excellent physician, a graduate of the College) who are of one mind in the matter and all among the best here, contemplate offering themselves to the American Board, under the leadership, possibly of Prof. Judson Smith, who has been approached on the subject, for the work in Shantung or some other one mission field where we may be sufficient to man the work.

Stimson argued that the advantages of enlisting the entire group, as opposed to a "straggling number" of "unacquainted" missionaries, would be "very great." They shared a common goal and were sure to work in harmony. Members of the "Band," he continued, had been meeting virtually every evening, discussing the plan. Their hope was "to be eminently successful in turning some portion of the world to Christ."[1]

It probably did not surprise the Board to hear from Oberlin. The school's founders were interested in creating a colony and college of Christian reverence "for the training of teachers and other Christian toilers for the boundless and most desolute [*sic*] fields" in the American West."[2] They named the school for John Frederick Oberlin, a French pastor who was a combination minister, teacher, doctor, engineer, and social worker who worked for sixty years among an isolated, illiterate population in the Vosges Mountains. The college's students—most of whom were from families headed by ministers or who were raised on farms—were expected, like Oberlin, to apply Christian moral principles to all human activities and institutions. And, indeed, the school attracted young men and women imbued with the sense of service to both God and mankind; they spent the school's long winter recess preaching and teaching in the hinterlands of the Midwest and South.

Oberlin College's name quickly became synonymous with piety. In the beginning, and for a long time, the students were governed by strict rules—no drinking, no smoking, and no activity of any kind on Sundays. All the college's classes began with a prayer, or at least a hymn, and some classes even held weekly prayer meetings. In addition, all students were required to take a Bible study course each week and to attend Monday night prayer meetings as well as both morning and afternoon services on Sundays. Morning prayers were conducted daily in the dormitories. If a male student boarded off campus, he had to room with a family that held a morning prayer meeting.

The school was also no stranger to religious enthusiasms such as the American Board depicted in China; for some thirty years, the college president, Charles Grandison Finney, was one of the leading revivalists in the country and the world. He believed that salvation was possible for everyone, even sinners. The faculty that served under him represented the pioneering spirit of New England Puritanism. Each year, a Day of Prayer was held—a Day that sometimes lasted a week. The founders of Oberlin hoped that its graduates would bear the message of salvation to people throughout the world.

Oberlin was, for the period, an unusual institution. Although its founders, many of its first teachers, and all of its trustees were Presbyterians, their views on salvation were considered heretical by church authorities, who also cringed at the fieriness and length of Finney's sermons. As a result, the college developed into becoming a prime mover in the establishment of an association of Congregational churches in the area.

The college had also, from its start, been innovative; its name connoted not only religious piety but also social reform. It was open to both men and women from its very beginning in 1833. It began admitting blacks as well the following year, and in 1835 the school was started on its way to becoming a center of abolitionism when a group of antislavery students and teachers bolted from the Lane Theological Seminary in Cincinnati and entered Oberlin. The college was soon a breeding ground of abolitionist preachers and the town a haven for runaway slaves that was second only to Canada. Oberlin graduates accompanied the slaves from the schooner *Amistad* when, after a much-heralded trial in 1841, the mutinous natives were freed and returned to Africa; there the Oberlin grads founded the Mendi Mission on the continent's west coast. Students and townspeople, both whites and blacks, rescued an escaped Kentucky slave from slave hunters in 1858 and then were indicted for violating the Federal Fugitive Slave Law. The case became a national cause célèbre and catapulted Oberlin into national Republican politics.[3]

Before the Civil War ended and for a dozen years afterwards, the astonishing zealousness displayed by Oberlin's students led to more than five hundred of them going into the South to teach and preach among the blacks. A branch of the Young Men's Christian Association was founded in Oberlin in 1881, and within a year it was the largest YMCA in the world.[4] Between 1877 and 1886, the one career that attracted more male Oberlin graduates than any other vocation was religious work; one out of every four seniors went into the ministry.[5] Many of the graduates of its Theological Seminary, which was established soon after the college started, became missionaries for the American Board. As of 1889, one hundred and sixty Oberlin men and women were currently serving in missions as far afield as Africa, the Sandwich Islands, Jamaica, Turkey, India, Haiti, Bulgaria, Micronesia, Japan, and India, as well as among the Blackfeet and Ojibwa in the American West.[6]

It was undoubtedly no surprise either that the Oberlin Band wanted to enlist Judson Smith to be their leader. He was a spellbinding lecturer who taught, among other courses, medieval and church history. He was particularly inspiring when he described the work of the Roman abbot Augustine, who landed with some thirty monks off the coast of Kent in the tenth century and proceeded to establish churches and schools throughout Britain. "We saw England, in fact all Europe converted before our eyes," a student of his recalled. "Unrolling the panorama of the Living Church, this enthusiastic professor became himself an evangelist of the Augustinian order. His fiery appeal tingling in the receptive ears of a thousand students raised an army of volunteers on the spot."[7]

It seems almost a foregone conclusion that Stimson's *"confidential"* letter to the American Board that January in 1881 would draw an immediate, favorable, and apt response—as, in fact, the letter did. The Board wired back: "I Chronicles 17:2."[8] ["Do all that is in thine heart; for God is with thee."]

A letter followed a week later. The Board was then focusing its missionary activities on North China. It had transferred most of its staff in Shanghai to the north and closed that station as early as 1863, and its oldest mission, in Canton, was suspended three years later. Home Secretary E. K. Alden wrote Stimson that the Board was already "working" the province of Shantung on the Yellow Sea that Stimson had suggested, but its North China Mission had recommended that it next reach out westward to neighboring Shansi, a "splendid field for new blood for the next generation." Alden said, "Should you find that a band of devoted well-equipped men can be found, whose hearts the Lord has touched, who are ready to go out to a New Province in No. China, you will be most heartily encouraged by us."[9] Alden also contacted Judson Smith, telling him that he thought that the Oberlin Band's work "might constitute an Epoch in our history."[10]

A few days later Alden again wrote Stimson, to emphasize the immense opportunity Shansi offered. The province, he noted, had a population of fourteen million people but no evangelists to speak of except for "a small beginning by the [China] Inland Mission who do good work as scouts." Therefore, he was sanguine about Shansi: "This will be a splendid field and can open the way for Shensi and for Honan, with 25,000,000 more yet little cared for, if the work expands."[11]

The members of the Oberlin Band, however, had other things on their minds for the moment than the missionary goal the Board foresaw. For one thing, Stimson informed the Board, while three members were ready to go to China "putting no limitations" on what their priority should be, several others "feel that they are unwilling to go to any foreign field unless they go with the express intention and reasonable expectation of building up a school of the higher grade within a limited number of years. If we can go with a view to an *educational* and miss'y work rather than to a *miss'y* and *educational* work, our Band would seem to promise success. Not that all of the Band are desirous to do educational work, more than evangelistic labor, but some feel that that is a phase of work for which they are specially fitted." Stimson wanted to know "whether it is probable we could work with the intention of developing a College in the course of a number of years"—an Oberlin-in-China, if you will.[12]

One of those who was especially concerned about the Band's priorities was seminarian Charles D. Tenney. "We hope to establish a *center of influence* for the Chinese Empire and we plan in time to found an *educational institution* which shall command the respect of, and so influence the higher classes of China." There were some who thought the plan chimerical, but Tenney said he had abandoned "other plans which I had formed for my lifework especially because of the large opportunities of doing good which I saw in our organization. This is the feature which is attracting others also."[13]

The Board had no objection to the Oberlin Band's goal in the long run, but it did not want to enter into a lengthy debate on the subject. If the Band did not occupy Shansi within a reasonable amount of time, other missionary societies "may push in and interfere with the steady development of our work westward from our base in No. China."[14] In other words, the Board, having accepted the idea of Shansi becoming an Oberlin preserve, now wanted its members to move as swiftly as possible to begin work there.

The Oberlin Band expressed another concern—one that would continually haunt its members in the future. The doctor Stimson had mentioned in his initial letter would not be going after all. The Band wanted one on hand to tend to the medical problems that were sure to arise because a number of the members were married, or about to be, and planned to have children. Stimson was assured that a physician would appear "in due time,"[15] and until then there was a CIM doctor stationed in Shansi's capital, Tai Yuan. Besides, the Band was told, "Best above all is a *healthy climate.*"[16]

Despite the Oberlin Band's entreaties, Professor Judson Smith felt he could not leave Oberlin at the time; but he soon afterwards accepted appointment as Corresponding Secretary of the American Board and moved to Boston, becoming the Oberlin Band's trusted link with the home office. Thus, it was left to Martin Luther and Emily Stimson to be the first to leave home to reconnoiter Shansi.

In early September 1881, nine months after he first wrote the American Board, Stimson and his bride said good-bye to families and friends and left for China, traveling across the Pacific by ship, and then by waterway and road into the interior, just as the Davises and the Prices would do several years later. The Stimsons took with them their prized possession, an organ especially made in Cleveland of seasoned wood boiled in linseed oil to prevent warping.

The couple arrived in Tientsin in October. There they were guests of Timothy Richard and his wife. Richard graciously helped the Stimsons to rent a large store in the grain market as a temporary residence. Although there was competition between various Protestant missionary societies—and there were more than thirty such organizations represented in China besides Richard's English Baptist Society and the China Inland Mission—their members in the field invariably found it expedient to cooperate with each other in an otherwise hostile environment. They formed close friendships and felt free to visit one another, to trade advice and gossip, to lend money when funds from home were late, and even, once in a while, to marry one another.

The Protestants' interdependence was in sharp contrast to their relations with Roman Catholic missionaries, with whom they did not associate at all, even when both Protestant and Catholic missions were situated in the same city and within walking distance of each other. The Protestants looked on the Catholics as Antichrist, while the Catholics believed the Protestants were dangerous heretics. It didn't help that most Protestant missionaries were Anglo-Saxons and spoke English, while most Catholic missionaries were French, and others were Italian or Spanish.

Communication was difficult. Besides which, the way they operated was different, and so, too, were their goals, a matter, generally speaking, of revolution versus evolution. Protestant missionaries felt an urgency to bring knowledge of the Gospel to all Chinese, to save souls, before it was too late. They opened their chapels and medical dispensaries to everyone, Christian and non-Christian alike, in the hope of attracting outsiders who could be taught about Christian beliefs. The Catholics, on the other hand, maintained a relative seclusion, concerned only with their own parishioners; the only exception was the orphanages they operated, which were totally out of keeping with the Chinese attitude about waifs and strays and were misunderstood by them. Catholic clerics were chiefly concerned with creating Christian communities that, by adapting as much of Chinese culture as possible within the limits of Catholic orthodoxy, would slowly spread and transform other Chinese into believers. Simply stated, the Protestants' chief aim was the immediate conversion of Chinese; the Catholics' was the birth of Christians to already converted Chinese.

Stimson waited until the worst of the winter was over before heading into Shansi the following March on a tour that he took with a member of the Board's North China Mission.[17] Their first stop was Tai Yuan, which was already occupied by missionaries of both the English Baptist Society and the CIM. Despite the presence of other missionaries, the Oberlin Band had been urged to settle there, as well. Stimson had been told that it was "usual for different societies to center on the capitals of countries or provinces."[18] The CIM, for one, purposely chose a provincial capital for its first station when it penetrated a new province; it would later branch out from there into *fu* or prefectural cities and finally into less important towns. Taylor, who was primarily interested in spreading the Gospel, believed that the establishment of a mission station at the focal point of a province's political and social life was the quickest way to spread the Word.

But Stimson was impressed by the fact that there were a number of cities with populations of between 10,000 and 15,000 people within reasonable distance south of Tai Yuan whose inhabitants seemed friendly. The communities and market towns between them were magnets for hundreds of tiny neighboring villages, all within a comfortable day's round-trip journey. Besides which, although the Catholics were a presence in the province, with as many as a dozen priests and 20,000 converts, there were only three Protestant mission stations and fifty of their converts in the entire area.[19]

Stimson and his companion examined six cities in six days, among them Taiku, a district city of about 20,000 people that was one of the province's banking centers. They then crossed the Fen and toured the west side of the river, passing through an area where signs of the Great Famine—broken-down, abandoned homes whose bricks had been sold for food—were still evident; in the prefectural city of Fenchow-fu alone, nearly a third of the population were believed to have died of starvation in the late 1870s.[20] Upon returning, Stimson felt so optimistic about the opportunities for working in the province that he immediately got off a telegram to Oberlin: "Forward Band."[21] He then purchased a house in Tai Yuan to use as a temporary base until other members of the Oberlin Band arrived and decisions could be made as to what cities to occupy.

The first from the Oberlin Theological Seminary to join Stimson was an eager group consisting of an undergraduate classmate of his from Dartmouth, Charles Tenney, and his wife, Annie; a bachelor, Chauncey Cady, and Cady's undergraduate classmate from Ripon College in Wisconsin, Iranaeus J. Atwood, his wife, Annette, and their son Karl. Atwood was to become the Mission's interim doctor until a physician arrived two years later. He studied for a while with a British missionary doctor in Tai Yuan and gained enough of a rudimentary knowledge to treat common illnesses; he was particularly successful in removing cataracts from eyes, using a procedure called couching that had been known to ancient Egyptians but about which the Chinese had apparently never heard. When he later opened a makeshift clinic in Taiku, Atwood saw more than a thousand patients within the first three months alone. He went home on furlough in 1888 because his wife was sick and took the opportunity of being in the States to study and receive a medical degree from Rush Medical College in Chicago.

In the fall of 1882, the Atwoods, the Tenneys, and Cady reached Paotingfu in Chih-li Province and after a journey of thirteen days arrived in

Tai Yuan that November in a caravan with "21 animals, including two mules, litters, one organ, eight mule packs, three horses, four donkeys, etc."[22] They all settled into the house that Stimson had found, but it was far from ideal for housing all the families. Typically, all the windows were of paper, with only a small square of glass in the middle that let in light. The walls seemed just as thin, for "every conversation" was "easily overheard in the rooms next on either side." There were also other nuisances that made their living together untenable. Tenney purchased a cow for milk and kept it in one of the courtyards "much to the annoyance of the Atwoods." The Atwoods were also bothered by how near their quarters were to a room occupied by the nurse for the Stimsons' first child, Leonard, who had been born that April. But then Tenney's wife began to feel "very poorly" in the stifling summer heat, so he moved his family to an apartment in a neglected temple in the hills west of the capital for the summer.[23] Stimson also eventually moved out, renting a house when his wife became pregnant again.

In December the seven missionaries, anxious to begin, held their first annual meeting, then quickly fanned out to begin their work among the Chinese. The Stimsons went to Ch'i Hsien, Cady to Ping-yao, and the Tenneys and Atwood to Taiku. But that arrangement didn't last long, because both Cady and the Tenneys eventually resigned. So it was decided to focus the Mission's operations on just two cities, Taiku and Fenchow-fu. Using them as hubs, over the years the Oberlin Band opened several outstations in rented quarters in nearby outlying villages that served as prayer meeting rooms, opium refuges, and chapels on Sundays. The missionaries toured them on regular journeys into the countryside. Meanwhile, Atwood's dispensary in Taiku became increasingly popular with local Chinese and provided the missionaries with a captive audience for introducing Christianity to its patients.

Even though the Shansi missionaries iterated as early as December 1883 that their "primary object" was the establishment of a school,[24] four years later they were no nearer their goal. They concluded that "the times are not now ripe for beginning educational work" and, instead, unanimously resolved that "the most profitable, present ambition of our feeble Mission is thoroughly to evangelize our field."[25] It was not until 1889—seven years after the arrival of the first pioneers—that the Mission finally opened a school, for boys only, in Taiku. The school was a beginning, but hardly the higher-education enterprise that the Oberlin Band had envisioned.

The reasons for the delay in establishing the school were many—the difficulty of finding capable teachers, problems of language, reluctance on the part of Chinese parents, and the upset in routine caused by a constant turnover in missionary personnel. Stimson blamed the American Board in part for the failure of the Shansi Mission to accomplish more because it hadn't sent out enough missionaries to man it. The Board promised to make up for the deficiency by sending fourteen families and seven single women missionaries to Shansi and to keep the field open to Oberlin as a "University Mission" for a "reasonable number of years."[26] But it never did meet the quota it set.

As it turned out, not all of the twelve original members of the Oberlin Band went to Shansi, but a total of thirty Oberlinites—missionaries, their wives, and single female missionaries—served there, at one time or another, in the two decades before the turn of the century. The average tour of duty was seven years, but some members stayed as little as two or three years, and others died or were forced to take furloughs in order to get medical treatment for themselves or their children. Only two couples served fourteen years. The roster of the Shansi Mission never went beyond a total of eighteen missionaries, including physicians, and then only in the four-year period 1893–1896. In truth, even that total was never in the field at any one time because of continual shifts in personnel and leaves of absence.

Following the arrival of the Stimsons, the Tenneys, the Atwoods, and Cady, four missionaries arrived in 1884—Charles Wesley Price's older brother Frank and his wife, Jennie, and, at last, after repeated requests, a doctor, Daniel E. Osborne, and his wife. But comings and goings became so constant that at one point the Mission was down to only three members and was forced to abandon Fenchow-fu and concentrate in Taiku. Chauncey Cady, for example, left to study Chinese in Tientsin in 1884 and never returned. The Tenneys departed the following year when Annie Tenney fell ill and required an operation; they also did not return.[27] The Frank Prices subsequently went on furlough home because of illness and, after returning to Shansi, remained only a few years more before Frank was stricken with a severe case of bronchitis and went back to the States again; he recovered, but he and Jennie then went to Micronesia as missionaries. The Osbornes stayed only until 1888. Atwood, in the meantime, transferred to a new station opened by the North China Mission, where he remained briefly before having to return to America because his wife was ill.

The long-awaited physician who replaced Osborne, Dr. James Goldsbury, reached Shansi in 1889 but died of typhus four years later. A similar fate befell one of the first single woman missionaries, Tinnie D'Etta Hewett. Tinnie, who had studied in both Oberlin College and its seminary, was another one of the Shansi missionaries who had been encouraged to go to China by Martin Luther Stimson. A female colleague of hers described her as a "dear little woman . . . just big enough to be loved."[28] Lydia Davis, who knew her well, considered Tinnie the "intellectual superior" of any of the men.[29] In Shansi, Tinnie met and married fellow Oberlinite James B. Thompson. When she was eight months pregnant with their third child in 1899, her twenty-one-month-old daughter Alma fell ill with dysentery and died. Then, shortly after giving birth, Tinnie came down with childbed fever. The Shansi missionaries sent for a doctor attached to an English mission, but he was sick himself, so Tinnie died. Thompson felt compelled to return to the States with their two surviving youngsters.

Death and disease were a constant. Part of the reason was the environment. Living beside cramped, narrow streets and alleyways in the midst of a crowded city was virtual suicide. Despite what the Board had said about the climate being healthy, the missionaries were surrounded by unsanitary and disease-ridden conditions—open sewers, contaminated wells, and streets filled with garbage scavenged by dogs and pigs that ran wild.

Even when a doctor was on station, he was sometimes so far away and took so long to get to a patient that he was too late to be of any good. Ten deaths were recorded by the Shansi Mission in the years preceding 1900. Besides Dr. Goldsbury and Tinnie and Alma Thompson, Leonard Stimson, who was born shortly after the Stimsons arrived in Shansi, died of bronchitis in 1884 at the age of twenty-two months. He was buried in a small cemetery in the hills outside Tai Yuan that soon was the site of the graves of a growing number of foreigners. Frank and Jennie Price lost a twenty-month-old daughter to typhus the same spring; she was buried

Oberlin Band missionaries at their annual meeting in 1893. Kneeling, left to right: *Tinnie D'Etta Hewett Thompson, Rowena Bird, and Jennie Pond Atwater, first wife of Ernest Atwater.* Seated: *Alice Williams, Annette and Iranaeus Atwood, and Jennie and Howard Clapp.* Standing: *George Williams, Mrs. Mary Goldsbury, widow of Dr. James Goldsbury, Francis and Lydia Davis, James Thompson, and Ernest Atwater.* *Courtesy Oberlin College Archives.*

next to Leonard. Frank's brother Charles and wife, Eva, suffered losses of their own—two sons aged three and twelve. The Davises lost their first two infants. Jennie Evelyn Pond Atwater, who arrived in Shansi in 1892 with her husband Ernest Richmond Atwater, died in 1896, leaving him with four daughters to care for. In addition, two of the Atwood children—Karl and a son born in China—died while the Atwoods were with the North China Mission in Shantung.

The list of fatalities might have been even greater. Francis Davis got seriously ill in 1893 with an attack of grippe and a subsequent bilious attack that was believed to be aggravated by his having fallen eighty feet from a yardarm when he was a young sailor. His colleagues first thought that Francis would be "a hopeless invalid with no chance of recovery," then, ominously, "that he would never be well again." Miraculously, Francis did recover, which Jennie Atwater credited to "how wonderfully the Lord" answered all their prayers.[30] That same year, Florence Price almost died while being born. Atwood was away when Eva Price went into labor. The infant was born with the umbilical cord wrapped around her neck and strangling her. Eva's husband, Charles, who was pressed into service as midwife, was beside himself and didn't know what to do. But Eva directed him and the child's life was saved. Then, when she was five years old, Florence skirted with death when she set fire to herself while trying to light a fire in a toy stove. Eva heard her screams and, running upstairs to where she was playing, smothered the flames by throwing her arms around the child and gathering her clothes in a tight wad.

When it did occur, death was a test of faith. Lydia Davis noted in her diary that her first baby, a boy, lived for only three and a half days, dying at 5 A.M. on Saturday, December 20, 1890, when "the angels came and bore our darling away from us to Jesus."[31] A second son, born in 1894, also died after three days. "But I know the Father knew best and 'He doeth *all* things well,'" she wrote.[32] "To-night I can but think of the dear ones gone before, waiting to welcome us when time shall have passed away."[33] Charles and Eva Price left China to take their son Stewart to sanatoriums in Nebraska and Iowa and a faith-healing institute in Chicago, when he came down in 1896 with either Bright's disease or "Diabetes Miletus"[34]—doctors disagreed on the diagnosis. But all to no avail. Charles was always proud of "the manly way he bore his sickness and his fearless way of meeting death has been a good lesson for me. I think I can never feel the dread of the end as I once did."[35] Eva, who was devastated when "God took" her son Donald in 1892,[36] said, "Our hearts look forward to the time so longingly when we shall see our boys again. Oh! the joy of this very blessed hope"[37]:

> When I paint my picture of "Age" it will not be an old couple in a boat looking *backward!* No! I shall paint them, in a boat maybe, but looking *across* the "River" to their *real,* Eternal home, with a reflection on their faces of all the beauty, glory, peace and satisfying happiness of that land which they are about to enter. Oh! it is infinitely *better.* Why *should* they look back, and have their faces pictured in the shadow of their earthly sorrows, when they might have

their eyes fixed on the "shining shore," and their faces glowing with His express image? Glowing with the blessed assurances of immortality?[38]

At almost the very time that the Davises and the Charles Prices were arriving in Shansi in 1889, Charles's brother Frank was looking back on the few accomplishments the Mission could boast and offered several reasons that its early goals had not been reached. One was the presence of a "mysterious providence" evidenced by the number of deaths that had occurred. A second reason was the fact that too many missionaries served an "exceedingly short" term of service. Then, too, there was the "slowness of the work," which was "trying to those in service." Price, a linguist who mastered more than half a dozen foreign languages, attributed the slowness to the "peculiarly difficult" Chinese language. He also blamed the lack of progress on the opium habit that had "enslaved multitudes," the worship of idols, and "the deceitfulness and vileness of the heathen heart," which "closes the ear to the Gospel message."

Finally, Price said, the Mission's work had been hampered by internal doctrinal disputes.[39] Charles Tenney was at the center of two of them. His theological views began to change, and, in questioning Congregational beliefs, he moved gradually to a Unitarian point of view. Tenney didn't hide his unorthodox opinions, becoming one of those, said Price, who caused "the entire brotherhood to suffer from their exceptional and erratic views."[40] Tenney also began expressing a great deal of pessimism about what Protestant missions were accomplishing in China. He came out against the hiring of native Chinese evangelists and street preaching; instead, he favored trying to win over the literati and gentry. His views put him in direct opposition to Stimson and set off a furious debate.

Stimson, who was anxious to use a direct approach in dealing with ordinary Chinese, paid a servant, who was a Christian, to act as a colporteur, distributing religious tracts, and to preach. Tenney argued that employing "natives" encouraged the unemployed—"empty cisterns which love no water"[41]—to profess Christianity so that they could get salaried jobs with the Mission. Such Chinese were called "rice Christians." Hudson Taylor was quoted as being told by his most reliable native converts not to pay native preachers with foreign money: "When you put a man into a street chapel on $5.00 per month, the fact is that everybody in the place soon finds out that he is the best paid and (according to their opinion) has the least to do of any man among them."[42]

The results of an experiment that the rival English Baptist Missionary Society attempted seemed to bear out that warning. The Baptists sent six native evangelists from Shantung into Shansi in 1882 but had to withdraw four of them two years later, and though the other two remained with the Baptist station in Shansi, they were of "doubtful advantage."[43] The lesson was not lost on the Oberlin Band. Other members of the Mission agreed with Tenney and voted against hiring Chinese to do missionary work. But Stimson, who thought the ban was a relic of medieval times, stubbornly continued the practice anyway and, despite objections, it eventually became standard procedure simply because there were never enough missionaries to handle the Mission's workload; and, in point of fact, native preachers attached to every Protestant missionary society were responsible for most conversions of Chinese.

The episode, though, left a sour taste in everyone's mouth. When Stimson sought to return to Shansi from furlough in America, his fellow missionaries agreed to let bygones be bygones if he agreed to cooperate, but Stimson felt "deeply wronged."[44] He never did return.

The Oberlin Band had set an unrealistic goal for itself—the establishment of an Oberlin-in-China college. But at least it was within the realm of reality, given time, perseverance, and resources. The American Board's goal, however—to drive a sizable wedge in the conversion of fourteen million Chinese in Shansi Province—was so wildly improbable that it can only be labeled as misdirected fantasy. But the missionaries persisted, undaunted by any obstacle, real or imagined, undeterred by the comings and goings of missionary after missionary, unfaltering in the face of constant illness and death, and ever-eager and welcoming to a new crop of recruits.

"Patience and faithful labor," Frank Price declared, "are needed and these with the blessing of God will bring this province to the Lord Jesus Christ."[45]

FIVE ❁ "Little America"

[Perfect virtue] is when you go abroad,
to behave to every one as if you were receiving a great guest.
—Confucius

When they arrived in Shansi in 1889, the Davises settled in the same house in Fenchow-fu that Martin Luther Stimson had lived in, while the Prices set up housekeeping in the Mission's main compound. Francis and Lydia were never happy with their living accommodations, but Charles and Eva quickly turned their quarters into a home away from home.

Fenchow-fu, on the western side of the Fen River and about three thousand feet above sea level, had a population then of fifty thousand, making it the second largest city in Shansi. As the "fu" in its name indicated, it was a prefectural city, with jurisdiction over a number of districts, and the site of periodic civil service examinations. The city proper was not large, but a number of substantial suburbs ringed it.

Stimson, who had scouted Fenchow-fu for the Oberlin Band, had trouble finding a house to rent when he first went there in 1885. Chinese landlords were reluctant to rent to foreigners. He spent seven months living in an inn until he was finally able to prevail upon the local *kuan* (magistrate) to persuade a homeowner to rent a place to him. The Davises lived in the house for several years before transferring to the Taiku station, but Lydia was never happy with the place. She thought it was "comfortable, but exceedingly primitive."[1]

On the other hand, Charles and Eva Price, who resided about a mile and a half away near the West Gate, took great pride in their quarters.

The Mission's main compound, which was surrounded by a fifteen-foot-high wall, was actually a little village in itself, consisting, in typical Chinese style, of a jumble of connecting walled-in courtyards that covered about two acres. Each courtyard was surrounded by rooms. A gate in the wall of the Prices' courtyard led out onto one of the city's narrow, crooked business streets, but they kept it shut tight because of the many thieves in the city, "too avaricious" people in general, and "too many famished dogs and beggars."[2]

Beggars posed a special, painful problem for the otherwise charitable Americans. Filthy, unkempt paupers were constantly trying to force their way into the Mission compound "to beg for pity," and sometimes at night "their pitiful cries" kept everyone awake. "Their name is legion," said one of the missionaries, who saw the dead body of a beggar being torn "limb from limb and eaten by dogs" within sight of one of the city's great gates. But, as he ruefully added, "The more one does for them the more he is besieged."[3]

When the Prices first moved into the compound, their courtyard was about fifty square feet, paved with gray brick, and surrounded by rooms of the same brick that included—before they renovated them—a bedroom, a kitchen, and a large sitting-dining room that was employed for church services and prayer meetings until a chapel was built. A brick stove ran along one side of the kitchen. It had three holes in it for cooking and two on which iron kettles rested for boiling water. The kitchen was inconvenient to the dining room, forcing a servant to take a circuitous route when carrying dishes back and forth.

Starting in 1891, the Prices hired Chinese workmen and began to clear off a back court in the compound. Walls that were covered with moss and lichen were torn down, and space was made for a playground as well as a tennis court and, off of it, a croquet field. A staircase against a wall of the croquet field led over an alleyway to where the Atwoods lived. Eva would climb it in order to see out of the compound, but the staircase fell down with a crash one night and was never restored.

The Prices evidently did not appreciate Chinese architecture. Eventually they had the main gateway of the compound, with its gracefully curved tile roof, torn down. They got rid of the "hideous" dragon heads that adorned each of its corners as well as the two "horrid" stone dogs that guarded the entranceway to the courts.[4] When they were finished, there was still ample room in the compound for a schoolboys' courtyard and housing, a separate women's court, a guest room, a servant's room, a recitation room, a storeroom, a coal house, a washroom attached to the kitchen, and a stable courtyard.

The Prices planted four evergreens by a well in a corner of the main courtyard. The Davises' first child, who died in 1890, four days after being born, was buried in the midst of the trees. His grave was surrounded by a little brick wall with a little tree in the middle. Eva planted this so-called House Court with the seeds of flowers brought from home. One of their friends said that the nasturtiums, zinnias, portulaca, sweet peas, mignonette, lady's slippers, and morning glories created "the prettiest flower bed I have seen in China."[5] Eva surrounded it with pots of roses, oleander, geraniums, and day lilies. In a back court she grew onions, radishes, cabbage, corn, potatoes, peas, lettuce and beets. The Prices also had chickens and a cow, though, as with all Chinese cows, it didn't provide milk unless its calf was with it and "helps to do the milking."[6]

It was impossible for the Prices to do away with every element of Chinese architecture in redoing the outside of the main house and courtyards, but the interior was another matter altogether. The American Board alloted $500 to outfit each missionary before he, or she, left for Shansi. Besides items they could not expect to find in China—lye, flea powder and kerosene—the missionaries also took cans of vegetables, sugar, and even tins of butter, though how it was preserved enroute is a mystery. They shipped ahead tools, locks, cooking stoves, iron bedsteads and mattresses, clocks, and organs.

So, walking into the Prices' rooms—or, for that matter, into the quarters of most any missionary—was like taking a step into another, but familiar, world. All the comforts of home were literally echoed—rocking chairs and bookcases, cushions and tables, bureaus and mirrored dressers, and paintings and family photos on the walls. Atop one of the end tables might be the *Oberlin News* and magazines such as *Scribners, North American Review,* the *Household, Wide Awake,* or the *Congregationalist.* Eva subscribed to all of them, though they were always six to eight weeks old by the time

Charles and Eva Price and their daughter, Florence, in their quarters in Fenchow-fu. The only noticeable oriental touch is the scroll on the wall. One of their sons who died is in the photograph hanging at the corner. Courtesy Oberlin College Archives.

they reached Fenchow-fu.[7] Except perhaps for some locally made mats on the floor, or the Chinese design in a curtain fabric, the impression was unmistakably small-town, middle-class America. Inquisitive Chinese neighbors loved to tour the rooms. The women were especially taken with Eva's "iron needle"—her sewing machine.

The major addition to the Prices' house was a second floor. They had added a bathroom and two bedrooms above their old downstairs bedroom. Pleasant as her garden was, it was the view from an upstairs room of her own that gave Eva the most joy. The compound was like a prison to her; indeed, the compound wall shut out the world from the Mission, isolating all its residents from even their closest neighbors and emphasizing their apartness from Chinese life. But now, at least, Eva said she had "something else than walls, walls, walls for me to look at."[8] She could at last "look out over these walls toward America."[9]

When the blistering days of summer came and the stench of Fenchow-fu—everything "from a dead dog to spoiled cabbage"[10]—became unbearable, the Prices retreated to the foothills outside the city about five miles away. There, in the village of Yü Tao Ho, they were able to purchase an old, abandoned mill by a little, tree-shaded "splashing" stream that was fed by a spring in the mountains.[11] The mill was one of about eighty decaying mills in a valley eight miles long that was then entirely given over to the growing of poppies for opium.[12]

"Water & trees, both a rarity in China," exclaimed Charles,[13] who believed that living in Fenchow-fu meant "certain death" even for people in comparatively good health.[14] In Yü Tao Ho, they drank water directly from a cold spring, the first and only times they could do so without boiling it first. The air, Eva declared, "makes one want to eat and sleep at all hours, making a refreshing change from this walled in city with its vile odors."[15]

In order to get the vistas she craved, the Prices cut a window into the mill's wall. But that encouraged curious local farmers, who had never seen a foreigner, to come by and peer into their rooms—hence the title she gave their getaway home, "Peeking Place."[16]

Eva had what she called a "regulation flag" made to encourage "patriotism of the house." It was a Revolutionary War flag of thirteen stripes and thirteen stars.[17] Later, for Charles's forty-seventh birthday, she had a full-fledged American flag of silk made for him (it had thirty-nine stars). She kept it draped over the front door of their house in Fenchow-fu.[18] Visitors from other countries called both the Fenchow-fu compound and its counterpart in Taiku "Little America."[19]

Unlike Fenchow-fu, which was chiefly a residential city, Taiku was a wealthy trade and financial center known as the Wall Street of China.[20] It was situated east of the Fen River on a fertile plain about two miles above sea level, and had a population of some twenty-thousand people. An old, walled city, it had narrow streets and, unusual for China, many houses of two and sometimes three stories. Because of the narrow streets and the tall houses, little sunlight penetrated the city.

The Shansi Mission's compound in Taiku was on busy South Street, near the city's South Gate. Behind it stood Taiku's famous landmark, a tall white pagoda. The *yamen* (courthouse) and post office were midtown, down South Street from the compound and just beyond a tower in the center of the city. Other than the pagoda and the tower, the city was a monotonous arrangement of high walls that shut in every house. One missionary was astonished at how little noise there was in the city. "You cannot hear a sound when approaching the city even when you come right up to the wall," he said. "It seems quite dead and silent. But go to one of the gates and there is considerable motion, shouting and business."[21]

The Mission compound was so crowded, it was fairly bursting. At one point it housed three missionary families, a single female missionary, and

The famed white pagoda of Taiku, as seen from the American Board compound on South Street. *Courtesy Oberlin College Archives.*

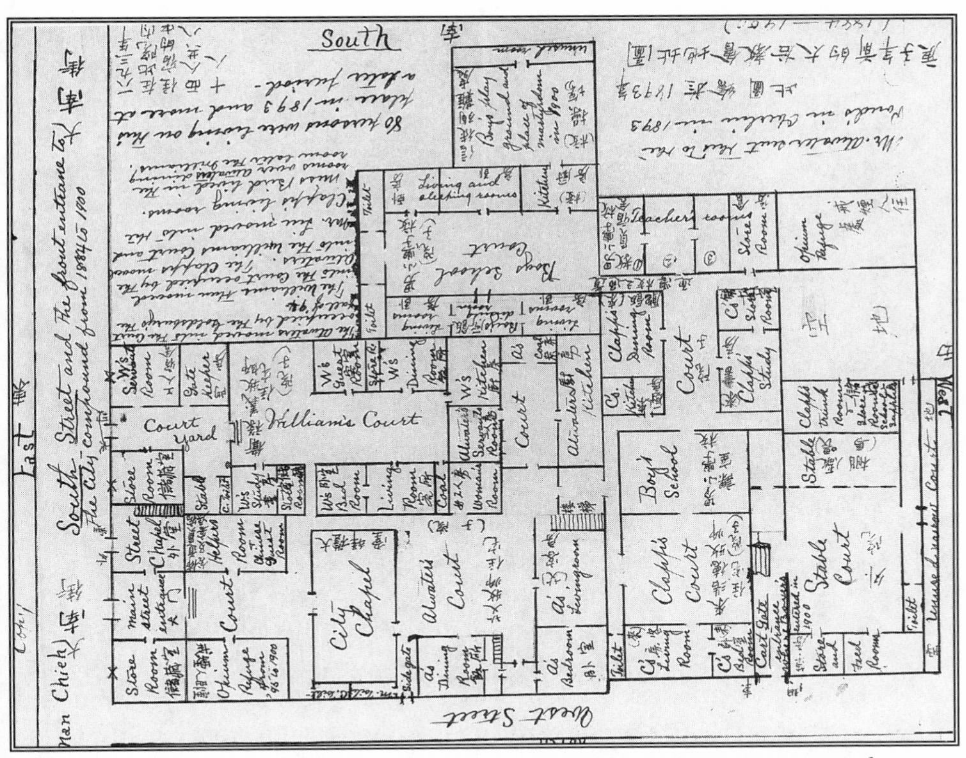

The crowded Shansi Mission compound in Taiku, drawn by Ernest Atwater in 1893. Note the "Boy's play ground" and "unused room" on the right. Courtesy Oberlin College Archives.

Chinese of all ages and both sexes in its schools, hospital, and opium refuge—a total of eighty people in all, plus six animals, in a compound of about twenty-nine thousand square feet.[22] Like Taiku itself, the compound rarely enjoyed the sunshine that, as one missionary put it, "we foreigners welcome so gratefully as one of God's good gifts to make our lives in China so much pleasanter than they otherwise would be."[23] The compound wall was twenty feet high, and most of the year the sun never touched the floor of any of the inside courtyards. Only eight of its nearly forty rooms ever received any sunshine in the winter.

Moreover, the window in the female missionary's bedroom, on a second floor, opened above a cesspool. Her study on the ground floor below it was next to an odorous Chinese water closet. In addition, one missionary couple suffered the inconvenience of having to live in two areas of the compound.[24] Their bedroom and sitting room were beside the compound gate, where almost constant noise from street traffic in the city was unavoidable. Their kitchen and dining room were in another court altogether, and their storeroom was even farther away.[25] After spending a summer in the outlying village of Li Man, a missionary wife unhappily complained about the prospect of returning to Taiku:

> We go back this fall into sunless courts, green with mould, small rooms and a study that in the summer heat without rain is so damp that we can scrape the whitewash off by the handfuls.
>
> A narrow passage way connects our court with the other courts. It is through this passage way that every one passes not only into our court but into the chapel, the opium court for men, and street chapel—people tainted with disease and contagion as well as those strong in body.[26]

Whether in Fenchow-fu or Taiku, the lives of the missionaries were circumscribed. Between September and May—before the heat of the summer drove them into the hills—they were busy virtually nonstop with their duties. The missionaries had to adjust their routines to a totally different concept of time and had trouble sometimes getting Chinese to put aside a day for Sunday services and prayer meetings. The Chinese did not measure time in weeks, nor did they observe any sabbath. They followed the 360-day lunar calendar and worked without respite until their New Year's celebration, which fell in late January or early February. It was then that a succession of festivities was held during which the images of old gods were discarded and new ones pasted up on doorways and in shrines; everyone was officially one *sui* (year) older no matter when they were born; debtors were expected to pay back what they owed; and everybody vacationed.

The missionaries thus enjoyed a lengthy midwinter holiday, a combination of their own Christmas–New Year's celebration and the Chinese New Year, when no missionary activity was possible. Otherwise, they worked almost without pause. The men usually ran the medical dispensaries, supervised the school programs, conducted church services, and toured the countryside to distribute tracts and, perhaps, with a Chinese helper as interpreter, to preach to any villagers they could assemble. Deacon Liu alternated leading sabbath services at Che Wang, the village where his family lived. It was one of the most encouraging outstations the Shansi Mission had because the villagers there—seven Christians plus a number of inquirers—were self-supporting. They paid for hiring a room on Che Wang's main street that was used for services and prayer meetings.[27]

Che Wang was only some ten miles from Taiku. Many other villages that the missionaries served were farther away and hard to get to. Charles Price spent most of a day traveling to one small community about twenty-three miles from Fenchow-fu, in the hills beyond a mountain pass, where the gorge leading to it was so narrow his horse could barely get through. The village had about sixty inhabitants, only a few of whom were Christians. The Christians were not able to get into Fenchow-fu for services very often, so the missionaries tried to visit them every few weeks. "We have learned not to despise small things," Charles said.[28]

Missionary wives and single females busied themselves with teaching Chinese women about the Christian faith, using so-called Bible women as their interpreters and trying, whenever they could get invitations, to visit the women in their homes. They distributed tracts and talked about Christianity to the women who sought treatment at the dispensaries or who committed themselves to the opium refuges. Some, like Jennie Clapp, toured villages as well.

At the end of a day, the missionaries were often weary, too tired sometimes even to keep up their correspondence with friends and families at home, which seems to have been their favorite leisure-time activity. Eva Price, who didn't think she worked as hard as any of the men or the single women, described a typical day as follows:

She had breakfast with her family at 7:30 in the morning, followed by prayers in English and the study of prayers in Chinese; after that she joined other missionaries and their Chinese followers in her sitting room for Chinese prayers, which lasted about half an hour. She read Chinese from nine to ten o'clock with her Chinese teacher, then did sewing chores, visited Chinese women in their homes, and, if she had time before supper, wrote some letters. After supper she spent two hours with her Chinese teacher and his wife, teaching them English.[29]

Studying the Chinese language, by the way, was a constant chore for many of the missionaries. After eight years in China, Eva's husband, Charles, said that he still felt the need "of persistent study of the language. This is one of the mysteries connected with this great people, how they ever came to form such a very difficult mode of expressing themselves." And, he added, "The people themselves are just as hard to read as their language."[30]

Charles was echoing the sense of frustration that the missionaries felt about what they perceived to be the many failings of almost every aspect of the Chinese way of life. None was more loathsome to the missionaries than the Chinese addiction to opium, though they never castigated the British for introducing the drug into China. At one point, before Shansi and other regions in China began growing opium, the British were selling more than 23,500 chests annually; each chest contained between 130 and 160 pounds of opium.[31] Poor, downtrodden peasants looking for some escape from their dreary, near-starvation existence were the chief users, but literati and gentry were addicts, too. By 1900 there were believed to be forty million Chinese who smoked or chewed opium, about fifteen million of whom were full-fledged addicts; thus, for every Chinese who converted to Christianity there were fifteen Chinese addicted to opium.[32]

Many of the men who were addicts sold their wives or children to pay for the opiate. Once, when Iranaeus Atwood was setting the broken leg of a man, he asked him if he had a wife to take care of him once he got back to his village. He had one, the man said, but he had sold her for money to purchase opium. "That is very bad indeed," remarked Atwood. "Wife was very bad also," the man retorted.[33]

Deacon Liu, who had broken the habit and never relapsed, was the exception rather than the rule. Eva Price bemoaned the fact that despite the refuges the missionaries operated, perhaps only one in a thousand addicts would fall off the habit permanently. "All we can do is to work and *trust,* but in the face of such facts you can readily see what discouraging work it is":

> They pay for the medicine, besides all the suffering they have to undergo; and some of them suffer dreadfully before they are rid of the craving. Bodily pains and aches, the craving and mental unrest make the ordeal anything but a pleasure I can assure you, and we would get disgusted and perfectly discouraged were it not for *the* occasional one who *sticks.* . . . If there is a place in the whole world where it is harder to do missionary work than right here in Opium

drugged Shansi province, which is probably one of the worst in the whole Empire, I do not want to know of it. . . .

There are five women on our place now, breaking off opium, one at least for the second time, and I spend two hours a day with them trying to teach them the Better way. I come away so often feeling discouraged and heart-sick. We go over the wonderful things Christ did for the world; we talk of Salvation and Eternal joy and Everlasting life, but it does not seem to make much impression. When I think of my lack in many points as a *teacher,* my inability to speak to them understandingly because they know nothing of the book language and I have so little of their local dialect, to realize the darkness of their minds and hearts, their inability to grasp the meaning of spiritual things, their utter ignorance of God and His purposes, I am filled with wonder that any good whatever can come out of it. But when I think of God and the way He often uses the weak things to bring great glory, and when I know that it is not by might nor by power but by *God's spirit* that these poor souls are to be lifted up, I must trust that the world of Life I speak, however imperfectly, many not return to Him void. (But I get awfully discouraged).[34]

"Shansi is a hard field to work," wrote a fellow missionary, "because of the almost complete dominion of the opium habit. It is like trying to save a race of drunkards."[35]

"Oh, that the holy light would shine through this seemingly inpenetrable fog bank of ignorance and foul miasmas of sin and superstition," wrote Atwood. "We labor on, walking still by faith, not yet by sight, hoping for a rift in the clouds to gladden our weary eyes and burdened hearts."[36]

SIX ❁ *Realities*

What you do not want done to yourself, do not do to others.
—Confucius

Most if not all of the Shansi missionaries were discouraged at one time or another, as early exuberance gave way to harsh reality. Some never wavered in their determination to bring the Chinese into the Christian fold, but others in time became frustrated. A few threw up their hands and quit.

Take, for example, Charles Tenney. He began with enthusiasm, writing that "we have always looked upon the conquest of the Roman Empire as the greatest achievement of the Church, and are in the habit of thinking that work must ever stand as the masterpiece of Christian triumphs. I have come to the sober conviction that the greatest work ever undertaken by the Church is the one she is now entering upon in the advance upon the Chinese Empire. I do not put the Chinese second to the Roman Empire in civilization, intellectual power, or future possible influence on the world's history."[1]

But Tenney soon had second thoughts. He resigned after three and a half years for a number of reasons—his disagreement over Mission policy, for one, his theological differences for another. But perhaps more fundamental were the complexities he foresaw as early as 1883, after only a year in Shansi: "In the Roman Empire the stream of Christian truth wore down a mountain of loose ashes, in this Empire it has to wear down a mountain of solid rock." The "only thing that is really effective is *spiritual power,*" he said, adding:

Of course, natural gifts and cultivated talents are good, but only as the machinery of the spiritual power within. . . . The Chinese cannot be overawed or taken by storm by any brilliancy of logic or rhetoric, but when they see a man actually controlled by the love of God and of souls so as to forget himself they are *impressed* by it. They understand brilliancy and ambition but they don't understand *love*."[2]

Tenney wrote to the Oberlin Band in Ohio that year:

What I have seen in China makes me feel very strongly about this, dear friend. Don't come if you are drawn only by the grandeur of the work and your ambition to have a part in moulding the future of a great nation. Come for the *love of Christ and of souls,* and you will be satisfied and the Lord will be *sure* to use you."[3]

Chauncey Cady also began missionary work optimistically when he first wrote the Band, "If there could be 2 or 3 families or individuals located in 7 or 8 of these hsien [district] cities and four or five more in the city or town where the central school is to be say by the end of 1888, I think the foundations of the future Oberlin-in-China would be fairly laid."[4] However, he soon came to the conclusion that establishing an Oberlin-in-China was dependent upon the introduction of advanced western technology. It was clear to him, for example, that farmers would not abandon the cultivation of opium and grow grains that could be shipped from the province and profitably sold until a railway line was built. Unlike Tenney, who put Christian fervor first, Cady thought that anyone from Oberlin joining the Band should make it a point to study natural sciences and practical subjects such as agronomy and engineering. He wished he had watches, clocks, a telephone, and other marvels to impress officials with western achievements. Before Cady left Shansi to work instead in Japan, he reflected on the dreams that the Band had shared:

I conclude there still remains a sort of ghost of that idea that about all we need to do is to have the proper buildings erected and sufficient men on the ground and presto! the New Oberlin University among the Celestials is there! in Shansi, of course. Now the sooner the truth is realized that the school system of our Mission such as we really ought and will have is *sure* to be *very slow in beginning,* and in *growth* so much the better.[5]

Cady left Shansi after only two years, saying that he found "nothing attractive in the Chinese people."[6]

The truth was that dreams, desires and determination aside, none of the Oberlin Band who came to China was ever prepared for the reality of living and working there. Incredibly, in spite of the fact that the American Board had been sending missionaries to China for nearly a half century, its officials seemed not to have learned any lessons. The Board never set up any system or procedure for indoctrinating its China-bound representatives before they left the States. It published no literature or brochures on the subject other than a guide as to what food items and medical supplies, clothing, furniture, and the like to take or send there in advance. It recommended no background material about China or its history; offered no information whatsoever about its people, politics, customs, mores, or culture in general; and provided no explanation of the country's religious heritage. There was no orientation course, and no attempt was even made to teach the missionaries the difficult Chinese language or to help them learn to read its complicated pictographs until they were actually on station in China. The Board relied solely on missionaries in the field—in Oberlin's case, those attached to the North China Mission—to orient new arrivals, and inevitably the information they passed was negative, dealing primarily with the obstacles and difficulties the newcomers would encounter.

The missionaries' efforts were further hampered by the Bibles and tracts that they gave away or sold—and thousands of copies were either distributed freely or sold below cost for a few pennies. Because the three major Bible societies—British, Scottish, and American—did not want to offend or stir up an unending controversy between the many denominations in China or their donors back home, the sacred literature contained no explanatory notes or even commentary of the simplest kind. The missionaries, who were never fully at ease in the Chinese language, found it a strain to explain anything as profound as the Christian faith to the Chinese in the simplest of terms.

In addition, the Chinese had never heard of prophets, had no idea where the Biblical lands were, and thought that certain practices, such as the washing of feet, strange. They were often confused by such elemental matters as the frequent allusion to shepherds in the Bible. In many areas of China the inhabitants had never seen sheep. What were they? Moreover, where there were sheep—as in Shansi—they were considered the lowest form of animal, and shepherds were not highly regarded.

And then there were references totally counter to Chinese customs. The missionaries spoke of the right hand as the seat of honor, and whoever sat at Jesus' right was special. In China, the opposite was true; the left hand was favored. Similarly, the missionaries regarded the dragon as an associate of the devil; though they didn't believe in saints, the allegory of St. George and the dragon was clearly a battle against evil. But the Chinese took the dragon to be the symbol of intelligence, beneficence, and power. The dragon was displayed on the national banner and royal coat-of-arms; the Imperial seat in Peking was the Dragon Throne.

The Oberlin missionaries repeated many of the very same practices that the Board's mission in Foochow, opened in 1847, had employed, and that added to their problems. They relied almost totally on Chinese teachers as interpreters, translators, go-betweens, and teachers of religion even though few of them were Christian. The missionaries had great difficulty in establishing ties with any Chinese, particularly among the literati and gentry, outside of their converts; and they were unable to recognize that their criticism of Chinese education—rote learning based entirely on ancient classics—antagonized the very literati whose authority and influence they needed. Added to all this was an attitude that they shared with almost every other missionary who ever served in China: contempt for virtually all things Chinese—their religious beliefs, morals, habits, manners, dress, speech, and the way they treated women.

Protestant missionaries in general had no idea how deeply the literati were offended when the missionaries took the opportunity of the triennial provincial examinations for government positions to distribute Christian literature as the candidates emerged from the exhausting tests. Missionaries also insulted the literati by criticizing the rote learning required to pass those examinations. Education played a dominant role in China, the prerequisite to the power and prestige that went with holding office in the country's immense bureaucracy. The competitive exams held in prefectural cities were the stepping stone into that bureaucracy. They were based on the memorization and analysis of texts attributed to Confucius or some of his early followers and some commentaries on those texts.

In essence, the literati, who were very influential in provincial cities, were the very persons the missionaries should have been courting if they were going to win over a sizable portion of the population. But the missionaries had very little success making inroads among them. Iranaeus Atwood once held a feast and staged a lantern slide exhibition about Christianity for the literati of Fenchow-fu and vicinity. He attracted a large audience. Afterwards, Deacon Liu, who accompanied Atwood, offered to answer any questions the attendees had or would send him, or to compare the Gospel with Confucius and his disciple Mencius if anyone were interested. "Alas! Alas!" Liu despaired. "All the time I was there not a man of them came around and not even a question did they send around. They enjoyed the good food and liked to see the pictures but that was the end of it."[7]

In addition, most missionaries exhibited no empathy for the profound feeling the Chinese possessed about ancestor worship and its concomitant, filial piety. The chief duty of a married couple was to produce a son to maintain the family line, and the chief duty of a son was to obey his father. A disloyal son could be punished legally.

As an American observer put it, "The spirits of the past rule this nation from their urns."[8] The Jesuits who followed the Italian priest Matteo Ricci to China in the sixteenth century would have appreciated that observation. They grasped the importance of the Chinese veneration of ancestors. Wisely, the Jesuits defined ancestor worship as a nonreligious practice and permitted converts to perform ceremonies for the dead. They likewise permitted at mass the Chinese custom of firing off firecrackers at religious celebrations. But the Pope put a stop to such practices in the early 1700s, ruling that ancestor-worship rites did indeed constitute worship.

For their part, Protestants never considered any alternative to banning ancestor worship outright. In demanding the abandonment of ancestor worship as a criterion for church membership, both Catholics and Protestants created enormous hostility among their Chinese neighbors, who believed that a person was an inseparable link in a long chain of ancestors and that the tablets and shrine to them were the most sacred part of a home.

The missionaries also failed to fully comprehend that the Chinese did not think in terms of sin, souls, and salvation. Nor did they appreciate the "three ways to one goal" that imbued their lives—Taoism, Buddhism, and Confucianism.[9] To a Chinese person, evil was a question of spirits who dwelled everywhere and schemed to interfere with a person's good fortune. The missionaries emphasized man's sinfulness and his dependence on God's mercy. The Chinese held to the Confucian belief in the essential goodness of man and his responsibility for his own destiny on earth.

"It is a saying of great antiquity in China," wrote a veteran missionary in the hindsight of almost three decades spent in China, "that upon entering a village one should learn what is customary, and upon entering a country ascertain what is forbidden—with a view, that is, to conforming to the custom, and eschewing what is for any reason taboo."[10]

One of the few differences between cultures that most missionaries did understand was how deeply shocked the Chinese were by the impropriety displayed by married missionary couples. Women occupied the lowest rung in their society, so inferior that it was not uncommon to find unwanted infant girls thrown outside a city's walls for wolves to eat. The father was a supreme autocrat, with strict control over family income and property. He could sell a daughter into slavery. His wife never appeared with him in public (even the Dowager Empress in Peking hid behind a screen at audiences), and any display of affection between him and her was considered immoral. Story has it that the wife of one of the Shansi missionaries suddenly departed for home when a serious domestic scandal occurred that the missionaries feared their Chinese adherents would learn about.[11] If it was true, it was hushed up so well that no one spoke about it.

The contrast between the two cultures, Chinese and Western, was best illustrated when it came to what to call God. There was a heaven and there were many gods in the Chinese pantheon, but no single God, no one Lord who was omnipotent. The missionaries wrestled with the problem of coming up with an expression that would adequately convey the idea of one deity. Protestants argued about whether to use the term *shen*—meaning "god" or "spirit"—or the term *Shang-ti*—"Lord on High." They finally settled on the latter, though both terms showed up in their translations of the Bible. Roman Catholics translated God as *T'ien Chu*—"Lord of Heaven."

In addition to abandoning the worship of ancestors, those Chinese who wished to be considered candidates for baptism—and they were almost always either peasants or laborers—were also obliged to shun all forms of idolatry and could not take part in, or contribute money to, religious processions, theatricals, and festivals. In fact, the Tientsin Treaties of 1858-1860 between China and several European powers and America specifically exempted converts from "taxes levied and contributions for the support of religious customs and practices contrary to their religion."[12] Few things irked their neighbors more. Local festivities were a shared expense. When the converts didn't chip in their share, the rest of the Chinese in the community had to pay more.

"It is monstrous in barbarians to attempt to improve the inhabitants of the Celestial Empire, when they are so miserably deficient themselves," wrote a member of the literati in the mid-nineteenth century:

> Thus, introducing among the Chinese a poisonous drug [opium], for their own benefit, to the injury of others, they are deficient in benevolence. Sending their fleets and arms to rob other nations of their possessions, they can make no pretensions to rectitude. Allowing men and women to mix in society and walk arm in arm through the streets, they show that they have not the least sense of propriety. And in rejecting the doctrines of the ancient kings, they are far from displaying wisdom. Indeed truth is the only good quality to which they can lay the least claim. Deficient, therefore, in four out of the five cardinal virtues [humanity, righteousness, decorum, wisdom, and good faith], how can they expect to renovate others? . . . Further, these would-be exhorters of the world are themselves deficient in filial piety, forgetting their parents as soon as dead, putting them off with deal [plank] coffins only an inch thick, and never so much as once sacrificing to their names, or burning the smallest trifle of gilt paper for their support in a future world. Lastly, they allow the rich and noble to enter office without passing through any literary examinations, and do not throw open the road to advancement to the poorest and meanest in the land. From all this it appears that foreigners are inferior to the Chinese, and therefore most unfit to instruct them.[13]

Not all Chinese were so negative. Some were ambivilant, willing to credit Westerners for the many advances they brought with them. A noted educator who grew up in Shanghai recalled his boyhood feelings: "The foreigner appeared to my mind half divine and half devilish, double-faced and many-handed like Vishnu, holding an electric light, a steamboat, and a pretty doll in one set of hands, and a policeman's club, revolver, and handful of opium in the other. When one looked at his bright side he was an angel; on the dark side he was a demon."[14]

Returning from a tour into the countryside, one of the Shansi missionaries recounted the reactions of three people he met that he thought were typical of the Chinese attitude toward Christianity. One, a scholar, told him that the doctrine of Christ was foolishness, that he himself knew more than Christ did. A second man said that half of the residents of his village were Catholic converts and that he and his family would probably become Christians eventually. The third person, a woman, said she would not be ashamed to become a Christian but that it was unimportant to her.[15]

One can only conjecture how much the attitude of the missionaries toward the Chinese was affected by their own reactions. New arrivals were invariably fascinated by the exotic differences between East and West: The Chinese ate with chopsticks rather than knife and fork; mourners wore white instead of black; their surnames came first, and often the given names of males were changed three times as they grew up, went to school, and married. Newcomers marveled that Chinese men shaved their heads, wore queues, and dressed in long, flowing robes, while their women wore trousers and bound their feet.

But, then, after living for a time in China, the opinions of many missionaries became increasingly negative, derived as they were from the perspective of Western mores and chauvinistic superiority. Charles Price, who was vocal about his affection for the Chinese, still felt uncomfortable with them. It wasn't "a lack of love," nor "any feeling of repugnance," he said: "There are many of the people very kind and cordial and seem to wish to be friendly and social. But their manner of life, their customs are all so different one cannot feel the pleasure in their society that we do for one of our own nationality."[16]

Others expressed their feelings in stronger terms. Lydia Davis had been repulsed when she first saw Chinese people in California, but she "mercifully" changed her mind. After she "saw the Chinese one by one in their native setting," she said, "all the feeling I had had in San Francisco miraculously vanished, never to return."[17] But Lydia's change of heart was based on her relationships with Chinese probationers and converts. When she talked about her house servants, she had some harsh things to say: "Their slowness, their filth, their incompetence, their cheating, makes one sick at heart, and they grow to be a weariness to the flesh. To be with people all day long who, until converted, all lie, and steal, and mistrust you, is that ease? To love them that hate you, is that natural?"[18] Lydia's husband, Francis, said that an old English lady missionary from Nangpo had told him that to govern servants, "'Don't get angry or excited, dont [*sic*] raise your voice but quietly and firmly insist with a falling slide of that is an end of the matter.' The falling slide shows your faith that you will be obeyed, but a louder tone is apt to have a rising inflexion which is really '*Will* you obey' instead of 'You *will* obey.'"[19]

George Williams, who joined the Shansi Mission in 1892, found "the dirt and filth of the street and home" to be "very trying to the sense of the Missionary." Once, while he was visiting the home of his language teacher, who was wealthy and aristocratic,

> A little child running about the room defecated on the floor. The thing seemed to be common occurrence and no notice was taken of the fact that we were present. A servant went to the door and called to a dog which came in and ate up the foul mess. The dogs and pigs of China scavenge the streets and live largely on human ordure.[20]

Williams's revulsion was echoed when, in the late 1890s, the president of Oberlin College, John Henry Barrows, made a lecture tour of India, Japan, and China. In Shanghai, he took a half hour's stroll outside the foreign enclave and into the native section of the city. "In all of my experience of humanity," he declared, "I have seen nothing so foul, so degrading, so unutterably filthy as this Chinese quarters." Upon his return to America, Barrows gave a series of lectures that was singularly critical:

> Seeing Japan after a visit to China, one feels that he has escaped from the mouth of hell. The Japanese people may be imitative rather than creative; it is true that they have originated but little. Still they have had the wisdom enough to imitate many of the best things. . . .
>
> The first impression which China makes upon the stranger is grotesqueness. Its people are spoken of as morally and physically our antipodes. "Their compass-needle points south instead of north, their soldiers wear quilted petticoats, satin boots, and bead necklaces, and go to a night attack with lanterns in their hands, being more afraid of the dark than of exposing themselves to the enemy. . . . Ladies ride in wheelbarrows, and cows are driven in carriages. When a man furnishes his house, instead of laying stress, as we do, on rosewood pianos and carved mahogany, his first ambition is for a handsome camphorwood coffin, which he keeps in the best place in his room."[21]

Barrows conceded that the Chinese were aware of the circulation of the blood before Harvey, inoculated against smallpox nine hundred years before Jenner, invented the printing press before Gutenberg, and made known the compass and gunpowder to Europe. China, he said, "is in many respects the most remarkable civilization the world has known. Its antiquity seems like that of the eternal hills. . . . It saw the empires of the ancient world blaze up in all their brief brilliancy—Babylonia, Assyria, Persia, Greece, Rome." Nowhere else in the world is education so highly valued or are people so devoted to the printed word as in China, Barrow said. But, he continued, "Endless imitation, as with Wordsworth's child, is the whole vocation of this nation of boys, imitation without improvement." In China, Barrows added, nearly everyone owes money to somebody else, lying is not an offense, and torture is part of the administration of justice. "China," he declared, "is the paradise of cruelty and conservatism."[22]

What the missionaries interpreted as a propensity on the part of most Chinese to lie was in reality a question of communication; by custom, Chinese tended not to answer questions directly. The missionaries never seemed to have grasped the subtlety of the Chinese oral tradition.

They were also troubled by what they labeled as cheating when they dealt with Chinese workers and shopkeepers. Eva Price complained that she and her husband, Charles, had to closely watch workmen renovating their home "to see that we are not *fleeced* out of our eye-teeth."[23] The ambivalent Charles said he was "constantly being surprised at the capabilities of this wonderful people,"[24] but at the same time said he could not "fully trust" any "of the natives." He feared that "even those who profess to love & serve God, are only professing with some sordid motive."[25] George Williams, who believed that "every one is trying to cheat you," said, "It takes lot of Grace to live in China."[26] Louise Partridge, who joined the Mission in 1893, believed it was "almost impossible for an American to realize the limitations of these people. I remind myself of it constantly, but don't seem then to take it in."[27] Jennie Pond Atwater thought that "all their civilization has done them very little good for they live in a distressing atmosphere of selfishness and hatred and distrust. In fact their lack of confidence in others and underhanded efforts to outwit others are so extensive as to paralyze business and make most public undertakings failures if attempted at all."[28]

The missionaries considered Chinese superstitions childish, if not self-defeating. Iranaeus Atwood was able to rent a house to open a dispensary in Taiku because it was believed to be haunted and no Chinese would live in it. Timothy Richard had had the same experience with a house that stood vacant for a long time because it was considered unlucky. "The foreign devil was supposed to fear no other devils," he noted.[29] However, the missionaries ran into difficulty when they had houses of their own design built because of the Chinese belief in *feng-shui*—the spirits of wind and water that accounted for both beneficial and harmful influences on the living and the dead. Buildings were supposed to have a proper relationship to the landscape, and the missionaries tended to build structures higher than surrounding Chinese ones and thus produced a harmful effect. Such superstitions were apparently not confined to the peasant class. A missionary related that the so-called Bismarck of China, Viceroy Li Hung Chang, visited a bridge that had been built across the Pei Ho (river) near Tientsin to accommodate a new railway line. Li was prostrated the next day with a "sick headache" that he blamed on the bridge, so it was torn up. "So much for progress in China," said the missionary.[30]

Considering the attitudes and adversities missionaries faced or expressed, it is no wonder that the work of conversion was snail-like. It took Methodist missionaries in China ten years before they baptized their first convert. The Methodist Episcopal Church South, which began evangelical work in Shanghai in 1848, took four years before its workers baptized a Chinese couple. The American Board's experience was less encouraging. The Canton station's hospital and dispensary treated thousands of Chinese every year, but it couldn't claim a single convert in that seaport until seventeen years after one of their missionaries began preaching there. Board missionaries labored for nine years before they baptized their first Chinese convert in Foochow.[31]

But as slow as the work was, Protestant missionaries continued to view China as a ready field for converting multitudes of non-Christians. In 1858, when treaty agreements with China were interpreted to allow missionaries to travel freely and preach throughout the country, there were only 81 missionaries, representing twenty Protestant societies, in all of China. Eighteen years later, 29 societies had 473 missionaries in the field. By 1889 there were nearly 1,300 Protestant missionaries working in all but one of the Empire's provinces. More than half of them were British, and more than a third American. In all, they represented 41 different societies. Driven by their ardent desire to spread the Word, resolute despite the obstacles and difficulties they faced, they claimed well over 37,000 communicants.[32]

Ten years later, in 1899, the various Protestant societies had more than 2,800 Protestant missionaries in China.[33] They operated some 500 mission stations, an almost fourfold increase in thirty years.[34] It was reported that the societies, again mostly British, had established 12 universities and colleges, 65 theological and training schools, more than 165 seminaries and high schools, and 30 medical training schools in connection with their hospitals. There were said to be 124 hospitals that, together with nearly twice that number of dispensaries, were treating nearly 2,000,000 patients each year.[35]

By comparison, the Shansi Mission's operations seem inconsequential. Understaffed, plagued by never-ending illnesses and death, the Mission, as the year 1899 ended, could count only ten members of the Oberlin Band on station in the province, the lowest number in more than ten years. They were Francis Davis, Charles and Eva Price, Howard and Jennie Clapp, Ernest and Elizabeth Atwater, George Williams, Rowena Bird, and Louise Partridge. They, together with five missionary children, lived and worked either in Taiku or Fenchow-fu, or in one of the outlying villages of those cities. There actually should have been twelve missionaries on duty, but two wives—Lydia Davis and Alice Williams—had returned with their children to America for medical reasons; they hoped to return to China in the new year.

The Mission was so far from achieving its original goal, an Oberlin-in-China, that it was not even talked about anymore. Instead, with the urging of the American Board, its focus was on turning its boys' boarding school into an academy at the high-school-level that would feed students to North China College in Tung Chow. Its crowning achievements had, in fact, been the establishment of the boys' school and, perhaps more importantly, a boarding school for girls.

SEVEN ❀ *School Days*

Among the educated, there is no distinction of origins.
—*Confucius*

As much as the male members of the Oberlin Band talked about their educational goals, the credit for starting the first two Shansi Mission schools went to two of their wives—Jennie Clapp and Lydia Davis.

After so many years of waiting, Jennie, who was a gifted teacher[1] and had taught in public schools in Ohio, was finally able to enroll fifteen youngsters for the boys' school that opened in Taiku in 1889. They were "all bright, lively boys."[2] Many were from families that had converted, though that was not a requirement. The "scholars" ranged in age from five years old to eighteen, and the instruction was on the elementary level—traditional Chinese classics in the morning; then, in the afternoon, the Bible and *tao-li* (doctrine) and perhaps a smattering of simple arithmetic and geography, or, later on, as the students progressed, Western history and science.

All the classes were taught through interpreters or by Chinese teachers like Deacon Liu, who was the first teacher hired; however, unlike Liu, many of the teachers in the beginning were not Christians. English was not spoken or taught. Jennie was by then proficient enough in Chinese to lead classes in the school along with Liu. She won a reputation among the schoolboys for being a stern disciplinarian, strict and demanding, though loved. "No one in Shansi," it was said, "did better work."[3] A native teacher, a Christian who later worked with her, said he could never "look into the face of 'Lai tai tai' [Mrs. Clapp] but that I think of the apostle John whom Jesus loved."[4]

Jennie Clapp and a friend seated on a kang. Courtesy Oberlin College Archives.

Jennie's fellow missionaries, however, saw her in a different light. To them, she was a timid woman, a worrywart.[5] Physically, she was "quite fleshy,"[6] with a plain, round face and hair parted in the middle. A passive person, she was liked by other missionaries, but the same could not be said for her husband, Dwight Howard Clapp. The senior member of the Shansi Mission, Clapp tended to antagonize his colleagues because of his inflexibility.

Born Mary Jane Rowland in East Clarksfield, Ohio, on February 18, 1845, Jennie—as everyone called her—was a student in Oberlin College's preparatory department in 1858–1859, and subsequently studied at Lake

Erie Seminary. She and Howard—she called him by his middle name—were married a few weeks after he graduated from Oberlin Theological Seminary in May 1884. He was thirty-five years old at the time, but she was thirty-nine—which may explain why they were the only couple in the Shansi Mission who were childless.

By the time of his graduation, Howard, who was born November 1, 1848, in Middlefield, Ohio, had spent almost ten years in school at Oberlin—first in the preparatory department, a dozen years after Jennie had studied there, then as a student in the college between 1875 and 1879, and later, after two years away teaching and preaching, as a seminarian. The few records available indicate that he was the equivalent of a *C* student in Greek and Latin in the 1874–1875 school term.[7] He would have studied Greek again in the seminary, as well as, among other subjects, the New Testament and the Old Testament, church history, theology, science and religion, and elocution. How well he did is not known; theologs were not graded.

Howard was an unpretentious person, generous and sympathetic by nature. But he was also a rigid moralist. He spoke on "Conscience in Politics" when he graduated from the college in 1879, deploring the lack of it in political life and emphasizing "the debasing influence of the press." A reporter who heard him thought Clapp "was entirely too sweeping in his denunciation of newspapers, but presented his views with an earnestness which commanded attention."[8]

When he graduated from the seminary in June 1884—at the same time that the inspiring Judson Smith, who was one of his teachers, was leaving Oberlin to join the American Board in Boston—Howard obviously had a clear idea as to where his future lay. He spoke then on "Missions as a Civilizing Agency."[9] The next day he was ordained, and that September he and Jennie left America to take up missionary posts in Taiku. They would return home only once, ten years later, when they spent sixteen months in the States before going back to China.

Like their colleagues in the Shansi Mission, who were avid letter writers, Howard and Jennie may have jotted down their experiences and related their feelings to friends and family in the States, but only a few items survive. What is known about them comes chiefly from impressions and remarks made by other missionaries or the few photographs that exist in which one or both of them appear. To an extent greater than any others in the Shansi Mission, the Clapps were private persons. Rarely did Jennie ever confide her feelings to others. Once, after their furlough home in the mid-1890s, Jennie admitted to a fellow missionary that it was more difficult in many ways to return to the Mission than it had been to go to Asia in the first place. For one thing, it was harder "to leave the beauty of the homeland and come back to dreary China."[10]

A photograph taken at the annual meeting of the Shansi Mission in 1893 (p. 35) shows that Howard grew a Chinese-style moustache and shaved his hair, but that is true of other male missionaries in the picture; some of them, such as Francis Davis, sported long beards, too. Both Howard and Jennie are wearing Chinese clothes, but again that was the usual practice for all the missionaries; they attempted to blend in as much as possible with their environment. When Martin Luther Stimson first toured Shansi, back in 1882, villagers made fun of his "grotesque attire, consisting of American trousers and shoes with a long Chinese garment as overcoat, topped by the huge, ungraceful pith helmet."[11]

Even so, some missionaries never felt at ease with the change of wardrobe, especially when they had to mingle with Western merchants or diplomats. When George Williams, who took the unusual step of growing a queue, went to Shanghai in 1899 to put his wife and children aboard a ship, he suddenly became self-conscious. "I am enjoying our stay here at this port with its 5000 foreign population as well as I can in my Chinese clothes and pigtail," he wrote home. "My clothes & cue [*sic*] are all right up inland. Out here they are well nigh intolerable. I am very anxious to get off."[12]

Howard Clapp, the Chinese said, had "a hot heart." By that, they meant that he was a well-intentioned, benevolent person. That is true. He was a kind man. But it is also true that he was a stickler for protocol, sensitive about his prerogatives, and sometimes as rigid in dealing with people as he was about matters of ethics. Howard in fact had a weak heart. Like his wife, Jennie, he was also a worrier. He became easily depressed when faced with a crisis, and crises became frequent as the Shansi Mission faced the final year before a new century began.

While Jennie's launching of the school for boys was the culmination of years of hopes, prayers, and plans, Lydia Davis's achievement in starting the school for girls, in 1893, was spontaneous. The Davises were still living in Fenchow-fu then. Lydia had already lost two baby boys in infancy, so after she gave birth that year to a third child, whom the couple named William, she was particularly protective of him. She and the baby stayed confined in her home. One day the gatekeeper inadvertently left the street gate open. While no one was looking, a young, blind beggar girl stumbled inside. Her parents had sold her to a family as a household servant, but she suffered some disease that blinded her and the family had thrown her out. The girl groped her way into the courtyard outside the Davises' quarters, her hand out beseechingly for the copper coins known as *cash.*

Lydia spotted her and reacted angrily, rebuking the gatekeeper for leaving the gate open. But then she had an inspiration. Lydia had recently read the life of Mary Lyon, founder of Mount Holyoke College, and was impressed by Lyon's perseverance in establishing a school of higher education for women. Although she didn't have to, Lydia was already trying to master the Chinese language so that she could tell the illiterate Chinese women she visited about *tao-li.* Male and unmarried female missionaries were required to learn Chinese and take examinations, but married women such as Lydia were exempted from the requirement. Nevertheless, Lydia, who didn't have a college education, was determined to pass the same examination that an unmarried female missionary took. She persevered, "oftentimes studying with a wet towel around my head," and passed with flying colors, the first married woman to do so.[13]

Lydia took to walking two miles to a village where there was a family willing to listen to *tao-li* and where the women were trying to learn to read. For some time she had agitated within the Mission about establishing a school for girls. But the Chinese attached to the Mission laughed at her; it was "quite sufficient," they said, "if girls can cook and sew." Besides which, "they couldn't learn any way." They told Lydia to take a book out to the stable and "hold it up before the donkey; if the donkey can learn to read, then the girls can learn."[14]

Francis and Lydia Davis with their newborn son. Courtesy Oberlin College Archives.

The remarks incensed Lydia. Now, seeing the blind girl, it occurred to Lydia that maybe she might become her first pupil, the beginning of a long-necessary revolution, for, like all her missionary colleagues, Lydia was outraged by the way Chinese women were treated. They were commonly referred to by an expression that translated as "commodity-on-which-money-has-been-lost." Sons, on the other hand, were prized; it was they alone who were permitted to perform the important acts of worship before ancestral tablets in the family home and at grave sites.

Daughters were held in such low esteem that in the nearby province of Shantung they were given numbers, not names, and when a child was born the question ordinarily asked was "Is it a pupil (boy), or a slave (girl)?" In South China, daughters were sold "as openly as cattle," and selling a child or a wife to pay off a debt, or to buy opium, was common throughout the country. Infanticide was so common—as a rule, a family allowed no more than two girl babies to survive—that a female missionary who spoke to forty women in one village alone learned that they had destroyed among them seventy-eight daughters by tossing them over the city's walls to scavengers. The only outlet a Chinese woman seemed to have, this missionary said, was "the exhibition of her wrath to her street and neighborhood." Chinese women, she said, lashed out in shriller tones than men did—and the men were notorious for their rapid, high-pitched chatter.[15]

The Chinese attitude toward women was perhaps best illustrated by their view of the world as the product of two interacting elements—*yin* and *yang*. *Yang* was the attribute of all things male—active, bright, strong. *Yin* was the attribute of all things female—weak, passive, dark. *Yin* and *yang* were complementary, but *yin* was by nature passive toward *yang*.

The missionaries were astonished that in a culture that prized learning, women were uneducated. They were completely without rights of any kind, totally subordinate to men, and often expected to commit suicide when their husbands died. In actuality, suicide was common among women whose husbands were alive. Mission dispensaries often treated women who swallowed massive doses of opium in an attempt to kill themselves. "Poor women!" a sympathetic male missionary exclaimed, "sometimes they even don't know their own by-marriage-acquired names."[16]

One missionary was astounded one day when a Chinese woman, curious as all Chinese were about things Western, stooped and took hold of his trouser leg and turned it up to see how it was sewn. "The idea of a Chinese woman touching a man's apparel was astounding in its audacity. Brothers and sisters hardly venture on too familiar intercourse in families where etiquette is understood and observed."[17]

The strictures against men and women commingling were so severe that Eva Price believed it was best not to have women patients at a dispensary, "for they have to mix more or less with the men which gives us a bad name."[18] Realizing how strongly the Chinese felt about the issue, Jennie Atwater was pleasantly surprised one Sunday when Deacon Liu and his wife sat next to each other in the Taiku church to witness their grandson's baptism. "It was a strange sight for China to see a man and wife together in a public meeting. Especially in such a way," she said.[19]

The missionaries felt compelled to condone the separation of the sexes in order not to offend any Chinese who showed an interest in Christianity. They had separate chapel doors for men and women, and inside a curtain or screen ran down the middle aisle, separating the men's section from female churchgoers and effectively blocking the two sides from seeing each other. An unmarried female missionary who objected to such segregation took silent pleasure when the curtain was accidentally torn from its rungs one Sunday in the overcrowded chapel. She was responsible for putting the curtain back up, but she said, with some satisfaction, that "it was never convenient" to repair it.[20]

Women missionaries as a whole found foot-binding especially horrifying. The tradition had begun at court in the tenth century, supposedly when an emperor expressed his pleasure at seeing his wife's feet encased in tiny slippers. Through the centuries, the shackling took on sexual overtones for Chinese men, and a woman who did not bind her feet was considered licentious. Girls as young as six had their feet bound by their mothers. The toes were curled under and so tightly wound with a strip of cloth that bones were broken and their feet permanently deformed. Many women required canes to walk. Steps were a special hazard for them.

One Christmas Day, Eva Price invited some Chinese women friends to dinner. Before they sat down to eat, she gave them a tour of her house, going upstairs to show them the bedrooms. The women were able to grope their way up the stairs, but descending them was another matter. "Some of them *sat down* and shuffled from one step to the other. It gave me a good chance to point to the bother, if nothing worse, foot-binding makes for them."[21] A colleague of hers bemoaned, "Poor slaves in bondage." She was dismayed when she "heard a child of six or seven sob and scream piteously because her feet hurt her."[22]

"The more I go among the women the more I realize the true misery of heathendom," wrote one female missionary after being in China for several years. "The first year I pitied them for their dark, dirty homes, and lack of all that is externally pleasant. Now, that we are able to talk together, I see that their real misery is their darkness within, the purposelessness of their lives without God and therefore without hope."[23]

Eva Price found herself constantly contrasting her life with that of Mrs. Chia, the nurse of a child of another missionary family.[24] Coincidentally, Eva's surname, Price, was Chia in Chinese, too:

> What if my lines were set in such hard places? What if, instead of an earnest christian, my husband were an opium user with a lot of other bad characteristics? What if, instead of my pleasant home, with all the comforts and advantages that come through christianity, knowledge, hope, faith, books, pictures, good food, comfortable clothes, beds, and cleanliness, I had to live in such a comfortless, poor, mean, barren home as hers? What if, instead of having plenty, with wide outlook and some aspiration for the future of my dear little girl, I had to go out sewing at seven cents a day, haunted by the fear that *maybe* when I went home at night I would find that my husband, the father of my children, had *sold* my girlie and was using the money for opium? She, this *other* Mrs. Chia, had that experience once four yrs ago, when her oldest girl eight years old was sold, and she lives in constant dread that one of the remaining two will soon share a like fate. . . . She is expecting another baby. What joy of motherhood is hers?[25]

Jennie Clapp pointed with pride to her housemaid, Chang Ta Sao, who used to accompany her when she worked with opium patients or visited women in their homes. A Christian, the maid had learned how to read Chinese at the Mission and told Jennie that "now when night comes I read the Bible, and have something to help me. Before I used to sit and think of trouble past and trouble to come, until I was most unhappy."

Jennie—disturbed about "all these poor women who cannot read, and have nothing to think of but their poor miserable lives!"—began a Thursday afternoon prayer meeting that was so popular with neighborhood women that the meeting turned into a beginners' class in Christianity. They prayed together, then the women read to her what Chang Ta Sao had taught them during the week.[26]

So, taking into account how she and others empathized with Chinese women, and how much she always wanted to begin an educational program for women, Lydia Davis seized the opportunity of the blind girl's presence in the compound and decided right then and there to start a school for girls. The girl's name was Ching Huan txu—she was called Golden Circle—but Lydia named her Lois, and everyone afterward referred to her as "blind Lois." She did indeed become the first student. Lydia quickly enrolled two more pupils: the eighteen-year-old bride of a servant, and the niece of a Christian woman from a nearby village. The three girls studied in Lydia's sitting room, where she could continue to tend to her infant son William while teaching them.

Blind Lois lived with the Davises and before long could repeat from memory all the Gospels. Later on, the Davises sent her to the missionary-run Bridgman School in Peking, and she eventually became a Christian and learned to play the organ. For a living, she made brooms and caned chairs.

In time, housing for Lydia's school was found, and in 1899 it contained sixteen pupils. The school was restricted to girls who had unbound feet, which the missionary ladies who operated the school considered a sign of liberation.

The Davises were an affectionate couple. A missionary colleague once remarked that Francis "is very evidently, still a lover, and they both seem very happy."[27] But Lydia never enjoyed living in their "exceedingly primitive" house in Fenchow-fu, so she was ecstatic when, after five years in that city, Francis was transferred across the Fen River to Taiku. Lydia took her schoolgirls with her. The couple lived in Jen Tsun, "a beautiful village" near the Mission station, in "a fine old family mansion rented for a song from a family ruined by opium."[28] It was there, in Jen Tsun, that their second surviving son, John, was born in 1896.

Although not quite thirty years old when she gave birth to John, Lydia had now gone through four pregnancies, and childbirth was apparently becoming more difficult for her. She was pregnant again in the spring of 1897, and experiencing difficulties, when she and Francis asked the Board's permission to return to Ohio on furlough; they had been in Shansi for seven and a half years. The Davises went home to live near her parents in Ravenna, expecting that once she gave birth and her health was restored, they would return to China. Their third son, Lewis, was born there on September 12.[29]

But Lydia did not rally afterwards. Her health was so "uncertain"[30] that Davis asked for, and received, a year's extension of their furlough. They fully expected to return and well in advance, they purchased steamer tickets to sail back to China in the fall of 1899. Lydia, meanwhile, began seeing a Cleveland doctor named Henry S. Upson. Upson reported that her uterus had slipped out of place and would require "a few stitches—a common occurence [*sic*]," but, he assured her, no stitches would be necessary for the perineum.[31] However, when the American Board suddenly decided that it wanted a doctor's letter certifying that she was well enough to return, Upson refused to provide one. She still needed rest and time to recuperate.

Accordingly, after thirty months in the States, Francis went back to Shansi on his own, anticipating that Lydia and the children would join him in the not-too-distant future. But he was very lonely from the start. Eva Price knew how close the couple were. One December day, shortly after Francis returned to China, Eva wrote Lydia to describe to her a visitor who was sitting nearby:

> Over there by the k'ang before the N.W. window, in a chair where the light falls softly on his work, sits a man mending his "ma kua erh." The picture would attract notice in America as quite oriental in tone and coloring, but here where we are so used to the beautiful blues and reds we might not think of the coloring but of the man himself. You might do the same. He has whiskers covering the lower part of his face, said whiskers very liberally sprinkled with gray, Time's finger marks; his eyes are keen and blue, and his fingers manage the needle cleverly. A dark blue long garmen[t], a crimson "k'an Chien tzu," and a black cap of curious shape, when compared with a "Derby" or "Soft Felt," are

> the chief points of his costume visible to me as I sit here glancing occasionally toward him. His feet . . . are somewhat prodigous [*sic*] as to size and are covered by leather shoes bought in the Occident. . . . He has a wife and three fine sons in America of whom he is very proud; in fact, on all occasions that will at all warrant it, he draws out a small picture of said wife, carefully wrapped in paper, and offers it for our inspection. . . .
>
> Can you guess who this man is? He is honest as daylight and as generous as the sun; two principles that covers a multitude of petty sins. . . .
>
> Glad! Yes, we were glad to see him and to have him with us once more. To see him coming as of old, reminds us of those days ten years ago when we all were "Tender-Feet["] in China together. If *you* were only here . . . [32]

But Francis didn't want Lydia to return to Shansi unless they were certain that medical care for her and the children would be readily available. He began pressing Judson Smith in Boston to have the American Board secure a doctor for Taiku. He wrote Lydia that if Smith contacted her, "Be sure & show them how far it would be in the States. Live in Denver and no doctor nearer than New York and Boston and only one doctor in each place, and he liable to be sick or away. Tell them of Mrs. Thompson's and Alma's death only 90 li from a doctor." (About twenty-seven miles. A *li* is half a kilometer.) Francis cautioned, "I think you had better stay in the States at some inconvenience to yourself rather than take the risks of living in a mountain station entirely out of reach of a doctor."[33]

At the same time, "in view of the difficulty of securing one new physician for the Taiku station," Francis proposed to the Board that he be transferred from the Shansi Mission to the post of treasurer of the North China Mission in Tientsin, where a physician was stationed. "I feel better qualified for the work at Tientsin than the position I now occupy."[34] His talents, he said, "lay more in the direction of business than the work I am now engaged in."[35] Francis asked that the Board's executive committee—its oddly named Prudential Committee—cable him as soon as possible about the transfer so that he could start for Tientsin before the rainy season started in the spring of 1900.

In truth, no sooner had he requested the transfer than Francis had second thoughts, which he confided to Lydia. For one thing, the schools their sons would have to attend in Tientsin were "English in management so that our children would waste their time attending them." There were other problems, too. Tientsin, he had learned, "is an unhealthy place, no cows, no good water, living expensive, a foreign community to associate with." Francis was torn by what to do. "All I want is to make you happy, and if Tientsin will do it we will go if the Board say '*Yes.*'"[36]

The Board finally did engage a doctor to cover the Taiku station, but his departure was delayed because his fiancée could not leave until the following year—and by then the issue was moot.

EIGHT ❁ "Paradise Cottage"

The wise find pleasure in water; the virtuous find pleasure in hills. The wise are active; the virtuous are tranquil. The wise are joyful; the virtuous are long-lived.
—*Confucius*

Charles and Eva Price, who accompanied Francis and Lydia Davis to China in 1889, were the next oldest couple in the Shansi Mission after the Clapps. In photographs taken of them, they look stiff and formidable, but nothing was further from the truth. Unlike the Clapps, who kept mostly to themselves, the Prices were so genial and hospitable that other missionaries—both their fellow American Board colleagues and those of other societies—made it a point to stay with them on visits to Fenchow-fu.

If the Prices looked formidable, it was because at one time both weighed over 180 pounds, and Charles, for one, kept putting on weight. He always had difficulty finding Chinese shoes big enough for his feet. Charles swore when he returned to Shansi from leave in America that he would never wear Chinese clothing again, but his weight undid him. "I have fallen. Strange how readily we turn to things vile. Now I am dressed in the long flowing robe of the ubiquitous Chinaman." Which was just as well, Price noted, because he was gaining weight and the robe "would about reach around an ox. It gives the body room to grow. I am growing a very large stomach—so large that civilized clothing is almost out of the question. Weight about 200. I suppose I do not present a very majestic appearance."[1]

Charles Wesley Price was a native of Richland, Indiana, born Decem-

Eva and Charles Price with their daughter, Florence. The photograph was taken in San Fransisco in 1897, when they returned to China after the death of their son Stewart.
Courtesy Oberlin College Archives.

ber 28, 1847. As a teenager during the Civil War, he served in the Union Army, but there is no evidence that he ever saw combat. His wife, who was seven and a half years younger, was born Eva Jane Keasey in Constantine, Michigan, on August 19, 1855. The couple were married in Altoona, Iowa, in 1873 and were living in Des Moines ten years later, when—against the wishes of her parents, who were not enthusiastic about evangelical Christianity—the Prices went to Oberlin to study. He wanted to become an ordained minister like his brother Francis, who had just graduated from the Theological Seminary and gone on to China as a missionary. Eva herself attended Oberlin College, but only briefly because she soon had two children to care for—Stewart and Donald—while Charles studied in the Seminary.

Charles used up his savings in order to complete the course. He delivered his final oration, "A Plea for a Closer Union of Churches," at commencement exercises,[2] and graduated on May 31, 1889—at the same time that Francis Davis did. Like Davis, he was persuaded by Martin Luther Stimson to apply for an American Board assignment to Shansi.

Eva—whose name was pronounced "Eye-vah" by the family[3]—was proud that the visitors who stayed in her home in Fenchow-fu called it either "Paradise Cottage" or "Rest Cottage."[4] One winter, she entertained guests from a dozen different countries. Her brother-in-law Frank said many missionaries "enjoyed and were refreshed and encouraged by the hospitality of their home." Eva, he said, was "a capable helpmeet and a rare hostess," and his brother Charles "a quiet, unobstrusive man, kind and a true friend."[5] However, another missionary who knew Charles saw a different person, one who was "so jolly and keeps everything lively."[6]

However they described them, almost everybody liked the couple. Francis Davis found himself growing "very strongly inclined to the Prices." Their daughter, Florence, he said, "is a sweet girl,"[7] a sentiment that was echoed by George Williams, who was "utterly surprised" that by the age of seven Florence could read "'God moves in a mysterious way' and other hymns and takes her turn in family worship in reading with the rest and knows the most [*sic*] of the words. It seems wonderful to me."[8]

The Prices enjoyed a special place in the hearts of the Chinese they dealt with, too. It was not unusual for Eva to entertain Chinese women in her home. "She had the happy faculty of always making them welcome," said another missionary wife. "They enjoyed her happy free way of conversing with them."[9] The Chinese called Charles Lao Han—Old Chinaman—a term of respect.[10] Florence was Nai Hua—Love Blossom.[11]

Eva called her husband Charlie and noted that by the time of his forty-sixth birthday in 1893—after only four years in China—he was already "white around the ears," had to wear glasses almost all the time, and was already referring to himself jocularly as "the venerable missionary."[12] As for herself, she began experiencing "change"—menopause—when forty-two in 1897, felt "*ten* years older, and my hair will warrant the feeling, for it is grayer with every setting sun." [13]

Both Charles and Eva saw themselves differently than their missionary friends did. "I always was unfortunate," he wrote a friend in 1893, "and probably will be to the end."[14] Charles never explained what prompted that remark; one can only surmise that, for one thing, he was referring at the time to the death of his son Donnie, which affected both him and Eva deeply.

As for Eva, for all her conviviality, she was often lonely and homesick. As a friend put it, she found it "hard to be reconciled to the thought of two homes, one in America and one in China, with an ocean rolling between."[15] She also felt inadequate. After almost a decade in China, Eva believed herself to be "so helpless and incompetent" because she had "so little of the language." Most of what she knew, she said, "is 'picked up,' here a little, there a little, in the midst of house-work, training 'boys,' tending babies, ect, ect [*sic*]."[16] She tried to help teach the Gospel at the opium refuge in Fenchow-fu, but "distracted by the numerous duties with green servants, babies, and household affairs," she was never able to study "so as to get much use of the characters." She confessed, "Do you wonder I tremble, hesitate and *shirk* at the thought of teaching these women characters?"[17]

Eva was just as candid about expressing her doubts about the Mission's role as she was about her own shortcomings. She was not, she wrote friends in Ohio, "an over-zealous missionary. I love nature and rural life so much, and companion-ship with congenial friends and all the other 'flesh-pots' of such an attractive 'Egypt'—that I find the isolation and environment of heathenism more than ever depressing."[18] She wondered about the "partiality" that God "seems to show for some in giving them so many advantages, while others, because of *environment,* exist and die with no hope in the world to come and with nothing but misery in this." [19]

Eva was fiercely sarcastic at the time of the Mission's Annual Meeting in April 1899. She talked embitteredly about staying in Fenchow-fu, "watching green grass sprouting two inches below the barren surface" of her backyard, while the other missionaries traveled to the meeting "over the bumpiest and humpiest of bumpsy and humpy roads" and would be "forced to spend the night in a filthy stable, into which donkeys, pigs, dogs, and dirty lousy people, come and go at will." She imagined, she added derisively, "a year of uninterrupted and successful work with hundreds, yes, thousands brought into the fold. Oh, Yes I see it all!"[20]

But if anything truly bothered Eva Price, it was the criticism she drew for the way she was bringing up Florence. She lashed out about "how easy it is for others to torture you almost to the verge of insanity with their lack of sympathetic interest in such questions [of child rearing]; and not only that, but who seem to be really gratified to call your attention to faults in your children; who overwhelm you with the feeling that your children are wicked and your manner of dealing with them foolishly inadequate and unwise, while *they,* and *they* have the opportunity, would show you just *how* it ought to be done!"[21]

Eva's protective attitude about Florence is understandable. The Prices were emotionally devastated by the loss of two sons, and Florence resembled one of them, Donnie, who had died suddenly in 1892 after being ill only eight days. Eva was constantly worried that her daughter would contract some terrible disease, also, and lived, as a missionary friend put it, "in a shadow that some dreadful calamity was to fall upon dear little Florence."[22]

Eva's fears seemed justified. There was the time the girl set herself on fire, and then for two weeks, when Florence was seven years old, Eva lay awake, beside her, transfixed, simply "*staring* from one spell to another," as the child, suffering from a severe case of whooping cough, gagged and fought for breath.[23]

As a result, Eva was strict about whom Florence played with. The child was ordinarily not allowed near Chinese children. An exception had been a schoolboy about fifteen years old named Ch'iao Ko Ling, who wheeled her as an infant in a carriage about the Prices' courtyard and was even allowed to take her in his arms, although, Eva acknowledged, "I don't as a rule let the Chinese hold her for they are dirty and usually lousy."[24]

Eva never indicated who in particular among her missionary compatriots she was mad at, but the hurt was there. After the couple buried their son Stewart in Oberlin in 1897, Charles never hesitated when he thought about returning to China—"to the people, we have learned to love so well, in 'Fenchofu.'"[25] But Eva entertained doubts. A benefactor of the Shansi Mission whom the Prices had befriended offered to help the Prices to settle in a community near him in Ohio when the couple decided to retire from the mission field. The offer, said Eva, was "tempting." She thought of it, she told him, "many, many times."[26]

NINE ❁ *The Associate Missionaries*

Of all people, girls are the most difficult to behave to.
If you are familiar with them, they lose their humility.
If you maintain a reserve towards them, they are discontented.
—*Confucius*

As early as 1884 the Shansi Mission began asking the American Board to send out "at least two young ladies earnestly consecrated to general missionary work and willing to do whatever work Providence may open for them."[1] Three years later the Mission renewed its appeal. This time it asked for eight single women. They and the twenty new missionaries and their wives whom they also requested would enable the Mission to open two new stations in addition to Taiku and Fenchow-fu "and to strengthen opium work."[2] Charles Price took it upon himself to write his friend, the Mission benefactor who lived in Ohio, to ask if he could recommend "a young Lady, or two," for the Fenchow-fu school. "It is not necessary that they be highly educated, but that they be prepared for hard study and are ready to work for our Master."[3]

Despite the appeals, the Board was never able to muster more than three single women for the Shansi Mission. Two arrived in 1890—Tinnie D'Etta Hewett and Susan Rowena Bird. The latter was an attractive graduate of Oberlin College who, everyone agreed, was a hard worker and usually "bright and chatty."[4] She was also something of a snob.

For a long while, when she was young, it looked as though Rowena would never get a proper education. Born in Sandoval, Illinois, on July 31, 1865, she was so frail as a child that it was impossible for her to attend school regularly. Her father, Rev. William Harrison Bird, a Presbyterian preacher, died when she was twelve years old. Her mother moved to Oberlin in 1884 so that her daughter, then nineteen, could take a business course in a small secretarial school and learn to support herself as a typist. College, they thought, was out of the question because of her health.

To avoid confusion with her mother, who was also a Susan, Rowena was called by her middle name. While in Oberlin she expressed interest in the missionary movement but was concerned that her physical condition would prevent it. To become a missionary, Rowena would have to attend college. Her mother prevailed on a noted member of the Oberlin faculty, Professor James Monroe, for advice. He recommended that Rowena follow her instincts, prepare for school with a tutor, and enter Oberlin. All of which Rowena did.

Rowena spent two academic years in the school's preparatory department before moving on to the college itself. She soon proved herself an able and talented student, with grades equivalent to almost straight *A*'s in courses as diverse as geometry, Latin, botany, physics, and the science of government. But her marks fell off dramatically, and mysteriously, in her junior and senior years. Perhaps her health was a factor. Nevertheless, she was able to graduate in 1890 despite low grades. By then she had already applied to and been accepted by the American Board, and that September, when she was twenty-five years old, she left for China.

Rowena's performance in Shansi belied her experience as a sickly child and her less-than-admirable grades in her final school years. For one thing, she never complained about her health, even though the musty rooms she occupied in Taiku had cracked walls and opened out onto a street with an open sewer that emitted foul smells. By the end of the first year, she was exhausted, but so was everyone else in the Mission; everybody was always tired after a busy year of carrying out their duties amidst an alien culture with a difficult language and customs. "I use my voice too hard," she acknowledged. "It is senseless[,] they would understand just as well if I spoke slower & lower. Friday I had a cold and of course taught as usual in the A.M. then in P.M. went out there & found all those women and of course forgot all about my voice and in the eve. could hardly talk."[5]

Rowena was able to spend at least one restful summer with the Prices in Peeking Place. Eva, who knew Rowena's mother in Oberlin, became "sort of her Chinese mother" in Shansi.[6] After spending ten weeks

Susan Rowena Bird. Courtesy Oberlin College Archives.

together, Eva remarked on how much better Rowena looked than when she arrived.

Then, too, although she was not an especially talented language student in college, Rowena became adept enough in Chinese to become Jennie Clapp's assistant in the boys' school at Taiku. She taught arithmetic and algebra. After school she spent time at the opium refuge in nearby Tung Fang, explaining the Gospel to the women there. "I asked for that kind of work because it did not require study and is more of a rest from my other work which keeps my brain working most of the day."[7]

Eva Price was impressed when, after less than two years in China, Rowena helped to teach the wife of the Prices' "second boy" and her twelve-year-old daughter the Ten Commandments. Rowena, said Eva, did "very well indeed," and between the two of them they got the woman and the little girl "to understand pretty well."[8] Rowena herself recalled the time she was explaining the Last Supper to some Chinese women who had observed the communion service at a Sunday evening meeting. Rowena spoke about Christ and the disciples in Gethsemane, then stopped because it was late and she was afraid she had told the women more than they could remember. But they remonstrated that they wanted to hear more. Even though it meant missing her supper, Rowena went on, telling stories about Jesus' death. "It is good to see them so touched by Christ's sufferings and his great love for us," she wrote her mother, "but it does not always follow that the impression lasts and brings real repentance. It sometimes does, however, so one always tells the story with hope, trusting that the good seed may lodge in some receptive heart."[9]

Rowena, moreover, took it upon herself to study Confucius' great disciple, Mencius, which no one else in the Mission apparently ever attempted. She became attached to one of the Taiku school's first pupils, a motherless youth who was unusually gifted, K'ung Hsiang Hsi. Hsiang Hsi, who was a direct descendant of Confucius—seventy-fifth in line—would play a critical role in twentieth-century China. He considered his "dearly beloved Miss Bird" an older sister.[10]

She was "like a beloved sister," too, to one of Hsiang Hsi's friends, Fei Chi Hao,[11] but in this instance her behavior raised eyebrows. Rowena's relationship with him prompted one of the two times that the Clapps found it necessary to take Rowena aside and reprimand her.

The first time had to do with Rowena's "alabaster box of conceit," in particular a predilection she had to brag about her relatives. Whom she boasted about is unclear. She had a brother who was a vice president with the Chicago, Milwaukee and St. Paul Railroad, but otherwise no other known family connections with anybody of note. But whatever Rowena was saying "was causing unfavorable talk among the Chinese." To Rowena's credit, she was chagrined. "Why didn't you tell me before," she said, and did not mention her relatives "in a bragging way" ever after.[12]

The Clapps had to speak to her again because of the "talk" caused by "her faithfulness to her work" with Fei. Fei—or Mr. Fei, as the missionaries called him—was a graduate of North China College who was hired to teach in the boys' school in Taiku. His sister's husband was one of the Mission's teachers in Fenchow-fu. Fei, who was not quite twenty years old, was himself married, but he lived alone because his wife was a student at the Bridgman School in Peking. To expand his knowledge of English, Fei took lessons with Rowena for nearly a year and a half. The lessons were held in her private sitting room—which apparently is what caused the "talk."

The very thought that anyone believed there was anything improper between the two of them shocked Rowena. She was "greatly surprised and felt very badly." The upshot was that Rowena and Fei agreed to hold the lessons in Jennie Clapp's room.[13]

A dedicated worker, Rowena was offered an extension of her furlough when she went home on leave in 1898. The Board voted to permit her to stay in Oberlin until better accommodations could be provided in Taiku, but she refused, saying that she wanted to return, that she "must be about her 'Father's business.'"[14]

Like Rowena, Mary Louise Partridge was the daughter of a minister, was the same age, and also wanted to be called by her middle name, even though her family referred to her as Mary. "Please ma'am," she told Lydia Davis, "my name is Louise."[15] In other ways, however, the two young women were total opposites. While Rowena obviously cared about how she looked, Louise paid little attention to her appearance, except, oddly enough, for her feet; her wardrobe included an unusual number of dress shoes. And while Rowena enjoyed working in the Taiku school, Louise—at first, anyway—abjured teaching, preferring instead to tour among the hundreds of tiny villages outside the Mission station, distributing pamphlets and texts, talking about Christianity to any group of women she could assemble, and holding prayer meetings. "She could caress and love these women and children as no other person thought of doing," said a fellow missionary. "Homes were soon open to her, and in villages, where only a few heretofore came, many were anxious to learn. She took special pleasure in touring and opening doors in villages, where never foreigner had entered."[16]

A tall, lantern-jawed woman, Louise was the Mission's independent spirit—"of a sprightly temperament, with a quick relish for humor," as Judson Smith described her.[17] Though she appears stiff in photographs, she was anything but that. "Have been more like myself to-day than for some time," she wrote her father, "laughing and joking and singing or whistling all over the court."[18]

Associate missionaries like Louise were free to express opinions at Mission meetings, but the women could not vote on any issues. But Louise had a mind of her own. She insisted, for example, on moving in 1897 to the village of Li Man, outside of Taiku, despite "all the hatred" she received from the men in the mission who opposed her. She was able to find "a little daisy of a place" there.[19] Her needs were simple: "The only thing I am extravagant in is kitchen utensils and the dressing of my feet. Well a good reason for that, for I have a mission. A woman with unbound feet is an example and the neater and prettier her feet look, the more influence she is likely to gain."[20]

Louise said she had made up her mind to go to Li Man because, for one thing, there was no room for her in or near the crowded Taiku compound. "Furthermore," she explained in a letter to Judson Smith in Boston, "my work just at present could be carried as well from Li man as T'aiku, yes, even better, with T'aiku to go to and stay over night occasionally, on my way somewhere."[21]

An expert horsewoman, Louise would ride off on her journeys from village to village, with only her servant, Kuo Hsiao Hsien, also known as T'sui, as escort.[22] "It's my hobby to open new villages," she claimed.[23] Eva Price referred to her constant touring as a "madcap career," and said

Mary Louise Partridge and her helper Kuo Hsiao Hsien, known as T'sui, about to set out on one of her village tours. Courtesy Oberlin College Archives.

Louise came back from one trip into the countryside "looking as though she had been through flood and flame."

Eva was pleased when Louise surprised the Prices, who were enroute back to Fenchow-fu after their furlough home in 1897. Louise showed up in Paotingfu to accompany them to the Mission station. She had forded rivers and ridden over mountains to be with them. But when the Prices stopped at an undesirable "emergency inn" because their Chinese carters didn't want to proceed farther one evening, Louise was so disgusted with the idea of "giving in" to the carters that, without waiting to unpack her bedding from a mule, she and Kuo Hsiao Hsien rode off into the dark and rain without the bedding or any food, and with little money. The Prices could do nothing about it but worry.[24]

Louise seemed destined for missionary work. She was born May 27, 1865, in Stockholm, New York, into a family deeply interested in missions at home and abroad. She was the firstborn of Rev. and Mrs. L. C. Partridge, and when she was only a day old a family friend, a minister, came to the parsonage where the Partridges lived and offered a prayer in which he dedicated the child to God. Louise's parents never urged her to be a missionary, but when she was only six years old, she told her grandfather, who was also a minister, that she was going to be one. She was persuaded to do so, she explained much later on, by "the life of my parents."[25]

Louise's dedication far outstripped her predisposition about her own schooling. She studied, according to American Board records, at several institutions, including Mount Holyoke Seminary, Rollins College in Florida, and Oberlin.[26] She attended Oberlin College for four years, between 1889 and 1893, but never graduated. Her marks were dismal. She never received above the equivalent of a *B* in any subject. The *B*'s she received were in political economics, logic, and rhetoric. She got *D*'s in Greek, Bible, and Hebrew studies, French, ethics, philosophy, and German. She flunked courses in Greek and German during two terms. She was, all in all, a low-*C* student.

Undeterred by her college record, Louise applied to the American Board. Its qualifications for missionary candidates were extensive: "an unimpaired physical constitution; good intellectual ability, well disciplined by education, and if possible by practical experience; good sense; sound judgment of men and things; versatility, tact, adaptation to men of all classes and circumstances—'sanctified common sense;' a cheerful, hopeful spirit; ability to work pleasantly with others; persistent energy in the carry out of plans once begun:—all controlled by a *single-hearted, self-sacrificing devotion to Christ and His cause.*" A candidate, whether male or female, was required to answer in writing thirteen specific questions dealing not only with family background, education, health, and marital plans, if any, but also with the Scriptures, the duties of a preacher of the Gospel, and the reasons for choosing foreign missionary service. "How do you regard hardship, suffering, and peril incurred in prosecuting the missionary work," its Prudential Committee wanted to know, "and to what extent are you taking them into the account and preparing yourself to meet them?"[27]

Despite Louise's poor academic record, the American Board, evidently desperate to find single women to send to China, approved her application. Undoubtedly, her family connections provided the testimonials the Board required about her sincerity in wanting to be a missionary.

Louise embarked for China in the latter part of August 1893 from Vancouver, British Columbia, taking the shorter and quicker northern sea route to the Orient. She arrived in Taiku in mid-October. She was twenty-eight years old.

Louise's talent lay with her natural ability to achieve a rapport with the Chinese people she encountered on her almost constant village tours. But much to her dismay, she had to abandon her jaunts into the countryside in the fall of 1899 after Tinnie Thompson died. Tinnie had taken over the girls' school in Jen Tsun when Lydia Davis left for the States for medical treatment. With Tinnie's death, there was no one else to call upon to run the school. Jennie Clapp had turned over the supervision of the boys' school to Charles Price and didn't want any teaching responsibilities anymore. Rowena Bird was the obvious choice to head the girls' school, but she was still needed to teach the boys. So it fell to Louise to take charge of the girls' school.

Reluctantly, Louise accepted the post and lived for a while in Jen Tsun, complaining at first, "It is the most confining work I have ever had in my life."[28] She finally brought the schoolgirls to Li Man, holding classes in her own quarters until she could rent additional space.

Miraculously, once she began work with the youngsters, Louise had a complete change of heart. She started thinking about how she would like most of all to start an orphanage. And as for teaching, Louise, who never was a great student, astonished herself: "I teach two hours and study four and a half. Would like to make it nine. My, I'm just wild over books, and get so interested in what I read. Have finished Biology and am reading Physical Geography. I hated it when I studied it, but its [*sic*] so interesting now."[29]

"The very thought of having a school for girls, 16 of them with unbound feet, a hope realized after long years of waiting, makes one want

Louise Partridge with one of her schoolgirls in Li Man. Courtesy Oberlin College Archives.

to shout for joy," she declared. Soon there were forty students with unbound feet "and almost every week adds to the number."[30] Overwhelmed by the increase in enrollment, Louise travelled to Peking to hire a Chinese teacher to help with classes. She returned with Ruth Fan, the niece of the pastor of a Tung Chow church who had studied at North China College.

Louise's schoolgirls had trouble pronouncing her name. It came out "Aunt Weze," but they also called her Pei Chao Shih—Precious Pearl Teacher.[31] "Dear girls," she wrote at Christmastime, "with faults and virtues so like those of their American sisters. They need the same training, the same advantages, and their need is greater because of their surroundings. How quickly they respond to lessons of gentleness and love. How soon they learn to love the Savior, and to live for Him. What large returns; how small the outlay, who can grudge it."[32]

Louise became so attached to the girls that when the Taiku missionaries considered assigning the school to Rowena Bird, she got upset. She wouldn't turn it over to anyone but Lydia Davis unless Lydia, when she came back, didn't want it. "The more I teach," Louise said, "the better I like it and I don't know how I shall ever be able to give it up to Rowena. She's set her heart on it. I wonder how it will turn out."[33]

TEN ❁ *Friendships*

By nature, men are nearly alike;
by practice, they get to be wide apart.
—Confucius

"The relationships on the mission field," Lydia Davis said, "are either very strong, or are soon forgotten. So small a group living so close together produces lasting friendships or the opposite."[1]

One of the few friends Lydia made was Alice Williams, the wife of missionary George Williams, who had been at Lydia's side when the Davises' second son, John, was born in 1896. Her friendship with Alice blossomed into "one of the most satisfying of my life," Lydia said, though she marveled that she and the firm, self-assured Alice developed such a close relationship. They were, she said, worlds apart "by temperament, she being very placid and practical, the best of cooks, and a perfect seamstress, making everything beautiful that she touches, quiet and calm under all provocation. No sister could have been more to me through all the years."[2]

Coincidentally, Alice Williams was yet another missionary who preferred to be called by her middle name. She was born Mary Alice Moon in Reedsburg, Ohio, in 1860 but grew up in Ashland, where her parents moved when she was two years old. Alice spent two widely separated years as a student in the Literary Department at Oberlin College and also attended the Theological Seminary for a year, but she was not a graduate of either. It was in Oberlin, however, that she met her husband, who was then a seminarian.

George Louis Williams was a perfect match for Alice—considerate,

Alice Moon Williams. Courtesy Oberlin College Archives.

well-intentioned, dedicated to his work, and the sort of husband who, like Francis Davis, was devoted to his wife. A native of Southington, Connecticut, born on October 4, 1858, George was a professed Baptist before he entered Oberlin College in 1882, but sometime in the next nine years that he spent there he switched his affiliation to the Congregational Church. He earned his A.B. from Oberlin in 1888 and graduated from its Theological Seminary in 1891.

As an undergraduate George was a student of mixed achievement. He excelled in elocution, German, French and modern history, getting the equivalent of *A*'s, but he was a *B* student in Greek orators, astronomy, English literature, and English constitution and government. He did poorly, in the *C* range, in Livy, Latin grammer, mineralogy, geology, and international law. He failed psychology. George's desire to be a missionary, however, never wavered. At his graduation from the Seminary, he spoke on "Our Mission and Our Inheritance."[3] Five days later, on May 26, 1891, he and Alice were married—he was then thirty-two years old, and she had just turned thirty-one. They left for China that July.

The Williamses spent a year in Tung Chow so that he could learn the Chinese language before taking up their posting in Shansi. No other Oberlin missionary had ever done so. The idea was evidently an experiment to better prepare him for his assignment. He studied Mandarin Chinese, which was spoken throughout North China, for many hours each day but was reluctant to participate in prayer meetings until he could speak it with the proper inflections. After six months he was finally persuaded to write a prayer in Chinese and to read it out loud at a prayer meeting with some servants. "Thank God," said one of the women who had never heard him say a word, "'Wei mu Shih' [the pastor] has his mouth opened."[4]

However, when George finally settled in Taiku, he soon regretted what he believed was a wasted year. Mandarin Chinese was spoken in Shansi, but in a regional argot that was totally unlike what he had learned. "At first I find this Shansi dialect so very different from the Pekingese that I can understand very little," George reported to Judson Smith soon after taking up his post. "I do so wish they would speak the tones and sounds clearly. These tones, which I have worked so hard the past year to master,

George Louis Williams. Courtesy Oberlin College Archives.

seem to be almost wholly ignored by the people here. I cannot say whether it was wise to remain at the coast a year or not."[5]

To his credit, when George was examined on his proficiency in the language by an English Baptist missionary a little more than two years later, he received a glowing report. The examiner, George B. Farthing, who was a colleague of Timothy Richard's, declared, "The English into Chinese shows acquaintance with Chinese idiom which one must praise," though he added, "The faults it manifests are common to us all—it is too redundant." Farthing gave George a grade of 90 in "Chinese at a Glance," 80 for English into Chinese, and 75 for the writing of Chinese characters.[6]

George was one of those missionaries who "went native." A handsome, dark-haired man, he had his head shaved, grew a queue, and let the moustache he ordinarily favored grow down from his upper lip in oriental style. The change made him look much older and grimmer than he was. Jennie Clapp chided him for going about in the sun "as the Chinese do—bareheaded or with a handkerchief tied over his head." So George purchased a hat, but that didn't satisfy Jennie either. It was "a small coarse coolie hat," she said, "that looks very funny, or would on most people."[7]

Judson Smith found George "full of missionary enthusiasm and growing zeal in its prosecution." Iranaeus Atwood described him as "one of the juiciest of men, having the milk of human kindness, and full of the love of God—an embodiment of the spirit of the thirteenth chapter of second Corinthians—an epistle of God to the heathen world, written on a fleshly tablet but known and read of all men."[8]

But, strange to say, while Lydia Davis and Alice Williams became the closest of friends, and remained so throughout their lives, their husbands, Francis and George, did not like each other. In fact, their relationship can best be described as outright hostility. One of the manifestations of their animosity was their reaction to the illnesses of their wives.

Alice's health problems first cropped up in 1893 when she was carrying the couple's first child, Gladys, who was born that August. George purposely took Alice to the Prices' summer retreat, Peeking Place, sixty miles from their home in Taiku, when she entered her seventh month of pregnancy because of her "delicate health." Atwood was staying nearby, and George wanted Alice to be close to a doctor. He complained afterwards to Judson Smith, "We are greatly disappointed that a physician has not

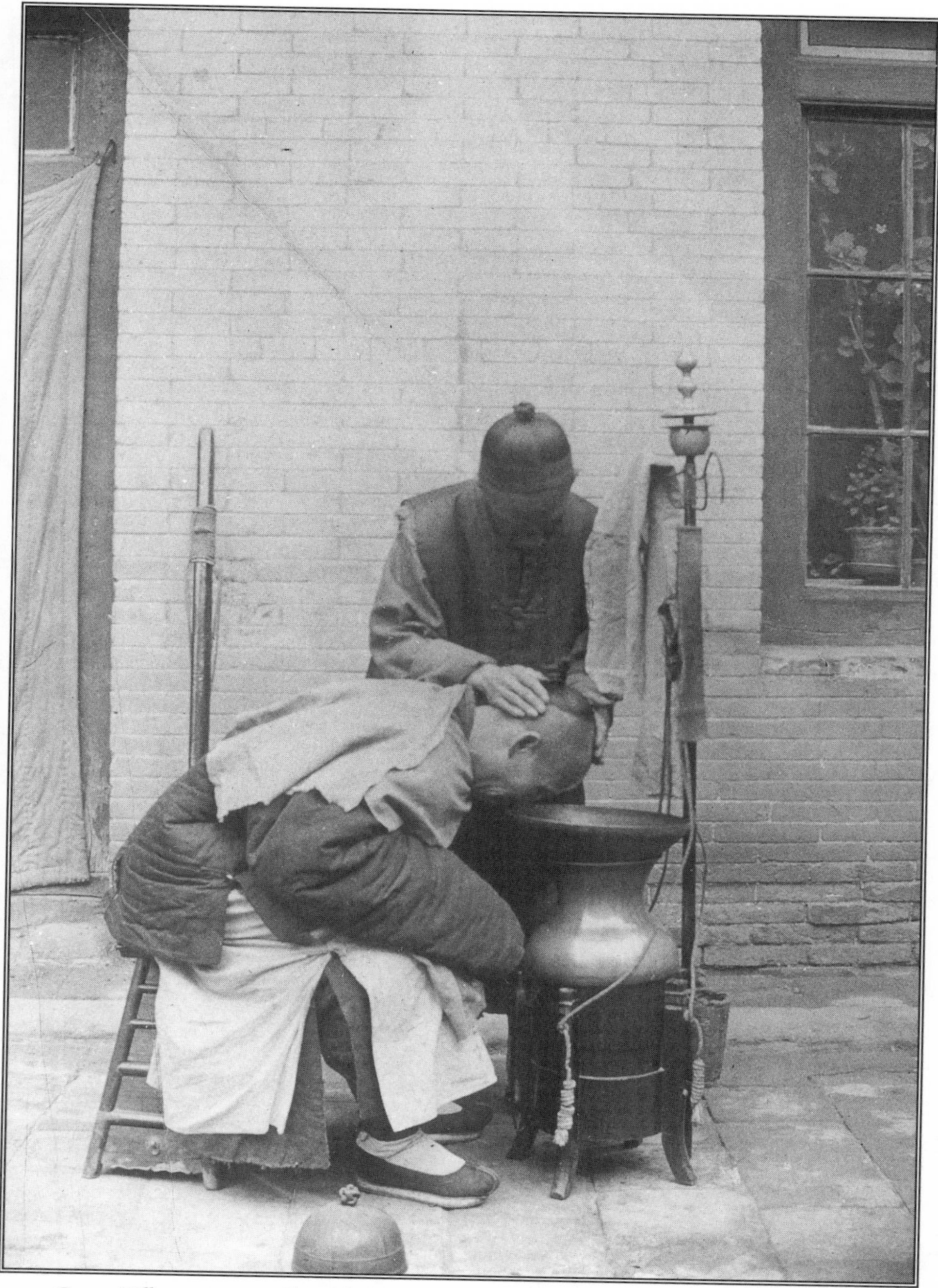

George Williams getting a Chinese haircut from a barber. Courtesy Oberlin College Archives.

yet been found for TaiKu. The fields are white, where are the laborers? By not having a Dr. here we lose much time in going to one elsewhere."

George pointed out that during the past winter he suffered a severe sore throat that was feared to be diptheria. Atwood had to be summoned from Fenchow-fu during "most trying Winter weather, leaving his own work at great risk to the welfare of his hospital patients." Atwood had, in fact, left the hospital in the care of an assistant who was just recovering from a fever and who subsequently suffered a relapse.

George told Judson Smith that he and Alice were forced to spend the entire summer near Atwood "because during the rainy season the rivers are liable to be unpassable at any time and we could not depend with any certainty upon the Dr's being able to reach us in the time of need." When Alice did give birth, he told Smith, she was "very ill, and, so far as we can know, the lives of both Mother and child were saved by the use of instruments in the skillful hands of Dr. Atwood. It is not pleasant to contemplate what the result might have been had we remained at our post in or near TaiKu."[9]

Alice gave birth to two more daughters, in the fall of 1895 and in the spring of 1897, when she was four days shy of her thirty-seventh birthday.[10] In the meantime, she contracted malaria, and, at one point, suffered so terribly that her friend Lydia said that she looked "dreadfully. Pale as can be and so thin in the face." Lydia blamed Alice's ill health on the crowded Mission compound in Taiku in which the Williamses lived. "Human beings ought not to live as they are there housed," she declared.[11] Both George and Alice had realized that for a long time, and made a number of appeals to the American Board for a grant to erect housing in a healthful locality.

The Board seemed to ignore them, but in truth it was continually strapped for funds. Realizing that, friends in Oberlin launched an appeal for $3,000 to build the Williamses a new house. When she felt well enough, Lydia Davis, who was then home on sick leave, made the rounds of women's church groups to gather pledges, and Rowena Bird helped to solicit donations, too, when she went to Oberlin on furlough in 1897. The money was eventually raised and turned over to the American Board. Williams was able to purchase land in the South Suburb of Taiku[12] for

400 *taels*[13] (about $300; a *tael* was worth about seventy-five cents). In the fall of 1898 he hired Chinese workmen to begin erecting his own house.

The Williamses' home was the first western-style building ever put up in Taiku, and George, who designed it, had to spend all his spare time overseeing its construction, making sure the local carpenters understood how to build it. Unlike Western design, Chinese architecure was based on wooden pillars and a system of interlocking brackets and beams that supported the roof and wide, flared eaves; walls did not contribute to the roof's support but were merely screens that separated one room from another. Williams's house—a two-story, forty-by-sixty-foot building with a one-story wing on each side—followed classic Western wall-supported construction. It had a modified peaked roof and verandas with railings and would have looked perfectly suited to its ambience had it been built in Ohio.

Alice, however, never got to live in their new home. As it was nearing completion in the fall of 1899, she left for the States with her three daughters to seek medical attention. "My house, my beautiful house with which I took such pains," George moaned, "it is built for others."[14] Instead of the Williamses, Rowena Bird and Howard and Jennie Clapp moved into it, able at last to find suitable, healthy quarters away from the hectic, cramped confines of the main Mission compound on South Street. Their moving left the main compound to the Chinese who lived in it and worked in its boys' school, opium refuge, and street chapel.

At a loss what to do now that he was living on his own, George finally moved into the house he built, also, residing in a fourteen-square-foot ground-floor room in the southwest corner.[15] But he was there as a boarder, taking meals with Rowena and the Clapps because he didn't have enough room for a cooking stove, or his organ, or much of the furniture that he and Alice had accumulated.

Alice, meanwhile, returned to Ohio and consulted a doctor in Cleveland, who diagnosed her problem as "'Impoverished' blood."[16] She and her children settled in Oberlin, living with her mother, and expecting that George would join her in the spring of 1901.[17] At almost the same time, Lydia Davis, who was under the care of Dr. Henry Upson, underwent an operation on her uterus in Cleveland, and George Williams was afraid that his wife might be persuaded to undergo some similar treatment. "D'ont, d'ont, d'ont, d'ont, [*sic*] go to too many doctors," he wrote Alice. "For they will tell you you must have all sorts of treatments and operations and what not. And I d'ont believe in it. What you want is good food to nourish and proper recreative [*sic*] and peace of mind. If you go to that old Dr. Upson and he puts you through all sorts of operations I shall be greatly displeased. It isn't what you need."[18]

Both George and Francis had wives who obviously would need medical supervision once they returned to China, but they argued over the necessity of having a doctor on station in Shansi. They also disagreed about Iranaeus Atwood, though their argument about him, or doctors in general, was probably symptomatic of a deeper enmity. Atwood had saved Alice Williams's life at the birth of their firstborn, and George appreciated his ability. But Davis thought otherwise about the doctor, who was going deaf. He didn't want his wife Lydia to come back to China if it meant it would place her and their children "under the bungling care of Dr. Atwood," who "can hardly take care of himself."[19]

Although Williams himself had urged the American Board to appoint a physician for Taiku, he mocked Davis for not wanting Lydia to return to China "unless they can live with a physician."[20] He said that Francis, in fact, was "loathe to go anywhere without a physician" even if he stayed in China without his family.[21] "I say it is all wrong," George declared. "And I will show them what I think pretty soon by my actions."[22]

What George meant by that last remark is a matter of speculation. Perhaps he was thinking of asking his wife, Alice, to return to Shansi with or without a doctor nearby once she was healthy. Davis, he wrote her, "thinks you are sure to have a collapse. But Pshaw! He talks that way about everything. I never saw a man who put so many things in the way of doing work."[23] He was sorry, he told Alice, that "I don't like him better."[24]

Davis was similarly critical of Williams, though on the surface they tried to maintain some semblance of cooperation. Once, after talking over Mission matters with George, Francis remarked, "We were both very pleasant both very cautious in statement, but there is no entente cordial [*sic*] and I am afraid there never will be." Davis made a point of saying that when he spoke with a missionary other than Williams, "it seems plain to both of us that we are each immediately ready to deal on the principles of the Golden Rule."[25]

On occasion, Francis evinced a certain amount of sympathy for George. When Williams, who was once ill with a stomach abscess, later suffered two fainting spells while overseeing the construction of his home, Davis commented that "life is uncertain to the best of us."[26] A few months later he worried that "Williams looks & acts tired and homesick."[27]

At one point in the fall of 1899, Francis even suggested to George that, now that they were both without their families, the two of them share living arrangements in Jen Tsun, where Francis continued to live. George demurred, even though he was very unhappy living with the Clapps. Jennie and Howard couldn't "bear" the house Williams had built. She complained that she had no curtains for the windows or for "this & that, and says it will take as much coal and 'it isn't so warm as a Chinese house is it?'"

Moreover, George was "especially annoyed" with Howard because he thought Clapp "put him in bad light with the Chinese" over sharing the cost of a holiday dinner. "It is very irritating," George said. He dropped by Clapp's study to discuss the matter with him. "I told him plainly what I thought yesterday and today he acts so estranged as though I had crossed him." George wrote Alice that he couldn't "live in sympathy of feeling with him, ever, *ever,* ever."[28]

However strong his feelings about Clapp, George was evidently willing to put up with living with him rather than with Francis Davis. When Francis broached the idea that he and George move in together, George adamantly refused. "I don't enjoy him as a companion," he wrote Alice. "I do not desire to keep house with him. He is so notional, has to have a hot fire, and hot water bottle to keep warm, then he must have foreign flour for the summer, and butter and raisins and what not. He is too full of crank." George thought Francis's "judgment is warped on many questions and I disagree with him so many times." Maybe, George reflected, "I shall get sour and cynical and sickly and lonesome and quit the whole business. But we need strong, hopeful, hearty, men in the Mission to hold on & push out or we shall be swamped."[29] As far as George was concerned, "it would have been better" if someone else had been sent to

Shansi in Francis's stead. "If he can get the position at Tientsin and another be sent here it will be best I think."[30]

It seemed as though almost every male missionary had something to complain about. The small, compressed world of the Mission compound exacerbated sensibilities, leading to personality conflicts between veteran missionaries and younger ones, between those who were theologically liberal and those of conservative bent, and between those who mastered Chinese and those who never felt at ease with the language.

Charles Price thought he knew another reason for so much bickering among members of the Shansi Mission: the climate and the altitude, which, he said, "render life here very trying to the nerves, that is if you have such a 'thorn in the flesh,' you would be sure to be reminded that you had them if you were to live here a few years. They develop and become more prominent the longer one is here. The intense heat of the summer with the dust of the winter makes it uncertain whether you will have much enjoyment during the year. And then the isolation of our life here is very trying."[31]

Relations between some of the Shansi missionaries became so strained at one point that Francis Davis wished he could avoid any dealings with his colleagues in Taiku anymore. He leveled his unkindest remarks at the last of the Oberlin Band to reach Shansi before the turn of the century—Ernest Richmond Atwater—though the reason for his hostility is unclear. Davis said that Atwater "is somewhat like Bret Harte's description of the Chinaman"[32]—Ah Sin, who, Harte wrote, slyly hid twenty-four packs of cards in the long sleeves of his robe while playing euchre:

> "That for ways that are dark,
> And for tricks that are vain,
> The heathen Chinee is peculiar . . ."[33]

Davis's odious comparison was strikingly different from the way Judson Smith felt about Atwater, whom he described as "a man of the fine scholarship, of high purpose, of great energy."[34] On the other hand, Eva Price, who was normally circumspect when it came to talking about fellow missionaries, expressed shock when Atwater became engaged and remarried so soon after his first wife's death.

Ernest, who came from an education-minded family, was, academically speaking, the best mind among the members of the Oberlin Band. Both his parents had studied at Oberlin College. His mother had been enrolled from 1853 to 1861; his father had graduated in 1863 and gone on to become president of two small colleges in Iowa and Missouri. Ernest, who was born August 20, 1865, in Oberlin, attended West High School in Cleveland before he himself entered Oberlin College in 1883. He was an excellent student and almost without exception received the highest grades in all subjects throughout his four years. He was almost a straight-*A* student, graduating as the class of '87 valedictorian.

After a year of teaching Latin and Greek in an Ohio normal school, Ernest entered the Oberlin Theological Seminary, graduating from there in 1892. While at the seminary, he married Jennie Evelyn Pond, a pretty, bespectacled young woman of twenty-two who was the eldest child of the Rev. and Mrs. Chauncy N. Pond. Jennie had been born while her own father was preparing for the ministry in the Theological Seminary. She herself began teaching Sunday school at the age of thirteen.

Jennie and Ernest were married shortly after her graduation from Oberlin College in 1888, and, since Ernest was still in the seminary, they lived with her parents until he finished his studies. They had two children right away, and, by the time they both celebrated their twenty-seventh birthdays in 1892, they and their two children, both girls, were enroute across the Pacific Ocean to Shansi.

Jennie relished the challenge of learning Chinese. She said that "really in spite of the difficulties under which I study I never enjoyed any study better, so well. It has a real living interest that no school tasks ever can have."[35] She wrote her father, "The more you get their language, you find common ground with them.":

> When God created Adam and the race was established by him, there were certain distinctive things[,] traits, tendencies, habits, which were to remain as unchanged to the end of time as are the distinctive traits, habits etc. of the sheep, the musk-rat, or the spider. Man is always man. He is never an imperfect monkey or anything of the kind. I expected to find very strange habits of thought

> even in common matters, not to speak of religion, when I got way off among the prime ordial [*sic*], unchangeable Chinese. I felt sure that I would get a new conception of what men were at the time of the flood. And I did. Only it was the surprising conception that men at the flood and men at the Chicago [*sic*] are absolutely identical. Adam and Noah and Moses and Job could just as easily fix up a little and do business in Boston or New York.[36]

Ernest learned quickly, too. Within a few months of their arrival, he was able to boast that he was "able to understand much that is said now, and begin to feel quite at home in China." The Chinese language, he insisted, "is principally for the eye, not for the ear." All that was required, he believed, was "a vocabulary of 4000 or 5000," which he expected to have in less than three years.[37]

Over the next four years Jennie and Ernest had two more daughters. The last child's birth in late November 1893 was especially difficult for Jennie. The Atwaters were living in Fenchow-fu at the time. Jennie had caught a "very hard cold" a week beforehand, and five days after giving birth came down with a slight fever. The fever first went down but then returned and could not be checked. She developed "a very peculiar cough, spasmodic in character," and no medicine she took could stop it. As a result, she couldn't sleep. Her milk gave out, but a Chinese woman from next door volunteered to nurse the baby. Rowena Bird sat by her bedside, while Ernest summoned Iranaeus Atwood and wrote to Jennie Clapp in Taiku to come as soon as possible. Nine days after giving birth to Bertha, Jennie's temperature shot up to over 104 degrees. The next day, Ernest wrote home to her parents, the Ponds, "The messenger is coming for our Jennie."

Atwood finally reached the Atwaters on Thursday, November 24, and diagnosed Jennie's illness as puerperal fever, commonly called childbed fever—an infection of the bloodstream and of the endometrium, the mucous membrane lining the uterus. By then, it was too late to save her. "The messenger" came at 2 A.M. the next day. "Jennie has passed on," Ernest reported to the Ponds. "A beautiful, peaceful end. No struggle. Just a gentle sigh and she was gone."[38]:

> As the last breath passed her lips, I almost saw her soul pass away, it left so marked a change in the body, her tabernacle, once so full of life. I stood face to

The Atwater children. Left to right: *Mary, Bertha, Ernestine, and, in front of Ernestine, Celia.* Courtesy Oberlin College Archives.

> face with that last great transaction, and I will say to the glory of God that I was not afraid. I felt that I was prepared in heart to lie down also and entrust my soul to the Father. I seemed to see that she had entered into a higher and better life, and that is ours to wait our turn.[39]

Jennie, who was little more than thirty-one years old at the time of her death, was buried in the foreigners' cemetery outside Tai Yuan, beside the grave of Dr. James Goldsbury, who had died three years earlier. Ernest was now faced with a dilemma: "'What shall be done with the little ones?'" Sadly, Jennie had died on their oldest daughter Ernestine's seventh birthday. "A mother can make an oasis in this desert of heathenism where children can grow up," Ernest said, "but when the mother is taken away the children must be placed among safer surroundings."[40]

At first, a nurse was found for the baby, Bertha, and both nurse and infant were taken in by the Atwoods. The other three children remained with Ernest, but the following April, after the Mission's annual meeting, the children were split up. Bertha and the next youngest, Celia, went to live with the Atwoods. At the same time, William L. Hall, the doctor who briefly replaced James Goldsbury, took the two oldest girls, Ernestine and Mary, to the village of Li Man outside Taiku.

The Atwater girls and two of Hall's children made up a fledgling "Liman Missionary Boarding School" under the tutelage of a twenty-seven-year-old Irish woman named Elizabeth Graham.[41] "Lizzie" was a native of County Down, had studied at the Royal University of Ireland and subsequently taught school both in London and in a town outside Bristol. She had come to China as the governess of an English missionary family.[42]

Ernestine and Mary were sweet youngsters who liked to read, draw, and play. Rowena Bird said that when they were told that their mother "had gone to be with Jesus in Heaven, they took it with simple faith, a pleasant rather than a bitter thing." Some Mission adults thought the youngsters didn't grasp what had happened, but Rowena believed otherwise: "They come nearer to the reality of things than we do—it is the child's heart that receives the light straight from Heaven."[43]

Like her mother, Ernestine had dark brown hair and eyes. Eva Price, who sat across from her in chapel one Sunday, thought that "if she wore glasses, the resemblance to her mother would have been almost perfect."[44] And like her mother, Ernestine seemed destined to be a missionary. Be-

Drawings made by Ernestine and Mary Atwater and sent to their grandparents, the Chauncy N. Ponds, in Oberlin, Ohio. Courtesy Oberlin College Archives.

fore Jennie died, she told her, "Mama, when I get big enough to go to Oberlin, oughtn't I to stay and teach people about Jesus?"[45]

Atwater called his daughter Ernestine "Sunshine."[46] She was, he said, "peculiarly strong in character. She is old for her years."[47] His pet name for Mary was "Sweetheart."[48] The three-year-old girl was "very tender and heedless and playful," he said. "She will look very steadily at you while you are giving her some good advice, and at the end entreat you to see her big toad out of doors."[49]

Lizzie Graham soon developed a close rapport with Ernestine and Mary. "They feel now that they have one mother in Heaven and one here, so near has Lizzie come to them," Atwater rejoiced.[50]

Ernest, then thirty-two years old, was also attracted to the young woman, and suddenly, in March 1897, he announced his intention to marry her—which Eva Price thought was precipitious. "The only disagreeable thought that creeps in my mind is that less than four months after his first wife died he was 'booked' for another one."[51] Eva admitted, though, that Lizzie "is a fine young woman and will make a good mother" for Atwater's children.[52]

In all fairness, Ernest and Lizzie waited until August 1897 to become officially engaged and then put off for almost another year the wedding itself. Unlike James and Tinnie Thompson, they didn't have to travel to a consul's office at a treaty port to be wed legally. The U.S. State Department had since rescinded the rule. Instead, they were wed late in the afternoon of July 8, 1898, in the chapel of the China Inland Mission compound in Tai Yuan. Theirs were the first foreign nuptials ever held in Shansi Province.

The ceremony, which began with the sounding of a gong, was marked by a spirit of Anglo-American unity. "The Union Jack & our own Stars and Stripes were significantly intertwined around a pillar near us as we took our places for the ceremony," Ernest wrote the Ponds. The American flag was made by Louise Partridge, who was one of the bridesmaids. Lizzie wore a cream silk dress trimmed with lace and ribbons. Louise had on a dress of pink silk she especially made for the occasion. The other bridesmaid, Ellen Stewart, the governess of the children of English Baptist missionary George Farthing, wore a Chinese dress. The men all wore Chinese attire, too.

Although it was the rainy season, the day was warm and bright, and, after the vows were exchanged, the newlyweds and their guests retired to the home of a CIM missionary for supper. The wedding cake was topped with frostings in the shape of orange blossoms, leaves and butterflies, with, appropriately, "the Am. eagle & British Lion hobnobbing on top."[53] The next day, in the rain, the newlyweds left for a honeymoon in a "pleasant valley home."[54]

Lizzie and Ernest decided soon afterwards that perhaps it was best for

The wedding of Ernest Atwater and Elizabeth Graham on July 8, 1898, in Tai Yuan. Seated on the steps in front of the couple are Dr. and Mrs. E. H. Edwards of the English Baptist Mission. Behind the newlyweds are, left to right: *George Williams, an English missionary named Underwood, Alice Williams, Howard Clapp, Louise Partridge, and Ellen Stewart, governess of the family of English missionary George Farthing.* Courtesy Oberlin College Archives.

Ernestine and Mary to return to their grandparents, the Ponds, in Oberlin for schooling, while they took care of Celia and Bertha. The two older girls could travel there with Iraneaus Atwood, who was returning to America. But the pain of being separated in distance and time from the two children was too much for either of the couple to bear. The girls and Lizzie had become so attached that without hesitation they called their stepmother "Mother." They were "Our girls" to her.[55]

When the Atwaters heard about a boarding school for missionary children that was started by the English family for whom Lizzie had first worked in China—the Pigotts—they jumped at the opportunity. Thomas Wellesley Pigott, a native of Ireland, was first connected with the China Inland Mission when he arrived in China in 1879, but some ten years later he decided to start his own independent mission in Shou Yang, a market town in a mountainous district about two days' journey outside of Tai Yuan, on the main road to Peking and the coast. He began the boarding school after he, his wife, Jessie, and their eleven-year-old son Wellesley William returned from a visit to England in 1898. They brought with them an English tutor and a French governess.

Lizzie Atwater was relieved to have the opportunity to send Ernestine and Mary to the Pigotts. "Mrs. Pigott is a beautiful woman, a noble consecrated lady," she declared. "She is highly educated herself & has travelled much in Europe and elsewhere. Mr. Pigott is a splendid man. I do admire his character so much. I feel that in their home Ernestine will be influenced for good & at a very susceptible age. I felt when I lived there that it was an education to be with such people."[56]

Soon Lizzie was able to report, "Ernestine & Mary are doing so well at Shou Yang. We are blessed to have such an opportunity for them so near."[57] Celia and Bertha were now with her and Ernest in their home in a suburb of Fenchow-fu, about a mile away from the Mission compound where the Prices lived. They were able to afford their own summer home, one of the old abandoned mills in the same valley that the Prices vacationed in Yü Tao Ho.

Now a missionary's wife and no longer a governess, Lizzie began to study the Chinese language seriously. She didn't yet "attempt to talk," Eva Price wrote the Ponds in January 1899, "but she is studying, and has the spirit to go about among the people which is proof that time only is needed to make her an efficient worker."[58] George Farthing, who later gave Lizzie a language examination, reported that she "has not learned Chinese by rote, but has taken a grip of it with the intellect." Her translations from English into Chinese, he said, "were without error."[59]

Lizzie was acclimating to her new role with ease. She "has such a quiet, beautiful manner with children that must endear her to them," Eva said. "We all love her very much."[60]

Lizzie's husband Ernest, however, was having problems getting along with some of the other missionaries, though the circumstances are clouded. One incident occurred in December 1899, involving a Chinese helper who had been Iranaeus Atwood's medical assistant at Fenchow-fu. The man went by several names. His full name was Li Yu. He was also known to the missionaries as Li hsien Sheng—that is, Mr. Li—but he was better known by his childhood name, Hei Kou, a nickname popular among Chinese, that translated as Black Dog.

Li/Hei Kou/Black Dog had been with the station longer than any other helper, Ernest Atwater acknowledged, and had attained "considerable skill in the treatment of diseases & some knowledge of the compounding of medicines."[61] For some reason, however, Ernest wanted to get rid of him. "But all to no purpose," Francis Davis reported. "The church members and Mr. Price stood by him and Atwater made a public apology to the black dog."

But the next day, Ernest retracted the apology. Charles Price then asked him to offer "some specified sin on which to discharge the black dog." Ernest's response, as Francis told it, appears petty: "At last he said that the black dog insisted on Atwaters going out of the chapel door ahead of the black dog when service closed on Sunday."[62]

Somehow, the matter smacks of a slight over prerogatives. But it prompted Davis to make his comparison of Atwater to Bret Harte's "heathen Chinee," Ah Sin. And there obviously was ill-feeling between other members of the Mission as well. At one point, Ernest proposed that Francis leave Fenchow-fu and open a new station, which would permit Francis to transfer from Taiku to Fenchow-fu with his family when Lydia and the children came back from America. Francis was amenable to the idea, especially to the thought of working with Charles Price. But, he said, the arrangement would mean that James Thompson—Tinnie's widowed husband—would have to work with either Ernest or Howard Clapp if he came back to China—"neither very agreeable."[63]

"There are three stages in missionary experience," James Thompson philosophized before he left for America following Tinnie's death. "First, welcome at Tientsin, second, beginning of criticism, third, when it gets so no on can work with him."[64]

Things might have calmed down had Atwater gone on furlough. He was granted leave by the American Board to return to the States in 1901.

By then, he would have been in China nine years. At first, he and Lizzie planned to take advantage of the furlough. Lizzie had never met her step-daughters' grandparents, the Ponds. "The time is not long now," she wrote them, "till we meet you all if God spare us. . . . We shall see each other face to face."[65]

But then the Atwaters started to have second thoughts, and Lizzie didn't think they would go at all. She soon had something else on her mind. Nearly twenty months after their marriage, Lizzie—now nearing her thirtieth birthday—was able to ecstatically announce that she was pregnant:

> We look forward to welcoming our first little one this Sept. It is so new & wonderful to me. Yet I can hardly realize it. We have longed for it & I shall be a happy woman if I live to hold my own darling baby in my arms.[66]

ELEVEN ❀ *Triumphs and Adversities*

Things that are done, it is needless to speak about; things that have had their course, it is needless to remonstrate about; things that are past, it is needless to blame.

—Confucius

As Christmas 1899 approached and the Shansi Mission's schools went into recess, the Oberlin Band took stock of the year's accomplishments and the work ahead. Members who headed committees or were responsible for the Mission's finances and educational programs started writing their annual reports to the American Board in Boston. There was a lot to feel sanguine about, particularly church membership and the school programs, they thought, but there were also some things that needed improvement.

The church in Taiku, organized in 1894, a dozen years after the Oberlin Band first entered Shansi, now had seventy-six Chinese communicants, seventeen more than when the year began. The number of Chinese who attended it on Sunday averaged two hundred. In addition, the Taiku missionaries tended eight outstations and places of meetings; their Fenchow-fu colleagues ran three outstations. Each of the two main stations also operated Sunday schools, with a combined attendance of one hundred and ten youngsters.

The boarding school for boys in Taiku now had twenty-four pupils. More students could have been accommodated, but the Mission did not have the funds to hire the additional teachers that would be necessary or the money to furnish another dormitory. Seven of the boys, all teenagers,

The interior of the chapel at Taiku. Courtesy Oberlin College Archives.

were in a special course of study that was being expanded on a year-to-year basis to become a preparatory academy for college students. Rowena Bird reported that the prospect of going on to college "has in itself been a stimulus to better work, and an incentive to those who felt they were getting a little old for school."[1] One Taiku student—Confucius' descendant K'ung Hsiang Hsi—was already in North China College, the first Shansi-trained Chinese youth to enter it.

Both Rowena and Jennie Clapp alternated in holding Sunday services in two outstations. Jennie, who otherwise devoted all her time to visiting Chinese women in their homes, was pleased to note that "a large proportion of the people of the little villages have given up their idols and some are hopefully Christians."

Meanwhile, in Li Man, outside Taiku, the girls' boarding school that Louise Partridge was running numbered sixteen pupils, more than one hundred families were being taught the Gospels, a number of women were taking reading classes, and forty of them, Louise proudly announced, had unbound feet. "This is the first time in all the years since foreigners first saw Li Man that such systematic work has been done," she triumphantly declared.

Louise, however, was troubled that superstitions about foreigners persisted. There were ugly rumors starting to circulate about foreigners' poisoning wells. "It is a hard place," Louise said. "One story that has gained credence is that foreigners are either going about themselves on horseback or hiring Chinese to go about dropping medicine into wells. Sometimes this is shaken from the sleeve, sometimes from a great green bottle inverted over a well."[2]

A boarding school for boys in Fenchow-fu, which Charles Price had run but which was discontinued when the Prices went on leave in 1896, was back in operation and had enrolled twenty-one pupils. Charles was encouraged that the students were "a better class of boys than at any previous time." Several of them, he said, had studied for two or three years in Chinese schools but could see the advantage of changing to the missionary school. There was also a noticeable increase in the number of the students whose parents were Christians. "It seems to me," Charles added, "our Fen Chou fu station work shows no more marked improvement in any line and nothing that is more hopeful for the general work of the station than this growing desire to have their children taught in our schools."[3]

In addition to the boarding schools, the Mission could also boast two day schools in outlying villages, which had twenty-five pupils between them.[4]

Ernest Atwater reported that the Fenchow-fu church, which had been in existence less than two years, had fifty-two probationers, among them Chinese in the outlying village of Liu Len Chen, where "men of influence were often in attendance." The membership roll had increased by six during the year and now numbered forty-one, though he added, it was really impossible to accurately identify and number the church members because of opium addiction. Members "break off opium in the winter & go back to it in the summer—a sort of Chinese back sliding."

The Fenchow-fu church, Atwater wrote, witnessed only one baptism service during the year, in which four men were baptized, but that didn't discourage him. He thought it best that the Mission be conservative in admitting people to full communion.[5] The trouble, Charles Price explained, was that "with many the idea of entering the Church depends on how much money can be got out of it[.] Men constantly ask, 'How much do you pay those who enter your Church?' "[6]

The missionaries had always found that conversions posed a thorny issue. Atwater's first wife, Jennie, believed that Chinese people were "so self satisfied it is very hard to reach them." Less than a year after arriving in China, Ernest was convinced that it would be "a long time yet" before there would be "a great Christian community" in China. "We had expected that there would soon be, we so little appreciated, so very little, the element of time."[7] The "heathen China farmer," he continued, "does not differ much from his brother in America who is without God and hope in the world. Both enjoy the good things of this life without much care for anything beyond."[8]

Ernest believed that the Chinese people did not understand why the missionaries were in China. "Most, rather all of the ideas that go to make up the good news are not in the Chinaman's comprehension. To him there are no such things. Communion with God, love of God, the necessity of salvation from sin,—all are foreign and all but incomprehensible well proclaimed. The moral people about do not want our gospel because they have the precepts of the ancients and what can they need more?"[9]

The validity of a conversion was a constant source of contention with other missionary societies. The Oberlin Band felt that some members of other societies indiscriminately accepted anyone who expressed interest in Christ and thus claimed hundreds of adherents of questionable faith. One Baptist missionary operating in south Shansi was said to have baptized more than two hundred Chinese solely because they came to him and "it was not his place to reject them."[10] A Bible Society agent doubted that "one in 15" of the six hundred converts in the province claimed by the China Inland Mission "was really interested in the truth."[11]

The Shansi missionaries were wary of such "make-believe work"[12] and followed a system to distinguish between inquirers, who evinced interest in the faith, and probationers, who were seriously studying for baptism. Probationers were required to study Christian doctrine for at least a year

The exterior of the chapel at Fenchow-fu, showing the entrance for men. Courtesy Oberlin College Archives.

and had to pass a stiff examination before being accepted into communion. Howard Clapp devised a number of questions to put to them: "What is it to be a Christian?" they were asked. "What is sin?, What is the meaning of baptism?, Why did Christ come into the world?, What is the work of the holy spirit?" and, finally, "Why do you love the Lord?"[13]

Still, the system was far from perfect. "We are constantly being disappointed in those we suppose to be sincere," said Charles Price. He thought the missionaries were able to offer the Chinese only "little of the truth" because of language difficulties. "But the hardest part," he said, "is to see them lacking in spiritual life. I feel sometimes like a man shoveling sand on the seashore. He will not find many *Pearls* though he work ever so faithful. We *scoop in* a goodly number and they are not all *Pearls*."[14]

When a Chinese man or woman was accepted as a communicant, it was an occasion for rejoicing. The first active work George Williams did upon reaching Taiku in 1892 was "the great privelege [*sic*] and joy" of baptizing his servant.[15] Even more memorable was the Sunday in 1893 that Deacon Liu's grandson was baptized. Eleven other Chinese—one woman, four pupils, four servants, and two teachers—were baptized at the same time. The woman was the first female to receive that rite in Taiku. Williams was touched as the twelve candidates stepped forward to receive the rite of baptism from Howard Clapp: "All our hearts were melted at the spec-tacle."[16] Nine other Chinese, including Deacon Liu's wife, who was an ex-opium addict herself, were accepted as probationers. The ceremonies that Sunday left Howard Clapp "so full of feeling, he could scarcely speak."[17]

Clapp, who headed the Mission's Depository, happily reported that the work of book and tract distribution in Fenchow-fu in 1899 had accounted for "the largest sales by far" in the Mission's history. Scriptures, calendars, scientific books, hymnals, and monthly magazines brought in 163,426 *cash* (approximately $81.70; twenty *cash* equalled a penny). Unfortunately, Clapp said, the sales in Taiku were minimal, chiefly because there was no money available to hire a colporteur "and no men fit for such work." As a result, the missionaries there only distributed a few cheap tracts and several hundred old American Bible Society books.[18]

Despite the backsliding Atwater reported in Fenchow-fu, he insisted that the record sale of tracts indicated that "the membership of the Church are interested in good reading & in the study of the Word & this will in time yield the harvest for which we so much long." He was also optimistic about an innovative helpers' class held in midsummer to train Chinese as Mission workers. He taught them elements of theology and advanced catechism; Clapp directed them in studying the exegesis of Luke and sermon preparation, and Fei Chi Hao instructed them in singing.[19]

The training of Mission workers was essential to the expansion of the Oberlin Band's operations, so Atwater's report was especially encouraging. But there were downsides to report, also. One was that, with the departure of the Atwoods earlier in the year, there was no missionary doctor any longer attached to the Shansi Mission, either in Taiku or Fenchow-fu. Moreover, the clinic and hospital in Fenchow-fu had to be discontinued. That was a serious blow to the Oberlin Band. The Mission's first contact with potential candidates for conversion was usually through the medical treatments it offered.

In addition, the dispensary in Taiku was now reduced to "a small scale." It was being run by Sang Ai Ch'ing and his wife—a couple trained by Dr. William Hall in Li Man before he left. Mrs. Sang was the more experienced of the two; she was called Dr. Sang. She had completed the medical course of a Presbyterian missionary society before she married Sang, who was then working with the China Inland Mission in Shansi. He helped Hall with male patients, while she tended sick women. With Hall gone—he had developed diabetes—the couple were nevertheless able to treat more than four hundred patients during the year. They had

Dr. and Mr. Sang Ai Ch'ing, who took over the work of Iranaeus J. Atwood when he left Shansi. *Courtesy Oberlin College Archives.*

successfully amputated the hand of a person whose wrist was shattered by a gun explosion. Still, the number of patients had decreased dramatically. Clapp, who was supervising the Sangs' medical work, said they had done "the best they could with the supplies given them."

The only good news to report about the Mission's medical service was that it was earning money. Clapp had decided to impose a fee for day patients who could afford to pay—30 *cash* (a penny and a half). In-patients were charged 50 *cash* (two and a half pennies) for fuel and lights. A fee of 1,000 *cash* (50 cents) "plus cart hire" was charged for opium poisoning cases that had to be brought into the dispensary. Sales of medicines—"mostly cod liver oil"—totaled a whopping 73,300 *cash* ($36.65). As a result, the dispensary, Clapp said, earned a profit of $147.98. The surplus was used for other Mission work.[20]

One discouraging note was that "Native contributions" for the upkeep and repair of the churches, school fees, and mission work totaled only $634.61.[21] By Chinese standards of the time, when workers earned only a few pennies a day, the sum was impressive—remarkable, in fact. But the contributions could not make up for deficits the Shansi Mission accumulated. Food for the boarding schools was going up in price, a result of a drought and incipient famine that were beginning to sweep through the provinces of North China.

The Mission's total budget for the year had been in excess of $14,650, slightly more than half of which went to salaries, which were by no means exorbitant. Married missionaries earned $1,000 a year. Those with children received additional moneys depending on the age of the children—for example, $500 for a child under seven years old. Unmarried female missionaries earned $500. To make up for the Mission's deficits, six of the missionaries were defraying expenses by contributing from their own salaries. To do so, they were drawing against their wages and were in debt to the American Board for "$585.06 Gold"—which "does not seem so much of a disgrace to the Mission as one might suppose," George Williams was quick to point out to the Board.[22]

Money happened to be very much on Williams's mind at the time, and for some time to come, but he didn't tell the Board anything about his concern. The Committee on Building, made up of Howard Clapp, Charles Price, and Francis Davis, reported to the Board that it was "a marvel that so few serious mistakes" were made by George and his Chinese workmen in building his new house in the suburb of Taiku. The committee praised him for his diligence, and said the house cost $2,800 and did not exceed the amount raised.[23] But that was stretching the truth, if not an outright fabrication, since Williams apparently never informed his colleagues of the true situation.

George toted up all the costs and came to the conclusion that he was "fully $1,000 in debt."[24] The debt weighed heavily on his mind and became a recurrent theme in his letters to his wife, Alice. He told her that he could not return to Ohio to be with her "till I get this debt paid off,"[25] that he was "straining every nerve to pay" it off,[26] that it "must be *removed.*"[27] He put up for sale the cow the Williamses kept for milk, tried to reduce the amount of lighting oil he consumed by going to bed at nine o'clock at night and rising at five in the morning, and made out a list of his books that he hoped to sell to raise money. "Nothing I have belongs to me," he finally wrote her in anguish. "Nothing I can call my own. *Things* that is. I have you and the children yet. Thank God for that?"[28]

The lack of funds was actually on everybody's mind, and thrift was the order of the day at Christmas that year. Ordinarily, the missionaries planned months in advance to have gift items for their family members and close Chinese workers forwarded to them from America. But 1899 was an exception. Jennie Clapp noted that the missionaries in Taiku exchanged few presents and gave none whatsoever to the schoolboys or their helpers. "We did not like to make a display among ourselves," she explained. "Another reason[:] the work runs our salaries so closely we do not have much to spend on the extras."[29]

Jennie did invite some seventy Chinese to Christmas dinner, a custom that began early in the Mission's life. But the Prices in Fenchow-fu had second thoughts about even that expenditure. The previous Christmas, about seventy male church members and probationers enjoyed a feast in the chapel under Charles's supervision, while Eva entertained a similar number of women in her home—by comparison, "more sinners than saints," she said.[30] But Christmas 1899 was another matter. Church members decorated the Fenchow-fu chapel with evergreens, lanterns, and banners with mottoes and gilt stars, but there was no sit-down meal for them or for anyone else.

Eva rationalized the break in tradition by saying that the Chinese have many feasts and the Fenchow-fu missionaries didn't want to associate eating with the purpose of Christmas, the celebration of Christ's birth. Then, too, there was the question of spending so much money on food when so many people had little to eat. "There are so many such vexing questions in the work here that we need to be wise as serpents and harmless as doves," she added.[31]

The missionaries' self-imposed frugality was a minor annoyance compared to an accident that occurred two days before Christmas. It colored the holiday week and, as the details about it emerged, almost wrecked all the progress the Oberlin Band had made toward creating a meaningful educational program.

A little ten-year-old boy named Hu'er, the son of one of the Mission's helpers, suffered severe burns from falling against a hot iron stove. Hu'er died the day after New Year's Day. The youngster's suffering was tragic and cast a cloud over the simple festivities the missionaries had planned. But then it came out that the accident was, in a sense, no accident at all.[32]

The boy's teacher, Fei Chi Hao, had made Hu'er stand by the side of the hot stove every morning for the past two months. The youngster was allowed to sit during morning prayers, but afterwards he was again compelled to stand by the stove all day and often into the evening until nine o'clock. He had to eat alone and was forbidden to talk to other pupils. Fei allegedly beat Hu'er, too, striking him thirty times, until a student of almost Fei's own age—Chang Cheng Fu, but better known by his childhood name, Er Wu—pleaded with him to spare the boy. Still, Fei continued to make Hu'er stand by the hot stove.

The reason for the excessive punishment, the teacher explained, was that the boy had told three lies. But Deacon Liu, who had never liked Fei, thought there was some other, personal motive behind the punishment.

As the details about the incident unfolded, long-smoldering feelings of ill will came out, involving not only Fei and Deacon Liu but also Howard Clapp. Unspoken, though evident between the lines, were questions of jealousy and authority that raised the issue of who was in charge of the Taiku station.

For some time, Howard Clapp felt that Liu was trying to run the station and automatically opposed him, according to Francis Davis, "in all cases, or at least enough to make trouble." At the same time, both Howard and his wife Jennie felt close to Fei Chi Hao. They had nursed him back to health that spring when he fell ill with typhus fever. The young teacher said they had treated him "like my own parents." Accordingly, Clapp despaired as vicious charges and countercharges were exchanged.

As details about Hu'er's death emerged, it turned out that Deacon Liu had kept a record of everything Fei "said or did that displeased him, and every fault he saw or heard of," even things, said Rowena Bird when she learned about them, that were "so trivial as to be ridiculous." According

Liu Feng Chih—Deacon Liu—with his crippled wife, left, and family. Note the bound feet of the wife and the woman next to her. Courtesy Oberlin College Archives.

to Liu, Fei, who was a graduate of North China College in Tung Chow, had taken offense to Hu'er's telling his schoolmates that "all Tung Chow students were proud."

But Liu also harbored a personal grudge against Fei. He claimed that the teacher had written a friend that the Taiku church would be better off without Deacon Liu.

Liu approached George Williams to complain about Fei, obviously believing that Howard Clapp would side with the teacher. Williams asked to see Er Wu, who corroborated "in almost every particular" what Liu said about Fei's punishment of little Hu'er. George immediately informed the Clapps and Rowena. Meanwhile, the deacon, believing that the missionaries would not take the matter seriously, "got all worked up and blurted out in morning prayers that God was higher than any 'mushih' [minister] and he was going to follow God." He then prayed, "asking the Lord to deliver us from 'this great wolf in our midst,'"—meaning, of course, Fei. He hoped no one would be "eaten by him" in the coming year.

Howard Clapp was incensed. He told Liu to remember that "God was above him, too," that "it was not good to thus talk in public." The deacon's prayer, he said, "was not the only instance when he had spoken with disrespect of the 'mushihs' in public."

Rowena, who taught Fei English, "boiled" when she heard what Liu had injected into the prayer session. She said that the deacon had not done "*one* thing all these months to have helped the young teacher, or shown *one bit* of sympathy with him in *any* thing."

Clapp didn't know what to do. For some time, he told Williams, he had felt that he had lost the respect of Liu, who had "frequently held him up to ridicule before the church." Williams was sympathetic. The deacon, he agreed, had "taken the attitude of sort of insulting Mr. Clapp all the year, that is by throwing out criticisms, remarks publicly, &c." Clapp had often remarked that "he felt he could not work with Mr. Liu much longer." He was so upset that he "could neither eat, sleep, nor work."

In an effort to resolve the matter, Clapp and Williams summoned Liu. The deacon apologized at once for his uncalled-for remarks at the prayer meeting. He denied that he had ever meant any disrespect for Clapp. But he was adamant about Fei's being punished. The case could be taken to the *yamen* (courthouse), but Liu felt that would embarrass the church. The fact of Hu'er's death would also fuel a widespread superstition that the missionaries killed children for their eyes and hearts and then used them in their religious rites.

Liu suggested an alternative: that Fei be made to stand by the hot stove for as many days as Hu'er did or that a tombstone should be erected in the boy's honor. When Clapp and Williams hesitated about what to do, the deacon threatened to take the matter to the *yamen.*

After the meeting was over, Clapp immediately ordered that a cart be hired to take Fei to Li Man, to get him out of the jurisdiction of local authorities. Williams, meanwhile, took it upon himself to go to the village of Tung Fang, where the parents of most of the pupils lived, to ascertain their feelings about the matter.

The parents were undoubtedly prejudiced against Liu, because when they first asked the Shansi missionaries to open an outstation in their village, the deacon had haughtily remarked, "I simply wipe my feet of the dust. They are not worthy to be taught."[33]

The parents told Williams that they were all for having Fei stay on "*if* he would only change and not punish the small boys so severely." To ensure peace, they also suggested that, after a few months, the teacher should be sent back to his home in Tung Chow. Deacon Liu became "violent" when he heard that the parents wanted Fei to remain, if only for a few months. "I am going to leave the Church," he declared.

Liu didn't go the authorities at the *yamen,* nor did he quit the church, but the crisis was far from resolved. He took the occasion of the annual meeting of members of the Fenchow-fu church to discuss the issue in public. The missionaries "dreaded" it when the deacon took the rostrum with a bunch of notes in hand and "began with the day after Mr. Fei had arrived in TaiKu and brought up point after point against him to remove our doubt." Williams thought he "acted like a baby." Was he just a nobody? Liu asked, sulking. Or a helper? Or a *chih shih* (deacon)? And then it came out that one reason for his vehemence was that he felt that the missionaries had done some things without consulting him and he wanted "to 'kuan' [control] things."

The meeting left Clapp "vexed and pained." He and Williams now summoned Fei in an effort to fathom what was going on. But the young teacher did not help his side of the story. He was not contrite at all. Fei "cooly admitted" punishing Hu'er. He said his conscience did not bother him and that "he would do the same to his own child."

Shaken, George began to think that the deacon was right about Fei. He told Fei that he would never allow him to treat one of his daughters the way the teacher had treated Hu'er. "The sight of him in his coffin was enough to melt a heart of stone," Williams said, "yet this man was unmoved & now says he would do it again." He said he was "getting to feel" that Fei should be "very severely" dealt with. The incident, he added, was "awful to my mind."

Again, Williams, the Clapps, and Rowena Bird conferred. "The great question" was what they were going to do with the Taiku school. Who could replace Fei? There was no other qualified teacher to handle the advanced classes essential to expanding the boys' school into a full-fledged academy. "If he showed any pity," Williams said, "it would be different."

Everyone involved was, at this point, sick with anguish. Liu was ill, "scarcely able to go out and looks like death, haggard and pale enough to make one's heart ache," said Williams. He suggested that the deacon remove to a village outside Taiku, but Rowena went there in advance and came back with word that the people there "were displeased with Mr. Liu though just what I don't know."

Williams was more worried, however, about Howard Clapp, who was so distraught he couldn't sleep. "I really fear for him," said Williams, who was also concerned about the consequences that the controversy would have on his own plans: "with the prospect which is before us how can I leave to come home even for a year. Who will take my place? No one can be spared."

Clapp thought that he could never work again with Liu, or ask him to preach or to teach classes at the opium refuge. But the deacon finally relented, making "a sort of public confession," and he and Clapp were reconciled. That left the question of what to do about Fei and the school. As Rowena Bird put it, "To dismiss school now would be like cutting off the right hand of our work." Clapp was so distressed at that thought that he was "almost ill over it."

A compromise was worked out, though Fei never repented his disciplining of Hu'er. In fact, he felt wronged, and too ashamed to face his parents. He said he could not find the words to pray and questioned whether he wanted to serve God anymore. But he accepted the compromise.

Fei went to Fenchow-fu, to teach in the boys' school there. In exchange, the Fenchow-fu missionaries sent to Taiku one of their teachers, the husband of Fei's sister, Liu Chang Lao. To avoid confusion with Liu Feng Chih—Deacon Liu—Liu Chang Lao was known as Teacher Liu. Rowena Bird, for one, was grateful. She wrote the Prices, "The quickness of you FenChofu people to appreciate our trouble, your ready sympathy, and timely aid, will, I am sure not soon be forgotten by us. Without it, it would have been darkness indeed for us."

But Howard Clapp was not happy with the solution. "I cant [*sic*] get over the feeling," he said, "that it is a graver mistake to allow prejudice to break up an important & prospering part of our work."

"I have felt rather 'blue' sometimes of late about our work," Howard reported to Judson Smith. He briefly recounted the events surrounding Hu'er's accident, saying that he thought that what had transpired was unfair to Fei Chi Hao. But there was so much prejudice against the teacher, he said, that the school might have entirely disbanded. "We felt compelled to send him away so we exchanged teachers with Fen Chou fu, & it is going on again—but it is no such school as we had last year," Clapp continued. "Now there is the anomalous situation of a second class teacher in a first class place & a first class teacher in a second class school.

"The probabilities are that we shall never have an Academy here in Taiku, at least for some years."

Hu'er's accident was but one of several tragedies that occurred during 1899. Any joy the Shansi missionaries experienced over their successes in evangelical and educational work seemed to be matched by the constant presence of death.

In May, Jennie Clapp paid a condolence call on Tinnie Thompson in Jen Tsun when she heard that Tinnie's mother had died. That night, while she was there, Tinnie's little daughter Alma was stricken with dysentery. With no doctor immediately available, Jennie stayed with the Thompsons for four days, watching over the young girl, until she suffered a series of convulsions and died. Then word came that Fei Chi Hao had come down with typhus fever in Taiku. Jennie hurried back home to help Howard nurse him without waiting to attend the funeral service for Alma. But even before the youngster was buried, her older sister Marion was suddenly stricken with dysentery, too, and for several weeks her life hung in the balance.

Both Fei and Marion Thompson recovered. But next, the children's mother, Tinnie Thompson, came down with childbed fever after giving birth. Jennie rushed back to Jen Tsun to be with her. While Tinnie was fighting for her life, Jennie received a letter from home that her own brother had died after an illness of two years. Somehow, despite her own grief, she managed to sit by Tinnie's bedside, watching her facing death "calmly, fearlessly, trustingly," until Tinnie died also.

"This has been a very trying year for us—full of work, anxiety and sorrow," said Jennie.[34] Eva Price echoed her pain: "So many calamities have overtaken this mission that one wonders who or what the 'Jonah' on board can be."[35]

As the New Year approached, an even more fateful death occurred, though it involved someone the Shansi missionaries did not even know. On the last day of 1899, Sidney Brooks, a twenty-four-year-old member of the Society for the Propagation of the Gospel, was on a road southwest of the prefectural city of Tsinan, returning to his post in Shantung Province. Brooks, a veteran of four years' service in China, had just spent the Christmas holiday in Tsinan with his sister, who had recently arrived from England after marrying a colleague of Brooks's.

Foolishly, Brooks was traveling alone. Two months earlier, in October, Imperial troops had fought a pitched battle in Shantung with a dissident group called the *I Ho Chüan*—Boxers United in Righteousness. Members of the same society had slain a gatekeeper and a Catholic teacher the next month.

The violence, aimed at Christian converts, was spreading rapidly. Diplomats in Peking were calling for the removal of the province's governor. Then, in the first week of December, missionaries of several nations telegraphed their legations in Peking: "Boxer rebellion twenty counties

Shantung, Chihli, rapidly spreading. Pillage[,] arson, murders increasing, avowed object kill Christians, exterminate foreigners, unless four legations combine pressure. . . . Americans consider situation almost hopeless."[36]

Brooks was morose as he made his way home on horseback. He had been that way all during the Christmas holiday, the result of a disturbing nightmare. He dreamed he was back in England and walking through his college when his eye was caught by a tablet on a wall bearing the names of all those who had gone from the school as missionaries. There was a companion tablet near it with the inscription, "To those who were martyred for the Faith." On it he saw his own name.

Brooks, who thought the dream was an omen, was suddenly surrounded on the road by a gang of young men. They were Boxers. What happened next is unclear. Apparently the youths wanted Brooks's horse and he refused to give it to them, or he got into an argument when they confronted him. The Boxers brutally beat Brooks, stripped him of his clothes, strung a rope through a hole they made in his nose and led him around for hours. Then, when he evidently got loose and tried to escape, they killed him with their swords and tossed his body into a ditch.[37]

The significance of Brooks's murder did not dawn on the Shansi missionaries at first, but its reverbations were felt throughout other areas of North China.

TWELVE ❁ *The Volcano*

The study of strange doctrines is injurious indeed!
—Confucius

Almost a decade earlier, nearly 450 members of Protestant evangelical societies had gathered far removed from Shansi—more than six hundred miles away in Shanghai. The occasion was the largest missionary conference ever held in China.

There was a lot to discuss. For one thing, the British Foreign Office was warning that the distribution of the Bible without interpretative commentaries and notes was dangerous. Chinese were misinterpreting it, and some places had banned it as a politically seditious book. But purists argued that it was heresy to think that God's Word could not be understood by everybody without any help.

The old argument about assimilating, or at least condoning, ancestor worship—the central tenet of Confucianism—cropped up again. Many delegates still felt that accepting ancestor worship was tantamount to accepting Confucianism itself, and that was an unheard-of admission.

Timothy Richard had a more urgent matter to call to the attention of the assembled missionaries, most of whom were English. Richard had resigned from the Baptist Missionary Society over a doctrinal dispute with his associates. He was now editor of *Shih Pao* of Tientsin, one of only six newspapers in the entire Chinese Empire. He hoped in that capacity to influence educated Chinese—the literati and high government officials—about the progress the country could achieve with railway systems and improved communications, such as telegraph lines. But even he sensed the stirrings of something that he felt compelled to communicate to the delegates: a growing xenophobia among officials of the Imperial government. It was being enflamed by Chinese conservatives who believed the Empire was being exploited by Western powers, the merchants who followed their flags, and the ideas they brought with them to China. They were especially hostile to Christian missionaries, who ran schools that taught about Western science and institutions.

Richard said—but no one seemed to listen—that the missionaries were "standing on a volcano" that could very likely erupt.[1]

One has only to look at a map of the Chinese Empire as it was when the nineteenth century drew to a close to visualize a major reason for the xenophobia. The rainbow of colors that depict the colonial possessions and spheres of influence of the various so-called Powers is striking. The German sphere, shaded in gray, is the smallest area of concessions, an oval-shaped slice of territory in the southern part of the province of Shantung. Yet it extends some two hundred miles inland from the coast of the Yellow Sea. British interests, in purple, cover a small portion on the northern coast of Shantung around the city of Weihaiwei as well as Hong Kong, on which Britain has a ninety-nine-year lease. But its purple tint also shades the vast Yangtze River Valley, reaching more than a thousand miles inland from the coastline of the East China Sea to the Kunlun Mountains. Japan's sphere, in red, covers a sizable part of Fukien Province on the mainland opposite the island of Taiwan, which she seized in the Sino-Japanese War of 1894–1895. The blue of France, which had already invested Indo-China by then, covers all of southwest China above it. The green denoting Russia, which had grabbed Darien and Port Arthur from China, colors Manchuria.[2] *Gua-fen,* the carving up of the melon, was almost complete.

How the map came to be drawn is a study of rampant imperialism. The Manchus who came out of the north to conquer China in the middle of the seventeenth century and established the Ching ("Pure") dynasty were always in the minority. The beginning of the Ching dynasty—second only to the Ming dynasty as the longest autocracy in the history of the world—marked a great economic upsurge and huge increase in China's population, from 100 million people in 1650 to 300 million in 1820

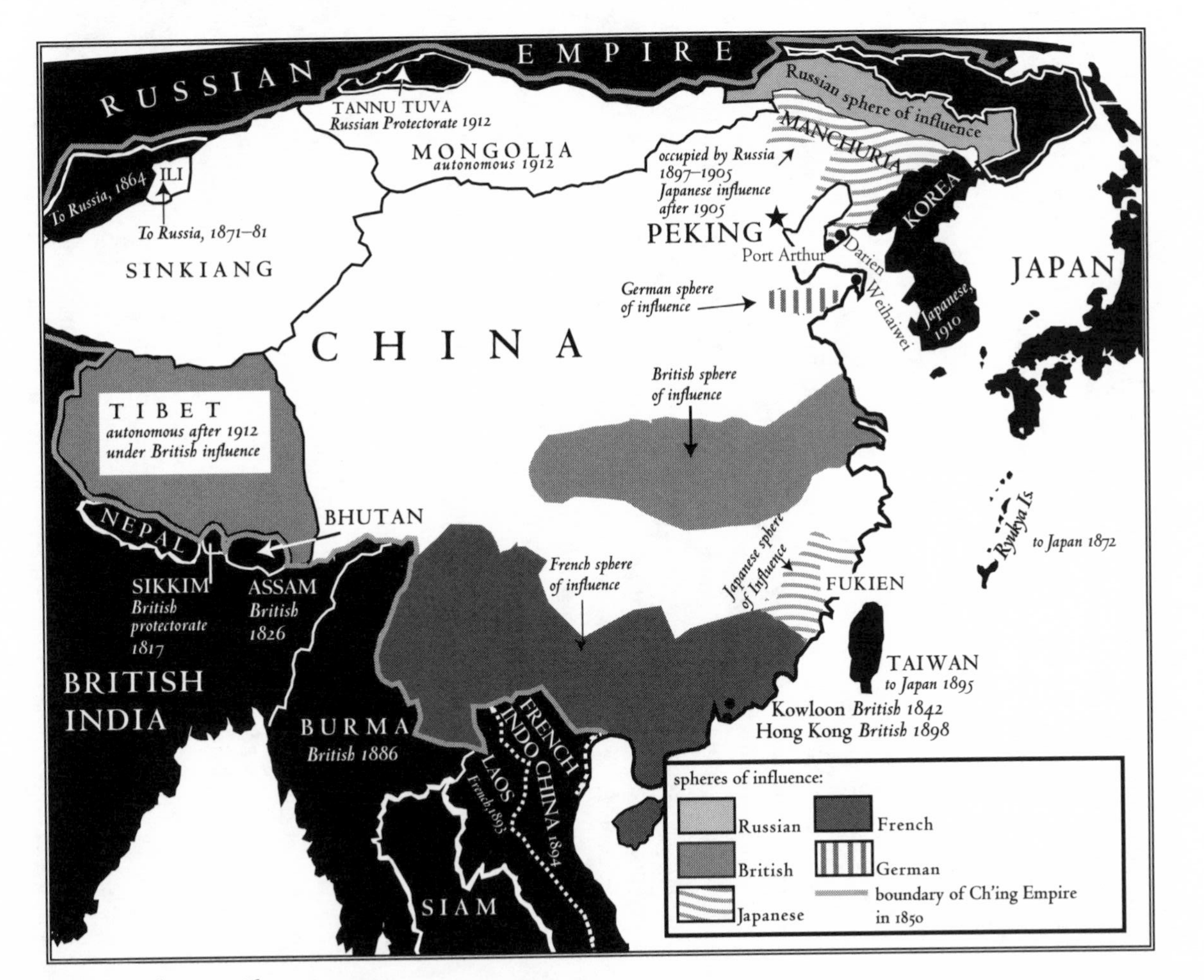

Spheres of influence in China, 1842–1911.

and to well over 400 million by mid-century. By comparison, the United States had a population of only 23 million by the mid-nineteenth century. Great quantities of tea, silk and porcelain were exported to Europe and America from the lone port of Canton.

China—the proud, tradition-bound, insular Middle Kingdom whose great sailing ships traversed the Indian Ocean long before Columbus set sail—prospered. But the financial burden of wars of expansion into Mongolia and beyond the Gobi Desert into Sinkiang, as well as the pressure of the growing population, produced hardships that led to a number of antigovernment revolts. To maintain control, the Manchus banned intermarriage and forced all male Chinese to shave their foreheads and grow a "twist," or queue, of braided hair as a sign of subjugation.

The dynasty's decline in the nineteenth century began with the White Lotus Rebellion, which started in 1795 and lasted until 1804. Until then, the Chinese refused to buy English goods in return for the tea that was being carried to Britain. As a result, Britain was losing vast amounts of silver currency. To make up for the loss, it began to import opium into the country, although the drug was outlawed in China. The British established a triangular trade similar to the one she had employed with her American colonies, when slaves, rum, and timber were carried in ships between Africa, the West Indies, and North America. The British shipped opium from India into China; they took back home from China tea, and sent India fabrics and hardware manufactured in England. The currency flow reversed.

The British, who dominated the commercial thrust into the Empire until the 1870s, pressured the Imperial Government to open China for legal trade. They saw its immense population as potential consumers, a perfect market for their textiles and other manufactures. (It was a myth that has never been realized; China was, and is, largely self-sufficient.)

When China tried to halt the opium trade, the British fought back, defeating it in the Opium War of 1839–1842. As a result, China was forced to open five so-called Treaty Ports in which foreigners could trade. The Chinese also ceded extraterritorial rights, allowing foreigners to govern themselves without Chinese interference. The concessions were the first, decisive breach in China's traditional isolation.

More ports were opened after the two fought again, the Arrow War, in the late 1850s. Western merchants now carried on their commercial activities in the interior, and where they went, missionaries soon followed.

What Britain wanted, her European rivals demanded, too. One after another, treaties were signed that whittled away at China's autonomy—the Treaty of Nanking, the Convention of Peking, the Chefoo Convention, the Treaty of Shimonoseki. The Ching dynasty was in trouble, both from foreigners outside its frontiers and from rebels inside its borders. During the Taiping Rebellion in 1851, a destructive conflict that lasted for thirteen years, some six hundred walled cities changed hands.[3] The rebellion was a particularly embarrassing and onerous one for Protestant missionaries because it was led by a mentally unbalanced, failed scholar who had studied with missionaries and claimed to be Jesus' younger brother.

That rebellion, the Arrow War with Britain, and other unrest convinced Western powers that the China of the Ching dynasty was on the point of collapse. Its armies were ill-equipped and old-fashioned, its government corrupt, bankrupt, powerless. In the midst of the Taiping Rebellion in 1856, British and French forces stormed the Taku forts, at the mouth of the Pei Ho River, occupied Tientsin several miles upstream, and then occupied Peking itself and razed the Summer Palace in its outskirts. The two governments forced the Manchus to open additional treaty ports and also compelled them to sign a treaty legalizing the opium trade.

One by one, the Empire's dependencies were cut away. Russia took a huge region north of the Amur River in 1858, the Maritime Province two years later, and finally part of Turkestan in 1871. Portugal won confirmation of her occupation of Macao in 1862. France annexed three provinces of Lower Cochin-China and gained control of the Mekong Basin in 1867, then seized Tonkin in 1885, taking control over all of Indo-China after a war with China. Britain annexed Burma the following year.

Despite their attitude toward diplomats in general, missionaries tended to side with them when it came to wringing concessions out of the Chinese. Protestant missionaries, in fact, were dependent on the legations in Peking to press their needs because the rigid hierarchy of control exercised by the Manchus prohibited them from dealing directly with local, district, or provincial officials. "We shall get nothing important out of the Chinese unless we stand in a menacing attitude before them," said S.

Wells Williams, a missionary who acted as interpreter and secretary of the American legation following the Arrow War. "They would grant nothing unless fear stimulated their sense of justice, for they are among the most craven of people, cruel and selfish as heathenism can make men, so we must be backed by force if we wish them to listen to reason."[4] When the Sino-Japanese War broke out, Charles Price said that "a good whipping would do a great deal toward Christianizing China":

> A defeat such as they would not fail to know of—one that left no doubt as to the superiority of foreign countries, would take some of their pride away and make them think there may be other countries beside China. For the present they have not yet learned this. They speak of Japan as a very small country and seem to think it impossible that they should be whipped by them.[5]

Japan's easy success in the war of 1894–1895 was devastating. Half-hearted efforts to modernize China's army and navy had failed miserably. The war was the fourth that the Chinese experienced during the century—and the fourth that they lost. Foreign skill and technology had again won out. It seemed clear that China would be divided into foreign colonies just as Africa had been. Germany took advantage of the murder of two German missionaries in 1897 to exert control over northern Shantung; the Russians threatened to send troops to take control of Port Arthur and Darien unless granted leases by China; France demanded anchorages in southern China. In all, by 1900, thirteen of China's eighteen provinces and three provinces of Manchuria were appropriated as spheres of influence.

The humiliation of China's defeat at the hands of Japan convinced a number of the Chinese intelligentsia that only a break with the past could save China. In 1898, a progressive faction secured the support of the young emperor—known by his reign title as Kuang Hsü—who instituted a series of reforms intended to start China on its way to becoming a modern nation. He issued edicts that called, among other things, for eliminating the antiquated examination system based on rote learning. Temples were to be turned into schools of Western studies, and Western-style institutions such as a patent office and translation board were to be set up. The reform movement lasted all of a hundred days. It was brutally suppressed by the Dowager Empress Tz'u Hsi, who deposed Kuang Hsü, assumed the regency, and had several reform leaders executed.

This was the second time that Tz'u Hsi had taken control of the empire, a singular achievement for a woman born to the family of a civil clerk, a Manchu who, after being promoted, was cashiered for deserting his post during the Taiping Rebellion. A striking beauty in her youth, she was selected as one of twenty-eight girls for the harem of Emperor Hsien-feng. She soon became his favorite and bore him a son. Motherhood gained her promotion from a third-grade concubine to one of first grade. When Hsien-feng died in 1872 and she was thirty-seven years old, she was one of two dowagers named as regents for the son, T'ung-chih. Though the young boy himself died three years later, Tz'u Hsi was able to retain her influence under his successor, her three-year-old nephew Kuang Hsü.

Much has been written about Tz'u Hsi, most of it critical, some of it spurious. The Chinese regarded her as "old Buddha," a term of affection. Westerners called her "Dragon Lady," a pejorative. By that they meant an evil, licentious woman who would stop at nothing to drive the foreigner out of China. Was she as bad as they said? The worst reports about her background and behavior were compiled through fraudulent Chinese documents and fabrications that a young English linguist named Backhouse, who was also given to hyperbole, passed on to a London *Times* correspondent. His dispatches, in turn, were copied by papers all over the world. So how close the vilification is to fact is questionable.

Tz'u Hsi was said to have hated foreigners all her life. She was especially resentful of missionaries, it was said, questioning what right barbarians had to teach the Chinese about religion. Tz'u Hsi, her critics claimed, was devious. She broke precedent, shocking court officials by her breach of the strict rules of etiquette, when she invited the wives of the foreign diplomatic corps to the Forbidden City. She moved among them, murmuring over and over, "All one family!"[6]

She was also reportedly a believer in the occult, had witnessed a demonstration of I Ho Chüan exercises, and believed in the Boxers' magical powers. In addition, she was, so it was said, maniacal in ambition and limitless in revenge. Ironically, when she participated, as she liked to do, in court theatricals and *tableaux vivants,* her favorite role was that of Kuan-yin, the Goddess of Mercy. One moment she could be charming to her ministers, the next she might furiously scream at them, or dissemble with tears. A woman in her mid-sixties, she was totally divorced from the people she ruled, and forced to rely on counselors for information and advice.

By assuming the regency again in 1898, ousting her nephew from power, Tz'u Hsi sided with reactionaries within the government. The Imperial Court was divided between them and a group of moderates who feared that open hostility to foreigners would only result in further incursions. The vacillation and byzantine political maneuvering that marked the Imperial Court's actions—opposing the Boxers in one instance, encouraging them in another—reflected the struggle between the two factions, and Tz'u Hsi's own insecurity.

Meanwhile, a newcomer to the *realpolitik* in the Far East entered the scene: the United States. The Spanish-American War had suddenly presented America with a strategic interest in the Far Pacific and Asia: the Philippine Islands. Afraid that discriminatory tariffs and other commercial barriers might be imposed by the competing Powers, in the fall of 1899 Secretary of State John Hay issued a series of notes to the Powers that embodied what became known as the Open Door Policy. They called for the securing of equal commercial opportunities among the different competing nations and also for the upholding of Chinese territorial integrity—a demand, in other words, for the status quo.

Timothy Richard's gloomy prediction about "a volcano" about to erupt seemed to be fulfilled the very next year after he made it, 1891. Three Catholics, one of them a priest, were killed not far from Peking. Then riots broke out in the lower Yangtze River Valley. Missionary premises in Nanking and I-ch'ang were burned and looted, and some missionaries were robbed and stoned; they had to flee for their lives. Under pressure from foreign diplomats, the Imperial Court in Peking issued an edict blaming the attacks on outlaws. The edict stressed the noble motives of the missionaries and the need to protect their churches. It said that local officials would be held responsible for any future incidents that occurred within their jurisdiction.

The riots were not the first anti-foreign demonstrations, nor were they the last. Missionaries and their Chinese supporters had been the target of disgruntled Chinese as early as 1864, when the first serious outbreak of violence occurred in Foochow in the South China province of Fukien. A mob seized converts at a Methodist street school and beat them up. Fourteen years later a mob destroyed a new college building in a suburb of the same city in a dispute with English missionaries over land that the missionaries wanted to build on. More seriously, in August 1895, again near Foochow, eleven British men, women, and children were slain during anti-Christian rioting.

Southern China was not the only scene of violence. In Tientsin in North China, twenty foreigners, most of them French nuns, were killed and the Catholic cathedral destroyed in 1870 by a mob incensed by the actions of a French consul. More than two decades later, in central China, a coolie called Yu the Wild led an uprising that engulfed large areas of Szechwan Province. The revolt was initially directed against Chinese Christians rather than the government, but it ran into conflict with the Chinese state, and Yu was eventually captured. His slogan—"Obey the Ching, exterminate the foreigners"—later became a rallying cry of the I Ho Chüan.

The massacre of the eleven British subjects in Fukien in 1895 prompted the British minister to Peking to threaten to use the Royal Navy against Chinese ports. The threat—it was called gunboat diplomacy—was never carried out, but when two German Catholic missionaries were slain in the North China province of Shantung two years later, Kaiser Wilhelm immediately dispatched his East Asian naval squadron there and used the murders as a pretext to occupy the area and demand leasing rights to construct railways and open mines. In the months that followed the German intimidation, the scramble for concessions in China began in earnest among the Western powers and Japan.

The attacks on missionaries—and there were others—were, however, sporadic, happening here and there without any pattern, relation to one another, or general sense of direction or purpose. The situation changed dramatically with the murder of Sidney Brooks on the eve of 1900.

The new year began in peace, but when the harsh North China winter was over, attacks on Christian converts broke out in Shantung Province, and the Boxer movement spread like some uncontrollable flood into the province of Chih-li, headed inexorably, village by village, north toward Peking and west into Shansi Province.

Early in 1900 a worried Timothy Richard left China to attend an international missionary conference in New York. He had a special task in mind, a plea for help. The volcano now—ten years later—was rumbling dangerously. Yet the diplomats in Peking continued to close their eyes to what was happening in North China and turned a deaf ear to the appeals of Protestant missions for help.

Dr. Arthur H. Smith of the American Board's North China Mission had drawn up a paper, warning of the gravity of the situation, but it was dismissed as crying wolf by the legations in Peking. The American minister to China, Edwin H. Conger, was personally fed up with missionaries' complaints—"bored," it was said, by their "verboseness." Conger shared with merchants and other diplomats the opinion that "missionaries are timid folk, listeners to idle tales and general mischief-makers."[7] He had a complaint of his own: Nearly half the business of the American legation was taken up with missionary matters.

Conger's lack of concern was supported at home in America by the State Department's Far Eastern expert, W. W. Rockhill. "I cannot believe that the 'Boxer' movement will be very long-lived or cause any serious complications," Rockhill advised Secretary of State Hay. "The day the Chinese authorities choose to put an end to it they can easily do so—I think they have now realized that they must act, and they will."[8]

"Strongly convinced of the dangers threatening missionaries and all foreigners," Richard carried Smith's report with him to the conference. He decided to plead the case before the Mission boards attending the world parley. He urged the conference's Executive Committee to press the various boards into taking some united action to avert a disaster. But the committee members decided that such action was tantamount to politics and, because it was a political danger that threatened, they could not break tradition and "interfere in politics."

Richard received a different reception in Boston, where he was invited in early May to explain the situation in China before the Twentieth Century Club. The members were so impressed by the gravity of the missionaries' position, as well as the peril to world peace, that he was given letters of introduction that supposedly "would open every door from the House of Representatives to the White House."

The very next day Richard went to Washington. So that there would be no misunderstanding about what he had to say about the situation and his request for aid, he had a statement printed out before he headed for the State Department's offices. Richard was able to hand the statement personally to John Hay, who expressed sympathy. But Hay said that the administration could not take any step without the support of two-thirds of the Senate. So Richard next went to the majority leader of the Senate, George F. Hoar of Massachusetts. Hoar expressed interest but said the Senate could not do anything without the support of leading cities, in particular New York, the most influential city of all. Richard rushed over to the Chamber of Commerce to confer with Morris K. Jessop, its chairman. But Jessop was pessimistic. "He feared the Government would not act on mere opinion, however strong," Richard later explained. "Nothing short of a massacre would justify it in immediate action."

Jessop's remarks were "the final blow" to Richard's hopes of getting America to avoid a "catastrophe." Two weeks after his round of meetings in Washington, telegrams arrived with news of the first outbreaks of violence in Shantung Province. Richard embarked for China, hoping he would get back in time to be able to do something to save the missionary community. By the time he reached Yokohama, there were reports of anti-Christian attacks in Chih-li, too, and it seemed likely that Shansi would be next.

"I was at my wit's end what to do next," he said, "as there was no communication between Peking and the outside world." Then, of a sudden, "God gave me a thought." Richard telegraphed the British Consul-General in Shanghai, asking him to announce to all Chinese viceroys and governors that the British government would hold them personally responsible for the safety of British missionaries. It was a ploy that perhaps would spare members of English missionary societies, if it worked. But it was too late.[9] The volcano had erupted.

THIRTEEN ❀ *The Boxers*

The high-mindedness of antiquity showed itself in a disregard of small things; the high-mindedness of the present day shows itself in wild license.
—Confucius

The I Ho Chüan—what Westerners called the Boxers—arose in Shantung Province. It was an area with a tradition of martial arts. Its people were reputed to be fearless fighters—though the area was also called the birthplace, ironically, of both Confucius and his disciple Mencius. The Boxers had no central organization, no defined leadership other than the leader that a local village band chose. Those in the north, a barren but crowded region where there were more than five hundred people per square mile, were known as Spirit Boxers.

The Spirit Boxers first appeared west of the Yellow River in the mid-1890s. They exhibited no signs of being anti-Christian, or violent; rather, they were interested in teaching only simple principles. They enjoined against covetousness, lust, drinking, and taking advantage of the young or the weak. On the surface, their rituals appeared simple. The members would bow to the southeast, toward Peach Flower Mountain, where there was a special shrine, six caves filled with the statues of gods. They chanted spells, burned incense, and wrote charms on paper, which were then burned. They drank the ashes with water.

The major feature of their rites, however, was spirit possession. Eyes closed, each Boxer would go into a trance, begin weaving and breathing rapidly until possessed by his own special god. The trances recalled the transformations experienced by the whirling dervishes of North Africa, or during the Ghost Dance of the American Plains Indians. "Suddenly,"

A typical Chinese shrine in a temple. Courtesy Oberlin College Archives.

wrote an eyewitness, "their faces got red and their eyes stared straight ahead as though they were having an epileptic fit. Foam dropped from their mouths as they shouted out, while their fists flew and their feet kicked." Eyes rolling, limbs flailing, the Boxer would fall to the ground, then leap up "as though drunk, or in a dream," and fight fiercely, mocking the battles fought on stage in popular operas.[1] The Boxers came to believe that this part of the ritual made them invulnerable, much as those trained in martial arts and heavily muscled by lengthy exercise could withstand sword blows and spear thrusts.

A Boxer always chose one of the local gods as his special idol. They brought the figurines of such gods out of temples for the operas or theatricals that were staged at village fairs and at the time of religious observances. The gods would be given seats of honor in the front row, under a tent or parasol, while on stage performers would act out battles of righteousness and honor.

When the drought that began in the summer of 1899 continued

unabated into the fall, and then over the winter into the new year, the Boxers had a cause. The Yellow River, swollen by melting snow from the mountains, flooded, and locusts swept in clouds through the region. Thousands upon thousands of peasants, farmers and artisans faced starvation. Ineffectual local authorities and the weak Imperial Court were too inept to handle the enormous task of arranging for emergency food supplies. A repetition of the Great Famine was feared.

In reaction, the Boxers became civil insurgents, intent on the overthrow of the Manchus. Then, as a result of disputes between Chinese Christians and non-Christians over contributions to local religious festivals and lawsuits over property and debts, they turned their venom on the converts. It was but one step from attacks on native Christians to attacks on the missionaries who had converted them. Shantung was in a state of virtual anarchy when Sidney Brooks left his sister and, traveling alone, started back to his post.

Whether Boxer or not, most peasants blamed foreigners for the drought; they believed the "barbarians" kept the rain from falling. But there was more to their xenophobia than that. Every slight or imagined wrong, even what a Westerner considered superstitious in nature, became another reason for despising the foreigner.

All the grievances and grudges that the Chinese harbored focused into open hatred. The women in Shantung who used to make a living weaving no longer had any work because of the importation of machine-spun fabrics from Europe. Artisans who made pots and lamps or any of a number of other crafted items were similarly affected by the influx of machine-made goods, some of which were made in factories that foreigners established in their enclaves in treaty cities. In Chih-li the boatmen and carters who made their living on the waterways and roads no longer had any means of livelihood once the railway ran through their district.

Moreover, the Chinese were outraged that the tracks of the "iron centipedes" were often laid over the sacred cemeteries that dotted the countryside. They believed that the telegraph poles that paralleled the tracks were strung with the tongues of murdered children; they said you could hear the children moaning when the wind blew and see their blood (actually rust from the wires) drip down the poles after a rain. Foreigners, so rumor had it, could cut a figure of a man out of a piece of paper and it would spring into life as an evil genie. The reforms that the Emperor had tried to institute in 1898 were attributed to a medicine foreigners had given him. It made the Emperor crazy, it was said; he put on foreign clothing, spoke a foreign language, and wanted to change all things to foreign style.

Some Westerners regarded the Boxers as a *hui*—a secret society—which was illegal in China, though many such organizations existed. They began chiefly as self-protection societies that villagers and urban neighbors formed to fight off bandits, to protect themselves from unscrupulous landlords and merchants, or to bring pressure on local officials. But the Boxers were hardly secret. They practiced their ceremonies in the open, on grounds in every village in which they appeared, drawing crowds of the curious and the interested. Ordinarily, someone who watched them perform would ask a Boxer who had mastered the technique to come to his village to train people there. The movement attracted the unemployed, the dispossessed, and the uprooted. Most of them were youths, their average age about twenty.

No one has ever traced the movement to any formal organization or individual, but there is no doubt that some literati and gentry who felt threatened by foreign ideas and intervention were in the background as *agents provocateurs* if not outright supporters. Placards, posters, and handbills that appeared in widely separated areas of North China often bore the same wording. A typical one, issued by "the Lord of Wealth and Happiness," did indeed hold foreigners responsible for the drought, but that was a certain way to incite a hungry, desperate people:

> The Catholic and Protestant religions being insolent to the gods, and extinguishing sanctity, rendering no obedience to Buddha, and enraging Heaven and Earth, the rain-clouds no longer visit us; but eight million Spirit Soldiers will descend from Heaven and sweep the Empire clean of all foreigners. Then will the gentle showers once more water our lands. . . .
>
> Hasten, then, to spread this doctrine far and wide, for if you gain one adherent to the faith your own person will be absolved from all future misfortunes. If you gain five adherents your whole family will be absolved from all evils, and if you gain ten adherents your whole village will be absolved from all calamities. Those who gain no adherents to the cause shall be decapitated, for until all foreigners have been exterminated the rain can never visit us.[2]

The battle cry of the Boxers soon became *"Sha! Sha!"*—"Kill! Kill!"

Diplomats in Peking protested strenuously the slaying of Sidney Brooks to the *Tsungli Yamen,* an agency that the insular Imperial Court, bowing to pressure, had reluctantly set up in 1861 to handle foreign relations. Brooks's murderers were caught, tried in the presence of a British consular official, and executed.

In addition, on January 11, 1900, an Imperial edict was issued denouncing unlawful violence. But the edict made a distinction between outlaw associations of "worthless vagabonds" responsible for banditry and disturbances, and those made up of "peaceful and law-abiding people [who] practise their skill in mechanised arts for the preservation of themselves and their families." The latter, the edict went on, were acting "in accord with the public-spirited principle (enjoined by Mencius) of 'keeping mutual watch and giving mutual help.'"[3] In effect, the Imperial Court, which had always banned private associations, was giving the Boxers carte blanche to hold meetings and recruit members in self-defense groups as long as they did not break any laws.

The trouble with the edict, Charles Price said, was that it did not differentiate between a *hui,* a secret society, and a *chiao,* a religious sect. "The Christian Church is also called by the same name [*hui*], and in the mind of the people is only on the same footing with the disadvantages of being foreign," he said. "But in the Edict no distinction is made between the Church and these lawless societies."

There were several reasons that the Chinese regarded the Christian Church as a *hui.* For one thing, the Church acted as a separate political entity with its own laws and punishments—the missionaries' ban, for example, on opium smoking, which was ground for excommunication. For another, the Church separated its adherents from their local community, not permitting them to take part in religious-oriented celebrations. Moreover, the Chinese thought that some Church practices, such as baptism, were bizarre.

As a result of the edict, said Charles, all the work of the Shansi missionaries almost stopped for a time because their Chinese followers "were afraid" to been seen with them. "Its effect is not small," he noted. "Another hindrance to our work." He said that the "wonder is that no violence was offered to us personally."[4]

Britain, France, Germany, and the United States joined in protesting the January 11 edict. Their diplomats repeatedly demanded that the government ban the Boxers outright. They were dismayed when Yü Hsien, whom they had successfully lobbied to have fired as governor of Shantung, was honored by being granted an audience before the Imperial Throne. They were shocked when, in mid-March, Yü Hsien was named the new governor of Shansi.

The man whose name would be forever linked with the fate of the Oberlin Band was a dour-faced civil servant with a reputation for being both an efficient, incorruptible administrator and a speedy, cruel enforcer of the law. An expert on martial-arts groups, he was the scourge of secret societies and bandits and had won the praise of the people of Shantung for his efforts to suppress the thieves that plagued the province.

Yü Hsien's father, a Manchu of the Yellow Banner, had been a minor official in southern China, and Yü Hsien could afford to purchase only the lowest possible degree for a career in government. However, in 1879, he was able to buy the rank of prefect in Shantung. His chief concern was to maintain order, and his policy was simple when it came to any societies that threatened to disrupt the peace: arrest the leaders and disperse the followers. At one time he backed the Big Sword Society, which was considered both a *hui* and a *chiao,* because of its activities against bandits. But when the society turned against Christians, he had its leader arrested and executed.

Yü Hsien's abilities were soon recognized. In 1895 he was promoted to administrator of the entire south Shantung area. The following year he became judicial commissioner of the province and even served as acting lieutenant governor of Shantung before being transferred to another province. He returned to Shantung to become its governor in mid-March 1897—a full three years before his appointment to Shansi.

In Shantung, Yü Hsien faced a precarious situation. Germans were brazenly asserting their privileges in a huge slice of the province that was considered their sphere of influence. They aggressively set about building railway lines and opening mines, lording their rights over local officials and appropriating land. At the same time, the Boxer movement was growing rapidly among the disenchanted, starving peasants of Shantung. Boxer attacks on Christian converts increased alarmingly. Yü Hsien was worried that the anti-Christian incidents might escalate into rebellion against the government, and he tried to prevent them. But he also believed that China should be repaid for any Chinese deaths or the destruction of any Chinese property that occurred at German hands, just as the Germans had demanded indemnification from China every time a German was injured or threatened or a Christian converted by a German missionary lost property.

In mid-October 1899 government troops and Boxers fought the Battle of Senluo Temple, a pitched battle that was handled so ineptly by the official in charge that Yü Hsien recommended that he be stripped of his command. Both the Boxers and the Germans interpreted his recommendation as a punishment of the official for trying to suppress the movement. The Boxers, who had not been pursued following their losses, felt encouraged to move north, attacking and robbing Christians and, in doing so, killing a non-Christian gatekeeper, the first civilian casualty of their violence. In the second week of November, they seized and killed a Catholic teacher, the first Christian casualty. The next day Catholic converts, whose mission stations were well-armed with repeating rifles, counterattacked.

Meanwhile, in Peking, a bitterly hostile group of anti-foreign Manchu princes took control of the central government. In a precedent-shattering move, the Dowager Empress named the son of its leading member, Prince Tuan, as the heir to the throne. Foreign diplomats viewed the move as a prelude to the eventual ouster of the liberal-minded Emperor. They refused to attend a celebration in the heir apparent's honor, which, as was bound to happen, only incensed the princes more.

In Shantung rumor had it that the Boxers attacking the Catholics carried banners with Yü Hsien's name on it. But when incidents between the two groups increased, Yü Hsien had three Boxer leaders arrested and executed. Their deaths in December halted Boxer activity in one section of Shantung, but the effect was like cutting off the tentacle of an octopus. No sooner was one "rebellion" contained then another sprang up to take its place. Incidents of Boxer violence broke out throughout the province. Angry that Yü Hsien's policy of arrest and dispersal was not working, missionaries and diplomats demanded his dismissal. The Imperial Court bowed to their demands, and a new governor was appointed to take his place. But within days of his appointment, before the year 1899 was out, Sidney Brooks was killed.

The Imperial edict of January 11, 1900, which made a distinction between lawful and unlawful groups, clearly symbolized a victory of the anti-foreign element at the Court, though official policy continued to waver. The rapid spread of Boxer sentiment worried both factions at Court. Malcontents could easily turn against the government. Should local officials try to manipulate them through a policy of pacification, or should they go to the other extreme and resort to military force to wipe out the society's members? The latter option, both factions feared, would only incite further violence. Accordingly, for several months, the Court's official attitude vacillated as the debate raged as to how to master the situation. The Court feared the Boxers but did not want to wage all-out war against them; at the same time, it rationalized that villagers had the right to organize in self-defense—and, covertly, the foreign-hating princes condoned the Boxers' anti-Christian hostility. Ordinary Chinese were apparently so confused by this contradiction that when a provincial official on occasion issued a proclamation banning Boxers or protecting the missionaries and their converts, they believed that foreigners had bribed the official to do so.

Stripped of his position as governor of Shantung, Yü Hsien was summoned to Peking about the time that the January 11 edict was being issued. When called upon to explain his efforts to maintain peace in Shantung, he must have acquitted himself well, because two months later, the anti-foreign faction at Court—without any hesitation—saw that he was named the governor of Shansi.

It is a measure of their insularity that it took the members of the Oberlin Band in Shansi so long to recognize the threat posed by the Boxers. They never did understand why the animosity was directed against them, or the reason for its intensity. They seemed to believe the underlying cause of the Boxer propaganda was the drought. It alone was to blame for the unrest, they thought. If only it would rain, they told each other, all would be well. Sowing the critically needed millet would be possible, the people would be busy tending to their farms, things would quiet down. The Chinese of Shansi, as one missionary said, were peace-loving:

> In disposition the people are more mild and amiable than those of any other portion of the empire. They are patient and uncomplaining to a high degree. The common people are tolerant in their attitude toward Christianity and foreign missionaries except when instigated by the monstrous misrepresentation of the literati and officials. Almost invariably their first judgment of us is "they are just like us, they do good to accumulate merit."[5]

Another thing that the members of the Band, like other Protestant missionaries, believed was that the persons the Chinese were really mad at were the Roman Catholics. There was good reason to believe that. Without a by-your-leave, Catholic bishops as long ago as 1860 had assumed the trappings of officialdom. They adopted official insignia—buttons and hat feathers—and had an umbrella, a Chinese sign of rank, carried ahead of them. They even had a cannon fired when they arrived in a town and issued their own proclamations.

In 1898 the French government pressured the Imperial Court into formally accepting such frippery and into granting the bishops a rank equal to that of viceroys and governors. The Court apparently acceded to relieve the nuisance of dealing with the continual demands that Catholic missionaries put on the Court. As a result, bishops could seek direct interviews with viceroys and governors rather than face the red tape of a diplomatic staff as Protestant missionaries had to do. At the same time, provincial priests were allowed to deal directly with provincial treasurers, judges, and *tao-tais* [circuit intendants], and ordinary priests could approach district magistrates without intermediaries.

The Protestants refused even trying to win similar privileges. By and large, they also refused to interfere when their adherents were involved in lawsuits, as Catholic priests did. The priests often entered into land and money disputes on the side of their followers or pressured magistrates when criminal charges were involved—causing, in the process, a great deal of resentment.

The Protestants made a point of not interfering in the legal process, as unjust as Chinese law seemed to them. George Williams went through mental anguish when a Taiku Christian named Yang Ze Jung got into trouble. Yang and two other men had attacked a man with a knife. Afterwards Yang fled into the Mission compound and hid in a storeroom. Williams debated whether to surrender Yang, deciding in the end that it was important that the local authorities "should know that the church is a law-abiding institution," and that church members realize that the missionaries would not protect them if they committed crimes.

Williams went to the *yamen* and told the magistrate where Yang was. Yang was seized, imprisoned, and beaten with three hundred blows, a not unusual practice. A person charged with a crime was usually beaten with bamboo poles or tortured with devices such as an ankle vise to extract a confession. An accused person was presumed guilty and had no advice of counsel.

Williams thought Yang had been going "from bad to worse for many months and deserved a severe punishment but this was cruel." It made him "fairly sick." Williams went to the prison to see Yang with the medical helper, Sang Ai Ch'ing, who opened the beaten flesh on Yang's back with a knife and applied medicines. "Many of the church people think we did wrong in delivering him up," said Williams. "They can not see how it will affect them hereafter."[6]

The missionaries also shrugged off the fanciful stories that were bandied about the streets outside their compounds. They never realized how profoundly most Chinese, who were superstitious, believed them. Rowena Bird, for example, did not understand the importance the Chinese placed on their operas and theatricals:

> A thing happened to-day which strikes me as exceedingly laughable. A theater, or more properly puppet show, has been banging away in our street for three days now. The stand is built right across the street high enough up to allow carts to pass under easily. The Music (?) and banging & noise has been very pleasing to the Chinese but tiresome to us. The performance was ordered and paid for by a family near, because the head of the house was ill and recovered; and this show is performed in the presence of the Gods, as a thank offering. Fluttering papers at the end of the street indicate the gods in whos [*sic*] honor and for whos amusement the performance is given. Well this afternoon as I was writing my Fen-chou fu letters, a man came rushing in without even knockin. [*sic*] He had a paper & pencil in his hand, called me by name, and said that they wanted to continue the show two or three days longer, but their money was not enough, and asked if I wouldn't give them a contribution. Of course I said that they were worshiping the gods with it & I could not help them to do

> that. . . . It is the first time I ever heard of a Missionary being asked to contribute to heathen worship & puppet shows.[7]

Louise Partridge had a laugh, too, when she heard what people were saying at the funeral service of the mother of a schoolboy in Tung Fang. "It was reported in the village that Mr. Clapp took out the woman's eyes and heart and gave them to me. The comical side struck me and I laughed, which amazed them greatly. Wasn't I worried? No I wasn't. Do? Do nothing, shouldn't even hear it. So they revealed some more, and I laughed again to hear that when we baptised folks, it made them baldheaded."[8]

Even though members of the Oberlin Band experienced some hostility over the years—being called "foreign devils" when traveling through the city or a village was common—they tended to dismiss the incidents as isolated expressions of hostility rather than xenophobic-inspired rage. They remembered the time that a grateful magistrate issued a proclamation in 1884 forbidding the use of violent language against them after Iranaeus Atwood successfully treated the diseased eyes of the official's son.

The thought crossed their minds that local Chinese might retaliate in some way when Congress enacted the Geary Act of 1892. The legislation extended a discriminatory ban against the immigration of Chinese laborers, the Exclusion Act of 1882, that Congress passed after pressure from California voters that bordered on hysteria. The Chinese government and American Chinese communities protested the Geary Act, but the Supreme Court upheld the law. In China, however, news carried slowly, if at all; telegraph lines connecting Shansi to the outside world were not strung until 1897.[9] No word about the American action ever seems to have reached the province. "We are not disturbed in the least living here," Eva Price assured her family in the States, "you get all the scares in your newspapers."[10]

Still, there had been some troublesome incidents. Ernest Atwater had a nasty encounter with some ferrymen while on his way to Li Man with his daughters in 1897. The boatmen at the Fen River ferry refused to let him and the children on board unless they paid what Atwater thought was "an exorbitant price." Atwater was incensed. These were the same boatmen who had once accosted Howard Clapp and another missionary. In a rage,

Atwater cut the ferry cable with his penknife. In retaliation, the boatmen grabbed him, bruising his upper arm. They bound him and led him to a local temple while they summoned a magistrate. Even though he had cut the cable, Atwater insisted he was not to blame. He demanded that the magistrate force the boatmen to set a fixed price for crossing the Fen and that they be prosecuted for treating him so roughly. The magistrate had the head boatman put in a wooden stockade-like collar. He and other officials at the local *yamen* were so afraid that they would be held accountable for what happened that they provided Atwater and the girls with an escort to see them safely across the river.[11]

A man with a rake threatened Louise Partridge when she was returning from one of her tours in 1898, shouting at her, "Female foreign devil." Fearless, Louise turned her horse, rode up to him and horsewhipped him.[12]

Charles Price was nearly mobbed the following year when he went for a walk outside the Fenchow-fu compound at the time of literary examinations in the city. Instead of wearing Chinese attire, he was dressed for once in clothes he had brought with him from America. He immediately attracted attention and was surrounded by several hundred persons. The mob "hustled him, jostled, crowded, and hooted at him and threw clods of dirt at him, hitting him in the eye, and were altogether impudent and daring." Seeing the danger Charles was in, a neighbor's teenaged boy led him away. A crowd of two hundred people followed them as they made their way by back streets and alleys to the Mission compound.[13]

More often than not, the crowds that the missionaries attracted were simply curious. When George Williams built his Western-style house in the South Suburb of Taiku, Chinese flocked to look. The missionaries kept the gate open because they wanted people to "feel free to come." Williams and Howard Clapp would usually show Chinese visitors around inside the house, but so many came one day in May 1900 that George shooed them away. So the Chinese took to peering in at the windows. Rowena Bird was trying to write at her desk on the ground floor. She drew the heavy curtains so that she could continue without their seeing her. But every time she got up, she saw a crowd of faces at the window. When she stepped out into the sitting room, there were men standing at all the windows. Unnerved by the staring eyes, Jennie Clapp went to her bedroom upstairs to get away from them.[14]

Rowena, the Prices, and the Davises had a similar experience when on a rare excursion to a pagoda outside Taiku. They traveled in litters and purposely opened the windows so they could see the landscape. Seeing there were foreigners inside, a crowd of men and boys gathered to peer in at the strange individuals as they passed by. So many of them crowded around them that the missionaries had trouble getting out of the litters when they reached an inn, where they stopped to eat. In order to keep the curious Chinese out of the room in which they dined, one of the men stood with his back against the door. An old beggar woman managed to get a knee in, but Eva Price put her knee against hers and pushed her out. When Eva saw that some boys had made eyeholes in the paper covering the windows, she flung a cup of water at them. "The crowd was perfectly good-natured and meant us no harm," Rowena said. "Most of them simply wanted to see, but one could not help thinking what such a crowd might do if they were bent on mischief."[15]

What worried the Shansi missionaries more was the drought and the vision of another Great Famine. "I am going to write you especially about something that distresses us very much and about which we need help," Rowena wrote to Jennie Atwater's parents, the Ponds, in late October 1899:

> There has been an extended drought here which is not broken yet at the setting in of cold weather and much distress among the people generally is unavoidable, and if the thing go on so it will be little less than a famine before the winter is over. Aside from the lack of grain it is desperately hard times and money much depreciated. We shall without doubt need funds to help the distressed this winter, but what is pressing on us more heavily just now is how we are ever to carry on our work, especially school work, with reduced appropriations and these frightful rises in prices. It is costing us now twice as much to feed a boy in school as last year and prices are steadily going up, and we cannot raise the price of tuition in these hard times.[16]

Even after Yü Hsien was appointed governor of Shansi in mid-March of 1900, the Oberlin Band did not feel threatened. A few days later, Francis Davis, Charles Price, and George Williams donned long riding habits with large red hoods that the Chinese called wind hats and set off along the dusty highway leading out of Taiku. The three men were on a nine-day tour of the eastern mountains, searching for a place to start a new Mission station. They traveled more than two hundred miles, investigated five cities, but found the population was "sparser" than they had thought.[17]

They were no sooner back in Taiku than they set out again, in the first week of April, this time to the western mountains on the same mission, going up into hill country where, Davis said, "Thank God they cannot raise opium with much success." They passed through numerous village and market towns, but no cities. Finally, after reaching the Yellow River, they turned south toward the Mission station in Fenchow-fu, "where comfortable beds[,] palatable food and no vermin awaited us."[18] Again, they did not find a suitable place to open a station.

At no time during either of their two trips did the three men feel threatened or even talk about the possibility of being assaulted. Moreover, the fact that the Oberlin Band was even considering opening a new station is evidence of how insignificant they regarded the Boxer threat. Reporting on their scouting tours, Davis told Judson Smith, "The Taiku people have harmed no one as yet; and as the Chinese say, 'At first everyone spoke ill of foreigners but now everyone speaks well of them.'"[19]

Howard Clapp, who had stayed in Taiku while the other men went out on the two trips, was unconcerned, too. "Notwithstanding the unrest & anxiety in Shantung & Chihli about the 'Boxers,'" he wrote Smith, "the people here seem as well disposed & friendly as ever. I donot [*sic*] think that organization is liable to spread to this Province."[20]

At the same time that the scouting party was out in the eastern mountains, Louise Partridge had gone on one of her now-infrequent village tours. She traveled about thirty miles into the countryside outside Li Man, which the Boxers had begun to infiltrate. Louise did not realize at the time, she wrote her father, that for four days she'd been "in the greatest danger of my life, and without the slightest suspicion of it, nor the least indication at the time."[21]

Unnerved, Louise next went to Peking, where she hired Ruth Fan to teach in the girls' boarding school in Li Man. She returned, accompanied by Ruth and blind Lois, and with word that Yü Hsien was on his way to the provincial capital of Tai Yuan. His pending arrival seemed to make no impression on her. Louise announced that she planned to start a summer session of the girls' school on May 1.[22]

Rowena Bird reported a week later, in early April, that a group of Boxers were only five *li* (about a mile and a half) from Li Man, but she wasn't worried. "There are reports that men have come up here from Chili to organize bands of Boxers," she wrote her mother. "No one seems to fear that that kind of thing will flourish here." Rowena noted that the Boxers had set themselves up in a large market village in Shansi and distributed notices saying they could teach their system. But the village people, she said, refused to let the Boxers stay in the village and sent them away.[23]

The Oberlin missionaries were so little troubled by what was happening that they held their annual meeting in Fenchow-fu in mid-April and, after six days of talks and prayers, decided that, as a result of the lack of success of the scouting expeditions to the east and to the west, they would open a new station in Yu tzu, a county seat twenty-one miles north of Taiku. They also took the formal step of appointing Charles Price as the head of what they now called the Mission Academy. The Academy, started at the boys' school in Taiku, would be based in Fenchow-fu, a move obviously necessitated by the transfer of Fei Chi Hao there after the young schoolboy Hu'er was burned and died. With their eyes on the twentieth century, the missionaries reported to the American Board, "We are the only mission that has thus far contemplated such advance in this Province and present indications point to our being the only academy for a number of years. We will thus have the field to ourselves."[24]

A few days later, Francis Davis took it upon himself to write Judson Smith, chiding him that the Shansi Mission "has languished" because of the Board's "lack of support." Davis warned that other missionary societies were occupying the best places for stations in the province. He said that more men and women were needed to man new stations if the Shansi Mission was to succeed.[25]

Nowhere in the report of the annual meeting or in Davis's appeal for help was there one word about the Boxers, about the threat they posed, or about any uncertainty the missionaries felt regarding the future.

Early in the second week of May, but unbeknownst at the time to the Oberlin Band in Shansi, a dispute that started at a theatrical in a village midway on the railway line that linked Paotingfu in Chih-li with the Peking-Tientsin rail line boiled over into a bloody confrontation between Catholic converts and Boxers. The Catholics took offense at the opera because it was being staged in front of one of their homes. They overturned the local gods set up in a nearby tent, and in the lawsuit that followed the bishop of Paotingfu pressured the local magistrate to decide the case against one of the villagers. The villager had to offer a five-table feast to the church members and their priest (a feast was a typical recompense in lawsuits) and to kowtow to them when presenting it.

Angered by the humiliating decision, the man's friends invited Boxers to open a training ground in a temple courtyard. They attacked the church and homes of the converts, killing all the members of some thirty Catholic families. Government troops subsequently closed the Boxer training ground, but the next day the Boxers reassembled and ambushed the troops. The government forces won the battle, killing about sixty Boxers and capturing twenty more, but the Boxers staged another ambush a week later and killed a colonel who was the brother of a noted Chinese general.

Emboldened by what they had done, groups of Boxers began to fan out along the railway line, attacking stations and trying to interdict bridges along the route. Foreign diplomats demanded that the Imperial government take immediate measures to restore peace, and soon three thousand troops were dispatched to the provincial capital of Paotingfu.

That same week a new magistrate arrived in Taiku. He was only twenty-eight years old, but the missionaries took heart from the good impression he made by not allowing his subordinates to take "squeezes"—the bribes customarily required to cut bureaucratic inertia. The magistrate took it upon himself to go to temples to pray for rain, and he had the South Gate, near the Mission station, closed as a precaution against undesirable outsiders.

Howard Clapp was away, touring, when the young magistrate took office. George Williams noted that Clapp's wife Jennie was, as usual, "pretty nervous" because of all the Chinese peering into their rooms. But Williams was so unconcerned that he busied himself tending a garden he had planted.[26]

Unfortunately, a scorching sun was already searing George's garden.

Day after day and week after week passed without any rain. The missionaries searched the burning sky, their hopes for rain excited by any cloud that appeared on the horizon but then dashed when the cloud was blown away. They held a three-day meeting to pray for rain and "to comfort the people and to help them draw near the Lord."

"We never watched the clouds and direction of the wind so closely before," said Jennie Clapp. "It is very sad and ominous to see so many uncultivated fields."[27]

FOURTEEN ❁ *Colleagues*

When one gives few occasions for blame in his words, and few occasions for repentance in his conduct, he is in the way to get emolument.
—*Confucius*

The complacency of the Oberlin Band missionaries in Shansi began to give way to reality in the last week of May, when roving bands of Boxers were able to tear up the tracks of the rail line connecting Paotingfu to Peking and Tientsin. At the same time, Boxers pulled down the telegraph poles linking the two areas. By doing so, they effectively cut off communication between the Oberlin Band and the North China Mission stations in Peking and Tientsin. Couriers made attempts to get through but turned back when they encountered roadblocks. Anyone the Boxers caught who was carrying letters and dispatches written in a foreign language was beaten if not killed.

Couriers were still able to reach across the mountains to the east to the North China Mission station in Paotingfu, but the reports from there were foreboding. A convert in a village outstation had to go into hiding, and landlords in the city itself were warning Christians that they would have to move out if they continued to receive any visits from the missionaries or their Bible women. A missionary from a Presbyterian society had been set upon and beaten by a mob.

Soldiers were protecting the American Board compound in Paotingfu, but there was concern nonetheless for the safety of its occupants, three colleagues and friends—a man and two single women, all in their thirties.

The two single females stationed at Paotingfu—Mary Susan Morrill and Annie Allender Gould—were such close friends that people who knew them always spoke of them as one. They shared a pleasant one-story house that the American Board had built for them in the compound. It was not that the young women were at all alike, though they were both comely. But they complemented each other. "What one lacked the other made up from her fullness," said a missionary who was stationed with them at Paotingfu for several years.[1]

The two women were both from Maine and to outsiders they seemed to be very shy, but there resemblances ended. Mary was an energetic evangelist, "patient and long-suffering to a fault," but frail physically. She suffered at times from swollen, inflamed eyes and constantly from "splitting headaches," possibly migraines.[2] As calm as she looked, there was still a bit of the frenetic about the way she refused to give in to "physical weariness." Hearing about riots in which some Catholics were killed outside Peking in 1891, she said, "There is so much to do, and if the end comes quicker than we think, we do not want to have left a single bit of work undone."[3]

Mary ignored her ailments as best she could and worked tirelessly, exhausting herself to the point of being emaciated, looking worn, and suffering a nervous breakdown that necessitated her going home on furlough in the late 1890s. Mary hated to leave but acquiesced, fearful that the Board would not permit her to return. "There is no work so blessed as the missionary's is there?" she said.[4] A colleague described her as being "absolutely without fear."[5] Louise Partridge said that Mary's evangelical work—preaching to the women in the waiting room of the dispensary or in the woman's ward in the hospital, ranging the countryside in Chih-li Province around Paotingfu, talking about the Gospel to anyone who would listen—was "my model, and [I] stirred myself to fresh endeavor by memory of her earnestness and activity."[6]

An avid reader since she was a child and a teacher by training, Mary enjoyed a reputation for scholarship even though she had not had a well-rounded college education. But she was an exceptionally quick learner. When first enroute to China to assume her post in the spring of 1889, she took lessons with a veteran missionary who was returning from furlough.

Mary Susan Morrill. Courtesy Special Collections, U.S. Military Academy, West Point.

Under his tutelage during the voyage, she mastered the four tones or inflections in which Chinese is spoken as well as 120 of the 214 basic characters, or radicals, of the written language—"slippery things" she called them, "little black things [that] seem alert with life, ready to laugh at your discomfort because you have forgotten their names."[7]

Mary's housemate, Annie Gould, admitted to being lazy and was considered unfeeling by those who did not know her well. Those who got to know her understood that her cold exterior hid "a warm and sensitive heart." Annie was especially close to her schoolgirls, with whom she often lived for periods of time.[8] A young student of hers said that Annie treated "her scholars as though they were her own children," and that all of them "loved her very much."[9] Chinese friends who accompanied Annie to Tientsin when she went to greet Mary on her return from sick leave at home were so embarrassed by the impropriety of Annie's behavior—hugging and embracing Mary over and over again "in pure abandon of joy"—that they turned their backs rather than watch the public demonstration of affection.[10]

Louise Partridge may have been drawn to Annie because she had "great, big, pathetic, brown eyes" like Louise's sister Cora, who died in 1896. The two had a number of "good talks" about the purpose of their missionary work.[11] "It is not in vain," Annie declared, "that we have washed offensive sores on feet or head, given medicine for frosted feet and in other ways cared for them."[12] Louise, troubled because most Chinese people doubted the existence of God, said that Annie made her see that God's goodness shone out brightly in "the dense darkness of heathenism." When she realized with Annie's help the meaning of their toil in China, she felt even stronger about leading "these people from darkness to light."[13]

Annie was a graduate of Mount Holyoke—Mary Lyon's "Protestant nunnery," a steady source of female missionary workers. A person who did not talk about personal matters, she developed such a close relationship with Mary Morrill that she considered her a "yoke fellow," too. They both realized how much they needed and relied on each other. Mary said of Annie: "She thinks that her yoke fellow is sometimes her back bone but I think that she is also mine."[14] Annie in return said of Mary: "She needs me to make her take care of herself when she is tired and working too hard. I need her to prod me out of my laziness and easy-going ways—pretty well mated!"[15]

The older of the two, Mary was born March 24, 1863, in a section of Portland, Maine, named Morrill's Corners after her family.[16] She was raised as a Universalist, but, while studying to be a teacher at a normal school, she switched to the Congregationalist faith. Her decision to enter missionary work was prompted by the reply of a Chinese pupil who was in her Sunday school class in Portland. Mary asked him if his mother knew about Jesus. "She only a woman," the boy replied, "she never know unless some woman go tell her."[17]

In the fall of 1888, two representatives of the American Board came to Portland to raise money for its foreign missions and to recruit workers. Mary, then in her mid-twenties, took the occasion to remind them that she had applied twelve months earlier for assignment as a missionary, asking specifically to be posted to China. That she even approached the Board members was unusually aggressive for her. Mary's "shrinking nature" was so pronounced that friends said her "struggle for self mastery, self poise, was almost pitiful." On the subject of Christ, though, she could speak fluently—"eloquently even, yet simply."[18] Whatever she said must have impressed the Board's emissaries because a few weeks later Mary received word that she was accepted. She then tortured herself about leaving her parents, but they encouraged her to go. Mary sailed for China in March 1889 a few days after her twenty-sixth birthday.

Mary's primary duty when she arrived in Paotingfu was to take charge of the Mission's boarding school for girls. But her great "passion" was touring, whether in the blistering heat of the summer or the freezing cold of the winter. She loved to go from village to village, telling the Gospel story to women who had never heard it. "I have seen such opportunities for work as an angel might be glad to use," she told a friend, "and I am only one woman, but I can do that one woman's work and leave the multiplying of it to the Lord."[19]

Early on, the Board concluded that, between taxing school responsibilities and touring, Mary's work load was too much for one woman. The Board was able to recruit Annie Gould to take over her school duties, allowing Mary to work almost entirely in the countryside.

Annie was born November 18, 1867, in Bethel, Maine, about fifty miles northeast of Portland, to which her family subsequently moved. Her father, a church deacon, worked as the cashier of a Portland bank. Her mother had been a teacher of freed slaves who taught blacks in a Union-occupied section of South Carolina during the Civil War. Both parents were volunteers in the Sailor's Bethel, a little mission church in Portland, and, once she was old enough, Annie herself was active in its Christian Endeavour Society, Sabbath School, and Mission Circle.

Annie Allender Gould. Courtesy Special Collections, U.S. Military Academy, West Point.

After attending public schools in Portland, Annie traveled to South Hadley, Massachusetts, to enter Mount Holyoke. She was already embued with a desire to "teach Christ and his redemption somewhere, if possible in foreign lands."[20] Annie was a good student despite the fact that her vision was so impaired that lessons had to be read aloud to her. However, the handicap did not deter her from graduating at the top of her class.

Annie's eyes never seemed to bother her in China. Neither she nor any missionary she worked with ever mentioned any debility. Her only trouble, she said, was that she didn't "bear pain or sickness well, no grit."[21]

Upon graduating from Mount Holyoke in 1892, Annie applied to the American Board, hoping to devote herself to missionary work in Japan. The Board, however, asked her to go instead to North China to be Mary's much-needed helper. Annie did not hesitate in answering: "I want to go where I am most needed."[22] She was twenty-four years old when she left for China in the fall of 1892.

When Annie arrived, the Board's North China Mission station in Paotingfu was undergoing a number of personnel changes. One missionary family was retiring, another was taking its place, and a new doctor had been assigned to the station as well. The station had a number of native helpers, including two brothers who were pastors—Meng Chang-chun and Meng Chang-so, whom the missionaries identified as Meng I and Meng II. Their father was the station's first convert. Their sister, a Mrs. Tu, was the station's first Bible woman.

In 1897, when the exhausted Mary Morrill was ordered to take an immediate furlough and left for Maine without contesting the Board's decision, Annie Gould took over her all duties. She was soon overworked herself, writing home: "At present I am devoting myself vigorously to sleeping and drop asleep as often as I sit down to study."[23]

Mary departed for home shortly before another missionary family assigned to Paotingfu reached China, an unusual couple "well favoured in personal appearance and in literary and musical accomplishments"—Horace Tracy Pitkin and his wife Letitia.[24]

Horace Pitkin was the exception to the rule. Most other American missionaries, who came from farms or rural towns, never were or could hope to be well-off. Francis Davis, for example, worked as a janitor to support himself while attending Oberlin Theological Seminary; Charles Price used up his savings while studying there; George Williams was worried that he would never be able to pay off the debt he owed on the house he built in Taiku. Pitkin, on the other hand, was from a wealthy Philadelphia family and was so well off that he donated to the American Board

Horace Tracy Pitkin. Courtesy Divinity School Library, Yale University.

the stipend he received from a supporting church. A lineal descendant through his mother of Elihu Yale, he was a graduate of both Yale University and Union Theological Seminary in New York. One of his older sisters was married to the son of the president of Harvard University.

The Pitkins could afford to take the long, eastbound route to China. They left New York in the fall of 1896, sailing across the Atlantic, and spent six months traveling through Europe, Egypt, and the Middle East. In their own version of the Grand Tour, they visited Paris, Milan, Venice, Florence, Rome, Naples, Pompeii, Athens, and Jerusalem, and toured parts of Egypt, Ceylon, and India. They sent ahead of themselves to China a Steinway grand piano. Eva Price, who was passing through Paotingfu, had tea with them one day and was almost struck speechless by the plush furnishings of their parlor:

> The luxurious couch, beautifully rich "Art Square" on the floor, Egyptian screen bought in Cairo, easy chairs and grand sweet-toned piano (made to order), and, what made me green with envy, the ability of Mr. Pitkin in playing and that of his wife in singing. She sings beautifully while he is nearly perfect in accompanying. What resources! When one is nearly frantic with the poverty in music, refinement, cleanliness, and uprightness of this benighted land![25]

Wealth aside, Horace was a dedicated Christian. His rooms both at Yale and Union Theological were the center for prayers and the gathering spot for other students interested in missionary work. While at Yale he taught youngsters in the Bethany Mission Sunday School and worked among the drunks and cast-offs at the Grand Avenue Mission. While at Union Theological he spent the summer working in a local mission. He regularly attended the annual summer students' conferences held in Northfield, Massachusetts, by the fiery evangelist Dwight Moody and eventually became a traveling representative of the Student Volunteer Movement that was launched there. When he applied to the American Board for appointment as a missionary, he noted in his application that his decision to go abroad was affected by two deaths in his family:

> I found that God has been opening the way for me by taking both the father and the sister to himself. My study has shown me the true depth and glorious possibilities of the missionary service, and I knew perfectly that God wanted me to work for Him in the uttermost parts of the earth. There has been no call from the clouds, but the facts of my life and the result of study inspired by, and carried on under God have been a sure and certain call to His work in the waste places."[26]

Horace was born October 28, 1869, in Philadelphia, the eighth generation descendant, on his father's side, of a Pitkin who came to New England from London in 1659 and was attorney-general of Connecticut.[27] Coincidentally, two distant relatives were Oberlin residents.[28] His mother's father, Rev. Cyrus Yale, was at one time a missionary among the Cherokee in Alabama. His mother died when he was a child, and he was raised by her sister.

Even as a youngster Horace displayed an intense interest in religion. He liked to attend church, and a favorite amusement of his when he was barely seven years old was to conduct services before a congregation of his playmates. He spent summers at the old Yale homestead in New Hartford, where, every day, he withdrew for an hour to study the Bible, meditate, and pray under an old ash tree. He gave to charity half of the twenty-five dollars that his father gave him every year as a Christmas gift. While a teenager at Phillips Academy in Exeter, New Hampshire, he professed his faith and was received into the Congregational church.

As devout as he was, Horace had no intention of studying for the ministry. He wanted to be an electrical engineer and dabbled in making mechanical devices. He contrived a system of pulleys that enabled his father to lock and unlock his bedroom door each morning without getting out of bed. However, a talk with his aunt's husband, a minister, changed his mind. He decided, after much thought, to work in "God's service."[29]

Horace entered Yale in 1888. Classmates called him "Pit" and remembered him as a gifted, articulate speaker and the leading spirit of the Yale Volunteer Band, which held weekly prayer and mission study meetings. He developed such a reputation for overcoming obstacles that his friends quipped, "If anybody kin, Pit-kin."[30]

Oddly enough, the first article Horace submitted to the *Yale Courant*, "An Episode in High Life," was a piece of fiction about a Chinese emperor and the power he exerted over the lives of his people. It was a fanciful tale but indicated some knowledge of Chinese law. It was about robbers who murder the family of a mandarin but are freed by a miscreant justice, whom the emperor then orders to be beheaded.[31] Horace never explained what prompted him to write it.

After his freshman year Pitkin went to Northfield as part of a Yale delegation to attend one of Dwight Moody's seminars. What the popular evangelist had started as a Bible study meeting had turned into a crusade among college students not unlike the fervor displayed several years earlier by the pioneer members of the Oberlin Band. A nondenominational organization, the Student Volunteer Movement that took shape soon spread to campuses throughout the country. Underscoring its zeal was the belief in the Second Coming of Christ. The conversion of heathens suddenly became urgent, so much so that the movement's slogan was "The Evangelization of the World in This Generation."[32] Students such as Pitkin fanned out across the country, stirring local churches out of their lethargy and indifference into taking an active role in supporting foreign missionaries.

Horace met Letitia E. Thomas in July 1895, when the college glee club that she led performed at Northfield. "Letty" was a native of Troy, Ohio, four years his junior. A pretty, cultivated young woman, she had just graduated from Mount Holyoke and was going on to study at the Woman's Medical College in Philadelphia. He still had a year to go at Union Theological. The two decided to devote their lives together to missionary work abroad. They were married a year later, in October 1896, at her parents' home in Troy. They went the next day to Toledo to attend the annual meeting of the American Board and then on to Cleveland, where Horace was ordained in the Pilgrim Church, which became his sponsor.

When the Pitkins reached China in May 1897 after their extended honeymoon trip halfway around the world, the missionaries of the North China Mission were already heading for their summer retreat in Pei-tai-Ho, so the young couple joined their colleagues there for the next several months. Pei-tai-Ho was an isolated seashore community not far from where the Great Wall comes down to Liaotung Bay, north of the Gulf of Chih-li.

For many years a favorite summer resort was the Western Hills, twelve miles from Peking, but it was convenient only to missionaries from Peking and Tung Chow. Pei Tai Ho, which was sixty miles by rail from Tientsin, was more accessible. Missionaries first started going there in the mid-1890s, when the rail connection was completed. They were attracted by its high bluff, fine sand beach, saltwater bathing, and picturesque gigantic rocks. Word spread quickly among foreigners about Pei Tai Ho's cooling breezes, and within a year the community grew from six houses to thirty, many of them expensive summer homes built by businessmen and diplomats attached to consulates in Tientsin and Peking.

The two groups—the missionaries on one hand and the merchants and diplomats on the other—did not, however, mix. A mile and a half away from the other foreigners, a dozen different American and British missionary societies purchased large plots of land and joined together in forming an association to share their missionary experiences. The association sponsored joint prayer meetings, Sabbath services, and conferences dealing with mutual concerns. The missionaries resided in modest one-story cottages in a section called Rocky Point. Annie Gould and Mary Morrill shared a cottage there, a gift from Annie's father and friends who raised the funds for her to build it.

Horace Pitkin, who was enthralled by the sunsets, immediately recognized Pei Tai Ho's beneficial advantages. It could get so hot in Paotingfu that a temperature of 109 degrees in the shade—and 146 in the sun—was not unusual. "Naturally when Rocky Point was found, swept by sea breezes, free from all disease and cool all summer," he said, "every one who could borrow or steal enough to put up a house has hastened so to do, and sends at least the wives and children every summer. With bathing, lovely hills not far off, green grass, flowers and freedom, Pei-tai-ho means health of body and saving of many a missionary's life."[33] In that sense, Pei Tai Ho provided the same well-earned respite for the missionaries of the North China Mission that Yü Tao Ho offered for the Oberlin Band stationed in Shansi.

Paotingfu, which was the capital of Chih-li Province and the residence of the Viceroy of China, was a veritable hub of activity compared to Taiku or Fenchow-fu. The city, known familiarly to the missionaries as "Paofu," formed a triangle with Tientsin and Peking. A railway line extending from just outside the Imperial City to Hankow, a thousand miles to the south, was being planned when Pitkin arrived. The line reached Paotingfu in March 1899 and was an occasion for excitement. There were two "fire wheel carts" daily, one at 6:15 in the morning, and the other an hour or so after noon, depending on delays. The train service cut the travel time to Peking from a three- or four-day cart trip to a half-day's journey. It was a little bit more to Tientsin, which was farther away and required a change of trains. The missionaries now received mail daily. Annie Gould was flabbergasted when she got a letter from Maine in just thirty-eight days.[34]

The American Board compound was extensive, occupying some 100,000 square feet. It was bounded by a high mud wall with only one entry gate. At the south end of the compound was the girls' boarding school. From it a walk ran down the center of the compound to a chapel and a house for a missionary family, both of which were on the west side of the walk. The chapel, with its peaked roof, small belfry, and tall arched windows, looked more Western than oriental. At the compound's extreme end were the boys' boarding school and the stables. On the east side of the walk was the home where Mary and Annie lived, a pleasant one-story brick house with a pitched roof and veranda that sported a round window in its triangular peak. Farther down was the residence of the station's physician, Dr. Willis C. Noble, where the Pitkins first lived. The doctor ran a dispensary and hospital in a small compound on a nearby street.

Horace waxed enthusiastic when it came to the environment surrounding Paotingfu, which was so unlike dusty, uninviting, loess-carved Shansi Province where members of the Oberlin Band lived and worked. He said the birds, flowers, and trees reminded him of the summers he spent as a youngster in New Hartford. "Everything looks like the United States—except no grass, to speak of—only weeds."[35]

Despite all his education Horace had difficulty learning the Chinese language. He and Letty spent their first months in China by the seaside in Pei Tai Ho studying the language, three hours in the morning, two in the afternoon. Their studies continued in Paotingfu; in fact, they demanded most of his time. It took Horace almost two years to master spoken Chinese, and it wasn't until the fall of 1899 that he was adept enough to assume supervision of the boys' boarding school. By then, he and Letty had a boy of their own, Horace Collins Pitkin, born in late March 1898.

Although the Pitkins lived surrounded by luxury, their quarters—three cramped rooms in the Nobles' house—made Letty claustrophobic. She also suffered from neuritis, an inflammation of a nerve that causes pain, loss of reflexes, and muscular atrophy. Her spirits must have been aggravated by the reports of violence and unrest that accompanied the spread of the Boxer movement from Shantung into Chih-li Province during the winter of 1899-1900. Many months before the Oberlin Band over the mountains in Shansi expressed any concern, their cohorts in Paotingfu were already troubled by what they heard. Reports that thousands of homes of Chinese Christians were being destroyed reached them in January. By early March groups of Boxers had established camps in Paotingfu near the American Board compound, though none of the Mission's converts was molested and government troops had arrested a score of the Boxers' leaders. "We continue the even tenor of our way," Mary Morrill reported.[36]

But it was all getting to be too much for Letty. She suffered a nervous breakdown, and after less than three years in China, she left. Letty took her son with her when she sailed from Shanghai in early April 1900. She and the boy were expected to spend several months with her parents in Ohio. Horace hoped they would return to China in October.

By the time Letty left, Dr. Noble and his wife were gone, too, on furlough, and the other missionary family in the compound was preparing to return home for reasons of health.[37] Horace was put in charge of the depleted Mission station—an incredibly extensive "parish" that was equal, he marveled, "to Connecticut, Delaware and Rhode Island—or to Massachusetts—or more than New Jersey."[38] He, Mary Morrill and Annie Gould had to run the various operations, which was becoming increasingly difficult as unrest spread throughout the province.

The three American Board missionaries were not alone in the city, though. The North China Mission compound where they lived and worked was on the boundary of the South Suburb of Paotingfu. Between it and the city wall was a narrow, shallow river, which was crossed by a span known as the Beggar Bridge. On the opposite bank of the river was a station of the China Inland Mission manned by one missionary, who lived there with his family. Seven American Presbyterian missionary families and a doctor lived an hour's walk away in the city's North Suburb, about a mile from the city wall there.

That spring Horace took to riding a bicycle back and forth between the different mission compounds, trading bits of news as a growing number of reports of trouble reached Paotingfu. But it was difficult to tell truth from fiction. "The wildest rumors are all afloat," he said.[39]

One of the most serious reports involved a Boxer attack on Catholic converts in a nearby village. It happened in the third week of April. A

Catholic who mended bowls got involved in a lawsuit with a client over an unpaid bill. He demanded that the client pay for a feast and some church repairs and enroll his family in the church. When the client refused, other converts killed a member of his family. Local Boxers joined friends of the client in attacking the converts. But the Catholics, as usual, were well-armed and killed at least twenty Boxers.

The Chinese in Paotingfu grew wary. The small American Board contingent couldn't find anyone they could preach to, attendance fell off at the chapel, and the Mission's day schools had to be closed for lack of students. The countryside was in such turmoil that the missionaries abandoned the touring of villages, though Mary Morrill continued to visit women in Paotingfu and the girls' boarding school that Annie ran was still in session. A missionary wife who happened to be passing through the city that May said Mary "went fearlessly about the city, as if no Boxers existed."[40]

At first the stories that reached them had to do with attacks on Catholic converts. Boxers were making their families pay heavy ransoms; if they didn't, the Boxers pillaged their homes, plundering everything imaginable, from grain and carts to windows, doors, and even thatches of roof, which they carried off and sold. The Boxers extended their threats to include entire villages where Christians lived; either the community as a whole paid ransom—as much as $300 for a small village, an impossible sum—or all the homes in it were looted. The Paotingfu missionaries heard that Boxers had ransacked more than three hundred villages in Shantung and seventy more in Chih-li.[41]

What surprised Horace was that the Christians being attacked weren't just Catholics. Protestants were being attacked, too. Horace, for one, never expressed any amazement when Boxers set upon a Catholic family. "It is paying off old scores," he said,[42] "for the priests take up and prosecute law cases for their converts. This creates great enmity and when occasion offers, the return blow is given with great severity."[43] But now Catholics and Protestants were suffering alike, which hadn't happened before.

Alarmed by the turn of events, American and British Protestant missionaries in and around Paotingfu started to deluge their consulates in Peking and Tientsin with appeals for military protection. But it wasn't until late April that the government responded. With Boxers only fifteen miles from Paotingfu, the city magistrate ordered the local militia to guard the various Protestant missions.

Five soldiers were sent to guard the CIM station, three more to the hospital compound in which the Presbyterians lived, and an additional nine others showed up at the American Board compound. But the troops were of little use. The American Board missionaries asked the soldiers to fire a salute when the compound closed down at nine o'clock at night, to demonstrate to others in the city that it was being guarded. But, incredibly, the soldiers had no powder for their rifles. The missionaries had to write the military official in charge, requesting powder for their guns.

Still, Pitkin refused to believe the mission was in any danger. He thought a stalemate had developed because the Boxers were not sure whether the soldiers would intervene to protect the missionaries. Personally, Pitkin didn't trust the soldiers to protect them, but the Boxers were not taking any chances. Thinking they were safe, both Horace and Annie Gould were planning to attend the annual meeting of the American Board's North China Mission in Tung Chow, though he wondered whether he ought to wait until one of the Meng brothers was on hand because he didn't want to leave the compound without a man in attendance.

Neither Horace, Annie, nor Mary spoke of trying to leave Paotingfu, not even when the Boxers were ordered to stop drilling in the city but refused, or when a friend of theirs, Frank E. Simcox, a Presbyterian missionary from Pennsylvania, was attacked. Simcox was pessimistic about the state of affairs—or, perhaps, realistic would be a better word. He believed the Chinese government was in sympathy with the Boxers and was certain that nothing could save the country. Nevertheless, Simcox insisted on attending a regularly scheduled prayer meeting at a village though the Christians there had warned him not to come. Boxers broke into the meeting, grabbed an inquirer, and beat him into unconsciousness. Simcox and an assistant fled to the roof of the house until the local magistrate appeared.

That was on May 18. It was a little over a week later that Boxers ripped up the rail and telegraph lines between Paotingfu and Tientsin and Peking. "We are now back where we were in the beginning,—all our boasted civilisation has been taken from us at one stroke," Mary Morrill moaned. "We are now minus daily mails, minus railway and telegraph."[44] Mary was worried whether her twenty-two schoolgirls would be able to return home safely.

The missionaries were well aware of the increasing danger but were determined to stay at their posts with their schoolchildren and converts. "Miss Gould and I cannot leave if we would and would not if we could," Mary declared.[45] They and some of their counterparts in the other Protestant missions did not comprehend the seriousness of the situation. One of them, Benjamin Bagnall, the lone China Inland Mission representative on station in Paotingfu, was urged by a Chinese friend to tell all the missionaries to flee from the city. But Bagnall, who had served in China for more than a quarter of a century and witnessed other periods of unrest, dismissed the warning.

Almost every day now a courier from an outstation or a Christian seeking refuge came bearing news about another violent attack. All across Shantung and Chih-li, foreigners were bolting for safety in an exodus through perilous North China. Some headed north into Manchuria, where Russian forces were, others to the south, to Chinese provinces that were not experiencing any unrest. Some escaped after incredibly close encounters with groups of Boxers and angry villagers. Others were not so lucky. A group of thirty-six Belgian and French railroad engineers and their families who tried to flee by way of the river route to Tientsin were waylaid in shallow water by Boxers. The engineers were armed and killed many Boxers, but, when their ammunition ran out, the Boxers, according to reports, slew every one of them—men, women, and children.

The attack on the foreign engineers and their families less than fifty miles from Paotingfu forced Horace Pitkin to realize that the killings "may be the beginning of the end."[46] On Saturday, June 2, he handed a letter to a courier, hoping that the man would be able to reach the American Board station in Peking. Even if he, Mary, and Annie thought of fleeing, he wrote, "the way is blocked by river and train." In addition, most of the troops sent to Paotingfu had left the city, leaving only a small, ineffectual unit to guard them. "God give us rain!" he declared. The Paotingfu missionaries were now totally surrounded by Boxers:

So now North of us, 160 li, is one band of plunderers; East, 160 li, on the river, another; South, 50 li, another, but more bent on local ravage; Southwest, 50 li, another pillaging railway.

As for Paotingfu, Boxers drill in temples in the city and officials are powerless. What our chances are, it is hard to tell. All along the officials have sent us a small guard, but they, although nice fellows enough, will be of no use. Whether the local Boxers will have courage enough to attack, don't know. But a firebrand from North, East, South, or West, will be sufficient, that's sure. . . .

One town, 30 li South of us, where the Catholics have recanted in a body,—firecrackers and great rejoicing! But Protestant natives are not touched. Everybody has been saying, that 'Jesus Church' is all right. Only want Catholics. All agree, that [if] the Catholics should be massacred, no telling whether the above pretensions would hold water. Fear they would not. Whether this trouble on the river will be an incentive to local talent, don't know. . . .

It is a grand cause to die in. Jesus *shall* reign, but we do hope a long life may be for us in this work.[47]

Pitkin was especially concerned that the Boxers might try a night attack: "The moon gets brighter every night—and—what—then!"[48] A measure of how desperate he felt was his plea that the American Board staff in Peking "press" the American minister, Edwin Conger, to get the Imperial government to send three to five hundred government troops at once. That despite the fact that the Chinese military had a dreadful reputation. Desertion was endemic; officers stole the pay of their troops, and looting by soldiers was so prevalent that many peasants hid their valuables and ran away when an army unit passed through their village. Mary Morrill and Annie Gould had had a frightening encounter with government soldiers in January 1895 when thousands of troops marched through Paotingfu on their way to Peking during the Sino-Japanese War. The soldiers were so filthy, said Annie, that their "vile odor" permeated closed windows.

More than any other confrontation between China and a foreign power, the Sino-Japanese War in the mid-1890s had caused missionaries great anxiety. They feared at the time that, although the Japanese were ancient enemies of the Chinese, the Chinese might turn against all foreigners. An Imperial edict was issued, assuring Westerners of their safety and commanding people to respect their lives and property. But army units were virtually undisciplined. One group of soldiers tried to force its way into the American Board compound. The Mission doctor, Willis Noble, was convinced that they were only curious to see how foreigners lived. He ordered the gate opened before it was ripped down.

Hundreds of troops rushed in and surrounded the house where Mary and Annie lived. Several of them broke a cellar window and crawled into the basement. They got upstairs to the dining room, where they stole some dinnerware and towels. Others stole utensils from the kitchen and robbed and hit the cook. One soldier tried to snatch Noble's eyeglasses from him.

Mary, who was trying to calm the frightened schoolgirls, rushed from the school and confronted the soldiers. They were surprised when she spoke in Chinese to them. One asked if she was afraid of them. "No, you are only men," she answered, smiling and doing her best to appear self-assured. While Chinese helpers scurried about, prodding the soldiers to leave, she stood resolutely on the veranda of her house, determined not to show any sign of fear. She was able to restore some semblance of order, but the troops did not leave until their general came and ordered them from the compound. The local magistrate issued an edict, notifying everyone that the Mission premises were off limits, but several weeks later another group of soldiers appeared, threatening to destroy the compound. The magistrate had to send officers and guards from the *yamen* to disperse them.[49]

More than five years passed between that incident and the disruption of Paotingfu's communication with Tientsin and Peking, but the memory of it was vivid. One night in late May 1900, shortly after the Mission lost contact with the outside world, Annie went to bed, thinking about what her mother once told her: "The nearest way to China is by the way of 'the throne,'—the mercy seat." Annie said her mother's words comforted her. "I can't tell you exactly what I fear; not death, nor even violence at the hands of a mob; for the physical suffering would be over soon, and God can give strength for that." Annie said the possibility of danger "does not weigh on me, or when it does I just cry out and pray for 'grit.'"[50]

"We live," Mary declared, "in the 91st Psalm."[51] (". . . He is my refuge and my fortress: my God; in him will I trust. . . . Thou shalt not be afraid for the terror by night; *nor* for the arrow *that* flieth by day; . . .")

Attacks multiplied. More Christian homes were burned, converts were killed, even non-Christians were attacked. Anyone who provoked rampaging bands of Boxers or incensed villagers was assailed. All the hostility against foreigners, their religion, and their converts that ever existed was climaxing in an orgy of bloodletting. Bands of Boxers were not only spreading through Shantung and Chih-li into Shansi but also approaching Tientsin and Peking.

The fate of the American Board missionaries at Paotingfu and across the mountains to the west at Taiku and Fenchow-fu was now bound up with events completely out of their hands, an international crisis of such proportions that the missionaries, in their far-off stations, were at last alarmed. They feared that in the catastrophe that was developing, they would be totally forgotten.

FIFTEEN ❁ *Under Siege*

A prince should employ his ministers according to the rules of propriety; ministers should serve their prince with faithfulness.
—Confucius

They were forgotten. Their missionary colleagues in Peking and Tientsin were also cut off from the outside world and caught up in their own struggle to survive. The fate of the Oberlin Band in Shansi and their friends in Paotingfu was now linked with circumstances that were complicated and rife with indecision, deceit, and blundering.

To make matters worse, the missionaries were confounded by confusing and conflicting signals from the Imperial Court. The Boxer attack on the Paotingfu-Tientsin-Peking railway on May 28 prompted the Court the next day to order all officials in the Empire to "annihilate" Boxers if they refused to disperse. It was the first time the Court used that word in connection with the Boxers and seemed to signal a dramatic victory for moderates. But when a day later foreign diplomats in Peking announced their intention to send for additional guard units to protect their legations, the Court quickly changed its mind. It never again made any mention of annihilating the Boxers, and on June 3 it explicitly warned against doing so.[1]

More than 470 foreigners—including 149 women and 79 children—lived in the Legation Quarter, guarded by a military contingent of about 450 men of eight different nationalities—American, Austrian, British, French, German, Italian, Japanese, and Russian. The Quarter was in the northern part of Peking known as the Tartar City. Through it ran the Imperial Canal, a sluggish, fetid waterway that was unnavigable. The foreign community was less than two hundred yards south of the walled Imperial City. In the midst of the Imperial City was the Forbidden City, which was actually a complex of buildings, in one of which the Dowager Empress lived.

The troops sent for by the legations were sailors and marines from an assemblage of foreign warships anchored off Taku Bar in the Gulf of Chih-li. On May 31 the men were ferried past the Taku forts guarding the mouth of the Pei Ho, then boarded trains for the brief trip to Tientsin, thirty miles away. The troops—in all, some 335 Americans, British, French, Italian, Japanese, and Russians—reached Peking, eighty more milesfarther on the line, that evening and immediately took up their guard duties. An additional 89 German and Austrian sailors arrived three days later.

In the meantime, word reached Peking of an acceleration of Boxer attacks. On June 2 the diplomatic community learned of the Boxer attack on the Belgian and French engineers who had attempted to escape with their families to Tientsin by riverboat. The next day, about forty miles south of Peking, two British missionaries were killed. Then, on the following day, June 4, Boxers attacked stations along the railway line to Tientsin. Government troops who were supposed to be guarding the line deserted. The Boxers severed through service on the line to Peking. The additional guards for the legations had made the trip from Tientsin just in time. Peking was now effectively cut off from the coast.

With the rail line cut and Peking virtually isolated, thousands of Boxers converged on the capital. On June 9 they attacked what was clearly a symbol of foreign encroachment: the grandstand of the International Race Course, a favorite social and recreational spot of the diplomatic community, three miles outside of Peking. Several young Englishmen riding there to see what had happened had to fire at the Boxers in self-defense.

The diplomats were outraged, evidently more disturbed by the incident at the racetrack than they were by the violence that missionaries and their converts were beginning to experience. Members of the diplomatic corps met that afternoon and agreed to ask the admirals of the various fleets off Taku Bar to send a relief force. Two thousand men of eight nationalities, led by the British admiral, Sir Edward Seymour, set off from Tientsin in five trains on June 10. But the next day, halfway to Peking, the relief force ran into Boxers and stalled. In a show of force, the Powers subsequently ordered their fleets to take the Taku forts, to protect the rear of the relief force, and to provide a staging area for reinforcements.

Meanwhile, in Peking, the chancellor of the Japanese legation went to the train station, expecting to meet Seymour and his international relief force coming from Tientsin. He was dragged from his cart by Imperial troops and cut to pieces. The soldiers sent his heart to their general. An Imperial edict was issued two days later, labeling his murderers bandits.

By then the first Boxer had appeared on Legation Street, in the diplomatic quarter. The German minister, Baron von Ketteler, was enraged at the sight of the man, who was dressed in a white tunic girded by a red sash, his hair tied up in a red cloth and his wrists and ankles circled by red ribbons. Von Ketteler attacked the man with his walking stick.

That same day hordes of Boxers burst through a gate east of the Legation Quarter, looting houses and shops of the Chinese who did business with foreigners, cutting down anyone in their path with their swords and pikes, and setting fires that soon engulfed thousands of stores and dwellings. As fire and acrid smoke filled the city, people fled, running for their lives, jamming the streets, shrieking in terror. The Boxers singled out hundreds of Chinese Christians. They speared them, hacked them to pieces, burned them alive. The Boxers set missionary premises on fire and burned the homes of foreign teachers at the Imperial University. They torched the East Cathedral, where hundreds of Catholic converts and an aged French priest sought refuge. The South Cathedral, which had stood for three hundred years, was set on fire that night, too, but all the missionaries there, including five sisters and twenty Chinese nuns, managed to escape.

The burning and killing turned indiscriminate as thousands of Boxers roamed through the city, attacking Christians and non-Christians alike. As Arthur Smith of the American Board put it, "Peking and Pandemonium were for the time synonymous terms."[2] That night the last telegraph line to the outside world—the line running north into Russian territory—was severed.

Up until then Imperial troops for the most part had played a passive role, doing nothing to stop the rampages and panic. On June 17, Prince Tuan, the leader of the conservative anti-foreign faction at the Imperial Court, submitted to Dowager Empress Tz'u Hsi an ultimatum that he claimed had been forwarded to him by the foreign legations. It purported to demand that the conduct of all military affairs in the Empire be placed in the hands of the foreign ministers and that the Emperor be restored to the throne. Tz'u Hsi was enraged: "Now the Powers have started the aggression, and the extinction of our nation is imminent. If we just fold our arms and yield to them, I would have no face to see our ancestors after death. If we must perish, why not fight to the death."[3] The Peking Field Force—made up of five armies—was ordered to surround the legations, supposedly to protect the diplomats but effectively sealing them off from the rest of the city. What Prince Tuan did not tell Tz'u Hsi was that the so-called ultimatum was forged.

Meantime the admirals of the fleets off Taku Bar demanded the surrender of the Taku forts, and, even before a deadline they set had expired, they landed troops and captured the forts. But afraid perhaps of being the one to report a defeat, the viceroy of Tientsin misled Peking. He informed the Court about the deadline issued by the foreign admirals, but he neglected to mention that the forts were already lost. He even went so far a few days later as to claim victories at both Tientsin and Taku, praising the cooperation he had received from Boxers.

As far as the Imperial Court was concerned, the deadline set by the admirals was the final insult. Provoked by it, but still unaware of the capture of the forts, the Court decided finally to expel the entire diplomatic corps and had an ultimatum of its own handed to each foreign minister: All diplomats and their families were to leave Peking and proceed to Tientsin within twenty-four hours.

The diplomats were also misinformed. Unaware that Admiral Seymour's sailors and marines had run into stiff resistance and were running out of supplies, they believed that the relief force from Tientsin was nearby. So they stalled for time and requested a meeting for the next day.

The diplomats waited anxiously for an answer to their request.

When it didn't come the next day, the impatient Von Ketteler set off to the *Tsungli Yamen* with an aide. Its offices were less than a mile from the Legation Quarter. The two Germans went in sedan chairs covered with scarlet and green hoods to denote their diplomatic status. As they passed alonga street, a lance corporal in the Peking Field Force—a Manchu Banner trooper in full uniform with a mandarin's hat and button and a blue feather—shot and killed the baron. His aide was wounded but got away.

That afternoon, June 20, the Imperial Court, on the basis of the erroneous information it had received from the viceroy of Tientsin, issued an edict that, in effect, declared war on the Powers. It blamed the foreigners for initiating hostilities. The Siege of Peking had begun.

Even before the edict was issued, it was clear that Prince Tuan and his cohorts—the "Ironhats"—were in control and that the Imperial government was intent on ousting all foreigners. Two of the most rabid antiforeign ministers at court had attended the burning of one of the Catholic cathedrals, and it was said that the Dowager Empress watched from her palace as the conflagration lit up the sky at night. Once they learned of the ultimatum regarding the forts, Imperial government officials distributed rice and money to the Boxers in Peking, and princes and grandees were put in charge of them. The two—the government and the Boxers—were irrevocably united.

Imperial troops were now on the firing line, surrounding the Legation Quarter. Its foreign community had been swelled by thousands of Chinese converts. They were refused admittance to the Quarter at first. The United States minister, Edwin Conger, resisted pleas to allow Protestant converts inside the Quarter. He ordered guards to escort Americans at the Methodist Mission to safety but said that the Chinese Christians there—more than eight hundred of them—would have to fend for themselves. He was persuaded to change his mind, however, after the Boxers set fire to the East Cathedral and killed hundreds of Chinese Catholics who had sought refuge inside. The missionaries arrived with their followers in procession behind them, reminding Arthur Smith "of the children of Israel as they departed from Egypt."[4]

The converts, in all some three thousand of them, were crammed into the palace of Prince Su, which was across the Imperial Canal from the

British legation. They became the target of the most severe artillery fire. To make sure that they would not be mistaken for hostile Chinese, the converts were given white armbands to wear with the word "Christian" on them. (Ironically, in Shansi, Yü Hsien had proposed, for another reason, that converts be identified in the same way.) The diplomats and missionaries set up committees to handle feeding the besieged. Work crews made sandbags and barricades, and a fire-fighting brigade was set up. Converts were assigned the most menial tasks, and for food they were given the leftover entrails and heads of the ponies and mules that were slaughtered to feed the diplomats, missionaries, and their families.

Meanwhile, Admiral Seymour's relief force, awaited so anxiously by the Peking foreign community, had to turn back. And the foreign settlements in Tientsin were under siege as well. There, an energetic young civil engineer, Herbert Hoover, was supervising the building of defense barricades, while his wife Lou worked as a nurse.

Several weeks earlier, shortly before the rail connection between Paotingfu and Tientsin was cut, Boxer posters calling for the extermination of all foreigners appeared in Taiku. Then, on Sunday, May 27, the day before train service was halted, an angry mob gathered outside the Mission as the Sabbath service was ending. They were led by a deranged man who claimed he was 108 years old. He had convinced the governor, Yü Hsien, that he could cause rain to fall, but after ten days of praying he had failed and was ridiculed. Blaming foreigners for his inability to bring rain, the man went through the city, flourishing a sword and yelling that all foreigners must be killed. A mob quickly gathered behind him. The man led it to the South Suburb.

Teacher Liu advised Howard Clapp to go the *yamen* for help. The mob shouted insults but did not threaten them physically. Liu and Clapp were each able to grab one demonstrator and drag him to the *yamen.* The magistrate wasn't in, but his chief assistant was. He had the two men Liu and Clapp brought in arrested and sent a corporal and four soldiers to disperse the other Chinese. All returned to quiet, or so it seemed. But that night, outside the house George Williams built, two men beat a gong, urging people to kill the foreigners. No one, however, responded to their shouting.

The next day a mob gathered outside the Mission compound on South Street, apparently emboldened by the fact that the two men arrested on the previous day had not been punished. This time Francis Davis wrote the magistrate and a proclamation was immediately issued, disowning violence and saying that foreigners would be protected. Once the proclamation was posted outside the *yamen,* on the compound gate and around the city, the mob again dispersed.[5]

However, on the following day, the deranged man confronted Williams on the street as he was leaving a bank. He grabbed the missionary by the sleeve and demanded money. When Williams demurred, the man dropped Williams's sleeve, stepped back and thrust his sword at the missionary, striking him on right side of his chest. Because the morning was cool, Williams was wearing a lined garment, so the sword point did not pierce his clothing, but the blow caused a bruise that turned black and blue. Williams was able to slip past the man and rush back into the bank, and the man was eventually arrested. "I shall never forget his devilish fierceness and the gleaming sword," Williams wrote his wife Alice. "There is a fearful amount of wild talk."[6]

The demonstrations and the attack on Williams failed to deter the missionaries' Chinese adherents. On the following Sunday, when Louise Partridge held services outdoors in Li Man, a large audience of almost sixty Chinese attended.

In Fenchow-fu, Eva Price was becoming increasingly anxious. In late May fifteen Boxers attacked a Christian in a village four days' journey south of the city, stabbing him in the side with a spear and robbing him. By the end of the month, Boxers were inside Fenchow-fu itself, drilling in several places and drawing large crowds of what she called "restless adventurers."[7] Rumors about unrest and talk reviling foreigners and their religion were beginning to be heard, all because of the drought, according to her husband, Charles. He said the Chinese believed storm clouds were being driven away by "fierce winds" that the missionaries created "by fanning with all our might."[8]

"Unfortunately," Eva said, "the people are made exceedingly restless and ready to believe the many wild stories about us, because of the drought, for which we are said to be the cause." Eva acknowledged that "the outlook is more than discouraging. It is serious." People, she continued, "say we are keeping the rain away; the placards that have already been posted in several prominent places in this city say, 'Drive out the foreigners and rain will come.'"[9]

Like her missionary colleagues, Eva wrote many letters to friends and family back home, hoping that eventually the mail would reach the coast and be forwarded to the States. Because regular courier service between Shansi and Paotingfu became haphazard at best, the missionaries added postscripts to their letters on almost a day-to-day basis until a courier became available. Several of the Oberlin Band—Howard Clapp, George Williams, Rowena Bird, and Louise Partridge—also began journals or diaries, making entries almost daily as a record of their ordeals.

The letters were forwarded to Horace Pitkin in Paotingfu, in the expectation that he would be able to send them on to the coast. Pitkin, however, could not do anything but let them pile up in his study. The words that the letters and the journals contained—which reflected the missionaries' hopes, fears, and prayers—were muted and would not be heard until it was too late. Eva Price, for example, sent a number of newspapers in Ohio an appeal for funds that was dated June 4. It took two years to reach them:

> We are isolated. We feel it more now than ever before. Were grain donated in America and shipped gratis, we are weeks from the port and there is a starving gauntlet to run. We have feared this very condition for months, and have hoped against hope that it would not be necessary to appeal for help; but we find we are not able of ourselves to be of help beyond the very little we can do. . . .
>
> You know what the expression, "Living in clover," means; many are realizing it in your land. But how many realize what is means literally to live on clover, the leaves of trees, etc., as some, yes, many, of these people are doing?[10]

The missionaries stationed in Fenchow-fu were already discussing the possibility of leaving for the coast but decided they would be safer in the city than on the road. Anyway, Eva said, "it would look like deserting the native Christians."[11] Her daughter Florence was curious to see a Boxer, but Eva said she hoped "she'll not get the chance."[12]

"The advent of the Boxers," Eva added, "and so soon after the arrival of the new governor who was responsible in large measure for the rioting in Shan Tung last year, makes us wonder if we, too, are to share with them in such persecution."[13]

On the other hand, Lizzie Atwater thought the Chinese in Fenchow-fu were acting "just as usual," and that there had been no effect on attendance at Sunday services although "threatening placards" were being posted throughout Fenchow-fu and surrounding villages.[14] Her husband Ernest insisted that he had seen "no special signs of hostility" against the missionaries on the streets of Fenchow-fu. He believed that they were safer staying where they were than trying to flee. The missionaries planned to "go on just as we have been doing. We do not plan to fortify our compounds," he said. "[A] kind of Providence can keep us safe even now. Though it does seem like living in the lion's mouth":

> It may be that our lives may not be spared to us. Be that as it may . . . I can see that the test is having a strengthening effect on a number of the Church members. . . . Numbers of them testify to the rest from anxiety that the Gospel gives them. They put their affairs into God's hands. . . . I have no doubt but that there will be a glorious Church in the land of China within another generation.[15]

In Taiku, Jennie Clapp also belittled the threats, though she admitted feeling uncomfortable. Her husband Howard was planning on going on a preaching tour into the mountains and saw no reason to cancel it. Writing to Alice Williams in Oberlin, Jennie said:

> We have been so wrought up with rumors of Boxers—and raids of madmen. . . . When I went to Tung Fang Sunday it seemed to me the people looked at me with more interest than usual—and I imagined something like this passed through their minds[:] "You've just escaped with your life! Don't you know the foreigners are all to be killed! I did not expect to see you out." The "yao yen" [rumor] comes from the drought—and prospect of suffering. Some say . . . the gods are angry because the foreigners do not allow the people to worship them. All sorts of foolish talk.[16]

Foolish talk aside, the reality was that there had been no rain at all except for some brief, scattered drizzles. All streams in the area were dried up, and the Fen River was a mere trickle, all its water used up for irrigating. "I have felt a *lump* of *disappointment* in my throat," said Jennie, "when I have watched clouds of promise rise and vanish away."[17]

On Tuesday, June 5, a Chinese man burst into the women's Bible class

Jennie was leading, warning that Boxers were coming to kill foreigners and their followers. Bible woman Chang Ta Sao reproved him, and the class went on as scheduled.

Neither Francis Davis nor George Williams felt alarmed at the incident. Francis, for one, didn't believe that the people of Shansi were going to "change the custom of centuries and begin to row and fight." He wrote his wife Lydia about her expected return to China, going into complicated detail about the cable she should send him in code so that he would understand what ship she would be on and when and where it would arrive. "It may be everything will be p'ing an [peaceful] before you arrive if you come," he said, but just in case he recommended that she purchase and bring a double-barreled shotgun or a .38-caliber revolver and smokeless-powder cartridges.[18]

By the middle of June, on the eve of the sieges of both Peking and Tientsin and with the relief force of Admiral Seymour blocked between the two cities, more ominous signs began to appear in both Fenchow-fu and Taiku, hundreds of miles away in Shansi Province.

In Fenchow-fu the first Boxers arrived on June 15. There were two of them; they tried to organize the young men of the city but were unsuccessful, so they started with boys ten years old. The new, young *kuan* issued a proclamation against the Boxers but almost immediately revoked it and gave them permission to recruit followers. Once that happened, people started openly insulting and threatening Christians on the streets of the city. They hurled taunts and threats at the missionaries, too. The missionaries were "plainly told" that they were to be killed. "Times," said Charles Price, "were very critical."[19]

On Sunday, June 17, it was Rowena Bird's turn to go to Tung Fang to conduct Sabbath services. Ordinarily, when she went, an old manservant escorted her the few miles from Taiku to the village. This time, however, she was accompanied by K'ung Hsiang Hsi, who was the friend of Fei Chi Hao and the first student the Taiku boys' school sent on to North China College.

Hsiang Hsi, who was nineteen years old, had known many of the

Fei Chi Hao, left, *and K'ung Hsiang Hsi. Courtesy Oberlin College Archives.*

Shansi missionaries for more than ten years. He came from a distinguished family in Taiku. Not only was he a descendant of Confucius, but his grandfather was wealthy, having acquired his money in banking and pawn shops. Hsiang Hsi's father, K'ung Ho-ting, taught school in a village outside Taiku. Three of his uncles were either businessmen or bankers, and a fourth was a government official. He, his father, and nineteen cousins lived with one of the uncles in an enormous compound in Taiku. His sister Chin Fêng was one of Louise Partridge's students in Li Man.

Hsiang Hsi's mother had died from tuberculosis when he was seven years old, and he himself was a sickly child. When he was eight, a friend of the family who was a Christian recommended that Hsiang Hsi be taken to the American Board dispensary in Taiku, where a diseased gland was removed from his neck. Hsiang Hsi was much taken with the life of the Mission and begged to go to the boys' school that was just being set up by Jennie Clapp. His grandfather consented.

Hsiang Hsi became especially attached to Jennie Clapp, who was like a mother to him, and then to Rowena Bird, whom he regarded as a sister. He spent college vacations with George and Alice Williams. He converted to Christianity and was baptized by Howard Clapp when he was only twelve years old, though he apparently did not inform his family. During his last two years in the Taiku school and for a time after he graduated but before he went to Tung Chow, Hsiang Hsi assisted in teaching in the mission school.

Once in college, Hsiang Hsi apparently got involved with young Chinese who supported the reforms that Emperor Kuang Hsü tried to institute. He reportedly put up the money for an assassination plot against the Dowager Empress that would have restored Kuang Hsü. His college roommate, a youth named Li, was supposedly the leader of the conspiracy. Hsiang Hsi, so it is said, was going to bribe a Court official to allow Li to enter the palace to kill Tz'u Hsi. But before anything could be done, Boxers struck the city of Tung Chow and all the students had to flee.[20]

Hsiang Hsi traveled from Peking to Paotingfu by train only a few days before the Boxers destroyed the rail line. While in Paotingfu, he met

Horace Pitkin and joined Pitkin, Mary Morrill, and Annie Gould for an evening prayer meeting. When he finally reached Taiku on a Saturday, June 2, he found only Chinese in the city compound. The Clapps, Rowena Bird, and George Williams had moved to the house Williams had built in the South Suburb. Louise Partridge was in Li Man, and Francis Davis, who had offered to share quarters with Williams and was rejected, was living by himself in the village of Jen Tsun. Hsiang Hsi stayed in Taiku, assisting the missionaries and helping Rowena in her Chinese studies.

That Sunday, June 17, when he accompanied Rowena to Tung Fang, he didn't tell her that he feared trouble, or that he was carrying a pistol he had gotten from his uncle. Rowena sat inside a small covered cart while he sat outside with the driver. As they rode along the dusty trail to the village, they were jeered. A bystander shouted out, "Still the foreigners go about, but they'll all be killed soon." Another called Hsiang Hsi a spy, and a third said, "Never mind, the native devils will all be wiped out too." A fourth man said, "See how dry the fields are; no wonder the heavens refuse rain while these church devils infest the land."[21]

Rowena and Hsiang Hsi reached Tung Fang without further incident, but that afternoon, after their return to Taiku, they came on a huge crowd of people swarming outside the Mission compound in the city. They were able to make their way to the South Suburb. Louise Partridge, riding in from Li Man about five miles away about the same time, found the city in an uproar. Foolishly, she suddenly realized, she was carrying with her a baby she was tending. A missionary with a Chinese child fed the worst of superstitions. Louise knew full well that many Chinese believed missionaries kidnapped infants and gouged out their eyes and hearts for use in religious rites.

Louise was cursed as she made her way through the mass of Chinese. Cries of "Kill the foreigners" rang through the air. Louise entered the Mission compound by the gate, trying not to show any sign of fear, purposely smiling and stopping to speak to anyone she recognized. "I was not afraid," she insisted with her customary bravado.[22]

Only Howard Clapp and a few Christians were inside the compound. They had postponed a communion service because of the noise outside. Howard had already sent a messenger to the *yamen,* asking for protection.

Jennie Clapp was with Rowena in the South Suburb and Williams was holding a Sabbath service in a village outside Taiku. Louise decided to see Jennie and Rowena. When she got to the suburban compound, she thought that the ordinarily timid Jennie was "much braver than formerally [*sic*], has passed through a good apprenticeship."[23] But when Rowena suggested that if anything happened, she and Louise should not be seen together—an obvious allusion to the possibility of rape—Jennie suddenly got upset.

Jennie tried to talk Louise out of returning to Li Man, but Louise did not want to leave her schoolgirls there alone. Both Jennie and Rowena urged her to close the school, but Louise said that was up to the parents. And even if the parents wanted the school to close and have their children sent home, Louise said she would remain to protect "my place. It would be a direct invitation for them to loot if I left and I don't care to extend such an invitation."[24]

So Louise returned to Li Man. She took with her three boys from the Taiku school who lived in the village. When she got back there, it was almost ten o'clock at night and all her schoolgirls were still up, excited and worried. She herself scarcely slept: "Another day gone and my life still spared."[25]

Strangely, Louise's behavior seemed to contradict her concern for her life. Two days later, Louise was studying after classes were over when there was a great banging at the gate of her compound. Without checking on who was doing the knocking, she unlocked the gate. A group of eight or nine men rushed by her, ran to the back court, found it locked and rushed out again.

Louise finally reacted. She locked the front gate behind them, but then she heard noise coming from the school courtyard. The men had climbed a wall and were looking down into it. The schoolgirls were frightened. Louise calmed them down, not knowing what would happen next. When she went back to the front gate, she could see boys peeking under it. A helper told her that the Chinese outside believed that she kept the gate locked because she was afraid, so without hesitating Louise flung the gate wide open and walked out into the street outside:

> Everyone followed and quite a crowd collected. We harangued a while and my man performed the monkey act and showed them how those men acted &

> raised a laugh. Then a lot of them came in to see and there was the friendliest feeling all around. There have been folks coming off and on all day & between times they've beat the gate and run. Interesting. My man got upon the wall and skied a brick at them & they called, "Kill the foreign devil.["] I don't know which came first or whether they had any connection. If it continues tomorrow I shall send for protection. All quiet now.[26]

But all was not quiet for long. Her Bible woman was later cursed when she went out into the village. The woman encountered many unemployed peasants, talking wildly about exterminating foreigners. "Poor things," said Louise, "they little know that with us dies their hope of help in famine." She began to wonder "how long we can live with the expectation of being killed day by day." Then, learning about the murder of the Belgian and French engineers fleeing by river to the coast, she became pessimistic: "I felt there was no hope for us. A horrible fear shook me for a minute."[27]

In truth, Louise's brave front was slowly dissolving. She was becoming unnerved. She had already slapped several of her schoolgirls one Sunday after services when the girls fell to quarreling amongst themselves.[28] She still insisted that "there's much 'yao yen' [rumors] and we've had one or two little fracases. But I am not afraid and mean to hold the fort."[29] But the next day after writing that, she "thrashed" two of the schoolgirls again. "I've got such a p'ao ing [negative] streak on," she said, "I can't sit still. It's first this and then that."[30]

In Taiku itself, the missionaries there had taken to holding their weekly prayer meetings in the sitting room of the Clapps' quarters in the South Suburb rather than going back and forth to the chapel in the Mission compound. Rowena Bird was beginning to get "a dreadfully isolated feeling." A courier from Paotingfu brought word from Horace Pitkin that he hadn't received any mail for three weeks, though the English Baptist Mission in the city of Tai Yuan had received a wire from Tientsin during a brief spell when the telegraph line was repaired. But the wire was five days old by the time it reached there. "There doesn't seem to be much use in writing," Rowena said, "but it is a relief to write."[31]

The missionaries were concerned because their bank in Taiku did not want to take any more drafts. But infinitely more terrifying was an Imperial edict issued on June 24. It called for the extermination of foreigners everywhere. The missionaries heard that a date for their elimination had been set.

The date set was June 27. The Sunday beforehand, students from the boys' boarding school started to leave the Taiku compound with their baggage. A rumor swept through the city that the foreigners were fleeing, and before Sunday services that morning an angry crowd gathered outside the Mission, throwing brickbats and shouting *"Sha! Sha!"*—"Kill! Kill!" Hoping to dispel the anger, the missionaries blithely opened the compound gate and invited the mob inside. Chinese jammed the chapel, while others roamed about the compound. They did not leave until nightfall.

Francis Davis, for one, decided that catering to a mob's whims was no guarantee of safety. He returned to his residence in Jen Tsun afterwards "determined to fight it out on that line." He had a revolver that was "in good condition" and thought he could make "a mob sick."[32]

The Taiku *kuan* was still friendly and responding to their appeals for protection, but, Rowena wrote in her journal, "These are most trying times":

> Everything in uproar—famine threatens the people with starvation—the dry, hot weather makes all ill, and the Boxers are threatening the destruction of the country by robbing and killing missionaries and Christians. . . . All the vicious element seemed to be aroused, and the whole province of Chih-li is one scene of confusion and danger . . . everything in uproar—no details. . . . As to our condition here, it is critical. . . . Proclamations protecting Christians and denouncing Boxers have been put up, but we have had to keep at the Yamen to get them to post them in the outstations. . . . The country is full of the wildest rumors and threats. The people have nothing to do but talk and they talk of nothing but killing the foreigners and the Christians and we all feel that the end may not be far off for many of us.[33]

Louise Partridge was now behaving irrationally. Of all times when she should have been on her guard, she made a major blunder on the eve of the day set for the extermination of the missionaries, June 27. She discovered the error when she awoke early that morning. After saying her prayers, she noticed that the gate to her compound in Li Man was halfway open. She had forgotten to lock it the night before. Anyone could have walked in. Louise tried to "laugh" off her "carelessness," but it was no joking matter.[34]

In Fenchow-fu the local magistrate was imploring local gods to produce rain. He cut off the head of a "Drought Devil" in a ceremony that Eva Price disparaged. "It seems at times as though the devil is really given the supreme power in this land, and that the faith of this heathen people is more honored in some of these ways," she said. "It is very trying at times to be living in what seems a very stronghold of the Evil One, fighting against powers and principalities that we truly know-not-of."[35]

Charles Price had armed himself with a shotgun, a rifle, and a revolver, which troubled Eva. The revolver was his brother Frank's, which Charles bought from him for shooting wolves before Frank went back to the States in 1890. Not knowing it was loaded, Eva once took the gun out of a trunk where it was stored and accidentally fired it, almost hitting one of her children who was playing nearby.[36]

While Price intended to defend his family, some of his missionary colleagues—in particular, Howard Clapp—were against meeting violence with violence, and in both Taiku and Fenchow-fu the members of the Oberlin Band hotly debated how to meet the threats to their lives and the lives of their converts. "We cannot claim that we are not anxious, that we are not at a loss to know what is best and right for us to do," Eva declared.[37]

Charles was determined to stay in Fenchow-fu unless ordered out by American authorities. But he wanted Eva to take their daughter Florence to Tai Yuan. Eva, however, wanted to remain with him. She was encouraged, she said, by the fact that "those actively engaged" in the Boxer drillings "are mostly boys—very few above 18 or 20."

One Boxer training ground was dangerously close—in back of where Ernest and Lizzie Atwater were living, a mile from the Prices. It was attracting more than five hundred people each day, and Eva was afraid that the drills might "like a flash of lightning leap into something far from being child's play." She said that it was difficult to know what to do. "One doesn't want to die unnecessarily, because of rashness."[38]

The Fenchow-fu missionaries knew about the engineers being killed enroute to Tientsin. They had also received a wire—when the telegraph line was temporarily restored—saying, "Travelling in Chihli unsafe; Warn all; Marines are being landed." But that was all they knew. All they could do was wait in "great suspense" until the next courier from Paotingfu arrived. Going to their summer home, "Peeking Place," in Yü Tao Ho was out of the question, though she and Charles talked of little else:

> The subject of "Boxers" is tabooed after the mid-day meal, and especially in the evening when the only reference we are allowed to make is "The big 'B'"—for it is not conducive either to sleep or appetite to bring it in the latter part of the day. But everything seems to revolve around the subject and it racks one's brains to think of anything else.[39]

Faced with the June 27 deadline for the extermination of foreigners in Shansi Province, Charles and Ernest sent a helper to the *kuan* with their cards, asking for an interview. They met him on Sunday, June 24. The magistrate assured them that they faced no danger, that the threats in the city were "only talk." The *kuan* promised to issue another proclamation to protect the missionaries. One was posted, but so apparently was a proclamation supporting the Boxers.[40]

The next day the missionaries learned that the magistrate had received a letter from Tai Yuan containing an account of the Boxers' successes in Chih-li Province—and that Boxers had been enlisted as government soldiers and had defeated foreign troops. Charles Price didn't believe it. "News from the coast vague and unreliable," he wrote in his journal.[41] But it was true. Admiral Seymour's relief column had failed and was headed back to Tientsin without ever getting close to Peking.

About this time, the American Board Mission in Fenchow-fu became the refuge for three missionaries who were fleeing ahead of the Boxers. One was Annie Eldred, a twenty-eight-year-old Englishwoman who had been in China less than two years and could barely read or speak Chinese. She was attached to a station in Hung T'ung, a district in southern Shansi. A "gentle little English lady," Eldred was having trouble sleeping and suffered from painful headaches.[42] She busied herself in Fenchow-fu helping Eva Price to cook, playing with Eva's daughter Florence and the two little Atwater girls, and giving Florence music lessons.

The other missionaries were Anton Peter and Elsa Nilson Lundgren, naturalized Americans who ran an opium refuge about eighteen miles outside Fenchow-fu. The Lundgrens were no strangers to members of the Oberlin Band. Before they were married, Elsa had stayed with the Prices for five weeks in 1895 and Anton courted her there. She and Eva Price formed a mother-daughter relationship.[43] Elsa was born in Sweden, Anton in Denmark. He emigrated to the United States when he was seventeen years old in 1878. He joined the Scandinavian China Alliance Mission four years later.

The Lundgrens were married shortly before they left China in 1896. They went to Chicago, where Anton studied in a theological college. The Lundgrens spent two years in America, then visited Anton's family in Denmark before they returned to China in the early spring of 1899 as members of the China Inland Mission. A friend of hers described Elsa as having "a peculiar fascination" for Chinese women because of her black hair and porcelain white skin. She spoke Chinese "very well" and, "above all, she had a gracious manner and real love for them."[44]

In the middle of the night one day shortly after the Lundgrens and Eldred arrived, there was an alarm in the compound that Eva, afterwards, thought was "a rather comical scene." But it demonstrated how nervous the missionaries were.

Some Chinese neighbors were having an argument while drawing water from a well. Eva herself heard the commotion, but she was accustomed to hearing men working at night during the summer when it was cooler. Annie Eldred and the Lundgrens were not used to such goings-on, and Anton Lundgren was especially edgy because a crowd had taken after him and Charles Price a few days earlier when they rode by a Boxer drilling ground. In a "nervous chill," Eldred ran to the Prices' bedroom, calling out Eva's name. Lundgren rushed from his room as well, partly dressed and with a cartridge belt wrapped around his waist. He and Charles armed themselves. The "two warriors"—the "nightshirt brigade," as Eva called them—sallied forth, she mockingly reported, "marching 'quick step'—'trail arms,'" and searched the compound area but "found every one in profound slumber."[45]

Eva poked fun at the incident and was feeling optimistic the next day because the missionaries heard that the Dowager Empress "had to skulk out of the back door and the former Emperor is back in power."[46] The report was totally unfounded, but the *kuan* apparently believed it, and, without being asked, he ordered the arrest of the father or older brothers of any boys found drilling with the Boxers.

The next day fresh rumors came in, and Eva's mood swung from one extreme to the other. There were "startling reports that all the foreigners in Peking had been killed," and that a Mission courier had been attacked and the mailbags he carried taken from him. Then the *kuan* came out publicly in favor of the Boxers, who were drilling in two or three places in the midst of the city. But that evening a Chinese friend who had been at the *yamen* heard that foreign soldiers had surrounded Peking. And later that night a messenger arrived from Tai Yuan with a letter from George Farthing of the English Baptist Mission, saying that sixty thousand Russian troops were in Peking. Nobody knew what to believe. And Eva didn't know whether to celebrate the news about the Russians or to grieve. Russians were of the Eastern Orthodox faith and openly anti-Protestant. "If Russia gets the upper hand we may be invited to step out," she said.[47]

Not knowing what to think, Eva decided to pack and store "the things we care for most and hide them under the k'ang here in the sitting room." She stuffed all their winter clothing into a trunk and had an empty trunk ready to fill with other clothing in case they received word to leave for the coast. "We could get off in short notice now," she decided, but they would need a "strong escort" to cross Chih-li Province to the coast.[48]

The other members of the Oberlin Band in Fenchow-fu, Ernest and Lizzie Atwater, were also preparing to leave. Lizzie was now in her seventh month of pregnancy and wanted to be near a doctor. The Atwaters planned to go with their two young girls to Tai Yuan, about thirty-six miles north of Taiku, where there was a hospital run by Presbyterian missionaries. Once there, they could be united again with their two older daughters, who were attending the school for missionary children that the Pigotts had established outside of Tai Yuan in the village of Shou Yang.

The missionaries' guests—the Lundgrens and Annie Eldred—were also planning to leave. They were thinking of heading some thirty miles south to Ping-yao. For some unexplained reason, none of the missionaries made any real effort to get away before the fateful June 27 that all foreigners were to be exterminated. Perhaps they thought they would be safer in the Mission compound than on the road.

Their decision was never tested, however, because the day passed in both Fenchow-fu and Taiku without incident. There would be several such aborted deadlines set in the future for the killing of foreigners.

However, as the missionaries soon learned, that day two young female missionaries of the China Inland Mission whom the members of the Oberlin Band knew—Edith Searell and Emily Whitchurch—were brutally murdered in a village near Ping-yao.

In anticipation of trouble, the CIM missionaries there—the two Englishwomen and a family by the name of Saunders—had already destroyed all the church registers and lists of students so that Boxers would not acquire the names of any converts or sympathizers. The Saunders family fled the station when some three hundred Boxers broke into their compound and ransacked it on June 26. The two Englishwomen were apparently away at the time.

On the following day several youths created a commotion at the compound's front gate. A helper rushed to Searell and Whitchurch and told them what had happened. The two immediately went to the *hsien kuan,* the district magistrate, to complain. The official personally went to the compound, but, when he saw that only the front gate was broken and nothing else damaged, he slapped the helper. Seeing that, a crowd that had gathered on the street to witness the official's inspection stormed the compound.

The Englishwomen appealed to the *hsien kuan* to stop the rioters, but he responded that his men were meant to protect Chinese, not foreigners. Villagers and Boxers rushed inside the compound and surrounded the two women. Suddenly frightened, they knelt, asking for mercy. Boxers struck them with clubs. Others smashed bottles over their heads. The two women were knocked senseless and died about an hour later. After they were dead, their watches were taken, their clothes were torn off, and they were reportedly raped.[49]

Early in the morning, four days later, Louise Partridge was asleep in her home in Li Man when there was a sudden knocking at her door. She sprang up, threw on a wrapper and went out to open her gate. It was Francis Davis. He sat down and made an effort to talk offhandedly. The two missionaries chatted about one of Louise's schoolgirls.

Davis then broached the real purpose of his visit. He had received troubling reports about an attack on English Baptists in Tai Yuan. He said he didn't know what had happened to them—actually, he did, but he didn't want to panic Louise—but she understood what he was getting at. "Well," she said, "that's my leading that I've been waiting for. I must dismiss my school and go into the city." Davis agreed. That was where he was going, too. He had packed some valuables, keepsakes, and pictures at his dwelling in Jen Tsun and was on his way to Taiku himself. He would wait while Louise hired carts for her students and would accompany them the few miles into Taiku. That, of course, was why he had purposely made his detour to Li Man, but he knew that he could not pressure the independent-minded Louise into a decision; she had to make it herself.

Louise quickly packed a steamer trunk and box and made bundles of the rest of what she wanted to take. She went through the house, gathering summer and winter clothing and her foreign clothes. She had actually donned foreign clothes the day before, when she first heard about war being declared.

Louise waited until after breakfast before she told her schoolgirls. They knelt and prayed together. She told them they must not cry or show fear, because that would only increase their danger.

Louise, Francis, and the girls arrived without any interference at the South Suburb in Taiku just as their Oberlin Band comrades were sitting down to their midday dinner. Francis confirmed reports they, too, had heard about the English Baptists in Tai Yuan. The news was grim, but grimmer news came while they were eating—a letter from Fenchow-fu telling of an attack on the Atwaters; they escaped unharmed to the local *yamen,* but it had been a close thing.

After eating, they all gathered for a prayer meeting, and afterwards George Williams and Howard Clapp went to the *yamen.* They weren't able to see the *kuan*, but the magistrate's *menshang* (secretary) tried to comfort them, pointing out that while other places had suffered attacks, the Taiku mission had not.

The missionaries didn't know what to do. While it was true that the Atwaters had been attacked, it was their house outside the Mission station that Boxers had pillaged, not the Fenchow-fu Mission itself. Both it and their own Mission compound in Taiku had been spared so far. "We consulted and consulted and argued, and talked and couldn't agree," Louise wrote in a letter to a friend. "Some said, 'come in the city.' We ladies were all opposed to it and one gentleman undecided, but the other two, with two Chinese on their side, over-ruled us. The only point on this side was that we would be near enough to flee to the court-house for protection. It was really funny how it went; deciding and changing; deciding and changing. One fifteen minutes it was go, the next, stay."

Louise sent four of her students to the school court in the city compound, where Deacon Liu, Teacher Liu, and others were. She went back and forth between it and the South Suburb to see that they were settled in, "glancing over my shoulder to see no one was in sight. It was scary. Then we went to bed with our clothes on and passed the most miserable night of my existence."

About midnight Louise heard a noise and saw a lantern. A cart was at the gate. She thought it might be the Saunders family, fleeing from the Ping Yao area. But it turned out to be Deacon Liu's wife, who was so crippled that she walked bent over. Hearing that Boxers were going to storm her home in Che Wang, she hired a cart and escaped with two granddaughters.

Only the Clapps had been asleep, but Mrs. Liu's arrival had roused them, too. Her flight seemed to settle the matter: They would abandon the South Suburb. Everybody started frantically packing, dragging boxes up and down the stairs, and calling out to one another. When anyone tried to catch some sleep, someone else would wake them up with news he or she had heard before. "It was one long drawn out horror."

At daybreak, the missionaries set off for the city compound "with heavy hearts," expecting the South Suburb house to be destroyed that day. They split into several groups, so as not to arouse attention. One cartload of schoolgirls and women went by way of the West Gate, another by the South Gate. The men went around through the East Gate. Louise, on horseback with her "man," Kuo Hsiao Hsien, as escort, rode straight up South Street to the Mission compound with a cart of goods.[50]

Once inside the large Mission compound, the men, Chinese helpers, and schoolboys spent the entire morning barricading the front gate and walls. After a late dinner and a belated Sunday service, they hoped to rest, but a distraught Christian woman named Kao Wei Hua showed up with word that her husband had been arrested.[51]

The previous night, Boxers tried to gain entrance into the Kao home in a village less than three miles away. In the confusion, someone threw a stone and killed a Boxer. The head man of the village had her husband, Kao Feng Cheng, arrested and put in handcuffs that were too tight; his arms were turning black.

The young student Er Wu went to visit Kao in prison. Kao told him, "I have committed my body and soul to the Lord and am at peace."[52] The missionaries sent a protest to the *yamen* in an effort to secure his release, but it was ignored. Mrs. Kao subsequently paid to have larger handcuffs substituted for the ones blocking her husband's circulation. She also paid to have irons that were riveted around his ankles loosened.

Later on the day Mrs. Kao arrived with the news of her husband's arrest, the missionaries were at supper when they received word that all the gates of the city were closed. Ordinarily they weren't closed until 10 P.M. Had the friendly *kuan* turned on them?

"We looked in each other's eyes and saw a horrible fear," Louise said. "Mr. Clapp expressed it. 'Well, friends, he's got us cooped up here so he can do it easily.' "

The missionaries prayed and then, Louise wryly remarked, "we went out and did what we ought to have done in the first place, inquired into the truth of the matter."

The truth was the South Gate was shut but the North Gate was open, and later the gates were open and shut several times during the evening and heavy guards placed on both the South Gate and the East Gate. It really looked like the *kuan* was trying to protect them. As Louise said, it was a "queer Sunday."[53]

Alarms and rumors and "reliable" reports were to become part of the missionaries' daily life in both Taiku and Fenchow-fu. Most were false; some were half-truths or distorted versions of the truth; only a few turned out to be true. The ones that were true were always the worst.

SIXTEEN ❁ *Paotingfu*
The First Losses

We are pilgrims and strangers in the earth.
—Rev. Frank E. Simcox

Horace Pitkin was getting desperate. On Saturday, June 2, he sent a wire to Tientsin. It was brief: "Situation still dangerous."[1]

Pitkin had no idea whether the telegram would get through, or whether he, Mary Morrill, and Annie Gould could count on getting any help. Telegraph communication to Tientsin was sporadic at best. Boxers would cut the line, repair crews would mend it, and then Boxers would cut the line again.

For almost a month after the rail connection to Tientsin and Peking was torn up in late May, Boxers drilled in private in Paotingfu rather than openly. They were apparently uncertain how city officials would react to their training exercises—at least that is what the missionaries posted there believed. About a thousand Boxers were in the city, and their numbers grew almost daily.

When virtually all government troops pulled out of Paotingfu and headed north to Peking, members of the missionary societies were so anxious that they started to shut down their school operations. Presbyterian missionaries in the North Suburb informed Pitkin that they were having trouble keeping their servants. Then came a rumor that a Catholic church about nine miles south of Paotingfu was going to be burned, that that would be followed by the burning of the cathedral in Paotingfu, and that afterwards all foreigners and Christians—Catholic and Protestant—would be slaughtered.

Horace hoped that his appeal might be forwarded to Peking and reach the American minister, Edwin Conger, but by then the foreign legations in the capital city were already isolated. The wire did reach Tientsin but could not be sent on to Peking.

On Monday, June 11—two days after Boxers burned the grandstand of the International Race Course outside Peking, and a day after Admiral Seymour's force set off on its aborted relief of the Peking legations—Horace decided to try again. Afraid now that the wire might be intercepted by Boxers, he wrote it in Latin, and signed it Immanuel ("God is with us"):

> Quaestor Province nonvult protegere. Ceteri volunt. Solum spes yoreciv statim imperat Nieh mittere milites. Sex mille pugiles ad orientem liu obsidentes Romanos. Hodie volunt pugnare. Si vincant pervenient.
>
> (The Provincial treasurer not willing to protect. Others are. Our only hope is that the viceroy orders General Nieh to send soldiers. Six thousand Boxers are at the village of Tung Lu beseiging the Roman Catholics. They wish to fight today. If they conquer they will come over [against us].)

A friend of Pitkin's, J. Walter Lowrie of the Presbyterian Mission in Paotingfu, happened to be in Tientsin when Pitkin's first message arrived. For the next week he tried unsuccessfully to get the foreign forces in the city to send a relief column to escort the missionary community from Paotingfu. He and a CIM worker also visited the American and English consuls in Tientsin, urging them to bring pressure on the Chinese viceroy to send troops to protect all Paotingfu missionaries (this was before the Imperial Court came out on the side of the Boxers). Soon thereafter, however, the foreigners in Tientsin were themselves under siege. Lowrie was certain that Pitkin could manage to escape by horse from Paotingfu at night, but he knew that Horace felt he had to protect Mary Morrill and Annie Gould.

Lowrie also pressed Hudson Taylor of the China Inland Mission to urge all missionaries—CIM workers, Presbyterians, and the American Board representatives—to flee to the southwest, but, with the telegraph line so unreliable, most messages were not getting through, and, as far as it is known, the missionaries in Paotingfu never received any such alert. Even if they had, it was probably too late to escape.

Boxers began drilling openly in Paotingfu once word reached there that the legations in Peking were besieged and that missions in the capital and Tung Chow had been burned and hundreds of Chinese Christians killed. Then, on June 24, the Imperial edict calling for the extermination of all foreigners was issued. Within a matter of days, it was reported, General Li Ping-heng, who hated foreigners and was a bitter opponent of appeasing them, visited Paotingfu to order that the edict be carried out.

Even if Li did visit the city, the missionaries were unaware of his presence in Paotingfu, or, for that matter, of the edict. But Frank E. Simcox sensed a gradual shift in the attitude of local officials. On June 24, a Sunday, Simcox preached a sermon at the Presbyterian Mission on the topic, "We are pilgrims and strangers in the earth."

Meng Chang-chun—Meng I—was packing books and furniture four days later in the street chapel that the American Board Mission operated in the center of Paotingfu. Meng I, the older of the two brothers who were pastors with the Mission, was rushing to get everything packed and removed for storage so that he could seal the premises. That morning Boxers had seized two helpers in their lodging near the Mission compound. Pitkin thought it best to close the chapel rather than to invite any attacks on it.

Meng was being helped with the packing by a young North China College student, Chang Ch'iang Hsiang, whose mother was a Bible woman who had worked with Mary Morrill for eleven years. Ch'iang Hsiang got hungry about midafternoon and left the pastor to get something to eat. Meng continued to work alone, stowing Bibles and tracts in boxes. Suddenly, Boxers burst into the chapel and seized him. They bound him with rope and carried him off to a temple they were using as their headquarters.

By the time Ch'iang Hsiang returned to the chapel, the Boxers were gone. The young student quickly found out from neighbors what happened and ran to tell Pitkin. Horace immediately went to the *yamen* to seek help to get Meng released.

Ch'iang Hsiang, meanwhile, went to the room of Meng's sister, the Bible woman Mrs. Tu, to tell her the news. She urged him and all the other young men in the Mission to flee. "Why should you young men who are educated for the service of the Church throw away your lives?" Mrs. Tu said. "You can protect no one by staying here. If all die, who will lay the foundations of the Church again after the storm has passed? The work of us old people is finished; yours is not."

Ch'iang Hsiang's mother agreed. "I have consecrated you to the service of the Lord and I can not let you sacrifice your life for me," said Mrs. Chang. She thought it was "almost" a miracle that Ch'iang Hsiang's life had been spared when the Boxers seized Meng. "God wills that you should live."

The mood in the compound that evening was somber. Anxiety had turned to hopelessness. Horace had been unable to get any official to intercede on Meng's behalf. "We are not reading anything but the Bible these days, and are giving ourselves much to prayer," Pitkin told a Chinese helper. "We are not talking 'hsien hua' [idle talk] either, but making all our plans for heaven."

Horace seemed calm. He cooked a meal for himself, watered flowers, and pulled up some weeds. But that was only veneer. "It will not be long now," he told another helper.

Mary Morrill was fatalistic, too; she told Ch'iang Hsiang, "We shall see the Lord soon." Mary, Horace, and Annie urged their converts and servants to flee while they had a chance. "You hurry and hide away in the country," said Horace, "we cannot escape—if God will we go to Him, it is well."

Ch'iang Hsiang was torn about what to do. He did not want to leave, but his mother's pleadings finally persuaded him. He left the compound and made his way on foot out of Paotingfu, heading west into the mountains that separated Chih-li Province from Shansi.

What he did not know was that, despite her age, his mother also decided to flee. That night, after dark, the sixty-year-old woman left the compound in the company of a niece. But the two women soon lost their way and wandered aimlessly from village to village.

Sometime that evening or the next day, the Boxers tortured Meng, cutting off the fingers of both his hands. Then they beheaded him. They threw his body into a ditch behind their temple.

❁

About a mile away, on the day after Meng was seized, Dr. George Yardley Taylor was working in a dispensary that the Presbyterians ran in the city when an official from the *yamen* came by. The official asked Taylor for the keys to the dispensary, saying that he wanted to remove the medicines and furniture before Boxers looted it. It was an obvious ploy to get hold of the drugs and property, but Taylor could not do anything to dissuade him.

The official also urged Taylor to appeal for protection to some of his friends among the wealthy Chinese whom he had treated, but the doctor was realistic. "My gentry friends," Taylor said, "are only friends in the dispensary." The one person he might have approached, he continued, had fled that morning in disguise from the city. All the doctor could do was lock the dispensary and hand the keys to the official.

Taylor returned to the hospital compound where he resided with two other American Presbyterian missionaries, their wives, and three children. One missionary was a fellow doctor and close friend, Cortlandt Van Rensselaer Hodge. Both Taylor and Hodge were natives of Burlington, N.J., had gone to Princeton, and received their medical degrees from the University of Pennsylvania. Hodge was about to celebrate his twentieth-eighth birthday the next day. His wife Elsie was a popular member of the Mission; she was known as "Bonnie" because of her cheerful disposition. Hodge, who had been in China only fourteen months, was slated to replace a Presbyterian physician in Peking.

The other missionary was thirty-three-year-old Frank Edson Simcox, the same fellow who had escaped atop a roof when Boxers burst into a prayer meeting at a Presbyterian outstation in mid-May. He and his wife, May, were from Pennsylvania and had met when members of the Student Volunteer Movement at Grove City College in that state. They had served in Paotingfu for six years. The Simcoxes had three children—Francis, seven years old; Paul, five, and Margaret, eleven months.

About four o'clock on Saturday afternoon, June 30, just two days after Meng was seized, about twenty Boxers approached the main gate of the Presbyterian hospital compound. They were carrying cornstalks. The Boxers' leader, Chu-tu-tze, was wearing a button that the *Nieh-tai* (provincial judge) Ting-Yung had given him in appreciation of his zeal and energy. As the Boxers marched down the street toward the compound, a veritable army of neighbors and passersby fell in behind them. On reaching the main gate, the Boxers piled the cornstalks against the gate and set them on fire.

Inside the compound the missionary families raced for shelter. Taylor found refuge in an empty house. He was armed with a gun that one of the other missionaries had given him, but he was reluctant to use it.

The Hodges and the Simcoxes meantime barricaded themselves in the Simcoxes' home. They had a rifle, a fowling piece, and one or two revolvers.

The fire the Boxers set weakened the gate. They were able to break it down and rushed into the compound. They, and the crowd that followed them, went from building to building, looting the chapel and hospital and setting fire to a number of the residences inside. They killed any Chinese servants and Christians they found hiding; as many as twenty, including two old women, were either cut down or driven to jump to their deaths in a well. Boxers waylaid Taylor's assistant trying to escape. They robbed him and buried him alive in a shallow grave.

Upon reaching the empty house, the Boxers found Taylor standing at a second-floor window. The doctor threw away his gun without firing it and instead remonstrated with the Boxers. They responded by setting the house on fire.

The Simcoxes and the Hodges, however, fought for their lives. They shot and killed Chu-tu-tze and wounded about ten of his followers, but other Boxers succeeded in getting close enough to the building to set it afire. As flames and smoke billowed up, May Simcox rushed from the front door with her baby Margaret in her arms. She begged the Boxers to spare the child, but they pushed her and the girl back inside.

A coolie who once worked for Simcox saw him walking to and fro by a window on the second floor, hand in hand with his two sons, as flames engulfed the building. All of the Presbyterians—Taylor, the Hodges, the five Simcoxes—perished in the fires.

That night, on the other side of Paotingfu from the Presbyterian compound, a sense of doom pervaded the American Board Mission. The missionaries seemed to be waiting for the inevitable. Ironically, it was raining hard. The rain that everyone—Chinese peasants and missionaries alike—had prayed for in their own fashion had finally arrived. The drenching storm continued all through the night.

The missionaries passed the time as best they could. They prayed, they wrote letters, then they went around the compound, searching for places to bury the letters.

Horace Pitkin prayed with the Chinese teacher of the girls' school, then busied himself writing letters. One was to his wife, Letty, another to his missionary brethren, and a third to the foreign soldiers who he believed would eventually come to avenge the killings. He and Kuo Laoman, an old courier and general servant, covered the letters with waterproof material and buried them in several places behind his residence, including a dovecote. They buried the communion plate with his letter to Letty in a deep pit in the floor of one of the outhouses in the rear of the compound. Horace hid the letters sent to him by the Oberlin Band in Shansi in the cellar of what had been Dr. Willis Noble's home, where he and Letty had first stayed. Then he returned to his house and prayed with Kuo.

The old man had earlier brought tiny shoes for two of the schoolgirls with unbound feet in order to disguise them as ordinary Chinese. All the other schoolgirls had by then left the compound for their homes. Nearly all the Christians were gone, too, except for Mrs. Tu and her three children, three of Meng I's children, and a seamstress, Mrs. Chien.

Mary Morrill was in the chapel with Mrs. Tu, praying, when Kuo came to bid good-bye. "Now we can only wait," she said. "Our lives are in God's keeping. He may ask us to lay them down very soon."

Afterwards Mrs. Tu approached Pitkin and asked him what could be done. "Nothing can be done,—we must prepare for the worst," he answered.

At midnight, at Pitkin's urging, Kuo fled over a wall and escaped into the night. Just before he left, Horace said to him, "My letter may be found and destroyed. If you learn that it is, send word to Pi Tai Tai [Mrs. Pitkin] that God was with me and His peace was my consolation. Tell the mother of little Horace to tell Horace that his father's last wish was that when he is twenty-five years of age, he should come to China as a missionary." The two men then knelt and prayed again. Parting, Pitkin said: "Silver is of no use; gold is of no use; stand firm in the faith."

Horace was planning to preach his first sermon in Chinese the next day, Sunday, July 1, but early in the morning, Boxers attacked both the front and back of the American Board compound, trying to break down the gates. The pelting rainstorm was still in progress as Mary opened the front gate and tried to reason with them. She pointed out that the missionaries only felt love and goodwill toward the Chinese. "Why must you kill us?" she asked a government officer who was standing by with some thirty soldiers, watching but not interfering. "Because you prevent rain," the officer answered, although it was raining. "Then kill me," she said, "and let the Chinese go."[2]

Mary's plea was in vain. The Boxers pushed past her, forcing their way into the compound. Mary ran ahead of them and, with Annie Gould, fled to the chapel.

Horace suddenly appeared, armed with a revolver, one that he had carried with him on his honeymoon trip with Letty across Europe and the Middle East. He tried to intimidate the Boxers by firing it into the air, but the Boxers chased him toward the chapel. Several of them came across Mrs. Tu. They slew not only her and her three children but the seamstress Mrs. Chien and Meng's children as well.

Accounts vary as to what happened next. Some say that Boxers seriously wounded Horace while he was on the stone steps of the chapel, defending it, and that they beheaded him there. Others say that he joined Mary and Annie inside the chapel and held the rioters at bay by firing through the windows of the building until his ammunition ran out. Then the three of them leaped through a rear window into the schoolyard and took refuge in a small room off of it. The Boxers found them and dragged them out.

However it happened, Pitkin's hands were uplifted in prayer as he was decapitated, and they remained in that position as rigor mortis set in. Boxers took his severed head into the city to Ting-Yung's *yamen* and afterwards the *Nieh-tai* reportedly gave it back to the Boxers, who carried it to a shrine.

Annie Gould, who admitted having no "grit" for pain, had in the meantime swooned, her body rigid in an almost catatonic state. Boxers trussed her like a pig being carried to slaughter. Her hands and feet were bound and a pole thrust through them. She was carried like that out of the compound and through the streets. Other Boxers seized Mary Morrill by her hair, which had become loose and flowing, and dragged her along. Bystanders clutched and tore their clothing as they passed through the city. Mary exhorted the onlookers, reminding people of the good works the missionaries had done, and even gave some silver from her pocket to a beggar in the crowd.

Across the river from the American Board compound, the missionary family manning the China Inland Mission heard the firing coming from the American side. They—Benjamin Bagnall, his wife, Emily, daughter Gladys, and a guest, William Cooper—were frightened and confused.

A Chinese friend had urged Bagnall to leave Paotingfu, but the white-bearded old China-station veteran had a stubborn streak. He was a British navy warrant officer who became interested in mission work among the Chinese while serving in Asiatic waters. He left the navy when twenty-seven years old and worked for a number of different missionary societies and also as an agent of the American Bible Society. Emily had been in charge of the CIM girls' school in Tai Yuan when they met. He was now superintendent of a CIM district extending to the borders of Mongolia in the north and to Shantung in the south. The couple had two older boys who were away at a CIM school for missionary children in South China. Their home in Paotingfu was well known as a rendezvous for all English missionaries journeying into Shansi.

Cooper was their current guest. He had recently completed an inspection tour of Shansi for the China Inland Mission and was enroute to Tientsin when the Boxer troubles began. Cooper was not a healthy man. He had never fully recovered from being stricken with typhoid fever, was hard of hearing, and also suffered somewhat from a "weak chest," the result of an accident during a furlough in England.

Bagnall finally decided that they should all flee from the CIM compound and head for an Imperial military camp not far away. He thought they could seek refuge there. The four Britishers made it to the camp without difficulty, but, instead of taking them in, the colonel in charge confiscated their valuables and turned them over to Ting-Yung. The *Nieh-tai,* in turn, surrendered them to the Boxers.

A group of Boxers had caught up with Ch'iang Hsiang's mother, Mrs. Chang, after she and her niece separated. Her feet were so swollen from walking that she couldn't stand. The Boxers came upon her trying to crawl from a yard to find food. They struck her with swords until her body was "literally minced."

They beheaded another Bible woman, Mrs. Kao, who was caught in the city, trying to escape with her nineteen-year-old daughter Jessica, a graduate of the Bridgman School in Peking. For some inexplicable reason, after killing her mother, the Boxers left Jessica at an orphanage. Several months later her father found her, dying.

The Boxers led Mary Morrill and Annie Gould to the temple Chi Sheng An in the southeast section of Paotingfu. Once inside it, Annie regained consciousness and was unbound. She was standing and walking around when, not long afterwards, the Boxers led in the Bagnalls and Cooper.

Late that afternoon a grim procession made its way from the temple, through the city gate and toward the southeast corner of the high, crenellated city wall. Thousands of Chinese watched as the missionaries were marched in single file, shackled like criminals, to an execution ground for convicted felons.

Two Boxers led Bagnall by a rope, which was connected to the others. The rope was passed and knotted around his clasped and uplifted hands, then around his neck and then similarly about the hands and neck of each of the others—Mary, Annie, Cooper, and Emily Bagnall. Only little Gladys was not tied. She trotted freely beside her mother. As the missionaries walked slowly out the city gate, guns were fired and shouts rang through the air.

Nearing the corner of the wall, where there were a few tall, sparsely leaved trees, the group reached and stopped at a large earthern mound, evidently the grave of the Boxer leader Chu-tu-tze, who had been killed the previous day during the attack on the Presbyterian compound.

Emily Bagnall pleaded with the Boxers to spare her daughter's life. One of them suddenly thrust Gladys through with a spear as her parents watched helplessly. Then the Boxers made the adults kneel and one by one beheaded them with long, curved swords.

Afterwards the Boxers threw the bodies of the missionaries into a shallow pit. And because the Chinese believed that a person could not rest in peace in the afterlife unless his or her body was intact, they disposed of their heads separately.

SEVENTEEN ❁ *The Flight from Shou Yang*

Pray for the Governor of Shansi and the Emperor. . . . Any kingdom that persecutes, does it to its own destruction, so we must pray for them. Remember the Saints of old in the fire and how God saved them.
—Rev. Thomas Wellesley Pigott

No place in North China seemed safe, not even the most remote towns and villages across the mountains from Paotingfu in Shansi Province. Thomas Wellesley Pigott was keeping a low profile in Shou Yang. The local *kuan,* a friendly official, warned him that members of his independent mission should exercise caution about what they said and where they went.[1]

Ernest and Lizzie Atwater could only pray for the best. Their two oldest girls, ten-year-old Ernestine and eight-year-old Mary, were still with the Pigott family, too far away for their parents in Fenchow-fu to travel to get them. The distance between it and Shou Yang was well over 160 miles—a four-day journey at the least, and impossible to venture through in Boxer-infested Shansi.

Although situated in a mountainous region, and almost sixty miles east of Tai Yuan, the market town of Shou Yang was on the main road between Tai Yuan and Peking—between Governor Yü Hsien in the provincial capital and the Imperial Court in the Forbidden City. From early June on, Boxers trooped along the thoroughfare, some headed for

Peking, others marching farther into Shansi. Wherever they went, rumors began circulating that Christians were poisoning wells and marking doors with mystic signs.

For several days Pigott and the converts attached to his mission fasted and prayed for rain, and, indeed, it did pour. But despite the much-needed rain, their efforts were misinterpreted. Another rumor spread that Christians were praying for drought and were even denying themselves food in order to drive rain away. Still another rumor said that Christians were throwing iron balls into wells that ignited and dried up the water.

In the last week of June, the Scottish missionary was able to send Wang-ten-ren, a convert associated with missionaries since the Great Famine, to Howard Clapp in Taiku, a three days' trip. Wang carried with him a letter asking to borrow some money so that Pigott could pay off contractors working on a new house he had built. Wang made it back and forth to Shou Yang without being stopped. He returned with six "shoes" of silver—about 300 *taels* (more than $225)—that Clapp gave him.

Wary of what the future might hold, Pigott put aside some of the money, just in case of an emergency. He halted all operations of his mission except for holding religious services and the work at the opium refuge inside its compound.

On Sunday, June 24—though unaware of the Imperial edict issued in Peking that day calling for the extermination of all foreigners—Pigott preached a sermon, mindful of the perilous times his mission was living through. Wang's wife, Wenchuen, recalled his talking about going "home"—a word that to missionaries was synonymous with the idea of joining God in heaven:

> If God wants us to go home we are willing. Pray for the Governor of Shansi and the Emperor. China must suffer if she persecutes God's people. The Jews crucified Jesus, and afterwards were themselves crucified. Any kingdom that persecutes, does it to its own destruction, so we must pray for them. Remember the Saints of old in the fire and how God saved them.

The situation in Shou Yang took an alarming turn three days later when Yü Hsien issued a proclamation under his own seal warning converts to recant. Those who did, and who paid a fee, received a certificate saying they were no longer Christians:

The Pigotts—Thomas Wellesley, Wellesley William, and Jessie. The Christian, *November 29, 1900.*

> The foreign religion is pernicious (reckless and oppressive)—it insults the gods and injures the people; the Boxers are right (good) to kill and burn (you); and your crime has come upon your own heads. The foreigners' preaching is an evil device to deceive man; it perverts the heavenly doctrine and destroys the five relationship.

The following Friday, June 29, the ordinarily friendly *kuan* in Shou Yang sent for Pigott and told him that Yü Hsien had sent him a copy of the Imperial edict ordering the extermination of all foreigners. The edict, and Yü Hsien's own proclamation, meant he could no longer protect Pigott, his family, or any of his converts.

After Pigott left, the magistrate, evidently under orders from Yü Hsien, put out a proclamation offering a reward of one hundred *taels* (about $75) for every foreigner's head, and twenty-five *taels* (about $20) for that of each native Christian. The issuance of the proclamation immediately sparked an outburst of hostility against Chinese converts. About eighty Christians, including some connected with Pigott's mission, were killed. Even the *kuan*'s secretary was alarmed. He talked the magistrate into recalling the proclamation, arguing that many non-Christians might be killed by greedy individuals, but by then the damage was done.

Desperate, Pigott was in a quandary about what to do. Out of sympathy for Pigott's plight, the *kuan* had offered to escort Pigott and his family "north, south, east or west" out of his jurisdiction. But where was safe? Pigott gathered together his wife, Jessie; the teacher of his boarding school, John Robinson; and the French governess, Miss Duval, to discuss what they should do. Pigott was against abandoning the mission, but his wife was worried about the children—their own son, twelve-year-old Wellesley, and the Atwater girls who were in their charge.

As the missionaries debated, a helper interrupted them to deliver a letter from Tai Yuan with frightening news: The Baptist hospital compound there had been burned to the ground, and one of the Englishwomen attached to the mission had been killed. The news propelled them into swift action. They would flee Shou Yang immediately, though they had no idea where to go except to head for the mountains.

Pigott asked a helper, Li-pai, to exchange the silver saved from the amount Howard Clapp had sent him. Li-pai was a shepherd who had been baptized by Pigott five years earlier and subsequently devoted all his time to assisting him in missionary work. Li-pai went from shop to shop in Shou Yang, but none of the proprietors would change their silver into *cash.* Meanwhile, a man named Yen, who was the husband of a woman patient being treated at the mission, invited Pigott and his family to his village, Peh Liang Shan, about fifteen miles from Tai Yuan. He said it was not only small and isolated, but also that five of the ten or so families who lived there were Christians.

Pigott accepted the offer at once. He told all the converts on the mission grounds to flee. His wife Jessie prayed with the women before letting them out the back gate. She told one opium patient, "All come back afterwards." As the women left, she kept repeating *"to tao-kao, to tao-kao"*—"pray much, pray much."

The four foreigners, three children, and Li-pai left Shou Yang about four o'clock in the afternoon of June 29. Ernestine and Mary Atwater rode on donkeys, while Mrs. Pigott, Miss Duval, and Wellesley William were on ponies. Pigott, Robinson, and Li-pai walked beside them. Neighbors seeing them leave later broke into the Pigott house and carried away everything it contained, including its doors and windows.

The missionaries reached Peh Liang Shan after dark. They moved into Yen's home, a *yao* dug into the hillside. They tried to conceal themselves, but villagers had seen them. The next day, from morning until night, hundreds of curious persons crowded the yard in front of the cave dwelling.

Within two days Boxers were less than three miles away, attacking Christians in villages on the way to Peh Liang Shan. The crowd's appetite was whetted by the news of Boxers in the neighborhood. More and more people came from the surrounding area, curious about what might happen to the foreigners. Several Chinese started pillaging their belongings despite Pigott's attempts to remind them of all the medical work they had done for them in the past. Finally he resorted to a show of force. "See, we have a revolver and could kill at least six of you, but don't wish to do so," Pigott said, pointing to a weapon that Robinson carried. "If you wish to kill us you may," one of the pillagers answered. "We don't want to kill you, but only to get your goods."

Pigott decided that the missionaries' only hope was to return to Shou Yang and put themselves under the protection of the friendly *kuan.* Li-pai saddled the ponies and donkeys—a villager had been paid to guard them from the pillagers—and accompanied the missionary party as they set out to return to their own home. It was already sunset by the time they left. Outside Peh Liang Shan, they all knelt down to pray. But the prayers were in English, which Li-pai could not understand, so Thomas and Jessie Pigott prayed separately with Li-pai in Chinese. Then Thomas told Li-pai to flee. He would be safer on his own. The missionary party was an obvious target for Boxers.

(The Pigott party left Peh Liang Shan none too soon. Boxers came the next day, looted Yen's home and those of his sons, then burned them. Yen, his family, and the families of his sons fled into mountain ravines, but the Boxers searched for them. They found Yen almost immediately and killed him. They captured and tortured one of his sons to make him tell where the rest were hiding; they burned incense on his back and then placed a heavy stone on it. In spite of the torture, the son refused to betray his family. His bravery was in vain. Boxers eventually found other members of the family and slew thirteen of them, most of them women and younger members.)

The road out of Peh Liang Shan was slippery from heavy rains. The missionary party reached a narrow river outside of Shou Yang after several hours, but the river was swollen. They managed to cross it with some difficulty, but, as they got to the other side, they heard the voices of men searching for them in the dark. Then there were shouts in the darkness: "The foreign devils have come back."

The missionaries eluded the searchers by entering the East Gate of the city instead of the South Gate near the mission compound as might be expected. They made their way to their compound, reaching there about midnight. They found the Pigott home closed and sealed.

There was only one thing left to do. They all went to the *yamen* to seek refuge. The *kuan* refused to see them personally, but he turned over two dirty rooms usually occupied by runners. The *kuan* confiscated Robinson's weapon. Jessie Pigott pawned a ring to purchase food staples.

The *kuan* let the missionaries stay for three days, but then he sent word that he could no longer protect them. He said he would have his men escort them from his borders. That way they would be protected from Boxers. As an added precaution, he suggested that Pigott and Robinson wear handcuffs so that they would look like prisoners under custody and would not be further molested.

Meanwhile, the loyal Li-pai had not fled. Unbeknownst to the missionaries, he had followed them into Shou Yang and was staying in an empty shed near the North Gate, going out only at night, when he wandered the streets, listening to conversations, trying to find out what had happened to the Pigotts. He finally discovered that they were at the *yamen.*

Hearing a commotion on the street outside on Tuesday, July 3, Li-pai sneaked out of his hiding place to find out what was going on. People were rushing to the West Gate, where Boxers were in the process of beheading seven Christians. Li-pai recognized one of the victims, a Mr. Mi, a helper of Pigott's and also a teacher in the Baptist boys' school in Tai Yuan, who refused to recant. In all, throughout the district, seventy-one Chinese Christians, including eighteen women and eleven children, were slain that day—husbands in the presence of their wives and children in their mother's arms. One woman was buried alive. Worried that he might be recognized, Li-pai left Shou Yang and hid in a sorghum field, eating grass and unripe wheat to sustain himself.

After the executions were over, the Boxers went to the *yamen* and demanded that the *kuan* turn the Pigott party over to them. But the magistrate put them off by contending that the fate of the missionaries was in the hands of the governor.

On the night of Thursday, July 5, Pigott's helper Wang-ten-ren visited them at the *yamen.* Pigott gave him a letter addressed to friends in England. Wang didn't want to carry it, but he promised to give it to his wife, Wenchuen, for safekeeping. (Although he was careful about not carrying anything that would associate him with the missionaries, Wang was later seized by Boxers and brought to trial before a mandarin, a military officer, and a Boxer. They ordered that a circle be made on the floor and inside of it a cross. They commanded Wang to micturate on it. When he refused, he was led away and executed.)

That same day, July 5, Li-pai heard from a friend that the Pigott party was going to be escorted by soldiers to Tai Yuan. After dark, Li-pai left the sorghum field and walked along the road to Tai Yuan. After about six miles he stopped and hid beside the road.

In gratitude for the *kuan*'s help, Thomas Pigott gave two ponies to him and one to the head warder. In return, the missionaries were given eggs and bread for their journey and also two pairs of large handcuffs for Pigott and John Robinson to wear. The entire party was put into a big country cart and, with an officer riding in front and more than thirty soldiers on foot and on horse around them, they set off for Tai Yuan.

Li-pai spotted them about ten o'clock that morning, coming down the road towards him. He watched them pass, then waited until nightfall and skirted around them and ran ahead to a temple a couple of miles east of a village named Shetieh to wait again for them to pass.

Several times on the journey, the Pigott party and the soldiers guarding them ran into Boxers, but the soldiers always protected them from harm. At Shetieh, Boxers stopped the caravan and demanded that the soldiers hand over the prisoners. The soldiers refused to do so, but the Boxers noted that the handcuffs Pigott and Robinson were wearing were loose. Without even consulting the soldiers, the Boxers tightened them so much that the cuffs cut into the skin of the two men.

Apparently deciding it would be wise to leave the main road to Tai Yuan, the soldiers turned off onto a side road, heading for the town of

Yu tzu, where they were to be relieved by another squad of soldiers. The new escorts actually joined up at a village about three miles outside of Yu tzu when the caravan stopped for the night.

In the meantime, a perplexed Li-pai was waiting patiently for the party to pass on the main road. Finally, when they didn't appear, he retraced his steps and learned of the detour. Again he raced ahead.

Early the next morning, Sunday, July 8, Li-pai was hidden so close to the road that, as the missionaries passed by in the cart, he could hear Pigott, who was sitting in the front, talking to the carter. He was complaining to the man that the *kuan* at Shou Yang would not do anything to save his son Wellesley.

A Christian named Yung Cheng recognized Pigott when the caravan stopped in a village for lunch. Yung, whom George Farthing of the Baptist Missionary Society had baptized the previous fall, had been living at the Baptist hospital compound but fled when it was burned. He was heading back to Tai Yuan that Sunday afternoon when he saw the Pigott party pause in the center of the village. The missionaries' cart stopped next to a food shop and the soldiers accompanying them—only about eight of them now—went inside and purchased some cakes and *mien.*

Jessie Pigott had to feed her husband the small cakes and the boiled strings of dough because his hands were so tightly cuffed. Robinson was able to feed himself. A group of villagers assembled to watch them eat. Pigott and Robinson started talking to them about Jesus and the Gospel. An astonished bystander said, "You are to be killed for preaching, and yet go on doing so."

As Pigott spoke to the onlookers, he spotted Yung. He signaled him to come to his side. He asked Yung about their friends in the English Baptist mission.

Li-pai was now traveling by daylight, figuring that he wasn't known in the neighborhood of Tai Yuan. He headed for the house of a relative who lived outside the East Gate of the provincial capital. Once there, he hid amidst the straw in the man's granary.

The Pigott party was stalled outside Tai Yuan. Boxers along the road became so threatening that the military escort had chosen to stop at a village about three miles shy of the city.

As a result, the missionaries did not reach Tai Yuan until the evening of Sunday, July 8. As they approached the city, two hundred soldiers, both on foot and on horses, met them and escorted them inside the city gate and through the streets. Guards were posted everywhere—on the city walls and in the streets.

The missionaries were taken to the district prison, a miserable compound that was off a little lane to the right of Yü Hsien's *yamen.* Atop its high mud walls were thorns to prevent the prisoners from escaping. Once inside, they were separated. Still handcuffed, Pigott and Robinson were put in a huge cell that housed other male prisoners. The prison governor came by to check on them. He assured Pigott that they were all going to be sent to the coast.

Jessie Pigott, her son Wellesley, Miss Duval, and Ernestine and Mary Atwater were placed in a cell in which two or three Chinese women were already incarcerated. It was next to a room with an idol that was used as a shrine. The walls and roof of the cell were black with the smoke of a cooking stove in the center. If nothing else, the smoke kept the cell smelling sweet. Its small windows were covered with wooden bars. To left of the door was a *kang,* on which the women and the girls were expected to sleep. The prison governor brought them meat and bread. He told Jessie that they were being detained for their own protection and would be escorted to safety. Later, the daughter of the warden, walking by the courtyard where the cell was located, saw Jessie talking to a woman accused of murdering her husband, telling her about Jesus.

Pigott asked to be taken to the home of the head of the English Baptists, George Farthing, but he was told that other foreigners were already assembled near the governor's *yamen,* in a compound that now housed not only their friends from the Baptist Mission but also all the Catholic clerics in Tai Yuan.

EIGHTEEN ❀ *Tai Yuan*

The Courtyard of Slaughter

My associate must be the man who proceeds to action full of solicitude, who is fond of adjusting his plans, and then carries them into execution.
—*Confucius*

The English Baptists spent a harrowing two weeks once the first news of the confrontations between the Imperial government and the international Powers in Peking and Tientsin reached Tai Yuan. An Imperial decree, posted in the city's telegraph office on Monday, June 25, said that war had begun at Taku and that Boxers had destroyed two foreign ships. (The Taku forts had been captured, and Peking was under siege, but no ships of the Powers had been destroyed.) The Emperor was pleased, the decree went on, and "now even children were able to use the sword and protect the country."[1]

Ominously, another decree was pinned up the next day, saying that Boxers were assembling in Tai Yuan and that officials were to see that they received 200 *tan* of rice (more than 13,000 tons; a *tan* was equal to 133.33 pounds). Moreover, the decree also said that on the first day of the sixth moon—that is, the following day, June 27—officials were to award Boxers 100,000 *taels* of silver (more than $75,000).

Hearing of the decrees, two English missionaries went to the telegraph office to read them for themselves. Neither of the decrees carried an official seal, so they decided not to take any notice of them. They were satisfied that they were false. Whether the decrees were legitimate or not, the import of what they inferred became clear the following day at the Baptist compound of the Schofield Memorial Hospital in the southeast section of the city.

Although the hospital compound was extensive, the Baptist contingent was so large—there were sixteen of them—that only four families and a single female missionary could be accommodated inside its walls. They included Rev. and Mrs. James Simpson, who had served in China for thirteen years; Rev. and Mrs. George W. Stokes, who were veterans of nine years' service; and Rev. and Mrs. F. S. Whitehouse. The lone female missionary was thirty-year-old Edith Anna Coombs of Edinburgh, who ran the mission's girls' school. The doctor in charge of the hospital was Arnold E. Lovitt. He, his wife, and son John (they called him Jack) also lived in the compound.

Visiting with the missionaries at the time were a Scottish couple, Dr. and Mrs. William M. Wilson, and their baby William. The Wilsons had planned to return home several months earlier but postponed their trip in order to help the Chinese during the famine. Wilson, who ran a hospital and opium refuge at his own expense in a desolate region of Shansi, had bought up large supplies of grain and donated them to the local populace. Their stopover in Tai Yuan was meant to be brief. The doctor was taking his family to the coast, where they intended to board a ship for England, but they were stranded in Tai Yuan for the moment because travel was impossible.

The remaining missionary family attached to the Baptist mission, the Farthings, resided in their own compound outside the hospital compound but not far away. George Farthing, who conducted the language examinations taken by several members of the Oberlin Band, lived there with his wife and three children—Ruth, Guy, and an unnamed baby. The children had a young governess, Ellen M. Stewart, who had been a bridesmaid at the wedding of Ernest and Lizzie Atwater. The Farthings also had guests, two middle-aged female missionaries who worked together for the China Inland Mission at an outstation in south Shansi—Mildred Eleanor Clarke and Jane Stevens.

Close by the Farthings were the only other English family residing in Tai Yuan, the Beynons. W. T. Beynon was a member of the British and Foreign Bible Society. He and his wife, Emily, had three children—

Daisy, Kenneth, and Norman, all of whom were ordinarily students at the Pigotts' school in Shou Yang, which had closed for the summer. They were playmates of Ernestine and Mary Atwater. Alexander Hoddle, an independent missionary who ran a religious bookshop, boarded with the Beynon family.

Late in the afternoon of the day after the rewards for the heads of missionaries and Chinese Christians were posted, the missionaries inside the hospital compound went about their duties without a break in routine, unconcerned despite the dire threats. Dr. Wilson's wife took her son over to the Farthings to play with the Farthing children and planned to spend the evening there. The girls' school that Edith Coombs operated closed as usual in the afternoon, but eleven pupils were still there, waiting to be picked up. One of their teachers, Chang Wen Ts'ui, a twenty-one-year-old graduate of the Bridgman School, went to take a nap. At six o'clock Coombs went to the Stokeses' house to join them for dinner.

In the street outside a great crowd began to gather. A helper who worked for Farthing, Liu-ching-hsuen, was just arriving on an errand, when he saw the people milling around. Liu rushed back to Farthing's home to alert him. The two men went at once to inform the *hsien kuan;* the district magistrate immediately told his superiors. At the same time, two local officials went to the *yamen* of Yü Hsien and asked the governor for permission to protect the foreigners. Yü cursed them and forbade them to do anything to help.

Emily Beynon was coming in a cart to visit with Coombs when she came in sight of the hospital compound and saw the crowd. She immediately turned back. Soon afterwards, the missionaries inside the compound, alarmed by the growing noise outside, spread the word for all to assemble in the Lovitts' courtyard, which was the innermost of the compound. Everybody—missionaries, pupils, Christian helpers, and servants—rushed there as the crowd, suddenly turning unruly, lit a bonfire at the front gate. It started to rain a little, which doused the fire, but someone rekindled it. The flames gradually spread from the roof of the gateway to the hospital building, the chapel, two school buildings, and the missionary houses.

Details differ as to what happened next. One story is that the prefect and about twenty or thirty soldiers reached the compound, saw the buildings on fire and simply stood by on a dustpile, watching.

By about nine o'clock, the flames approached the courtyard where the missionary party was hiding. The missionaries unlocked a little gate opening onto a barren plot off the street and urged the Christians to escape. But one old man, Lao Chen, the schoolgirls, and their teacher Chang Wen Ts'ui remained, afraid to leave on their own. About an hour later, the Lovitts' house was set on fire, and the missionaries retreated to the only refuge left, a tiny kitchen close to the back wall of the compound, where all of them squeezed together into the cramped space. Coombs and Wen Ts'ui tried to calm the frightened schoolgirls, who were crying.

As the flames crept closer and closer, the missionaries decided to make a break for it. Stokes and Dr. Wilson guarded the rear while the other missionaries walked in front; Mrs. Simpson carried little Jack Lovitt because his mother was ill. The schoolgirls were in the middle. Lao Chen was carrying one of them, a sick child who was too weak to walk. Edith Coombs was helping Ai T'ao, a teenager who was lame; her feet had recently been unbound.

Amazingly, the group made its way from one courtyard to another without hindrance. All around them buildings were burning and Chinese were rushing about, shouting and looting. But once they reached the gateway leading to the street, they stopped abruptly. The gateway was ten feet wide, but Boxers had set such a great bonfire there that only a passage of about three feet was left at one side. The missionaries decided to make a rush for it. They were pelted with bricks and struck with sticks as, one by one, they edged by the bonfire and ran the gauntlet in the street.

As she passed through the gate, Mrs. Lovitt's dress caught fire, but she was able to extinguish it quickly. A man tried to block their path, but one of the missionaries shot him. The smoke was so dense that Wen Ts'ui could not see anything in front of her or hear anything but the howling of the mob and the sound of shots. In the confusion, the missionaries did not notice that Edith Coombs was not with them.

Wen Ts'ui stumbled over the body of the man who had been shot, but she managed to get to her feet and reach the corner of the street. She heard a voice calling her name and, out of the smoke, came Lao with the sick girl on his shoulder. "Where is Miss Coombs?" she asked.

Edith Coombs had gotten out of the gate but turned back when she realized that Ai T'ao and another pupil, Fu Jung, had not followed her through the narrow gap by the bonfire. She went back inside for them. The two girls were huddled near the wall, too scared to move. Coombs carried Fu Jung to the street outside. Then she went back for Ai T'ao, who was bigger and heavier. She was supporting the lame girl as they passed through the gate when she stumbled suddenly and fell to the ground, pulling the girl with her. The crowd started to throw brickbats at them, then a man rushed up and struck Coombs over the head. Coombs covered Ai T'ao with her body and whispered into her ear, "Don't be afraid; we shall soon be where there is no more pain or sorrow. We shall soon see Jesus."

Coombs rose to her feet and begged the crowd to spare the girl's life. Someone led Ai T'ao away. Several men then seized Coombs and threw her on the bonfire. She managed to get up from the burning pile, but they shoved her back on it. She staggered to her feet again, walked a few steps, then knelt and started to pray. "See, she is pleading for her life," someone called out. "It is no good." Coombs was thrown back on the flames. People piled a door, tables, and boards on top of her so she couldn't move. They watched as she burned to death.

The other missionaries split up; some sought refuge in the home of the Beynons, others went to the Farthings'. George Farthing and Dr. Wilson went to see the *tao-tai.* The circuit intendant promised to send soldiers to protect the missionaries, but he said that he could nothing else for their safety unless he received specific instructions from Yü Hsien. The next day, Yü Hsien sent three minor officials to inspect Farthing's house.

Wondering what was going on, Farthing wrote a message on a slip of paper and gave it to Hei Kou (Li Yu or Black Dog) whom the missionaries in Taiku had sent to Tai Yuan to find out what was happening. Hei Kou had somehow managed to slip into the city without arousing any suspicion. Farthing was afraid to hand him any letters, but he made out a simple cable message on a tiny piece of paper in the hope that the Taiku missionaries would be able to get it through to Tientsin.[2]

Farthing and, this time, Dr. Lovitt went to see the same *tao-tai* the following day. As they went to and from his *yamen,* a great throng of people formed behind them, shouting *"Sha! Sha!"* Yü Hsien sent word that he could only promise to protect the missionaries if they would go to the *kong kuan,* a compound that enclosed a residence house for officials that was near his own *yamen.* The house was once the railway bureau and used also as a residence by visiting engineers. Yü said he could keep a protective eye over them there.

Yü's offer was repeated on Thursday, July 5, by the three minor officials, who again visited Farthing's house. "If you ask for protection you must go to a house in Chu Teo-hsiang street," they said. The government house had four courts, they explained. The Baptists could occupy two of them, and the Roman Catholics, whose mission was near the North Gate of the city, could use the other two. Farthing was skeptical. "If you order us to go, we will go; and if you mean to kill us we must still go." The officials replied: "Oh, no, that is not our intention. We really mean to protect you."

Farthing acceded. The Protestants planned to move into the *kong kuan* the next day, but it was raining so hard that day that they asked for a delay until Saturday. But it rained also on Saturday. The missionaries asked for another delay, but Yü Hsien refused another postponement: the word came that "even if it rained swords they must at once move to the new house."

Although it was still raining so hard that few people were out on the streets, the Protestants were afraid of being spotted and waited until dark to move. It was nearly midnight when the carts carrying them and their goods set off from the Beynon and Farthing compounds for the center of the city where the *kong kuan* was located. Five Chinese helpers accompanied them.

When they reached the government house, they found that the inner courts were already occupied by the Catholics—two Italian bishops who had been in China more than thirty years each and went by the Chinese names of Ai and Fu; two priests; a lay brother; seven Sisters of Mercy who had arrived in China a year earlier; and five Chinese attendants.

As the Protestant contingent of twenty-seven persons settled into the compound with the Catholics, the Pigott party was stopped for the night in a village outside Tai Yuan. They were taken to the prison near the *yamen* the next day.

Farthing and his colleagues kept busy early in the morning a day later, Monday, July 9, cleaning up their rooms and the courtyards at the *kong kuan.* Several of the women were in the kitchen, preparing for lunch. Shortly before noon, a subprefect arrived to make a list of all the foreigners and Chinese in the compound. Once he left, Farthing sent a servant to summon a mason and a painter to make some repairs. The two workers were in the compound, fixing a wall and whitewashing it when, at about two o'clock, Yü Hsien, dressed in official robes with all his signs of rank, appeared at the *kong kuan* accompanied by a number of officers and soldiers. At least they were dressed like soldiers. Actually, they were Boxers that the governor had recruited and outfitted.

Afraid that Catholic converts might attack to free the bishops—Chinese Catholics were known to be well-armed—the governor had taken a circuitous route to reach the *kong kuan.* He mounted his horse and surrounded by his troops proceeded as though he was going out of the city by the North Gate. But before reaching there, he wheeled around and headed to the *kong kuan.*

Once inside, Yü Hsien ordered the arrest of everybody—Protestants, Catholics, helpers, and servants, even the mason and the painter. No one resisted. They were tied together with a rope like criminals and led, single file, out of the *kong kuan* and toward the governor's *yamen.*

Liu-ching-hsuen had gone to check on Farthing's home that morning. He found soldiers looting it. He started back to the *kong kuan* to inform Farthing, but when he reached Chu Teo-hsiang Street he found it full of soldiers. One of them, with a shield and sword in one hand, was dragging a young Catholic girl by the hair with the other hand. Unable to enter the *kong kuan,* Liu watched in horror as two soldiers with drawn swords led Farthing from it. Behind him were two of his children being carried by soldiers. Frightened, Liu fled.

The schoolteacher Chang Wen Ts'ui had sought refuge in the home

The notorius Yü Hsien, governor of Shansi. Courtesy Oberlin College Archives.

of a photographer who was a friend of the English Baptists. Suddenly, a young Christian man, pale with excitement, came running there with terrible news. He was walking down the street by the governor's *yamen* when he saw all the foreigners and some Chinese tied up and coming towards him in a long line similar to the way condemned criminals were led to execution.

Yü Hsien's *yamen* was at the end of a narrow, crowded street that was bordered on both sides by single-story, slope-roofed houses. A wide open space separated the *yamen* from its neighbors. Overlooking it and in front of the gateway was a huge screen with a dragon's face on it that was intended to keep evil spirits out. The screen was bracketed by two tall poles.

Yung Cheng, who had spoken with Thomas Pigott just days before in a village outside Tai Yuan, was in a street near the *yamen* when he saw a large crowd gathering. Yung went to see what was happening. The crowd was following the Protestants and Catholics from the *kong kuan.* Yung heard people say that they were going to be executed. He tried to fight his way out of the crowd, but it had become so dense that he couldn't. He was dragged along with it as people pushed and shoved their way toward the open space in front of the *yamen.*

Each of the missionaries, men and women alike, had been stripped to the waist, as was the custom with condemned criminals about to be beheaded. No one cried out, not even the children, though they covered their eyes with their hands. Transfixed, Yung couldn't help but witness what happened next:

> The first to be led forth was Pastor Farthing. His wife clung to him, but he gently put her aside, and going in front of the soldiers, himself knelt down without saying a word, and his head was struck off by one blow of the executioner's knife.
>
> He was quickly followed by Pastors Hoddle and Beynon, Drs. Lovitt and Wilson, all of whom were beheaded with one blow by the executioner. Then the Governor, Yü Hsien, grew impatient and told his bodyguards, all of whom carried big beheading knives with long handles, to help kill the others. Pastors Stokes, Simpson, and Whitehouse were next killed, the last one by one blow only, the other two by several.
>
> When the men were finished the ladies were taken. Mrs. Farthing had hold of the hands of her children who clung to her, but the soldiers parted them,

and with one blow beheaded their mother. The executioner beheaded all the children and did it skilfully, needing only one blow; but the soldiers were clumsy, and some of the ladies suffered several cuts before death. Mrs. Lovitt was wearing her spectacles and held the hand of her little boy even when she was killed. She spoke to the people saying, as near as I can remember, "We all came to China to bring you the good news of salvation by Jesus Christ; we have done you no harm, only good; why do you treat us so?" A soldier took off her spectacles before beheading her, which needed two blows.

When the Protestants were killed, the Roman Catholics were led forward. The Bishop, an old man, with a long white beard, asked the Governor Yü Hsien why he was doing this wicked deed. I did not hear the Governor give him any answer, but he drew his sword and cut the Bishop across the face one heavy stroke; blood poured down his white beard, and he was beheaded. The priests and nuns quickly followed him in death.

None of the members of the Pigott party had any inkling of the executions of the Protestants and Catholics until they were lined up at the prison by soldiers and escorted from it to the *yamen.* The ground in front of Yü Hsien's compound was soaked in blood, and in cages atop the poles were the severed heads of their friends. Portentously, before the Pigotts returned to Shou Yang from England in 1899, their precocious son Wellesley, who, though only twelve years old, taught Chinese boys in Sunday school, had told relatives, "We can't be martyrs in England, but my father and mother and I might be in China."

Yung Cheng was still trapped in the crowd as soldiers pushed their way through it, leading Pigott; his wife, Jessie; John Robinson; Miss Duval; and the three youngsters. Wellesley was holding his mother's hand. Ernestine and Mary Atwater clutched the hands of the Frenchwoman. The children were crying:

> He [Pigott] was still handcuffed, and so was Mr. Robinson. He preached to the people till the very last, when he was beheaded with one blow. Mr. Robinson suffered death very calmly. Mrs. Pigott held the hand of her son, even when she was beheaded, and he was killed immediately after her. The lady and two girls were killed also, quickly.

Afterwards, all the bodies were stripped of clothing, rings, and watches and were dragged to a vacant lot just inside the South Gate of the city. The heads of the four adults were put in cages that were slung from each of the city's four gates. On the next day all the bodies were tossed on the execution ground outside the city, where wolves and dogs roamed, and soon their remains could not be distinguished from the remains of criminals who had been executed there.

In all, that day, Yü Hsien had personally supervised the slaying of thirty-three Protestant and twelve Catholic missionaries, as well as numerous Chinese, including those who were seized along with the Baptist missionaries. One of them was a fifteen-year-old boy who was a student of Pigott's in Shou Yang. No one was spared, not even the mason and the painter.

The orgy set off a frenzy of bloodletting in Tai Yuan and its neighboring villages. "A carnival of crime" was the way Chang Wen Ts'ui described it. The young teacher was still at the photographer's house when Boxers raided it. Wen Ts'ui was able to escape to an abandoned village, where she hid in a cellar room. When she was finally able to go home, to a village south of Peking, she discovered that her father, mother, and younger brother had been killed.

In and around Tai Yuan alone, nearly fifty Chinese Christians of all persuasions were killed in the next twenty-four hours. Hundreds of others were slain in the days that followed, including a colporteur who distributed tracts for Pigott; a church probationer whose two sons attended the Baptist school; the mother, father, and older sister of one of the schoolgirls who escaped from the hospital compound; and nearly all of the forty-odd members of the church in Shetieth, among them Li-pai's brother, who had been baptized barely three weeks before.

It is said that a number of the governor's subordinates had tried to intercede on behalf of the missionaries and that Yü's mother, a woman in her eighties, had also tried to dissuade him from executing the foreigners. It is also said that afterwards she made him kneel in front of her for an hour.

Whether any of that is true cannot be verified. One thing is indisputable. The man who became known both as the Butcher of Shansi and the Chinese Nero was not through yet by any means.

NINETEEN ❁ Taiku

Cornered

The blood of the martyrs
is the seed of the Church.
—Tertullian

Some thirty-six miles away in Taiku, the Oberlin Band missionaries were wrestling with a serious moral issue: whether they should resist any attack on the compound with force or turn the cheek and accept their fate. In other terms, should a Christian resort to violence when faced with violence? The dispute dragged on for weeks in the face of increasing attacks on missionaries and their converts. "We are a very divided company," Louise Partridge sadly remarked at one point.[1]

On the fateful Sunday of July 1, when Horace Pitkin, Mary Morrill, and Annie Gould were slain across the mountains in Paotingfu, George Williams hastily buried the Mission ledgers and roster of Christian converts in a hole by the back wall of his house in the South Suburb of Taiku. Then he and all the other members of the station moved into the main Mission compound on South Street in the city. The *kuan* assured them that he could protect them if they were inside the city gates, but his assurance did not allay the fears of many of the missionaries. Those like Howard Clapp, who was opposed to meeting violence with violence, argued that they should trust the *kuan.* But others, like Williams and Francis Davis, insisted that the missionaries prepare for the worst and fight to save themselves.

A "council of war" was held the first night they were all gathered in the city compound, and a compromise of sorts was worked out: No one was to fire at any attackers unless the gates of the compound were broken in. Night patrols were set up with the men and schoolboys taking turns on the walls; counting the missionaries, teachers, and students, there were twenty-four males who could be called upon. Davis was responsible for the watch by the front gate. Williams took the back gate. Each of the Chinese was given a white piece of cloth to wear as a headband to make identification in the dark easy. To supplement the few revolvers the missionaries had, they stocked bricks, tiles, stout clubs, and bottles of ammonia near the gateways and walls. The beating of a gong was to signal an attack. Women and children were to go to a certain room, while the men manned the barricades; to mask the women's hiding place, blinds were put up to cover the windows.

As a last refuge the missionaries chose a ramshackle old mill shed that adjoined the exterior of the rear wall of the Mission compound. It was on the premises of a deserted temple next door. The windows and doors of the building had been bricked up, leaving only a small opening that could be easily covered. The missionaries put some benches in the building and placed a ladder near the back wall so that they could quickly climb over it and into the temple courtyard. All were supposed to sleep in their clothes, with a candle and a bundle of necessities nearby in case flight became necessary.

Clapp, who was a steadfast pacificist, was not happy with the arrangements. He refused to budge on the issue of putting up any resistance. The missionaries had only six revolvers—two of them unreliable. When someone suggested that they purchase more weapons to defend themselves, Clapp was adamant. "We who believe in the Lord," he said, "ought not to put our trust in foreign arms, but we should meet death trusting in the Lord."[2]

Davis, whose home in Jen Tsun was looted once he left it, was just as firm in believing that they should defend themselves and argued against giving up without a fight. Rowena Bird agreed. She said she wished everyone had "a good revolver."[3]

Deacon Liu and some of the Chinese teachers and helpers offered another solution to the dilemma: The missionaries should escape into the hills. George Williams tried to act as the peacemaker between the groups, but the dispute flared continually as the weeks passed. "Mr. Clapp got up and *declared* he wouldn't resist, all against him, much dissatisfaction," Louise Partridge noted in a diary she started to keep.[4]

The arguments raged back and forth, putting everyone on edge. One day their spirits were up, the next day their spirits were down. The constant mood swings created an atmosphere of short tempers and frequent quarrels.

Rowena Bird woke up on the morning of Monday, July 2, feeling momentarily encouraged. It had rained heavily during the night, and many of the Mission people were able to get some sleep at last. But at breakfast Rowena found that Clapp had "seemingly given up hope," and that Sang Ai Ch'ing, the medical helper, and Teacher Liu looked "gloomy" as well.[5] Clapp was saying that no matter what the others did, he was not going to resist. Deacon Liu, who agreed with him, was praying against putting up resistance, and neither Sang nor Teacher Liu was cooperating with defense preparations. "I will not fly," Teacher Liu insisted. "Outside everywhere there are Boxers and God can take care of us as well in one place as another. I shall stay and die here."[6]

"Mr. Clapp rests very little and is almost beside himself," said Louise.[7]

Clapp, in fact, was becoming increasingly depressed, and his sense of hopelessness was beginning to become infectious. "I have felt for several years that Satan would stir up a great persecution for China," he wrote in a diary he began. He believed it likely that their "fate" would be "settled" before the message that George Farthing had written on a tiny slip of paper and handed to Hei Kou for forwarding to Tientsin ever reached Tientsin.[8]

The division finally became so serious that a private council and prayer meeting were held "unbeknownst to leader"—that is, without the senior member of the Mission, Clapp. The others—Davis, Williams, Bird, and Partridge—obviously felt it necessary to take the initiative. "Mr. Williams thot [*sic*] it just for strengthening," Louise noted, "and said little & prayed little."[9] Rowena said that although "the strain is hard," she felt "more & more that I can confidently trust my future with God[;] I believe also more & more in strenuous self defence."[10]

That is exactly what they decided on—"strenuous self defence." If Boxers tried to get into the compound, the missionaries would not wait until attacked personally but would fight back immediately. The decision was made on July 4, ironically another day designated for their extermination. "The glorious Fourth" got Rowena to thinking: "If some American soldiers could march in here today, wouldn't we celebrate though."[11]

Ignorant of the deaths of their three American Board colleagues in Paotingfu, the missionaries tried to relay Farthing's brief cable message. Davis sent the tiny slip of paper to Pitkin with an accompanying short note: "Americans alive but in great and imminent danger." He added a postscript intended for the eyes of the American minister, Edwin Conger, in Peking: "Cant [*sic*] you make Peking officials order him [Yü Hsien] to spare us? Our Mission number 15 souls." (The fifteen referred to the members of the Oberlin Band in both Taiku and Fenchow-fu.) Williams added his own postscript to the note, a request to a bank in Tientsin, asking for $500 in Chinese money.[12]

The messages were never carried out of Shansi Province. The helper picked to take them across the mountains—Louise's "man," Kuo Hsiao Hsien, whose home was in Paotingfu—dawdled at first, started out finally, but eventually turned back after several days on the road, saying he had run into Boxers. Unaware of the full extent of Boxer infiltration of the countryside, the missionaries did not believe him.

They were, however, very nervous. About 10:30 on the night of July 5, when everyone else was asleep, one of the Chinese women heard some noise outside the compound on South Street and, frightened, went to the head of the stairs leading to the second floor of the main house. The woman called out in alarm that Boxers were coming.

Jennie Clapp, Rowena and Louise were asleep together in an upstairs bedroom. At the sound of the alarm, they panicked and rushed hurriedly toward the stairs, evidently without lighting any candles. Rowena raced downstairs in the dark ahead of Jennie and Louise, in a rush to help the Chinese women and children. Jennie followed, with Louise behind her. Jennie started down the stairs but in the dark she missed her footing on the topmost step and fell the entire length of the staircase.

Dr. Sang and her husband were summoned. At first, everyone thought that Jennie had suffered only a sprained foot, but she said her arm felt bruised, too. Dr. Sang took off Jennie's dress and discovered a deep, wide, three-inch-long cut just under her armpit, where Jennie tended to be quite fleshy. Blood streamed from the wound, soaking her undergarments. It took five stitches to sew it up.

The accident so traumatized Jennie that she needed constant attention. "Poor Mrs. Clapp," Rowena said, "timid at any time, and now feeling so helpless."[13] Jennie could not walk without assistance and was so weak from the loss of blood that Rowena felt it necesssary to sleep next to her on a cot. Her accident seemed to doom what little hope anyone had for fleeing. "If it should come to running as a last chance of life, what could we do now?" Rowena wondered. "Why can't any word be got to the coast?"[14]

Jennie's husband consoled her with the thought that her accident might be a godsend. She had always thought that seeking refuge in the *yamen* was their only hope, but Howard believed that "would mean death in the most horrible way." Now that she couldn't walk, she had to stay put in the compound, which he thought was best anyway.[15]

There were constant reports now of converts in outstations being so intimidated that many of them were recanting. None of the missionaries, however, ever wavered in his or her faith. Louise, who admitted that she was getting "awfully irritable under this close confinement,"[16] said:

> If you want to know how folks feel facing death . . . [a]sk someone who has been there. Mr. Williams says that it is strange how little it affects us and it is. . . . I am ready & not afraid. Thats [*sic*] all I can say.[17]

Louise wrote her parents:

> We still hope and shall as long as breath remains in us but the clouds seem thicker. We know God can save us but are not sure it is ordered in His plan. Why should he save us alone from among so many[?].

"Oh, my darlings," she added, "I have not once 'looked back' and I'm ready to go forward still if God spares my life."[18] Louise hoped, she said, "I'll never become a broken down missionary and have to spend years sitting with folded hands. No, no, let me die with the harness on, laboring to the last to let the divine light into the souls of men; that would be worth while."[19]

On watch duty one night, George Williams told young Er Wu, "I must die in China, but if I die in China my wife will not grieve to distraction. She is too well-informed for that and will know that I have not died eternally but that in the hereafter we shall meet again in heaven." He was "very glad," he added, that his wife and three daughters were not in Taiku "to endure this terrible suspense. That is exceedingly fortunate."[20]

Every afternoon at three o'clock, the missionaries prayed together with their church members. At five in the afternoon, they held a Bible reading. One day, Howard Clapp read from Luke 9:23–27, exhorting the Mission Christians "with a perfect heart and with a strong heart to trust in the Lord"[21] :

> And he said to *them* all, If any *man* will come after me, let him deny himself, and take up his cross daily, and follow me.
>
> For whosoever will save his life, shall lose it: but whosoever will lose his life for my sake, the same shall save it.
>
> For what is a man advantaged, if he gain the whole world, and lose himself, or be cast away?
>
> For whosoever shall be ashamed of me, and of my words, of him shall the Son of man be ashamed, when he shall come in his own glory, and *in his* Father's, and of the holy angels.
>
> But I tell you of a truth, there be some standing here which shall not taste of death till they see the kingdom of God.

Together, American and Chinese alike, they committed to memory John 14 and 15:

> Let not your heart be troubled: ye believe in God, believe also in me. . . .
>
> And if I go and prepare a place for you, I will come again and receive you unto myself; that where I am, *there* ye may be also. . . .
>
> If ye love me, keep my commandments:
>
> And I will pray the Father, and he shall give you another Comforter, that he may abide with you for ever; . . .
>
> . . . Let not your heart be troubled, neither let it be afraid. . . .
>
> Abide in me, and I in you. . . .
>
> This is my commandment, That ye love one another, as I have loved you.
>
> Greater love hath no man than this, that a man lay down his life for his friends.

No matter how deeply they seemed to be resigned to their fate, the missionaries could not avoid being profoundly shaken by reports of new incidents of brutality. They were particularly upset when a member of the Taiku church, a Mr. An of Tung Fang, was attacked while he was tending his sheep. Thirty men and boys pounced on him, tied him up, and cut him to pieces; afterwards they burned his body. An was the first Taiku church member to be killed. Later, Boxers looted two shops in Tung Fang and killed a man, a non-Christian who frequently attended Sunday services. For some reason, afterwards a rumor spread through Tung Fang that vengeful foreign troops were coming; several Chinese women and girls jumped into wells and drowned themselves.

Boxers also burned two men in another village for supposedly poisoning wells at the behest of Christians. Kao Wei Hua, whose husband was imprisoned and tortured, was betrayed by a brother, who identified her as a Christian to Boxers; they hacked Mrs. Kao to death on South Street and burned her home.

On the other hand, there was some solace in the fact that their friend, the young *kuan* himself, was said to be out every night, checking that order was being preserved on the streets. He had some insolent Boxers arrested and punished with twelve hundred blows. It was a relief of sorts when Louise could jot in her diary: "Still safe, slept well, no relaxation of diligence. Very warm[,] sweat profusely sitting quietly in room."[22]

One morning a Christian merchant came by with the news that proclamations against the Boxers had been posted, forbidding the Boxers to practice or to spread wild reports about Christians poisoning wells. That was favorable news, indeed. But the missionaries later learned that the proclamations turned out to be nothing but instructions to shopkeepers to hire private watchmen, because Boxers had been going around destroying any goods, such as oil lamps, that were imported from Europe. "I suppose," commented Rowena, "a bit of good news rests one and does one good even if in a short time it proves to be false."[23]

Ominous signs began to appear. The missionaries watched as shopkeepers started moving out of stores neighboring the American compound on South Street. Then the night patrols became aware that two men were keeping an eye on the compound. And one day a man asking for Teacher Liu was allowed into the compound. He purportedly had come all the way from an American Board station in Shantung Province. But the missionaries were suspicious of his behavior and through questioning they discovered he was a spy, evidently sent to reconnoiter the compound's defenses. He was politely shown the gate.

The missionaries didn't know what to believe. Each report or every rumor that their helpers heard out in the street seemed to be contradicted the next minute by a new report or another rumor. Was it true, as they heard one day, that legation buildings in Peking had been burned and that foreign troops had destroyed the southern part of the city in retaliation? Fearing that it might be true, and that a full-scale war might break out, Rowena wrote her brother, "I cannot think that England and America will be thoughtless of the fact that there are hundreds of foreign residents in interior China and rashly proceed to a measure that would mean certain destruction to them."[24]

The missionaries learned of the massacre in Tai Yuan on July 11. Rowena wondered whether their converts would stand by them now that government soldiers were involved in killings. "It takes all the courage out of them," she noted in a journal she was keeping.[25] That same day, the police chief sent a friend to suggest that the missionaries withdraw into the hills until the danger was over. "But it looks too much like a trick," Howard Clapp thought. "It will be no harder to die here on our premises than in the hills."[26]

Even though Jennie Clapp was better, Howard was still against fleeing. But the other members of the Mission finally decided to try to make a run for it, and they made plans to do so with or without the Clapps. On July 12 they and the students in the compound prepared food and packed clothing and bedding. In the hope of not arousing suspicion, they planned to set out in groups of two or three and rendezvous at the South Suburb compound. From there they would head into the hills together. They planned to travel with six horses and two carts. To protect them, six of the older students were going to don soldiers' uniforms and act as a bogus military escort. Where they hoped to procure the uniforms was not clear.

However, someone mislaid a package of silver that was going to be left for the native helpers. The missionaries searched all over for it without success, wasting so much time that they decided to delay their departure until the next day. On the following day, one of the native teachers who was halfhearted anyway about going suggested that first they should check again with the *kuan* whether they would be protected if they remained in the city compound. "O, yes," the magistrate responded, "I will give them protection. Are they not all Americans?"[27]

The *kuan*'s promise calmed the fears of some of the missionaries. Louise Partridge, for one, was persuaded to remain. "We won't go," she wrote in her diary. "No thanks, we prefer protection." But she may have had second thoughts because the sight and sound of a motley troop of government infantry marching through Taiku later that day *"frightened"* everyone.[28]

Clapp was more concerned about the increasing number of converts who were recanting than he was about his or Jennie's safety. He urged the Mission Christians to hold fast in their faith. "'The blood of the martyrs is the seed of the church,'" he reminded them. "If that is the way I can best serve Christ, I am ready to die."[29]

But the reign of terror was working, and the Chinese Christians were scared. Late in the night of July 12, the Mission got word that Yü Hsien was ordering not only the deaths of the missionaries but also the death of any Christian found with them. People were reported to be gathering at the *yamen* with knives, and the streets were said to be hung with red lanterns.

The Chinese at the compound were "all much depressed" by the news[30] and the next day a "general breaking up" started.[31] Women who had fled Tung Fang when the Boxers attacked the village started back home. Teacher Liu and his wife were planning to leave, too. The teacher was reluctant, but he decided that perhaps he ought to go with his family to the country. He took the teacher Ruth Fan and blind Lois (Ching Huan txu) with him. The Sangs left, too, heading for the hills. But none of the refugees had any food with them, and they aroused suspicion when one of the men had to buy a hundred small bread cakes each morning. They hid in a mountain cave, but their arrival caused talk: All the women had unbound feet. After several days they felt so uneasy that they decided to return to Taiku. Mrs. Liu; her daughter-in-law; Ruth Fan, and Lois went to the Lius' home in Che Wang, while the rest made for the South Suburb compound.

The missionaries were again confused about what to do. "We talk of fleeing can't decide," Louise noted.[32] "Terror everywhere," Rowena reported. "The whole province is in uproar and no one's life is safe."[33] The missionaries revived their plan to escape, hoping to travel south and then work their way to the coast. This time Howard Clapp had a change of heart, and he and his wife decided to go, too. But no sooner was the decision made to leave than the *kuan* ordered all the city gates closed early, effectively blocking the missionaries from escaping.

Among the Chinese who were trying to convince the missionaries to leave Taiku and escape into the hills was K'ung Hsiang Hsi. All this time, despite the importunings of his family, the young college student stayed with the missionaries, helping to build the barricades and running errands. His sister Chin Fêng was with Louise Partridge when Louise abandoned Li Man. She had unbound feet, a sure sign that she was a follower of the missionaries. Hsiang Hsi hired a cart to take her to her grandmother's home in an outlying village. Upon returning, he was questioned by a man at a shop, "Don't you Christians say that there are no gods?"

"No, but we say there is only one God," Hsiang Hsi replied. "Haven't you heard the first commandment?"

The man called out to some Boxers nearby that there was a Christian in their midst. Three of them rushed toward Hsiang Hsi; two were brandishing clubs, the other a huge knife. Hsiang Hsi drew his pistol from his belt and aimed it at them. They stopped in their tracks, and he was able to get away.[34]

Together with Er Wu, Hsiang Hsi went back to the South Suburb one afternoon to retrieve some clothing, medicines, and other articles for the missionaries. They loaded the items in trunks, which they covered with hay. On the way back through the South Gate, soldiers halted the cart and spotted the trunks under the hay. Hsiang Hsi made certain they also saw the pistol in his belt. "Do you search all the trunks that go through this gate?" he asked. In the background came the cry *"Sha!"* It was picked up and repeated by a crowd that started to form. *"Sha! Sha! Sha!"* But an officer, sensing trouble, approached and permitted Hsiang Hsi and Er Wu to pass through with the cart.

The incident at the South Gate had an unexpected result. A rumor spread that the two young Christians had brought six huge cannons into the city compound. For several days there was comparative quiet.[35]

Day after day Hsiang Hsi's father, K'ung Ho-ting, came to the compound to plead with the youth to leave the missionaries. The uncle with whom Hsiang Hsi lived wrote stern letters reminding him of his responsibilities. "Are you not of the noble clan of Confucius, the only son of your father, his hope and pride?" he asked. "Where is your filial love?" The uncle threatened to have Hsiang Hsi arrested for unfilial conduct, which was a crime.[36]

Hsiang Hsi visited the uncle after the missionaries learned of the massacre at Tai Yuan, to find out if the uncle, an influential member of the Taiku gentry, knew what the *kuan* would do. The missionaries had heard that Yü Hsien had sent the magistrate strict orders to have them killed. The uncle was pessimistic. The situation had changed, he said. The missionaries could no longer count on official protection from the *kuan.* The gentry had already appealed to him to send the foreigners away rather than see them murdered because of all the good works they had done. Besides which, their presence in Taiku was a peril to the entire city. Once they smelled blood, Boxers went on a rampage, killing indiscriminately and pillaging and destroying shops no matter whether they did business with foreigners or not. The *kuan* agreed—he had evidently inspired the visit of the police chief and the suggestion that the missionaries leave the city—but he said that the missionaries had feared treachery and refused to leave.

Hsiang Hsi's uncle demanded that he stay in the K'ung compound, but the youth refused. Actually, he wasn't sure what to do. He visited Jennie Clapp, who told him he must decide for himself. But George Williams urged him to flee. So did Rowena Bird. "I don't want you to stay and die with us," she said. "When the end comes I want you to try to escape over the wall."[37] So that he would have money to make good his escape, Rowena gave Hsiang Hsi a belt into which she had sewn several pieces of silver. As for herself, Rowena said: "If the work which the Lord wants me to do in China is not yet finished, the Boxers cannot harm me. I will just trust in Jesus. The suffering will not be long, then I shall be with Him."[38]

Both Rowena and Louise gave Hsiang Hsi letters they had written to their families. Watching Rowena writing a farewell note to her mother, he began to cry. "Hsiang Hsi, do not grieve so for me,—I am not afraid to die," the young woman said. "And whatever comes to me, I know that my mother will not regret my coming to China. I do not know whether I have helped a single soul, but if I have, I do not regret coming."[39]

Hsiang Hsi planned to escape into the mountains with Er Wu. But Ruth Fan gave him some clothes for his sister, and the Sangs asked him to secrete their surgical instruments. So Hsiang Hsi tried to sneak into his uncle's courtyard at dawn to leave the items there. He got inside, but his father and a servant saw him. His father had Hsiang Hsi immediately locked in a room. The young man was distraught but helpless. He asked his father to take a message to Rowena Bird: "I am a prisoner. Fly? I have no wings. Die? Death will not come to me."[40] In turn, Rowena asked the father to tell Hsiang Hsi that he would find the thoughts in her heart if he started reading the first chapter of Philippians, beginning with the nineteenth verse:

> For I know that this shall turn to my salvation through your prayer, and the supply of the Spirit of Jesus Christ,
>
> According to my earnest expectation, and *my* hope, that in nothing I shall be ashamed, but *that* with all boldness, as always, *so* now also, Christ shall be magnified in my body, whether it *be* by life, or by death.
>
> For to me to live *is* Christ, and to die *is* gain.[41]

On Tuesday, July 17, Boxers attacked Che Wang, where Teacher Liu's family lived. The family was warned that the Boxers were coming and fled before their arrival. But Liu's daughter-in-law remembered that she had left some money in the house, and she foolishly returned to retrieve it just as the Boxers appeared. She was killed. Blind Lois—the young woman who was Lydia Davis's first pupil in the girls' school she founded in Fenchow-fu—was killed at the same time. "When will the end come?" Rowena asked.[42]

The latter half of July was comparatively peaceful, though little is known about what new rumors and fears gripped the members of the

Taiku Mission during this time. There is no evidence to suggest that they were aware of the fact that foreign troops had finally seized control of all of Tientsin and were massing to march on Peking. If they did write home during this time, the letters were lost.

The last surviving letter that Francis Davis wrote, to his wife Lydia, was dated May 28, 1900, but it included additions he made through June 10, and ended: "With love unbounded and full of joy in your sweet and precious love and love to all the folks. God be with thee till we meet again."[43]

Rowena Bird, in a continuing letter that she began to her brother on June 24, made almost daily entries. She closed off the letter on Friday, July 13, with:

> There is so much I would like to say but cannot, though it may be the last word from me you will ever get. Hsiang Hsi offers to send to his home any letters we may wish and when the country is restored to peace, if it ever is, they will be sent to Tientsin. I must say goodbye to you all, dear mother and all of you. . . . Our people are scattering. We cannot wonder. I think some of them would die for us if they could thus save us but to feel that staying simply means being killed with us, as the Tai-Yuen-fu Chinese were, without being able to is more than they can do—poor people these are dreadful times for them. All will be protected who deny their religion. . . .
>
> If you never see me again, remember I am not sorry I came to China. Whether I have saved anyone or not, He knows, but it has been for Him, and we go to Him.
>
> Darling ones—goodbye.[44]

A journal Rowena also kept runs from June 25 through Wednesday, July 18, and echoes much of what she wrote her brother. She began to add to the journal the next day, but never got beyond writing "Thurs. 19." Why she stopped so abruptly is unclear, unless it was to hide the journal or to send it to K'ung Hsiang Hsi for safekeeping.

Louise Partridge's diary—with its short, almost cable-like notations—stops on Saturday, July 14, after a recitation of all the converts who had fled from the Mission: "men nearly all gone."[45] Howard Clapp, who started his diary—addressed to "Dear ones at home"—on "July 4, 12:30 A.M.," wrote his last entry on Sunday, July 15:

> We still live. . . . I arose this morning very much perplexed and for a couple of hours was very unhappy but after breakfast we foreigners met and read John 14

> and again cast ourselves on the Lord and now my heart is at peace. I have never enjoyed such peace at a time of anxiety and trial. The Lord is very good to us. . . . I am anxious now to keep my heart stayed on Christ. He is our help and our shield. This very likely is the last I can write unless the Lord should see fit to deliver us in a miraculous way.[46]

There was a final flurry of messages from the Oberlin Band in Taiku in the last week of July, when a courier was evidently able to travel between Taiku and Fenchow-fu. Rowena wrote to Eva Price there on Friday, July 27: "We are still here & the city quieter than last week though dreadful things are still going on around us." She reported on the murders of blind Lois and Teacher Liu's daughter-in-law as well as the massacre at Tai Yuan: "No words can express what we feel and there is no use trying to write." The missionaries had been told that foreign troops were on the way and that the Dowager Empress had abandoned Peking and might be in Tai Yuan. "We hear our Magistrate has gone to Tai-Yuen today," she wrote. "It is not sure that it means anything bad for us & we hope not." She added, "We have been kept so long ought we not to hope for the best."[47]

The report about the Dowager Empress was, of course, untrue. The siege of Peking was still going on, and as yet no troops were on their way to relieve the legations there.

Both George Williams and Francis Davis also sent notes to Fenchow-fu that Friday—to Charles Price. Both men were so concerned that their American Board colleagues there would worry if they learned what their messages contained that each man added to the top of his brief remarks the admonishment, *"Don't read aloud."* Undoubtedly, they were afraid of upsetting the Atwaters, whose daughters had been slain.

Davis reported on the "sad news" from Tai Yuan, but, he said, "We are all well." The Taiku Mission had experienced "a comfortable month. We have had all sorts of rumors but no wars."

He hoped the Fenchow-fu missionaries were well "and that the day of our deliverance draweth nigh."[48]

"Oh! The horrors of these days!" the letter from Williams began. "Will they ever end?" Williams repeated a number of other false rumors—all learned from the local *yamen:* that the foreign settlement in Tientsin was burned and that not a foreigner was left in Peking, though it was surrounded by foreign troops. He graphically described how the Tai Yuan missionaries were "beheaded like criminals" and "their heads put in cages in the city gates." Williams said, "All are well here but ugly as can be," an indication that everyone's nerves were on edge. George was not bashful about saying where his feelings now lay. In an uncharacteristic moment of vindictiveness, he confessed, "I pray for vengeance."[49]

On Monday, July 30, a neighbor identified a man named Tai to Boxers as a Christian who attended the church in Taiku. The Boxers immediately seized Tai but promised him his freedom if he told them whether the missionaries had cannon, dynamite, mines, guns, or any other "foreign magic." Terrified, Tai told what he knew. The Boxers then killed him.[50]

That same day K'ung Hsiang Hsi's uncle told him that there was a report on the street that a proclamation to protect the foreigners had been issued, and that Hsiang Hsi would be able to visit his friends in the American Board compound the next day. Hsiang Hsi was excited. His only contact for almost two weeks had been with a senior from North China College who had showed up at the K'ung compound about the middle of July after trekking hundreds of miles from Paotingfu. The young man was Chang Ch'iang Hsiang, whose mother, Mrs. Chang, a Bible woman attached to the American Board station there, had been killed by Boxers.

Ch'iang Hsiang had escaped to a mountain inn outside Paotingfu and, while there, heard men talking about a fire back in the city. He climbed the mountainside and saw off in the distance the Presbyterian mission in the North Suburb burning.

Ch'iang Hsiang set off immediately in the only direction he thought was safe: out of Chih-li and across the mountains into Shansi. He reached Tai Yuan several days after the massacre there. Seeing Boxers dragging a Catholic woman away to be executed, he took to the road again, heading farther into Shansi. He came to the Mission compound in Taiku on July 19. It was raining hard and no one was in sight. Ch'iang

Hsiang knocked and knocked, but no one answered. In despair, he went to a shopkeeper and asked where the home of the K'ungs was.

K'ung's uncle was suspicious. Ch'iang Hsiang's shoes were worn to shreds, his stockings in tatters. His legs were swollen, his feet bleeding, and five of his toenails had fallen off. He hardly looked like a college schoolmate. The uncle sent for Hsiang Hsi and had him hide behind a screen to observe Ch'iang Hsiang, just in case the bedraggled-looking youth wasn't who he claimed to be. Hsiang Hsi recognized his friend at once. "He came out with a bound as soon as he saw my face," Ch'iang Hsiang later recounted. "We had strange, sad stories to tell."[51]

Ch'iang Hsiang stayed the night. The next day, refreshed and newly outfitted, he left with money Hsiang Hsi gave him, heading toward the school where Hsiang Hsi's father taught, about three miles away in the countryside.

The visit cheered Hsiang Hsi. For the past two weeks he hadn't been able to eat or sleep and had left his hair unshaved and unkempt, as though he were in mourning. Friends thought he was losing his mind. Hsiang Hsi longed to do something to help his missionary friends, so when his uncle informed him that he could rejoin them, his spirits lifted.

Hsiang Hsi rose about midmorning the next day, Tuesday, July 31, the sixth day of the seventh month according to the Chinese calendar. He bathed, shaved, and changed his clothes for the first time since being locked up by his father. He ate a morning meal about eleven o'clock, as was the custom, and then was so weak that he lay down again for a brief rest before going to the Mission compound.

His uncle went that morning to the examination hall and was working on an essay when a shout ran through it that Boxers were coming. He rushed home to stop his nephew Hsiang Hsi before he went to the Mission compound. A sleepy Hsiang Hsi was roused with the cry, "The Boxers have come!" A cousin said they were burning the compound in the South Suburb. Hsiang Hsi shrugged off the news; the burning of the abandoned residence and other buildings there had been expected for weeks. But then someone else came in with word that it wasn't the compound outside the city that was on fire but the Mission on South Street.

Hsiang Hsi started for the door, but his uncle stopped him and had him locked in a room in an inner court. It had a latticed window that looked out toward the city. From it, Hsiang Hsi could see smoke rising a half mile away. He could even hear the howling of a mob and rifle reports.[52]

Er Wu was at the Mission that morning.[53] After his friend Hsiang Hsi was confined in his uncle's house, Er Wu tried to flee with the Lius. He had turned back when they did.

There was no indication that morning that anything was awry. Everyone gathered in the chapel at nine o'clock for the usual morning worship service. Deacon Liu led the Bible reading. A day or so before, according to one story, he was called to the *yamen* and offered protection if he would recant; he had refused. Liu read from Ephesians and spoke at length of Paul's captivity, early martyrdoms, and the history of persecutions from the earliest times to the present. The service ended with the singing of the hymn, "My soul be on thy guard." The missionaries "were very happy together," Er Wu recalled.

Afterwards the youth went to the South Suburb to get some stores from the compound there. His trip there and back was uneventful. The streets were quiet. Before noon a servant who had worked for Thomas Pigott arrived, asking for help. He was robbed of everything after the Pigotts left Shou Yang for Tai Yuan and barely escaped with his life. Louise Partridge went upstairs to her bedroom to get him some money. It was the last time Er Wu ever saw her.

The day was very hot, and, after the usual one o'clock dinner, some of the Christians drifted out into the courtyards to rest. A servant was putting irons on the stove in preparation to do some ironing. Deacon Liu was in his room, sipping tea and fanning himself by a window. It was Rowena Bird's thirty-fifth birthday, but there is no indication that any special celebration was planned.

Suddenly a watcher cried out: "The Boxers are coming in a great crowd." Marching down South Street were not only Boxers, but also soldiers. The soldiers, members of the *kuan*'s military escort, were in the vanguard under the command of a leading Taiku landowner, Meng Ta Hsi, who hated foreigners. Behind them came the Boxers, some of whom were on horses. A man identified as T Chieh tzu led them. Some of the Boxers were from the city and some from neighboring villages. In all, there were anywhere from two hundred to a thousand Chinese heading determinedly toward the compound, the soldiers with rifles, the Boxers with swords and pikes. They were shouting *"Sha! Sha!"*

Er Wu and some of the other youths ran to the missionaries to alert them. They found them "perfectly quiet." Er Wu went next to Deacon Liu. He sat motionless, as though nothing was happening, his face "a picture of peace."

"Be quiet, keep your hearts at peace," the tall Chinese pastor said. "It is all right, don't be afraid."

Er Wu's older brother, sixteen-year-old Chang Cheng Yü, a pupil in the boys' school who was known familiarly as Fu Ssi Ching, ran across Er Wu in a courtyard. He was armed with a knife. The teenager urged Er Wu to flee. He said he wasn't going to run away; he wasn't afraid.

The Boxer horsemen were wearing red turbans and red sashes. Each carried under his arm a roll of matting plundered from the shop of a Christian mat seller about a block away. The Boxers stood the rolls of matting against the front gate and lit them with matches. Others threw wood from a restaurant across the street onto the flames. Fan P'ei Ch'eng, a Mission courier, climbed to a roof overlooking the gateway and threw some bricks down on them. But when the fire spread to the building he was standing on, Fan had to climb down. He ran to the rear of the compound.

Er Wu and some of his school companions were already at the rear wall and climbed the ladder to see what was going on. They could hear the hideous shouts of the mob and saw that flames and smoke were starting to spread through the large compound. Realizing that there was no hope of staying without getting killed, Er Wu said they started over the wall:

> My heart failed me. I ran up the ladder, got into the temple court, climbed a tree near the outer wall, and jumped from its top into another tree several feet below, and so escaped into the street. Two others followed me in this line of escape. The city gates were closed and guarded, but we scrambled up the city wall, jumped into a tree-top, slipped to the ground, and made our way to the mountains.

The Boxers swarmed inside the compound. A cripple, Wu San Yuan, stepped in front of them. Wu was already an old man when he had converted. His hope was to see the face of Jesus. "Brothers," he said, hobbling up to the Boxers, "let me go first to Heaven."

They struck him down and killed him.

Some Boxers and soldiers spied Deacon Liu, sitting unperturbed, still fanning himself, by his window. They ran into his room. T Chieh tzu's son killed him with his sword, then beheaded him, cut out his heart, and dismembered his body. "Who ever thought," his father gloated, "it would fall to my lot to have the happiness to know that my own son should kill Liu Feng Chih!"

The other Christians and the missionaries had fled to the rear wall and were starting to climb the ladder into the courtyard of the neighboring temple. Two cousins, Shieh hsing heng, who had worked for a time as the gatekeeper at an outstation, and Shieh hsing san, whom Howard Clapp had baptized, ran up and told the missionaries that soldiers were killing Deacon Liu.

Stunned by the news, Jennie Clapp looked at the cousins "too much overcome to say anything." Rowena Bird and Louise Partridge urged the Shiehs to leave the missionaries and save their own lives. Howard Clapp gave his diary letter to Shieh hsing heng, who stuffed it behind an ankle strap underneath his robe. The two Chinese men took off over the wall.

Fan reached the rear of the Mission compound to find a confused and bewildered Jennie Clapp. "P'ei Ch'eng, what can we do?" she asked. "Where can we go?" Someone helped Jennie up the ladder and over the wall.

Fan didn't think he could be of any more help. He vaulted over the wall, into the temple courtyard and over another wall to the West Gate of the city. It was closed, so he started to climb it, but he was caught by soldiers and imprisoned. Fan was unusually fortunate; the soldiers were sympathetic and hid him from the Boxers.

Meanwhile, the missionaries and some of the remaining Chinese, about twelve of them in all, hid in the bricked-up shed. With the afternoon sun beating down on the windowless little structure, it must have been stifling inside. But as sweltering and cramped as it was, they felt safe for the moment at least—the Boxers were too busy looting the compound.

One Boxer, however, got curious about the ladder propped against the back wall. He went to investigate it. He climbed the ladder and dropped into the temple courtyard. He then climbed to the roof of the shed, perhaps to see if he could spot any of the fleeing Christians and missionaries from there. His weight was too much for the decrepit roof. It broke in. Francis Davis looked up as it did, saw the Boxer and fired his revolver, wounding the man.

The sound of the shot brought other Boxers to the spot. They tore open the roof. The Boxers rained bricks and pikes down on the penned-in missionaries and Christians. It is not known whether the missionaries tried to fire back, or if they did, whether they wounded or killed any of the Boxers.

Accounts vary as to what happened next. Some say the Boxers kept at it, heaving bricks, until everyone was dead; then they broke open the shed and beheaded the lifeless bodies. Others say that the Boxers broke a hole in the wall of the shed, filled it with straw, and set the straw on fire. The fire flushed the missionaries and Chinese from the structure. They were already "beaten half to death." The Boxers stoned them until they were dead. T Chieh tzu's son, who had already killed Deacon Liu, is said to have personally slain Rowena Bird. After that, the Boxers cut off all their heads.

The toll was great: Deacon Liu, Rowena Bird, Howard and Jennie Clapp, Louise Partridge, Francis Davis, George Williams; Er Wu's brother Chang Cheng Yü as well as his sister and her husband; a student named Kuo Ma Erh; helper-teacher Lin Chen; old and crippled Wu San Yuan; a woman from Tung Fang, Mrs. Wang, and her little son; and church member Ch'ang Pao Erh.

To impress people that the missionaries were criminals of the worst class, the Boxers hung the head of Francis Davis over the North Gate and Jennie Clapp's head at a village south of Taiku identified variously as Nan Ti Ts'un or Nan Hsieh. Her husband Howard's head was hung for a time at a temple in the village of Chao Yang, where the Boxer leader T Chieh tzu lived. Later their heads and the heads of Rowena, Louise, George, Deacon Liu, and a student—either Chang Cheng Yü or Kuo

Ma Erh—were sent as a gift to Yü Hsien. A Chinese evangelist, a member of the English Baptist Mission who had stopped at an inn on his flight from Tai Yuan, saw a cart passing by with a grizzly cargo, the seven heads. The cart was enroute to the governor's *yamen.*

The heads of the others who had died with the missionaries were strung "right and left" about Taiku. All the bodies, missionaries and Chinese together, were dumped into a pit at an ash heap and refuse pile that extended nearly the entire length of the city wall outside the South Gate.

The bloodbath didn't stop with Taiku. The Boxers were unremitting. They roamed the countryside, searching for converts, attacking anyone who showed the least indication of being Christian or being sympathetic to Christians, or who worked for the missionaries. They killed five converts in Li Man, including the mother-in-law and daughter of medical helper Li Yu (Hei Kou/Black Dog), and Louise Partridge's servant, Kuo Hsiao Hsien, and his blind, eighty-year-old mother. Francis Davis's helper at Jen Tsun, Tsui Hen Tai, tried to hide with his family in a thicket of thorn bushes, but a relative revealed where they were, and Boxers killed the entire family, seven persons in all.

At Che Wang, Boxers found Teacher Liu's wife and Chun Sao, the daughter-in-law of Deacon Liu. They cut them with swords and then went on to another village a few miles away. On their way back, they discovered that Chun Sao was still alive, so they beheaded her with a straw knife and threw her head into a privy.

Teacher Liu and a child; Ruth Fan; and the Sangs with their two children had sought refuge in the South Suburb compound, but when they heard about the attack on the city compound they headed south on a little-used road. They reached the village of P'ang Ts'un the next day, where they were identified as members of the Mission and forced to return to Taiku. Boxers took them to an altar by the East Gate of the city. The adults were said to have recanted, but the Boxers didn't believe them and all seven, including the three children, were executed.

A helper of Howard Clapp's known by his child's name, Er Lai—his adult name was Liang Chi Tai—was caught by Boxers at a Taiku outstation. Boxers dragged him to a temple, gave him incense sticks to hold, and told him to bow down before the idols. He threw the sticks away and wept. The Boxers took him out and killed him.

A former pupil of Jennie Clapp's, an eighteen-year-old youth, the son of a gambler, drunkard, and adulterer named Wang Pao Rung who repented his ways and converted in 1895, was among six persons of Wang's family that were killed. The youth tried to hide in a sorghum field, but Boxers surrounded it and flushed him out. They ripped out his bowels. His father's head was chopped into bits and, with his heart, ground to a pulp on a stone mill.

The wife of a church member, Mrs. K'ang, and her oldest daughter, who was a pupil in Louise Partridge's school in Li Man, were slain.

A wealthy Christian landowner, Mr. Li of Wu Chia Pu, ten miles west of Taiku, was thrown from his roof, dragged through the street and killed. (His wife afterward offered forty *mou* of their land—almost seven acres; a *mou* was one-sixth of an acre—as a burial ground for the missionaries, but local officials would not let their bodies be interred.)

The two Wang brothers of Ching shen Tsun—Wang Shan and Wang Yu—were not converts, but they had broken off the opium habit and no longer worshiped idols. Boxers killed them. Another former opium addict, Ch'eng Chung Jen, was in the Taiku compound when it was attacked. Ch'eng was a convert who walked to church every Sunday from his village a few miles from Taiku. He managed to escape from the compound and hurried to a village where an uncle lived. Someone informed on him. The Boxers found him and cut him into pieces.

A neighbor informed on another church member, Li Heng Chang, a blind, seventy-year-old man who lived in the village of Nan Chang Ts'un. The neighbor said Li had two small, suspicious books. Boxers confronted Li and asked whether he had any Bibles. He said he didn't, which was literally true; one of the books was a catechism, the other a Chinese classic. The Boxers doubted his answer and said they would practice the art of "devining [*sic*] over him." If the smoke from an incense stick went straight up without wavering he would be freed; if not, he would be held guilty. The smoke wavered. They took Li into his yard and chopped off his head with a straw knife.

Church member Shih Shou Chi was killed at the village of Hsiao Pai. Another church member, Yang Chien Chung, who served as the Clapps' gatekeeper, was slain together with his mother and two younger brothers. The brothers were pupils in the boys' school.

The list of brutal murders is incomplete. Between seventy and one hundred Chinese Christians and members of their families are believed to have been killed in the attack on the Taiku compound and in its immediate aftermath in the villages where Mission converts, helpers, and sympathizers lived or sought refuge. Not all their names, however, were recorded. One of the anonymous victims was George Williams's gatekeeper, who was caught with his Bible wrapped in a bundle of clothing; Boxers hacked him to pieces and burned his body with millet stalks in a temple courtyard.

There were only seven members of the Oberlin Band now left—the two missionary families at the American Board's station in Fenchow-fu: Charles and Eva Price and their daughter, Florence; and Ernest and Elizabeth Atwater and the two younger Atwater girls, Celia and Bertha. With them were Anton and Elsa Lundgren and Annie Eldred of the China Inland Mission; the teacher Fei Chi Hao; Li Yu, the medical helper better known as Hei Kou or Black Dog, who had been carrying messages back and forth between the Oberlin Band members in Taiku and Fenchow-fu, and two church members known only as Chang and Tien.

TWENTY ❁ *Fenchow-fu*
Escape to Tragedy

The pain will soon be over and oh,
the sweetness of the welcome above.
—Elizabeth Graham Atwater

Lizzie Atwater was tormented. The past month had been an agonizing ordeal. She and Ernest had not heard from Ernestine and Mary, and the situation in Tai Yuan, they knew, was critical. The missionaries in Fenchow-fu had heard a number of conflicting reports—everything from the deaths of the English Baptists stationed there to the death of Yü Hsien himself. They hadn't known what to believe until the letter Rowena Bird wrote on July 27 confirmed their worst fears "concerning our dear ones at Taiyuen." It was "hard, God knows how hard, for us to bear," she said. She and Ernest had "passed a terrible night."

Lizzie, who was in her ninth month of pregnancy, was so distraught that she did not sleep that night, and the next day the local *kuan* threatened to make the missionaries evacuate Fen-chow-fu. That was too much for her:

> I could do nothing but cry to God. It seemed as if I could bear no more in present condition. No one talked at meals. We seemed to be waiting for the end, and I for my part longed that it might come speedily. . . . .
>
> There will be a joyful welcome for us all above. I am fixing my thoughts more and more upon the glorious hereafter and it gives me wonderful peace.[1]

Lizzie's anguish was expressed in a letter that she wrote her friends Jennie Clapp, Rowena Bird, and Louise Partridge on the eve of the massacre in Taiku. They never received it.

The members of the Oberlin Band stationed in Fenchow-fu first started to worry about Boxers in the last week of June when the *kuan* sent word that the missionaries should be careful and not venture outside the Mission compound. Charles Price believed it was better to heed him than not. "If we do anything counter to his wishes it will give him a good excuse for not giving us protection," Charles wrote in a journal he began that week. "Claims he cannot control the people."[2]

Like their colleagues in Taiku, the Prices and the Atwaters argued about what they should do if attacked. Charles and Ernest had two shotguns and a pair of revolvers between them, but the women didn't want the men to shoot anybody, so the two men buried the weapons. However, as the Boxer movement spread to the west side of the Fen River and the situation in Shansi deteriorated, Charles and Ernest dug up the arms and prepared to defend themselves. The women remained adamant against fighting fire with fire, but Charles, for one, "felt convinced we were not doing right to let our wives and children perish without an effort to save them. So we again prepared to sell our lives as dearly as possible."[3]

The Prices packed two trunks with valuables, wrapped the trunks in oilcloth and buried them together with eighty ounces of silver. "We shall not resist if they only take our goods," Charles noted. "If they attempt violence we shall fight if God gives us strength, unless they are better organized than now appears." He knew he could count on the help of Anton Lundgren, the CIM missionary who was staying with the Prices, and, if Atwater came over from his home half a mile away at the East Gate of the city, "we would be three men against thousands. But our trust is in One to whom numbers are of no importance whatever."[4]

That same night Atwater's dwelling was surrounded by a mob. His family was at supper when they heard noise outside their compound. They went out into the courtyard just as some bricks and pieces of tile came sailing over the wall. One almost struck little Celia, another just missed Ernest's head. They then heard pounding on a side gate. As it burst open, their cook urged the family to flee. Incredibly, they were able to follow him out of the front gate, through hundreds of screaming Chinese on the street, and make their way in the dark to the *yamen* without even being touched.

In the meantime, word of the attack had gotten back to the Prices. They sent Han, an evangelist who was with them at the time, to the local *yamen.* The magistrate responded at once. He immediately left for the Atwater compound without bothering to don his official robes or to ride in his official state chair. He left accompanied by a militia unit.

By the time the *kuan* reached the scene, the mob was pillaging the place. The magistrate personally grabbed a man who was making off with a rug under his arm. Others, though, were able to steal valuables. What they didn't take, they destroyed. They smashed windows, dishes, and lamps. The remnants were strewn all over the courtyard.

The Atwaters reached the *yamen* just as soldiers were hurrying to their home with the magistrate's official chair. They were not allowed to enter the government building, so they sat around an outer court. Lizzie, who had Bertha on her lap, watched the tumultuous scene. She thought it was like watching a play: Lanterns flashed weirdly, loud voices called out excitedly, people hurried to and fro.

After the mob dispersed, the magistrate returned to his *yamen* and offered to provide the Atwaters with an escort so they could return home. But they were afraid another attack might occur, so instead Lizzie took Bertha and Celia and set out in the dark to the Mission compound by the West Gate to be with the Prices. Atwater finally decided to return home so that he could guard his house against further looting, but he too moved into the Mission compound the next day.[5]

All the while the attack was going on, the Prices, the Lundgrens, and young Annie Eldred waited in suspense, convinced that the Mission would be assaulted next. The Prices' servants sharpened knives and bound up their heads with dark cloth to prevent being seen; they tucked their queues inside the makeshift turbans so that they couldn't be seized by them.

Things calmed down after Lizzie and the two girls arrived about midnight. But the next morning a servant came with the news that a man, a foreigner, had been killed and dumped in a grave in a village only three or so miles away. Who could it be? Some missionary they knew? One of the Oberlin Band from Taiku?

Soon afterwards the *kuan* asked Han to accompany him to the village to identify the man. He had the evangelist put on an official hat so he wouldn't be molested, and they set off in a cart with an escort of soldiers.

When they got to the village, the headmen said the foreigner had been killed because he was found poisoning wells. The *kuan* was skeptical. He ordered the man's body dug up and taken to a temple. The body was hacked up, the face so mutilated that it was impossible to identify him. But his clothes appeared to have a foreign cut; the sleeves were tight rather than loose. Han opened the outer garment to get a better look. He quickly surmised that the man was not a foreigner: the fingernails were too long, the teeth black from opium, and the hair was that of a Chinese.

Sitting nearby, drinking tea, the *kuan* was furious when he heard what Han discovered. He threw the pot into the face of a village elder. He had several women who taunted him beaten with thorns on their backs and across their mouths. The murderer was pounded over the head with a spade and led away to be executed. Four other villagers received a thousand blows each. Once back in his *yamen,* the magistrate had the men caught looting the Atwater house beaten, too. The one he captured had a wooden collar fastened around his neck and was made to sit in front the Atwaters' place every day.

The *kuan*'s behavior—his immediate response to the mobbing of the Atwater compound and his reaction to the murder of a "foreigner"—should have calmed the missionaries, but the opposite was true. As Eva Price put it, "Nights are continual hours of anxious suspense, starting at every sound, and imagining an unruly mob surrounding us and taking our lives in revenge for the way the Kuan has seemingly favored us."[6] The only joy they experienced occurred when, at long last, it started to rain one day—"a glorious shower of rain." The missionaries burst into singing "Praise God from whom all blessings flow."[7]

The month of July brought one terror after another. First, an incendiary rumor spread through Fenchow-fu that the Mission housed seventy foreigners "armed with all kinds of guns" and "ready to take the city and destroy the I ho chuan." The *kuan* immediately quieted possible repercussions by sending word out that missionaries were to be protected. "He is doing all he can for us," Charles reported.

But two days later the magistrate issued a proclamation asking all converts to recant "till the excitement dies out." Charles didn't think the magistrate understood "how great a matter it is to turn from the Gospel to serve idols." The proclamation also repeated that foreigners were to be protected, "but what comfort can it be to us if our Christians are to pay the price for us," Charles said. "There is one thing in their favor—they can hide for a few months till the storm blows over and no one would know they are Christians, but we would be known wherever we go." He reported that there were seventeen Christians at the Mission "ready to fight for their lives but say they will die rather than give up their belief in Christ."[8]

However, in the third week of July, the magistrate had four converts in a village outside Fenchow-fu beaten and then made to bow in front of idols in a temple. Charles thought at the time that the magistrate had the men beaten to prevent them from worse harm at the hands of Boxers. But except for a few Christians—Fei Chi Hao and Hei Kou, among them—the other converts began to desert the Mission compound. Han the evangelist, whose piety Fei anyway thought was a little dubious, recanted. He was given a card as proof that he had renounced Christianity. Han pinned the card to his jacket and went about telling people that he was no longer a Christian. Other converts soon followed his example.

Then, in the last week of July, the district magistrate was fatally wounded while trying to arrest several Catholics in an outlying village. Fearing reprisals, several more Christians immediately left the American Board compound. Charles, who had been so proud of the seventeen Christians who had stayed with the missionaries, was saddened as one by one they left. "It now seems that our work is to be altogether destroyed," he said.[9]

Yü Hsien immediately replaced the murdered *hsien kuan* with a personal friend and instructed him to expel the foreigners once and for all. That evening the missionaries received word that they were to be escorted to the coast "by order of Emperor." Did that mean they were going to be led out of Shansi to safety? "We have very little faith in it. It may be a blind to put us off our guard," Charles said. "Will be well for us to be careful how we fall in with a plan to escort us to the coast which may only be a plan to get us to the capital to kill us."[10]

The new official summoned Hei Kou to the *yamen.* He was gone for three hours, and when he came back he said that the official had offered to provide a small escort and to help the missionaries hire litters.

The missionaries debated what to do when, on July 29, another proclamation was issued: *"Mieh Yang Sha Kuei"* it said—"Destroy the foreigners." Charles despaired. "Nothing can be plainer," he said.[11]

Price urged the few Chinese left in the compound to leave at once. He gave each one some money, and to one servant he gave his horse. They were in tears as they said good-bye. Twice he told Fei Chi Hao to flee. Twice the young teacher went and twice he returned, saying he preferred to be with the missionaries and help out.

With no servants left, Eva Price took over the cooking chores, preparing three meals daily. No matter how hot the day was, she stood by the stove, her face flushed and wet with perspiration. Elsa Lundgren and Annie Eldred helped cook. Fei and Hei Kou washed dishes and clothes and at night kept watch with Charles, Ernest, and Anton. Hei Kou also did all their shopping in the city. Two church members named Chang and Tien showed up one day and stayed to assist the missionaries.

The missionaries tried to get word about their situation to the coast. They gave forty ounces of their "precious silver" to a man to induce him to carry messages to Tientsin. Instead, the man went into the hills and worked in the opium fields. He never returned the silver.

"It was like one long, dark valley of the shadow of death that month," said Fei, "with not one ray of news from the outer world to brighten it."[12]

The women tried to put their worries aside for the sake of the children. When they could, Annie Eldred and Elsa Lundgren romped in the courtyard with the three children "to cheer them up."[13] Fei played with them every evening after supper, carrying them around on his shoulder. The girls would kiss him good-night when their mothers called them to bed, wishing him pleasant dreams.

But Annie Eldred wasn't having pleasant dreams. She could barely sleep. When she did, she dreamed so often of being killed by Boxers that she said, "I feel half dead already."[14]

The second time Fei had left, he encountered the former evangelist, Han, and despite his reservations about Han's piety made the mistake of talking about the missionaries' plight with him and another recreant,

Wang, a one-time deacon. Both men contended that they still loved the missionaries.

Wang, who lived about ten miles from Fenchow-fu, offered to conceal the Prices in his home for a day or two, then lead the couple and their daughter Florence to an abandoned temple in the mountains. When Hei Kou heard of the offer, he proposed to lead the remaining missionaries to safety in another place in the mountains. Fei approached the Prices with the plan. They were reluctant to separate from the others, but Fei finally convinced them.

The escape was planned for the night of July 31—the day of the massacre at Taiku. The compound was being guarded outside by *yamen* troops, but the missionaries planned to elude them by leaving by an old gate at the back of the compound that was no longer used. That night Fei unlocked the gate and removed a stone that helped to keep it shut. He then gave a bundle of his belongings to a Christian inquirer named Jen who was still with them in the compound. He asked Jen to care for it while he went to summon the Prices.

Wang saw Fei give the bundle to Jen, who then put it in an empty room nearby. After Jen came out of the room, Wang went in and stole the bundle. Jen saw him rush from the room, leap over the wall and run away. Jen set up a loud wail, shouting at the top of his voice. Outside, four soldiers heard his screaming and rushed into the compound. The missionaries joined them at the rear of the compound.

Jen was jumping up and down, slapping his legs and crying. He said that Wang had stolen Fei's personal belongings. The soldiers took up lanterns and began to search for Wang. They spied the unlocked back gate. Believing it Wang's doing, the soldiers locked the gate, replaced the stone, and left two men to guard it. There was now no hope of the missionaries being able to sneak out of the compound without the soldiers spotting them.

In his zeal to help the missionaries, Hei Kou went the next day to the *kuan,* who he believed was friendly, and confided to him about the aborted escape plan. Much to Hei Kou's shock, the magistrate, who was under pressure to rid the city of the missionaries, immediately demanded that they turn over all their weapons to him. When Hei Kou insisted that the missionaries would need the guns for protection on the road if they were going to the coast, the *kuan* had Hei Kou beaten three hundred blows. Eighty blows across his face were added when Hei Kou made a slip in etiquette, speaking of himself as "I" instead of "the little one" or "your humble servant." He was then thrown into a cell.[15]

The magistrate sent to the Mission for the guns, and the missionaries felt they could not refuse him. They were now without any weapons to defend themselves.

That day, August 1, the Prices and Atwaters received another blow when they learned of the massacre of their Oberlin Band comrades at Taiku. Jennie Clapp's cook, who had fled, reached Fenchow-fu with the news. He didn't know all the details, just that no missionary survived, but another man brought them a full account two days later. It was then that Fei first learned that his sister, who was the wife of Teacher Liu, was dead; both she and her child had been killed.

Charles Price's journal ends on July 31: "Reported. Pekin in hands of foreigners. Hard fighting around Tien-tsin."[16]

His meaning—that Peking was occupied by foreign troops, and that fighting was going on at Tientsin—was no more accurate than any other rumor he heard. The legations in Peking were still under siege. However, Tientsin *was* in the hands of foreign troops, and, after many delays and squabbling, an International Relief Force of some twenty thousand men from seven nations was about to leave to rescue the diplomats and missionaries in the capital. They finally set out, following the banks of the Pei Ho northward, at dawn on August 4.

Sometime in the second week of August, as the International Relief Force slowly fought its way toward Peking, Dowager Empress Tz'u Hsi slipped out of the Forbidden City with an entourage of ministers, courtiers and the Emperor, Kuang Hsü. Legend has it that she fled before dawn in a common cart in the guise of a peasant woman just as foreign troops reached the capital. The royal caravan headed northwest at first, and once in Shansi Province turned south. The caravan paused when it reached Tai Yuan. There, as guests of Yü Hsien, the Imperial party dallied for several weeks before continuing south into Shensi Province and refuge in the city of Sian.

Tung Chow fell to the International Relief Force on August 12. The next day, foreign troops were at the walls of Peking. They liberated the besieged diplomats, missionaries, and Chinese Christians on August 14.

That same day, hundreds of miles away in Fenchow-fu, the missionaries at the American Board compound were ordered to leave the city. Ernest Atwater went to the district magistrate to request a delay, pleading that his pregnant wife Lizzie was in no condition to journey over the primitive mountain roads. The official refused to consider any further delay in their departure. He was already angry at the local *kuan* for not getting rid of the foreigners sooner. Yü Hsien's orders had been explicit.

Charles Price sent Fei to ask for an audience with the official, but he wouldn't see him. He said that if the missionaries did not leave the next day, Wednesday, August 15, he would send troops to "flog them out of town."[17]

The missionaries counted their silver. They had only 150 ounces, not nearly enough to hire carts to carry them and the three Chinese Christians still with them. Negotiating through an intermediary, they asked the official for money to hire carts, but he turned them down. They offered to sell their homes, but he said that the houses were going to revert to the government and be used to house troops. They finally got him to give them another 150 ounces of silver in payment for the summer homes the Prices and Atwaters owned in Yü Tao Ho; the property was worth at least ten times as much.

Lü Chen San, a middle-aged member of the gentry who was friendly to them, was on hand on the morning of their departure. He was considered a man "of unusual ability and power" but also greedy and deceitful.[18] Before the missionaries started out, Lü rode off, leading a troop of men.

Lü's appearance must have prompted Charles Price to have a premonition of some danger. He gave Fei Chi Hao several ounces of silver and a little piece of blue cloth meant to identify Fei as a friend should he meet any foreign troops. Charles wrote on it, "This is a trustworthy man, he will tell you of our fate."[19] Fei put the cloth in his shoe.

Anton Lundgren gave Fei a horse and some clothing, but, when Fei went to mount the horse, soldiers took it away from him.

As the missionary party left the compound, ten thousand people lined the streets of Fenchow-fu, watching silently as two carts with the foreigners in them rumbled by. Behind them, men from the *yamen* sealed the compound, ostensibly to keep it from being looted.

Fei later related to the wife of an American Board missionary in Peking what happened next:

> Mr. and Mrs. Atwater, Mrs. Lundgren, little Celia and Bertha, teacher Fei and the carter, made up the seven on the first cart. In the second were Mr. and Mrs. Price, Miss Eldred, Florence Price and Mr. Lundgren, the carter, two church members [Chang and Tien] and the baggage. They went together seven miles, and, little thinking what was before them, visited cheerfully as they went, one lady saying playfully, "What a turnout there was to escort us!" another one adding, "What fine new uniforms the soldiers wore." Little Celia and Bertha and Florence used to ride on Mr. Fei's shoulders and were his dear little sister play-fellows. He drew out their artless prattle about where they were going, from the two who rode with him.
>
> As Mr. Fei was riding along in the back of the cart, he noticed a Chinese soldier eyeing him intently. It was the man who had taken his horse. He inquired where Fei's house was, and, on learning that it was in Tung Chou he remarked: "Just ride this horse and you will soon get there," meaning that he would ride to certain death and then his soul would revert to his ancestral home, but Fei did not take it in. Later he said: "Such a pity for one so young as you to be bewitched and follow foreigners." Another man wanted Mr. Fei's boots, but when he objected a third said: "Never mind taking them from him; they will be ours in a little while anyway." Later, a fourth said plainly: "Escape with your life! We are about to kill the foreigners!" Two li ahead was the village where twenty soldiers were waiting to kill them all.[20]

Lü Chen San had ridden ahead of the missionary caravan. Under orders from the *hsien kuan,* he was to escort the missionaries as far as the Fen River, kill them, and throw their bodies into the river, where nobody would find them. But the avaricious Lü had another idea in mind. At every little community he and the soldiers passed through, he demanded a ransom from the village elders. If they didn't pay it, he said he was going to kill the foreigners in their village and let the responsibility for their deaths fall upon them. One after another, villages gave in to the extortion, until Lü and his men reached the village of Nan Kai Shih. The

Chinese there said they would pay only half of what he demanded. Angry at their response, Lü posted his men in a sorghum field on the edge of the village.[21]

> At this point he [Fei] took his last look at the kind faces and left. No words were possible in presence of the guard, but he thinks they saw him go. Must it not have seemed to them a sure premonition of the end when this faithful one turned aside?
>
> When he had gone a short distance the soldiers stopped him and wanted his money. He protested he had only enough for his journey, but he gave them his watch. One took his boots and gave him a wretched old pair of shoes, much worn and far too small, in place. He went on half a li, when they pursued him; one seized his queue and one held an arm, while they took his silver, all but one ounce, left at his pleading. About a li from the village he heard shots fired.[22]

Lü fired the first shot, a signal to the ambushers to attack. As they rushed out of hiding, one soldier hesitated. He had been a pupil in the boys' school at the Mission. Lü beat him furiously with a whip.

A soldier struck Ernest Atwater on the forehead with his sword. The missionary struggled with the man until he was overpowered.

Ernest was the only one to put up any resistance. The others were immediately either shot or cut down. The soldiers killed everyone—Ernest and Lizzie Atwater and their daughters Celia and Bertha; Charles and Eva Price and their daughter Florence; Annie Eldred; Anton and Elsa Lundgren; and Chang and Tien. The two carters were evidently slain, too.

Afterwards the soldiers stripped the bodies and carried away the baggage in the carts. They were going to leave the bodies lying in the road for carrion to feed on, but the villagers kowtowed and implored them to be allowed to bury them. The soldiers consented. The villagers took the bodies to a deep pit and tossed them into it.

The last word from the Oberlin Band came from Lizzie Atwater in a letter to "Dear, dear ones" in Oberlin, written two weeks before her death:

How am I to write all the horrible details of these days? I would rather spare you. The dear ones at Shou Yang, seven in all, including our lovely girls, were taken prisoners and brought to Taiyuen in irons and there by the governor's orders beheaded. . . .

The pain will soon be over and oh, the sweetness of the welcome above. My little baby will go with me. I think God will give it to me in heaven and my dear mother will be so glad to see us. I cannot imagine the Saviour's welcome. Oh, that will compensate for all the days of suspense. . . . I do not regret coming to China, but I am sorry I have done so little. My married life, two precious years, have been full of happiness. We will die together, my dear husband and I; I used to dread separation. . . .[23]

TWENTY-ONE ❁ *Aftermath*

In the ceremonies of mourning, it is better that there be deep sorrow than a minute attention to observances.
—Confucius

For all intents, the Boxer Rebellion ended with the lifting of the siege of Peking on August 14. Of the more than 900 foreigners in the capital—diplomats, troops of eight nations and missionaries—56 were killed; 2 adults and 6 babies died, and more than 150 others were wounded during the eight weeks of the siege. No record was kept of Chinese casualties within the defense perimeter.[1]

It was months, however, before the unrest was quashed, and the rescuing allied forces replicated in many ways the horrors unleashed by the Boxers. As thousands of Boxers fled Peking, disappearing into the countryside, international troops pillaged the city. Then some foreign units set out after the Boxers, ostensibly to track them down, but looting, raping, and murdering indiscriminately, with no regard for innocent Chinese.

The greatest loss of life among foreigners throughout North China during the Boxer Rebellion was suffered by missionaries. Precise death-toll figures were never ascertained, because some missionaries worked independent of established organizations, but it is known that at least 134 Protestant missionaries, the majority of them English, and most of them members of the China Inland Mission, were killed. In addition, at least 52 of their children died with them. Total Catholic losses were 5 bishops, 31 priests, 9 European sisters and 2 Marists.

The greatest losses among converts were suffered by Chinese

Catholics—a staggering total in excess of 30,000 men and women. Six thousand Catholics were buried in one cemetery alone in the outskirts of Peking. As far as can be determined, more than 1,900 Protestant converts were also killed.[2]

No tally of the number of Boxers who were killed was ever made, but it is believed that the total reached into many thousands. Likewise, no tally of the number of innocent Chinese who died during and after the Rebellion was ever made, but the figure is believed to be in the thousands, also. They were victims of both the Boxers and the International Relief Force. During the rebellion Chinese with grudges against a neighbor frequently identified the neighbor to Boxers as a Christian. Other innocent Chinese were slain by Boxers or the peasants and villagers who joined them during attacks on villages. After the rebellion foreign troops made little effort, or failed to be able, to tell innocent Chinese from Boxers who went into hiding in villages and in rural areas throughout the northern provinces. "It is safe to say," an American general said, "that where one real Boxer has been killed since the capture of Peking, fifteen harmless coolies and labourers on the farms, including not a few women and children, have been slain."[3]

More than 2,500 Protestant missionaries survived, though many suffered harrowing experiences. Luella Miner, a missionary from Oberlin who served with the North China Mission in Tung Chow, believed that Horace Pitkin and Annie Gould could have been among the survivors if they had left Paotingfu and gone to Tung Chow, as they planned, for the North China Mission's annual meeting that spring. Like Miner, they would have fled Tung Chow when the Boxers attacked the city and would have sought shelter in the British legation in Peking, where they undoubtedly could have survived the siege, as Miner did. She believed that Horace and Annie didn't try to reach Tung Chow before the rail line north was cut because they did not want "to leave the Christians in their trouble."[4]

Henry D. Porter, an American Board missionary in Tientsin, believed that the members of the Oberlin Band in Shansi might have been spared, too. He blamed himself for their fate. He said that it did not dawn on him, or indeed to anyone else connected with the Board, to check whether the telegraph line into Shansi from the west through Shensi

Province might still be operational after all other lines were cut. Porter said he realized afterwards that, if the Oberlin missionaries had been alerted in time about the serious danger the Boxers posed, they could have escaped by traveling first west into Shensi and then south and east through central China to Han-k'ou on the coast of the East China Sea. All missionaries in provinces along the Yangtze River were able to reach safety because the Chinese viceroy in the area deliberately altered the meaning of the June 24 Imperial edict. Fearing that the spread of the xenophobic Boxer insurrection would lead to the invasion of all China by foreign forces, the viceroy purposely changed the words *mieh yang*—"exterminate the foreigners"—to *hu yang*—"protect the foreigners"—when he had the edict disseminated.[5] Belatedly, Porter rued his lapse:

> Had we known that the telegraphic communication by way of Shensi was so complete we could have advised them to fly westward. They could have escaped by way of Hankow as early as the end of July. Alas! They were inaccessible and we practically gave them up long before the end came to them. They met their end serenely and faithfully and the Lord will reward them for all the bitter suffering.[6]

Foreign soldiers finally reached Paotingfu in Chih-li Province in mid-October 1900. It was then that the remains of the bodies of Horace Pitkin, Annie Gould, and Mary Morrill were formally buried. Horace's body was found in a pit with the bodies of eight members of the Meng family, six of whom were children. Horace's hands were still uplifted in prayer. His head was found buried under the ruins of the southeast tower of the city. The tower—which overlooked the site where Mary, Annie, and the Bagnalls and William Cooper of the China Inland Mission were beheaded—was destroyed. It, the gate towers, and a portion of the city wall were all blown up, as was Chi Sheng An, the temple where the Boxers held the missionaries before taking them out to be executed. The *Nieh-tai* (provincial judge) Ting-Yung was decapitated for his complicity in the massacre. The colonel who refused to protect the Bagnalls and Cooper and stole their valuables was also beheaded.

Some five months later, on March 23, 1901, a memorial service was held for the Presbyterians who died—the Simcoxes, the Hodges, and Dr. Taylor—at the North Suburb where their mission compound had been.

Their names were inscribed in Chinese in a makeshift shrine, and over the names was written *"Ling shuang tsai t'ien"*—"Their spirits are happy in heaven." Pots of flowers, presented by merchants, surrounded the shrine. French officers attended the rites, and a German brigade band performed.

Luella Miner attended the commemoration and was appalled at the destruction. "What a scene of desolation!" she said. "There are hardly enough broken bricks left on the place to mark the site of the house."[7]

The next day a similar service was held at the American Board compound for Horace, Mary, Annie, and the members of the China Inland Mission who were killed with them, as well as for thirty-six Chinese who died in the carnage associated with their murders. The bodies of only twenty-six had been found; of some of the others, only the queues of men were discovered. Coffins bore the names of the twenty-six that could be identified. Among the Chinese were Pastor Meng Chang-chun (Meng I) and all his children but for his son Ti-to, who escaped; Meng's sister, the Bible woman Mrs. Tu, and her children; Chang Ch'iang Hsiang's mother, Bible woman Mrs. Chang; and Bible woman Mrs. Kao and her daughter Jessica.

Banners with testimonials to the martyrs were hung along the sides of the courtyard where the service was held. One of them was from the schoolgirls that Mary and Annie had taught. All the bodies—American, British and Chinese—were buried together in a new cemetery located between the ruins of the two compounds.

In memory of Pitkin, students and faculty at Yale University launched in 1902 an independent, nondenominational association, the Yale Foreign Missionary Society—known familiarly as Yale-in-China—to establish a center of Christian education in the interior of China. The group chose the capital of Hunan Province, the center of violent anti-Christian propaganda, as its base of operations. (Seventeen years later, a young Mao Tse-tung, whose own periodical was closed by government orders, was made editor of the Yale-in-China's review, the *New Hunan.* It, too, was suppressed, but Mao continued to work in three rooms that the society rented to him. He established a bookshop in them, and later seven branch stores, which sold Marxist books and periodicals.)

A German army pressed into the mountain passes of Shansi Province from Paotingfu in January 1901, but it wasn't until July 9, a year to the day of the massacre at Tai Yuan, that a party of missionaries entered the city at the invitation of a new governor to attend memorial services for the Pigotts, Ernestine and Mary Atwater, and all the other missionaries and their families who died in that one day of slaughter.

Iranaeus Atwood, who volunteered to return to China to help restore the Shansi Mission, headed the missionary delegation. Dr. E. H. Edwards of the China Inland Mission, who had hosted the wedding supper of Ernest and Lizzie Atwater, accompanied him. They were met ten *li* from the city by minor officials. Their carts were exchanged for litters that became part of a procession into the city that was half a mile long. As they neared the great South Gate of the city, soldiers with banners of welcome opened ranks and the Shansi mounted police stood at present arms.

After a memorial service Atwood and Edwards went to Shou Yang, where Atwood was reunited with his old medical assistant, Hei Kou. The two missionaries stayed overnight in Shou Yang, when, ironically, considering all the blame for the Boxer troubles that missionaries had put on the drought, it rained—"such a rain," said Atwood, "as the Christians told us they had not seen for two years. When we left on Monday morning the fields never looked more beautiful since I came to China in '82. I have never seen the crops looking better at this season of the year. May it be a token of the spiritual blessings that the loving Father is about to send down in his infinite love upon the whole land."[8]

As Atwood and Edwards traveled through Shansi, they were met with the same ceremonies and obsequies, all tokens of mourning, apology, and humiliation. At one village north of Taiku, soldiers were carrying twenty-four flags, two of which were the Stars and Stripes. "A detail of soldiers kneeled on one knee with one hand to the ground [and] gave the royal 'Awh,'" Atwood wrote, "as I entered the sedan chair that the Hsien had provided for my entrance into the city."[9]

The services in Tai Yuan were held in a large pavilion erected about fifty yards from the *yamen* where the forty-five Protestants and Catholics and an unrecorded number of Chinese had been beheaded in Yü's presence. Silk banners with their names inscribed in gilt letters hung in its inner court. A short service was held afterwards on the spot of the massacre; then a procession was formed that passed through the city and out of the East Gate to a newly prepared gravesite about two miles outside. There mandarins read an apology for the crimes that had been committed, and representatives of the gentry came forward to express their humiliation by making a low bow.

The resting place of the missionaries who died in Taiku and Fenchow-fu was a beautiful, nine-acre private park that became known as the Flower Garden, just east of the city, that a number of Taiku families, including the K'ungs, owned and used as a retreat. It contained Chinese moongates, little shrine temples, and a miniature lake. Trees a hundred years old shaded its walks, and flowers of all kinds bloomed in spring, summer, and fall.

The principal owner of the garden was Meng Ta Hsi, who had commanded the soldiers who took part in the attack on the Taiku compound. He later carried off most of the property he found inside it, claiming that it was his. At the urging of Atwood and Edwards, the local *tao-tai* (circuit intendant) ordered the entire garden confiscated. It became, in Edwards's words, "another 'God's Acre'" consecrated as the resting place of those who "loved not their lives unto the death."[10]

The bodies of those killed at Taiku—Howard and Jennie Clapp, Rowena Bird, Louise Partridge, George Williams, and Francis Davis—were found by Christian survivors in the pit outside the South Gate, where they had been dumped. Er Wu and Hei Kou were on hand when all the bodies were later removed to a gravesite outside the West Gate. The remains were dug up again for reburial in the Flower Garden, as were the bodies of those Chinese that were found and could be identified—Deacon Liu, the Sangs, Ruth Fan, and Ching Huan txu (Lois). The bodies of their comrades from Fenchow-fu—Charles, Eva, and Florence Price; Ernest, Lizzie, Celia and Bertha Atwater; and Chang and Tien—were brought to Taiku for reburial, too.

The reinterments took place on August 9, 1901—a year and nine days

The graves of the Oberlin martyrs in the Flower Garden outside Taiku. Courtesy Oberlin College Archives.

after the Taiku massacre, and six days shy of the anniversary of the ambush of the Fenchow-fu missionaries.

The coffins with the bodies were carried from a pavilion outside the South Gate of the city, from which banners of richly embroidered silk were draped. More than five hundred Chinese formed a procession to carry the coffins and heavy catafalques. A government official, with his runners bearing his insignia of office, led the procession. Behind them came soldiers bearing memorial banners, and behind them a large group of foreign and Chinese mourners.

The procession wound its way through the streets of Taiku and by the Mission compound on South Street. Services were held there in a pavilion erected on the site, and then the procession continued on to the Flower Garden outside the city. There the magistrate ascended a platform and made three low bows towards the graves. After him, scholars, gentry, and merchants ascended the platform and bowed, too.

The coffins were lowered into graves and covered with mounds of earth. Each grave had a low sandstone monument at its head with the name of the deceased person inscribed in Chinese on a black marble headstand. Howard Clapp's grave was the first, at the southeast corner of the garden. His wife Jennie was placed next to him. Beside her was Rowena Bird. A white lilac bush that was growing by it and left undisturbed separated it from the grave of Louise Partridge. That of Annie Eldred followed, then the graves of George Williams, Francis Davis, and Deacon Liu.

Those who died in Fenchow-fu, the Atwaters and the Prices, were aligned in a row west of these. A semicircle of graves was formed at the end of the foreign graves and in it the coffins of the Chinese who had been killed were lowered. They included Hei Kou's little daughter and Ching Huan txu. Knowing how concerned Lydia Davis was about Lois—the girl who had inspired her to start the girls' school in Fenchow-fu—Atwood took the time to write Lydia that "the remains of our poor little blind girl now repose in a beautiful spot in a grove of trees."[11]

The crippled widow of Deacon Liu was given a small building in the Flower Garden to live in, and there she remained, in sight of the graves of her husband and the other martyrs, with her grandchildren who had survived. (One grandddaughter, Lan Hua Liu, later attended Oberlin College and became dean of women at Shantung Christian University.)

The graves in the Flower Garden remained undisturbed for half a century—until the Chinese Communist government had them obliterated.

In the months that followed the ceremonies at the Flower Garden, burial rites were held for slain Christians in nine villages within a radius of ten miles of Taiku, all of which were attended by local officials, soldiers, and converts who had survived. Those who died at Tung Fang were buried in land confiscated from T Chieh tzu, who had boasted about his son killing Deacon Liu and whose son also killed Rowena Bird. T Chieh tzu himself had bragged that he had killed thirty Christians.

Dowager Empress Tz'u Hsi and her weak-willed nephew, Emperor Kuang Hsü, were allowed to return to Peking from their refuge in Shensi

Province. The Empress, the Emperor and their retinue returned in pomp in the fall of 1901. Some reforms, such as the suspension of the arcane examination system and the establishment of new schools, were instituted, but the conservative faction continued to dominate the Imperial Court. The Boxer Rebellion left the elite fearful of any participation of ordinary Chinese citizens in the nation's politics. Even reformers distrusted the huge majority of peasants who made up the nation.

The Boxer Protocol that the Imperial government agreed to that fall called for China to pay a staggering indemnity of $333 million over the next forty years at interest rates that would more than double that amount. As part of the treaty, the government was to erect monuments to the memory of all dead foreigners and to ban all civil service examinations for five years in cities where atrocities against foreigners had occurred. The Protocol also called for the execution of ten leading government officials and the punishment of a hundred others; Prince Tuan, the leader of the "Ironhats," was sent into exile.

One of those singled out for punishment was Yü Hsien, whom the Dowager Empress visited in Tai Yuan during her flight south into Shensi. She was his guest for three weeks, during which time he is said to have regaled her with his account of the massacre of the Protestants and Catholics. The heir apparent—Prince Tuan's teenage son—reportedly pranced around the courtyard where the slaughter took place, brandishing one of the swords that had been used for the executions. "Your Majesty's slave caught them as in a net, and allowed neither chicken nor dog to escape," Yu is said to have told her. After hearing the details of the beheadings, T'zu Hsi was quoted as saying, "You did splendidly in ridding Shansi of the whole brood of foreign devils."[12]

A number of stories surround Yü Hsien's final days. One story says that when he was finally dismissed from office and reported to Peking, he was escorted out of Tai Yuan by thousands of its residents, that his boots were hung by a city gate to commemorate his virtues, and that a stone tablet was erected to glorify his achievements in clearing the province of hated foreigners.[13] Another story says that upon reaching Peking, he was received at the Imperial Court and that the Dowager Empress presented him with a scroll she herself had written, a rare honor.[14]

Yü Hsien was to be banished for life under an edict of punishments issued that November, but the Powers objected and he was finally sentenced to be executed for being "guilty of cruel deeds."[15] He was supposedly visiting an old friend, who had arranged a banquet, when the order for his execution reached him sometime in 1901. He finished eating and went into seclusion for the rest of the day. He was decapitated the next day.[16]

Other terms of the Protocol—a ban on the importation of arms into China and the right of foreign legations to station permanent guards at their offices—clearly indicated that matters were back to where they were before the Boxer Rebellion. Foreign encroachments continued, particularly in the north, where Russia and Japan pressed their demands for more concessions.

Not everyone believed that indemnities should be sought by the Powers. Neither Hudson Taylor nor Timothy Richard, for instance, believed compensation should be sought for lives lost or property destroyed. At Richard's suggestion, half a million *taels* (about $375,000) was set aside to establish a university of Western learning in Tai Yuan, where, hopefully, the prejudice and ignorance that had led to the Boxer Rebellion might be disspelled. The school was built on a site near what had been Yü Hsien's courtyard, where the massacre of July 9 had taken place.

However, a number of American missionaries were so zealous in their demand for restitution that missionaries in general were heavily criticized for their venality. The American minister, Edwin Conger, had given missionaries in Peking the right to sell off confiscated goods to help pay for food for starving converts. The auctions were misinterpreted, and the Protestants became the butt of denunciations by the Western press, despite Conger's assertion that he was prepared "to justify the conduct of the American missionaries before the siege, during the siege and after the siege."[17]

In all, claims amounting to more than $1.5 million were awarded to Americans, both missionaries and nonmissionaries. American missionary societies received slightly more than $500,000 for property damage. In contrast, a total of only $20,000 was awarded to servants of the missionaries for their losses. In the main, the compensation to an American heir was usually $5,000. However, both Lydia Davis and Alice Williams received substantially more: $15,000 each for the death of their husbands, and more than $1,000 each for personal property that was lost.[18]

Some missionaries sounded positively bloodthirsty in their desire for revenge. One of them was Elwood Tewksbury of the American Board, who became the target of some of the severest criticism in the Western press. An American captain who accompanied Tewksbury and W. S. Ament, also of the American Board, into the countryside claimed that the "bloodthirsty" missionaries wanted him to shoot any suspected Boxers on the spot and burn down any villages in which they were harbored.[19] Both missionaries defended their viewpoint. "Jesus," Tewksbury said, "would have approved the punishment of criminals . . . in terms that common heathen can understand." Ament, who was against conciliation, revived the old shibboleth: "The Chinese do not understand . . . leniency."[20]

Tewksbury and Ament were not alone in their opinion. One especially vindictive missionary, Gilbert Reid, wrote an article apologizing for not having looted more. Loot, after all, was the spoils of war. "For those who have known the facts and have passed through a war of awful memory," he declared, "the matter of loot is one of high ethics." Reid even defended German and French troops, the worst offenders when it came to pillaging. He said the sack of Peking, which followed on the heels of the siege being lifted, might "have been the greatest good for the greatest number."[21]

The mild punishments meted out to some of the local Boxers such as T Chieh tzu troubled some missionaries. Atwood, for one, was not satisfied with the sentence given to the man who led the Taiku Boxers. He was imprisoned for one year—a token punishment considering the brutal sentences ordinarily given out by Chinese magistrates. Atwood acknowledged that there was a "great reluctance to punish officials or literary men, however deeply involved, on account of the fact that they were acting on orders from superiors . . . tho [*sic*] in some few cases the men exceeded their instructions in the rancor shown in their execution of these orders."[22]

The fate of Lü Chen San, who led the ambush against the Fenchowfu missionaries, created a quandary many years later for another Oberlin missionary, Watts O. Pye. By the time Lü was captured, the Powers had agreed that no more Chinese would be executed. Lü was imprisoned for life. Twelve years later, when Tai Yuan was captured during a revolution inspired by reformers, he escaped from prison. According to Chinese law, he could not be returned to prison unless his accuser again pressed his arrest.

Lü returned to his home, "grey and badly broken in health by his prison life, unable to walk but a short distance at a time." Pye wrestled with the problem of what to do about him. There was no question of Lü's guilt: He had confessed to it. But the time to determine his punishment was when he was first taken into custody. On the other hand, whether judged by Chinese or Western law, the penalty he received was not commensurate with the nature of the crime—the cold-blooded murder of nine persons. Yet, Pye went on, enumerating the pro's and con's of the case, nothing would be gained by prolonging the punishment. Instead, forgiveness might provide an example of Christian charity.

Pye finally decided to put the question before a panel of twelve gentry and merchants, who—if they agreed to let Lü remain free—would have to put up a bond guaranteeing that he would not molest the church or seek revenge for his imprisonment against any church member. The panel agreed to the plan, which was then forwarded to the American minister in Peking for approval.

Pye consoled himself with the thought that Lü "little guessed that the Christian religion once here cannot pass away; that in one form of another it will endure thru all time; that as in Scripture, so also in the heart of man, is written 'The gate of Hell shall not prevail against it.' The burning of a little straw may hide the stars of the sky; but the stars are there, and will reappear."[23]

During the ordeals of the summer of 1900, Lydia Davis, at home in Ohio, suffered day after day of anxiety. The last letter she received from her husband Francis came in mid-June, and by then the letter was six weeks old. Lydia continued to write Francis, expressing her concern over his safety and promising to return to him in China with their children once she was better (she was experiencing periods of hemorrhaging). Hoping against hope that she would hear from him, Lydia told him:

> I waked in the night not long ago and it was raining hard & I thought of how it was the rainy season & I wondered if you had had to flee & were traveling now.[24]

August 14 was a special day—the Davises' eleventh anniversary. Lydia, of course, had no idea that Francis had died two weeks earlier in Taiku, yet she couldn't help but think that the worst might have happened:

> My own dear beloved—I wonder where you are to-night and what doing. Would that I knew you were safe. I have just been playing "Abide with Me" and how I love that hymn. Oh, Francis, today is our wedding day. Where are you? Perhaps safe in far-away China, perhaps suffering intensely there, and perhaps looking down upon me from the heaven, which wherever it is, is only a little way off for Christ said, "Today thou shalt be with me in Paradise."[25]

It wasn't until Saturday, September 8, 1900—on what would have been Francis's forty-third birthday—that Lydia was informed by a minister friend that Francis was dead. The State Department confirmed the news in a letter two days later. Two years later Lydia received Francis's last known letter, which he had started on May 28 and added entries through June 10.[26]

Francis's letter was found amid the rubble when the American Board compound in Paotingfu was being rebuilt. Horace Pitkin had hidden it in the cellar of Dr. Willis Noble's house together with other letters forwarded to him by the missionaries in Shansi. Horace's own letters, including the one he wrote to his wife, Letty, were never found. No letters that Mary Morrill and Annie Gould may have written were found either.

K'ung Hsiang Hsi was able to retrieve a number of letters written by Rowena Bird, Louise Partridge, and Jennie Clapp from his uncle's compound in Taiku and carry them to safety. Rowena's diary was found seven years to the day of the massacre in Taiku in an old curiosity shop in a temple yard there. A servant of a friend of an Oberlin missionary came across it while browsing among some second-hand books. Together with the diary were some poems Rowena had written, extracts of sermons by Deacon Liu, and the record book of the Taiku Mission's treasurer. The shopkeeper sold the lot to the missionary for the equivalent of sixty cents.[27]

Lizzie Atwater's last letters were saved by the son of the gatekeeper at Fenchow-fu, who reached Tientsin more than two months after she was killed. The originals were sent to her father in Ireland, and copies to the grandparents of her stepchildren, the Chauncy N. Ponds, in Oberlin.[28]

If it hadn't been for those and other fortuitous discoveries, little of what the members of the Oberlin Band experienced and thought during their last months would be known. What other information exists about them comes from the accounts of Chinese Christians who witnessed their ordeal and survived—among them, Chang Ch'iang Hsiang, Er Wu, Fan P'ei Ch'eng, Fei Chi Hao, Hei Kou, Kuo Lao-man, K'ung Hsiang Hsi, Li-pai, and the Shieh cousins, one of whom saved Howard Clapp's diary. Iranaeus Atwood heard some of the eyewitness accounts when he returned to China. To varying degrees, the fate of some of them is known.

Er Wu helped to identify the remains of the slain victims at Taiku, a task that was so traumatic that it emotionally paralyzed the youngster. The new governor of Shansi had first had the bodies of the missionaries disinterred and placed in cheap coffins for separate burial in a plot of waste ground outside the West Gate of the city; the Chinese who died with them were buried there, too. Er Wu enlisted the help of Hei Kou to set up small stones to mark the area where the bodies lay. Hei Kou had been released after the massacre of the Fenchow-fu missionaries but was rearrested when he tried to salvage supplies from the medical dispensary. He was beaten so terribly that he was now a permanent cripple.

When Er Wu and Hei Kou objected that the bodies were buried without their heads, an agent of the governor went to Tai Yuan, where it was known that some of the heads had been taken. He returned with seven heads in a sack—one for each of the missionaries who were killed and one for Deacon Liu. Er Wu and Hei Kou demanded to see the heads. The agent opened the sack and dumped the heads on the ground. To their disgust, the heads were not of the missionaries but of criminals that had been executed.

The two Christians traveled to Tai Yuan to search for the heads of their friends. They had to grope through the confused heap of the remains of Catholics and Protestants who had been decapitated. They were able to recognize the heads of some, but not all, of their Taiku friends, and these they brought back and placed in coffins with the bodies.[29]

The experience traumatized Er Wu. Atwood arranged for him to continue his studies in Peking but could not convince the young boy to go, or to even find regular work.[30] Later Atwood was surprised to learn that Er Wu tried to blackmail a former Boxer leader out of six hundred *taels* (about $450).[31]

Fei Chi Hao survived a perilous journey home only to find that his mother and father, who were Christians, had committed suicide at the request of the rest of the members of the family, who were not Christians and feared the couple would endanger them all.

Fei and his schoolmate, K'ung Hsiang Hsi, eventually journeyed together to Oberlin College to study, sponsored by Luella Miner, who had to fight American immigration authorities to get them into the country. The proceeds of a book she wrote about them, *Two Heroes of Cathay,* helped to pay for their education. Both men graduated in 1906 and went on to Yale, where they earned master's degrees in education the following year.

Fei subsequently returned to China, where he worked both in the field of education and in government service. Among other things, he was president of Chih-li Provincial College from 1908 to 1911 and was later attached to the YMCA in Peking. He was director of the Bureau of Stamp, Tobacco and Alcohol Taxes in Peking in 1936. His home was confiscated by the Japanese in 1938, and his family barely escaped with their lives, according to a note in his alumni file in Oberlin.[32] When last heard from, in 1941, he was living in Chungking, in Szechwan Province.[33] Fei named one of his daughters for Luella Miner, and two others for Lydia Davis and Alice Williams. He named one of his sons Oberlin. Another son, Samuel, attended Oberlin, graduating in 1949, after which he returned to China; Samuel Fei was, in 1992, a senior economist for the Bank of China in Beijing; his wife was a senior editor for the Chinese news agency Xin Hua.

Hsiang Hsi's career was even more distinguished. He turned down a number of government and academic offers. Timothy Richard, for one, wanted him to join the staff of his university in Tai Yuan. Instead he chose to become head of the Ming Hsien Academy in Taiku, the successor to the schools that the Oberlin Band had established. Its name meant "Remember the Worthy." With K'ung in charge, it was the only foreign school then with a Chinese principal. It flourished so that it outgrew its quarters and was moved to roomier buildings in the Flower Garden.

K'ung became involved in politics following the Revolution of 1911, when he served as head of volunteer troops in Shansi. He became even more committed after the death in 1913 of his first wife, a former teacher at the North China Woman's College. He met and married Soong Ailing, the eldest of three famous Soong sisters. One of the others, Chingling, married Sun Yat-sen, the founder of the Republic of China; the third, Mei-ling, wed Chiang Kai-shek, the republic's first president. K'ung, who subsequently became a banker in Shanghai and reputedly the wealthiest man in China, held a number of government positions, first in Shansi, then on the national level. At one time in the late 1930s, he was China's premier and later the country's finance minister. By then, he had westernized his name to H. H. Kung and was known as "Daddy" Kung.

Before his death in 1967, Kung made a number of gifts to Oberlin and established scholarships in the names of Rowena Bird and Luella Miner. The middle name of one of his daughters was Rowena.

The Boxer Rebellion failed to swerve the purpose of missionary societies or change their attitudes. China was still Satan's fortress and the key to worldwide salvation. In fact, the societies viewed the Rebellion as an aberration, a deviation from the norm caused by rampant heathenism. In no way did they interpret it as a reflection on their evangelical goals or on themselves. If anything, the grim fate of missionaries such as the members of the Oberlin Band fired the enthusiasm to serve in China.

No less a figure than Judson Smith—who had inspired the formation of the Oberlin Band two decades earlier—reported to the annual meeting of the American Board at St. Louis barely two months after the massacres in Shansi:

> The old-time conflict of Heathenism and Christianity is here renewed; conservatism and reverence for the past struggle against progress and the forces that animate and unite the western nations. . . .
>
> [W]e are reminded of the greater persecutions of the early church under Decius and Diocletian, when the church was bleeding at every pore. . . . We can no more retreat or abandon the work than the church could abandon

Rome when its martyrs fell, or than our Lord could abandon the world because it received him not. . . .

Are missionaries responsible for the things that have been done and suffered?

. . . There is nothing but these outbreaks to suggest even that they are not welcome guests in the land, and these outbreaks are confessedly the acts of law-breakers and violent men. . . .

But missionaries, we are told, have no business in China, forcing a foreign and hateful religion upon the people; their very presence and work naturally arouse resentment and hatred. This is an astonishing statement. Had the Apostles no business to preach the gospel when they went forth from Jerusalem, turning the world upside down? Had the martyrs and missionaries of the early church no business in that dark and loveless Roman world, which they presently filled with heavenly peace and glory? Were Augustine and his followers embarked on an impertinent errand when, at the peril of life and fortune, they came to England and preached the gospel to our savage and pagan forefathers there? . . .

No! search the missionary records as we may, make all the allowance due to human infirmity and mistakes, set down every slip and every fault; not one of them, nor all of them together, gives any rational explanation of this great anti-foreign outbreak in China. . . .

"The blood of the martyrs is the seed of the church." How thickly that precious seed has now been sown. What harvests await our faith in Pao-ting-fu and all its borders; in Shansi far and near, around Peking and Tung-cho, from the Yellow River to the Great Wall, from the sea to the far mountains of the West. . . .

When we went to China with the gospel it was to stay and conquer; and nothing has happened to change our purpose. We have met a stunning blow; great losses have come upon us, and a temporary check; but it is no crushing is the Bull Run and the Fredericksburg of our campaign; the Wilderness, Richmond and Appomattox lie before us. And all the voices of earthly wisdom, and all the trumpets of the skies, and all the examples of Christian history, and the blood of our martyred dead, summon us to these later and greater deeds, until the night is gone and China is won.[34]

By 1906 there were 3,500 Protestant missionaries in China—700 more than in 1900. They included the great majority of all the missionaries who had survived the Rebellion, including many who had suffered imprisonment. The missionaries claimed nearly 180,000 converts.[35] By 1917 that number had grown to more than 6,000 missionaries, who served a Christian community numbering more than 600,000 Chinese.[36] Between

1903, when Oberlin missionaries began returning to China, and 1917, no less than 28 men and women from the college served in Shansi.

However, as attractive as the ethical teachings of Jesus were to Chinese, Christian doctrine remained alien to their way of thought and tradition. In spite of the record number of adherents the Protestants could claim, no more than about one percent of the total population of China ever converted to either the Protestant or Roman Catholic version of Christianity.

Missionaries did gradually shift their emphasis to practical and social reforms rather than evangelism as the result of anti-imperialist pressure after the Revolution of 1911, when, after 260 years, the Ching dynasty fell. The Boxer Rebellion, it turns out in hindsight a century later, was one of the major factors, a watershed, in the bridge between ancient and modern China.

Dowager Empress Tz'u Hsi and Emperor Kuang Hsü died within days of each other in November 1908, he first, supposedly poisoned or strangled at her instigation, but that is believed to be another canard leveled at her. Following the overthrow of the Ching dynasty in the Revolution of 1911, China became a republic. But even Nationalists who inspired the revolution, many of whom were Christians themselves, continued to condemn missions as an arm of Western imperialism, and during the 1920s, several anti-Christian movements developed.

The old American missionary societies that continued to labor in China focused in the early part of the twentieth century on operating schools and hospitals, encouraging agricultural development, developing cultural ties, establishing newspapers and publishing plants. But their efforts were plagued by continued unrest in China and then by war.

Japan, which never abandoned its ambitions on the mainland, seized Manchuria in 1931 and invaded China proper six years later. The country was subsequently devastated by World War II, and, even though Japan surrendered all its acquisitions at the end of the war, internal unrest arose, particularly between the Kuomintang (Nationalist) party headed by Chiang Kai-shek and Communists led by Mao Tse-tung. After a long and bloody civil war, the Communists drove the Nationalists from China and in 1949 set up the People's Republic of China. The United States refused to recognize the new government for thirty years. Today in China the government tolerates the few citizens who are Christians, but it strictly controls their activities; foreign clerics are forbidden. Missionary societies no longer wield any influence whatsoever in the country's future.

For nearly a century scholars have debated the impact that missionaries had on China. Were they a help, bringing Western ideas and methods to a stagnant empire? Or did they disrupt an ancient, honorable way of life, pitting Chinese against Chinese? Prior to 1980, the "politically correct" view was unabashedly negative. As one Chinese critic expressed it:

> There is no group of foreigners who have done more harm to China than modern missionaries, either directly or indirectly. It is in connection with their subversive activities that China has lost the greater part of her dependencies. By their teaching they have denationalised hundreds of thousands of Chinese converts, and have thus been instrumental, to a great extent, in disintegrating not only the body but also the spirit of the nation.[37]

Since then, a much more balanced assessment has arisen among scholars in China, one that stresses the missionary movement's role in introducing modern medical knowledge and printing technology, educational reforms, and modern curricula—all invaluable in the development of modern China. Moreover, the high standards of academic performance in Christian colleges and universities within China, these scholars now acknowledge, were a model that Chinese institutions felt compelled to emulate—and thus likewise contributed a positive, constructive influence in the emergence of China into the modern world.

Still, these same scholars view the missionaries in a negative light. The missionaries are considered as being culturally arrogant, as being imperialist in their attitudes toward the Chinese, as well as being almost totally insensitive to the social structure in which they found themselves.

❁ *Epilogue*

A youth is be regarded with respect. How do we know that his future will not be equal to our present?
—*Confucius*

Despite wars, revolutionary upheavals, and civil war in China throughout the twentieth century, the spirit that sparked the young seminarians who wanted to start an Oberlin-in-China has never died. For a half century after the Boxer Rebellion, Oberlin missionaries continued to serve in Shansi as representatives of the American Board. In the early years of the twentieth century, many worked under K'ung Hsiang Hsi at Ming Hsien Academy.

Lydia Davis and Alice Williams were active in the establishment in 1908 of the Oberlin Shansi Memorial Association. OSMA, as it is more familiarly known, was established to support educational work connected with the American Board's operations in Shansi Province, in particular Ming Hsien Academy. The Board's link was eventually severed when the school came under the regulations of the national government in 1927 and mandatory Bible courses and church attendance had to be abolished. In time, the influence of the Christian faith in Oberlin College's goals gradually diminished, too, and Oberlin's graduate theological school—breeding ground for the Oberlin Band—declined so much in the post-World War II period that it was eventually merged with the Divinity School of Vanderbilt University in Nashville, Tennessee, in the mid-1960s.

However, as early as 1918, Oberlin College began sending civilian representatives—or "reps"—to Ming Hsien to teach English. The first to go was Lydia Davis's son Lewis. He was followed the next year by her son John. Lydia herself served as executive secretary of OSMA from 1929 to 1941.

The Oberlin reps served in Shansi for terms of two or three years, and since 1928 they have included both men and women. In addition to their teaching assignments, they have led a number of extracurricular activities, including sports. None was ever a missionary.

Lydia returned to China in 1924, mainly to visit the girls' school in Fenchow-fu that was named after her. She died in November 1952 at the age of eighty-five, some ten months after the death of her lifelong friend Alice Williams.

Alice had returned to China in 1909, serving there until 1912, when she went back to Oberlin as matron of the college's dormitories. She visited China in the mid-1930s, escaping from Japanese armies on the last train out of North China. Her daughter Gladys later served in China as head of a school for married women that was founded in Alice's honor and named for her. Alice was ninety-one years old when she died.

Ming Hsien Academy included both primary and secondary schools that became coeducational, a revolutionary step at the time in China. Its programs were expanded to include an agriculture department, which developed better strains of fruits and corn and a breed of sheep that gave more wool; an industrial department, which helped to improve irrigation techniques; and a rural service department, which promoted literacy and public health.

The Japanese invasion of China in 1937 forced the school to move south, in a trek by train, truck, and on foot that covered thirteen hundred miles until it finally reached Szechwan Province. There, in 1940, K'ung tried to make a reality of the Oberlin Band's dream of a half-century before, a college. He founded a three-year school of agriculture and industry; it was later expanded to a four-year college with the addition of a commercial department. But the war, inflation, and inadequate financial resources caused its failure after a few years.

Oberlin's involvement in China was abruptly curtailed when China sided with North Korea in the Korean War in 1950. Instead, during the next three decades, Oberlin reps became part of student and faculty exchange programs with schools in Japan, India, Taiwan, and several other Asian and Pacific nations. Reps were able to return to Shansi in 1980, after the United States resumed diplomatic relations with China. By then the Communists had turned Ming Hsien into Shansi Agricultural University, a logical extension of the program that the Academy had initiated. An exchange program was set up between Oberlin College and the university and the Taiyuan Institute of Engineering.

Shansi Agricultural University occupies the old Ming Hsien campus in the Flower Garden, where the bodies of most of the missionaries as well as those of several of their Chinese friends lay undisturbed until the mid-twentieth century. Each year Oberlin continues to send two reps to Shansi.

In May 1903 a monument, the Memorial Arch, was dedicated at Oberlin in commemoration of the eighteen members of the American Board and their families who died in China during the Boxer Rebellion. The Arch, constructed of Indiana limestone and bracketed on both sides by a gently curving line of columns, was erected on the west side of the college campus, Tappan Square. Some money to build the Arch was raised among students and faculty, but by far the greater part was donated by a New York philanthropist who was vice-chairman of the American Board and who believed the missionaries deserved a fitting tribute for the sacrifice of their lives.[1] Oberlin was selected because all but three of the martyrs were either Oberlin students or members of their families.

In the cornerstone of the Arch is a box containing the missionaries' last letters and accounts of their ordeal by Chinese Christians who survived; the rosters of churches in Ohio and Maine to which the missionaries belonged; biographical sketches, and photographs. Their names appear on bronze tablets inside the Arch. Epigraphs carved into the stone read:

> "The Blood of Martyrs—The Seed of the Church"
> "More than Conquerors through Him that Loved Us"
> "Neither Count I My Life Dear Unto Myself"
> "If We Died with Him We Shall Also Live with Him"

For many years the Arch remained a symbol of Oberlin's faith in changing the world for the better. It became traditional for graduating classes at commencement exercises to parade through it.

The dedication of the Memorial Arch on the campus of Oberlin College, May 14, 1903. Courtesy Oberlin College Archives.

But the Arch has taken on other meanings in the last half-century. In the early 1950s it became the rallying point for a group of students opposed to the Korean War. Then, as awareness of minority oppression and minority rights grew, it was seen as a symbol of Western aggression and imperialism. One student called the Arch a "blatant example of Oberlin's ethnocentricity and institutional racism."[2] Another declared that it "acknowledges the Chinese only as irrational barbarians and not as people working towards the realization of new political and social realities. . . . It fails to consider the complexities of the colonial situation and its role in precipitating the [Boxer] movement."[3] A third student denounced the Oberlin martyrs, saying:

> Good intentions aside, the missionaries represented a completely alien culture which not only misunderstood but also condemned Chinese culture in totality.[4]

Why, asked still another student, were no Chinese commemorated? He suggested that a separate monument be erected as a memorial to the Chinese Christians who also were slain.

Students have, in fact, put up commemorative arches and plaques in honor of the Chinese. In 1958, for instance, a wooden Chinese-style archway was erected directly across from the Memorial Arch "in memory of the Chinese killed in the Boxer Rebellion," apparently including in its commemoration converts, innocent non-Christians, and Boxers.[5]

A more sensational protest occurred in the fall of 1993, when an Asian-American student took credit for using spray paint to write "dead chink—good chink" and "death to chinks memorial" across the bases on which the columns of the Memorial Arch rest. The student said the decoration was intended to protest that the monument "glorifies white accomplishment" and makes no mention of "the thousands of Chinese who were killed or raped, either Boxer or Christian."[6]

Since the 1970s many graduating seniors have refused to march through the Arch on commencement day. Their reluctance to do so—and their desire to see Chinese also remembered—is the subject of annual demonstrations.

In that sense, the Arch symbolizes the disturbing legacy of the brief moment in history that was known as the Boxer Rebellion. The clash of cultures is still unresolved. Westerners still do not understand the complexities of Chinese civilization and tend to interpret its government, culture, and mores in ethnocentric terms. Chinese still do not trust foreigners.

If nothing else, one can view the Arch as a symbol of the attitudes of a time that are no longer acceptable—and a reminder of the long road to understanding and tolerance that still lies ahead.

❁ *Appendix*

The following is a partial list of those slain during the summer of 1900 as the result of attacks on mission stations in the provinces of Shansi and Chih-li. The list includes the missionaries associated with the American Board of Commissioners for Foreign Missions and members of their families, all of whose names appear on the Memorial Arch in Oberlin, Ohio, as well as missionaries attached to other societies, independent missionaries, and Chinese—Christian and non-Christian—who died with them or because of their association with them.

The list of the Chinese is by no means complete: Scores died. Indeed, nearly two thousand Chinese associated with Protestant missions throughout North China were killed in addition, it is estimated, to more than thirty thousand Chinese connected with Roman Catholic missions. Many other Chinese were innocent victims unconnected with any foreign mission. However, the names of most Chinese who perished were not recorded, and even the names given below are sometimes incomplete or may be incorrectly identified because of transliteration into English.

PAOTINGFU

American Board

Rev. Horace Tracy Pitkin
Mary Susan Morrill
Annie Allender Gould
Rev. Meng Chang-chun—*pastor known as Meng I; also three of his children*
Mrs. Tu—*Pastor Meng's sister, a Bible woman; together with her three children*
Mrs. Kao—*Bible woman*
Mrs. Chang—*Bible woman, mother of Chang Ch'iang Hsiang*
Mrs. Chien—*seamstress*

Presbyterian Board

Dr. Cortlandt Van Rensselaer Hodge
Elsie Sinclair Hodge
Rev. Frank Edson Simcox
May Gilson Simcox

Simcox children—*Francis, Paul, Margaret*
Dr. George Yardley Taylor

China Inland Mission
Rev. Benjamin Bagnall
Emily Kingsbury Bagnall
Bagnall child—*Gladys*
Rev. William Cooper

TAI YUAN

American Board
Atwater children—*Ernestine, Mary*

British and Foreign Bible Society
Rev. W. T. Beynon
Emily Taylor Beynon
Beynon children—*Daisy, Kenneth, Norman*

China Inland Mission
Mildred Eleanor Clarke
Jane Stevens

English Baptist Society
Edith Anna Coombs
Rev. George B. Farthing
Mrs. George B. Farthing
Farthing children—*Ruth, Guy, unnamed baby*
Dr. Arnold E. Lovitt
Mrs. Arnold E. Lovitt
Lovitt child—*John (Jack)*
Rev. James Simpson
Mrs. James Simpson
Ellen M. Stewart
Rev. George W. Stokes
Margaret Whittaker Stokes
Rev. F. S. Whitehouse
Mrs. F. S. Whitehouse
Dr. William Millar Wilson
Mrs. William Millar Wilson
Wilson child—*William*
Chang Ch'eng Sheng—*helper*
Liu Hao—*helper*
Liu P'ai Yüan—*helper*
Wang Hsi Ho—*helper*

Independent Missionaries, others
Alexander Hoddle
Rev. Thomas Wellesley Pigott
Jessie Kempt Pigott
Pigott child—*Wellesley William*
John Robinson
Mme. Duval
Ch'ang An—*student, Shou Yang*

TAIKU

American Board
Rev. Dwight Howard Clapp
Mary Jane Clapp
Susan Rowena Bird
Mary Louise Partridge
Rev. George Louis Williams
Rev. Francis Ward Davis
Mr. An—*Christian of Tung Fang, first martyr of Taiku*
Chang Cheng Yü—*known also as Fu Ssi Ching, pupil in boys' school, brother of Chang Cheng Fu (Er Wu); also the Chang brothers' sister and her husband*
Ch'ang Pao Erh—*church member*
Ch'eng Chung Jen—*baptized Christian*

Ching Huan txu—*known as "blind-Lois"*
Chun Sao—*daughter-in-law of Deacon Liu*
Fan Liu Te—*teacher, known as Ruth Fan*
Mrs. K'ang—*wife of member of Taiku church, killed with oldest daughter, a pupil in the girls' school in Li Man*
Kuo Hsiao Hsien—*servant and traveling companion of Louise Partridge, with his blind, eighty-year-old mother*
Kuo Ma Erh—*student*
Kao Wei Hua—*wife of imprisoned Kao Feng Cheng*
Li Heng Chang—*blind seventy-year-old church member*
Mr. Li—*Christian*
Liang Chi Tai—*Christian*
Lin Chen—*helper and teacher*
Liu Chang Lao—*known as Teacher Liu; also his wife, child and daughter-in-law*
Liu Feng Chih—*pastor known as Deacon Liu*
Dr. and Mr. Sang Ai Ch'ing—*medical assistants, together with their two children*
Shih Shou Chi—*church member*
Mr. Tai—*church member*
Tsui Hen Tai—*helper of Francis Davis, together with his family, seven persons in all*
Wang Pao Rung—*church member, together with his family, six persons in all, including a former pupil of Jennie Clapp's*
Wang Shan and Wang Yu—*brothers, both former opium addicts from Ching shen Tsun*
Mrs. Wang—*of Tung Fang, with her little son*
Wu San Yuan—*church member*
Yang Chien Chung—*church member and Howard Clapp's gatekeeper; also his mother and two younger brothers, pupils in the boys' school*

FENCHOW-FU

American Board

Rev. Charles Wesley Price
Eva Jane Price
Price child—*Florence*
Rev. Ernest Richmond Atwater
Elizabeth Graham Atwater
Atwater children—*Celia, Bertha*
Chang—*church member*
Tien—*church member*

China Inland Mission

Annie Eldred
Rev. Anton Peter Lundgren
Elsa Nilson Lundgren

Notes

When you know a thing, to hold that you know it; and when you do not know a thing, to allow that you do not know it;—this is knowledge.

—Confucius

Anyone reading the letters and journals of the missionaries will find a city or village—and Chinese individuals—spelled differently by different persons. Frequently, however, when the letter in question has been copied by hand or on a typewriter, the person doing the transcript made typographical mistakes. I have corrected such errors when they were obvious; otherwise, I have adhered to the original text of the letters and journals.

The interest in the massacres of 1900 was so widespread that photostats, carbon copies and handwritten copies of many documents were deposited in a variety of archives. As a result, copies of a number of the letters and journals cited in the notes that follow can be found in more than one file in the Oberlin Archives, in the Papers of the Board of Commissioners for Foreign Missions, and in other repositories. When possible, I have used the clearest of copies, the most complete, or the one freest of typos.

There is some minor confusion of dates of certain events among the accounts left by the members of the Oberlin Band and the Christians who survived them. I have attempted to bring some order out of the conflicts.

The following abbreviations are used in the notes:

ABCFM — American Board of Commissioners for Foreign Missions: Missions to Asia, 1827–1919: Shansi Mission (ABC 16.3.15), vol. 1–6, reels (microfilm) 316–23, Oberlin College Library

Bird — Papers of Susan Rowena Bird, 1893–1898, Oberlin College Archives

Clippings	Clippings, 1897–1902: Boxer Martyrs, Oberlin College Archives
CL	The Congregational Library, Boston
Corbin	Papers of Paul L. Corbin, 1904–1936, Oberlin College Archives
Davis	Papers of Lydia Lord Davis, 1862–1944, Oberlin College Archives
Fei	Mrs. Arthur H. Smith, *Mr. Fei's True Story.* Chicago: Women's Board of Missions of the Interior, n.d., Oberlin College Archives
Fitch	Papers of Florence M. Fitch, 1807–1951, Oberlin College Archives
Hale	Papers of Jonathan Hale Family, 1763–1950, Western Reserve Historical Society, Cleveland, Ohio
Houghton	Papers of the American Board of Commissioners for Foreign Missions: Missions to Asia: 1827–1919: Shansi Mission (ABC 16.3.15), vol. 1–6, Houghton Library, Harvard University, Cambridge, Mass.
Leith	Papers of J. C. Leith, 1851–1954, Oberlin College Archives
Miss'ys	Missionaries: Miscellany, Oberlin College Archives
OC	Files in the office of the Archivist, Oberlin College
OCA	Oberlin College Archives, Oberlin, Ohio
OCL	Oberlin College Library, Special Collections
Ohio	City Missionary Society: Letters, 1888–1897, written by Jennie Pond Atwater and Ernest R. Atwater, Ohio Historical Society
OSMA	Papers of the Oberlin Shansi Memorial Association, Oberlin College Archives

Pond	Papers of Chauncy N. Pond, 1892–1916, Oberlin College Archives
USMA	Special Collections, United States Military Academy Library, West Point, N.Y.
Williams	Papers of Mr. and Mrs. George L. Williams, 1883–1952, Oberlin College Archives
WRHS	Western Reserve Historical Society, Cleveland
Wright	Papers of George Frederick Wright, 1911–1921, Oberlin College Archives
Yale	Yale Divinity School Library, New Haven, Conn.

PREFACE

1. Clifton Jackson Phillips, *Protestant America and the Pagan World: The First Half Century of the American Board of Commissioners for Foreign Missions, 1810–1860* (Cambridge, Mass.: East Asian Research Center, Harvard University, 1969), 204.

1. THE NEWLYWEDS

1. Lydia Lord Davis, "Letters to My Grandchildren," typewritten, paginated manuscript, p.36, Davis Papers, OCA.
2. Ibid., 35.
3. Archibald L. Love to Lydia Davis, March 14, 1904, Davis Papers, OCA.
4. Judson Smith to Lydia Davis, Nov. 30, 1888, Davis Papers, OCA.
5. Remarks of William E. Barton at memorial service, Leavitt Street Congregational Church, Chicago, n.d., Davis Papers, OCA.
6. Archibald L. Love to Lydia Davis, March 14, 1904, Davis Papers, OCA.
7. The classmate was Charles Wesley Price.
8. Remarks of William E. Barton, Davis Papers, OCA.
9. Francis Ward Davis to American Board of Commissioners for Foreign Missions, May 16, 1889, ABCFM, reel 316.
10. The letters quoted between Francis and Lydia Davis are dated June 20, June 25, June 28, July 6, July 10 and July 19, 1889, Davis Papers, OCA.
11. Lydia Davis, "Letters to My Grandchildren," p. 35, Davis Papers, OCA.

12. Lydia Davis diary, kept in a student's notebook, Davis Papers, OCA. The entry is dated Oct. 20, 1889.

13. Tientsin is now Tianjin.

14. Liu Feng Chih's story is an amalgam of a sketch written by Iranaeus Atwood for the *Christian Union,* a handwritten copy of which is in Williams Papers, OCA.; a memorandum of his Christian experience that Liu wrote in his diary when examined for baptism on Feb. 25, 1891, as translated by Atwood, Williams Papers, OCA; and an unspecified newspaper clipping, Clippings, OCA.

15. Alice Williams to Florence Fitch, March 3, 1909, Fitch Papers, OCA.

16. Ernest Atwater to "Folks at the Old Home," Feb. 12, 1895, Ohio. Atwater added, "Oh, that China were full of such men. She would be a blessing to the whole world rather than what I fear she may be, the permanent strong hold [*sic*] of materialism."

17. Jennie Clapp to "My dearest Mary Ella," Nov. 10, 1899, Pond Papers, OCA.

2. SHANSI

1. Lydia Davis, "Letters to My Grandchildren," p. 38, Davis Papers, OCA.

2. Charles Price to C. O. Hale, Dec. 3, 1895, Hale Papers, WRHS. C. O. Hale was Charles Oviatt Hale (1850–1938), a benefactor of the mission school in Fenchow-fu, who was elected to the Ohio House of Representatives in 1892 and 1914.

3. Lydia Davis, "A Martyr's Children," *Missionary Dayspring* 20:4 (Apr. 1901), 39, Davis Papers, OCA.

4. Eva Jane Price, *China Journal 1889–1900: An American Missionary Family During the Boxer Rebellion* (New York: Collier, 1989), 160–1.

5. Ibid., 12.

6. Ray F. Downs, "Oberlin in China, 1880–1900" (senior thesis, Oberlin College, 1954), 9.

7. Robert E. Speer, *A Memorial of Horace Tracy Pitkin* (New York: Fleming H. Revell, 1903), 210, Yale.

8. Lydia Davis, "Letters to My Grandchildren," p. 38, Davis Papers, OCA.

9. Downs, "Oberlin in China, 1880–1900," 9. The person being quoted is Rev. Chauncey Goodrich of the North China Mission.

10. Charles Price to C. O. Hale, Jan. 1, 1895, Hale Papers, WRHS.

11. Speer, *A Memorial of Horace Tracy Pitkin,* 222, Yale.

12. Mary Tarpley Campfield, "Oberlin in China, 1881–1951" (Ph.D. diss., University of Virginia, 1974), 15.

13. Ibid., 16.

14. Charles Price to C. O. Hale, Mar. 13, 1894, Hale Papers, WRHS.

15. George Williams to Judson Smith, Nov. 23, 1892, ABCFM, reel 321.

16. Francis Davis to Rev. McInnes Neilson and Ravenna Congregational Christian Endeavor Society, Mar. 30, 1900, Davis Papers, OCA.

17. Alice M. Kyle, ed., *In Memory of Miss Mary S. Morrill and Miss Annie Allender Gould* (Boston: Woman's Board of Missions, n.d.), 28, USMA.

18. Eva Price to "My dear friends," Feb. 25, 1899, Williams Papers, OCA.

19. Eva Price to "Our dear friend," Mar. 27, 1900, Williams Papers, OCA.

3. THE GREAT FAMINE

1. Paul Richard Bohr, *Famine in China and the Missionary: Timothy Richard as Relief Administrator and Advocate of National Reform, 1876–1884* (Cambridge, Mass.: East Asian Research Center, Harvard University, 1972), 21.

2. Ibid., i.

3. Ibid., 65.

3. Ibid., 119.

5. Ibid.

6. Timothy Richard, *Forty-five Years in China* (London: Unwin, 1916), 155.

7. Ibid., 158.

8. L. D. Chapin, "The Missionary Call from China," pamphlet distributed by the American Board, 1880, CL.

9. Phillips, *Protestant America,* quotations from pp. 1, 10, and 12, respectively.

4. THE OBERLIN BAND: THE FOUNDING MEMBERS

1. Oberlin China Band Recording Secretary's Book, OSMA, OCA. Stimson's fiancée—and soon-to-be wife—Emily Brooks Hall was the sister of Charles Martin, founder of the Aluminum Company of America (Alcoa) and a major benefactor of Oberlin.

2. Campfield, "Oberlin in China, 1881–1951," 2.

3. See Nat Brandt, *The Town That Started the Civil War* (Syracuse, N.Y.: Syracuse Univ. Press, 1990).

4. John Barnard, *From Evangelicalism to Progressivism at Oberlin College, 1866–1917* (Columbus: Ohio State Univ. Press, 1969), 28.

5. Ibid., 30.

6. *Oberlin Record,* June 27, 1889. Because missionaries were posted so far from schools, many of them sent their children back to Ohio to be educated, so a home for them was formed in Oberlin in 1890. It became the nucleus of a "missionary compound" of several buildings known collectively as the Tank Home that housed the youngsters and missionary families on furlough.

7. Susan F. Hinman, *Ming Hsien: Memorial to Heroes of Three Nations* (New York: n.p., 1958), 5.

8. American Board to Martin Luther Stimson, OSMA, OCA.

9. E. K. Alden to Martin Luther Stimson, Jan. 12, 1881, Recording Secretary's Book, OSMA, OCA.

10. E. K. Alden to Judson Smith, Jan. 12, 1881, Recording Secretary's Book, OSMA, OCA.

11. E. K. Alden to Martin Luther Stimson, Jan. 17, 1881, Recording Secretary's Book, OSMA, OCA.

12. Martin Luther Stimson to E. K. Alden, Feb. 9, 1881, OSMA, OCA.

13. Charles Tenney to E. K. Alden, Apr. 14, 1882, OSMA, OCA.

14. N. G. Clark to Martin Luther Stimson, Mar. 5, 1881, OSMA, OCA.

15. N. G. Clark to Martin Luther Stimson, Apr. 9, 1881, OSMA, OCA.

16. N. G. Clark to Chauncey Cady, June 8, 1882, OSMA, OCA.

17. Stimson's companion on the scouting trip was Isaac Pierson.

18. N. G. Clark to Oberlin Band, Apr. 19, 1882, OSMA, OCA.

19. Campfield, "Oberlin in China, 1881–1951," 25.

20. Ellsworth C. Carlson, *Oberlin in Asia: The First Hundred Years, 1882–1982* (Oberlin, Ohio: Oberlin Shansi Memorial Association, 1982), 8.

21. N. G. Clark to Oberlin Band, Apr. 19, 1882, OSMA, OCA.

22. Downs, "Oberlin in China, 1880–1900," 9.

23. Martin Luther Stimson, "Early Days," *Schwenkfeldian,* 104, OSMA, OCA. The article was written in 1934.

24. Minutes of Dec. 29, 1883, special meeting, Shansi Mission, OSMA, OCA.

25. Minutes of Annual Meeting, May 10, 1887, Shansi Mission, OSMA, OCA.

26. *Oberlin Record,* June 27, 1889.

27. Tenney was subsequently tutor to the children of Viceroy Li Hung Chang. He was asked to enter Chinese government service after China's defeat by Japan in 1895. He organized the University of Tientsin, and later, in 1902, a regular system of schools in the interior, including a provincial high school at Paotingfu.

28. Louise Partridge to Lydia Davis, Jan. 6, 1893, Davis, OCA. The letter is misdated. It should be 1894. Louise did not leave for China until August 1893. A number of times the missionaries misdated their letters when writing shortly after the start of a new year.

29. Lydia Davis, "Letters to My Grandchildren," p. 80, Davis Papers, OCA.

30. Jennie Atwater to "Dear Grandma," Oct. 17, 1893, Pond Papers, OCA. The daughter of the Frank Prices who died was named Frankie. Charles and Eva Price lost sons Donald and Stewart. The other Atwood boy who died was named Kenneth.

31. Lydia Davis, "After Death of Children," entry for Jan. 1891, Davis Papers, OCA.

32. Ibid., entry for June 20, 1894.

33. Ibid., entry for June 23, 1895.

34. Charles Price to C. O. Hale, Apr. 16, 1896, Hale Papers, WRHS.

35. Charles Price to C. O. Hale, Jan. 1, 1900, Hale Papers, WRHS.

36. Eva Price, *China Journal,* 74.

37. Eva Price to "Dear Friends, one and all in the Pond homestead," Jan. 4, 1899, Pond Papers, OCA.

38. Eva Price to "My dear friend," Mar. 1, 1899, Williams Papers, OCA.

39. Rev. F. M. Price, "Mission Work in Shansi," typescript, OSMA, OCA.

40. Ibid.

41. Grace McConnaughey notes, OSMA, OCA.

42. Ibid.

43. Rev. F. M. Price, "Mission Work," OSMA, OCA.

44. Downs, "Oberlin in China, 1880–1900," 13.

45. Rev. F. M. Price, "Mission Work," OSMA, OCA.

5. "LITTLE AMERICA"

1. Lydia Davis, "Letters to My Grandchildren," p. 39, Davis Papers, OCA.

2. Eva Price, *China Journal,* 201.

3. George Williams to Judson Smith, Jan. 18, 1893, ABCFM, reel 321.

4. Eva Price, *China Journal,* 39.

5. Charles Price to C. O. Hale, June 21, 1899, Hale Papers, WRHS.

6. Eva Price, *China Journal,* 40.

7. Ibid., 22.

8. Ibid., 201.

9. Ibid., 175.

10. Ibid., 19.

11. George Williams to Judson Smith, June 20, 1893, ABCFM, reel 321.

12. Lydia Davis, "Letters to My Grandchildren," p. 42, Davis Papers, OCA.

13. Charles Price to C. O. Hale, Mar. 19, 1894, Hale Papers, WRHS.

14. Charles Price to C. O. Hale, Apr. 16, 1896, Hale Papers, WRHS.

15. Eva Price to "My dear friends," June 22, 1900, Williams Papers, OCA.

16. Eva Price, *China Journal*, 46.

17. Ibid., 22.

18. Ibid., 126.

19. Ibid., 85.

20. Campfield, "Oberlin in China, 1881–1951," 25.

21. Ernest Atwater to Dr. F. S. Clark, undated, Ohio.

22. The compound housed the families of Howard and Jennie Clapp, George and Alice Williams, Ernest and Jennie Atwater (before they moved), Susan Rowena Bird, and Deacon Liu, the rest of whose family lived in Che Wang. The room of the single female missionary subsequently mentioned was that of Bird.

23. George Williams to Judson Smith, Nov. 23, 1892, ABCFM, reel 321.

24. The Clapps were the couple inconvenienced by the layout of the rooms in the compound.

25. "Three Thousand Dollars. A New House Needed for Rev. and Mrs. G. L. Williams, Taiku, Shansi, China," Williams Papers, OCA.

26. Alice Williams to Charles Price, Aug. 21, 1896, ABCFM, reel 321.

27. George Williams, extracts from undated letter to Congregational Sunday School in Southington, Conn., Williams Papers, OCA.

28. Charles Price to C. O. Hale, June 21, 1899, Hale Papers, WRHS.

29. Eva Price, *China Journal*, 187.

30. Charles Price to C. O. Hale, Jan. 5, 1899, Hale Papers, WRHS. As with some other letters of missionaries written at the start of a new year, this one is misdated. It refers to the edict of 1900, so the date should read Jan. 5, 1900.

31. Jonathan Spence, *The Search for Modern China* (New York: Norton, 1990), 129.

32. John K. Fairbank, *China: A New History* (Cambridge, Mass.: Harvard Univ. Press, 1992), 234.

33. Charles Price to C. O. Hale, Jan. 5, 1899 [1900], Hale Papers, WRHS.

34. Eva Price to "My dear friend," Dec. 4, 1899, Hale Papers, WRHS.

35. Downs, "Oberlin in China, 1880–1900," 16.

36. Ibid., 14.

6. REALITIES

1. Downs, "Oberlin in China, 1880–1900," 10.

2. Ibid., 10.

3. Charles Tenney to Oberlin Band, Jan. 13, 1883, OSMA, OCA.

4. Chauncey Cady to Oberlin Band, Jan. 13, 1883, OSMA, OCA.

5. Chauncey Cady to Oberlin Band, May 11, 1884, OSMA, OCA.

6. Stimson, "Early Days," *Schwenkfeldian*, 104, OSMA, OCA.

7. Ernest Atwater to "Folks at the Old Home," Feb. 12, 1895, Ohio.

8. Charles P. Fitzgerald, "Opposing Cultural Traditions, Barriers to Communication," in Jessie G. Lutz, ed., *Christian Missions in China: Evangelists of What?* (Lexington, Mass.: Heath, 1965), 98.

9. John Henry Barrows, *The Christian Conquest of Asia* (New York: Scribner, 1899), 192.

10. A. H. Smith, *China in Convulsion* (Edinburgh: Oliphant, Anderson and Ferrier, 1901), 1:34.

11. Eva Price, *China Journal*, xxii.

12. Sidney A. Forsythe, *An American Missionary Community in China, 1895–1905* (Cambridge, Mass.: East Asian Research Center, Harvard University, 1971), 62.

13. Lutz, *Christian Missions in China*, xiv.

14. Paul A. Cohen, "The Contested Past: The Boxers as History and Myth," *Journal of Asian Studies*, 51:1 (Feb. 1992), 107. Jiang Menglin is the person quoted.

15. Downs, "Oberlin in China, 1880–1900," 17.

16. Charles Price to C. O. Hale, Dec. 3, 1895, Hale Papers, WRHS.

17. Lydia Davis, "Letters to My Grandchildren," p. 37–38, Davis Papers, OCA.

18. Forsythe, *American Missionary Community*, 27.

19. Francis Davis to Lydia Davis, undated, incomplete letter, Davis Papers, OCA.

20. George Williams to Judson Smith, Nov. 23, 1892, ABCFM, reel 321.

21. Barrows, *Christian Conquest of Asia*, 190–91.

22. Ibid.

23. Eva Price to "My dear friends," June 28, 1898, Hale Papers, WRHS.

24. Charles Price to C. O. Hale, Jan. 1, 1900, Hale Papers, WRHS.

25. Charles Price to C. O. Hale, July 4, 1893, Hale Papers, WRHS.

26. George Williams, undated letter, apparently written in 1894, when the Clapps returned to the United States, Williams Papers, OCA.

27. Rev. L. C. Partridge, "Memorial of Miss Mary Louise Partridge, one of the martyrs of China," n.d., n.p., Williams Papers, OCA.

28. Jennie Atwater to Lydia Davis, Dec. 13, 1892, Davis Papers, OCA.

29. Richard, *Forty-five Years in China*, 159.

30. Kyle, *In Memory of Mary Morrill and Annie Gould*, 22, USMA. Mary Morrill letter of June 14, 1889, is quoted.

31. Paul A. Varg, *Missionaries, Chinese, and Diplomats: The American Protestant Missionary Movement in China, 1890–1952* (Princeton, N.J.: Princeton Univ. Press, 1958), 6.

32. Kenneth Scott Latourette, *A History of Christian Missions in China* (New York: Macmillan, 1929), 405–406.

33. Joseph W. Esherick, *The Origins of the Boxer Uprising* (Berkeley: Univ. of California Press, 1987), 93.

34. Latourette, *History of Christian Missions in China*, 406.

35. Undated, unnamed newspaper clipping from 1900, OSMA, OCA.

7. SCHOOL DAYS

1. "In Loving Remembrance," reprint of *Missionary Herald*, Nov. 1900, issued by the American Board, 440, Williams Papers, OCA. Judson Smith is quoted.

2. Campfield, "Oberlin in China, 1881–1951," 28.

3. "In Loving Remembrance," 442, Williams Papers, OCA. Francis Price is quoted.

4. "History of Miss'ys Martyred 1900," handwritten draft of biographical sketches written for *Advance* of Sept. 27, 1900, OSMA, OCA.

5. Louise Partridge to "Dear friends," June 19, 1900, Williams Papers, OCA.

6. Rowena Bird to "To My Dear Brother," June 24, 1900, OCA. Hereafter referred to as Bird Letter, Bird Papers, OCA.

7. An incomplete series of record books detailing the courses and grades of students is kept in the Oberlin College Archives and is the source of the data here as well as the marks received by other members of the Oberlin Band.

8. *Oberlin Weekly News,* June 13, 1879.

9. Commencement programme, June 21, 1884, Dwight Howard Clapp file, Alumni Records, 1836–1977, OCA.

10. Eva Price, *China Journal,* 137.

11. Hinman, *Ming Hsien,* 8.

12. George Williams to "Dear Ella," Oct. 27, 1899, Williams Papers, OCA.

13. Lydia Davis, "Letters to My Grandchildren," p. 81.

14. Ibid., p. 40.

15. E. C. Parsons, "The Condition of Women in China," pamphlet, n.d., n.p., CL.

16. Speer, *A Memorial of Horace Tracy Pitkin,* 188, Yale.

17. Annie Allender Gould to "Dear Ones," Feb. 16, 1899, USMA.

18. Eva Price to "My dear friend," Mar. 26, 1900, Pond Papers, OCA.

19. Jennie Atwater to "Dear Ones at Home," Feb. 7, 1893, Williams Papers, OCA.

20. Kyle, *In Memory of Mary Morrill and Annie Gould,* 93, USMA. Mary Morrill letter of Apr. 1900 is quoted.

21. Eva Price to "My dear friends, one and all in the Pond homestead," Jan. 4, 1899, Pond Papers, OCA.

22. Louise Partridge to "Dear Grandma Thompson," Feb. 28, 1895, Williams Papers, OCA.

23. Kyle, *In Memory of Mary Morrill and Annie Gould,* 38, USMA. Mary Morrill letter of Apr. 1891 is quoted.

24. Mrs. Chia was the nurse of Bertha, hired by Ernest and Lizzie Atwater.

25. Eva Price to "My dear friends," Dec. 30, 1899, Pond Papers, OCA.

26. Jennie Clapp to Alice Williams, Apr. 25, 1900, Williams Papers, OCA.

27. Jennie Atwater to Lydia Davis, Dec. 13, 1892, Davis Papers, OCA.

28. Lydia Davis, "Letters to My Grandchildren," p. 41, Davis Papers, OCA.

29. In an alumni questionnaire that Francis Davis made out on Mar. 19, 1900, he gives the names of his children and their birth dates as William Potter Davis, born Feb. 1, 1893; John Lord Davis, born Aug. 12, 1896; and Lewis Eleazer, born Sept. 12, 1897. However, Lydia Davis, in "Letters to My Grandchildren," p. 43, says, upon returning to Ravenna, Ohio, "your father, George, was born . . ." Is it possible that Lydia renamed one of her sons after George Williams?

30. Lydia Davis, "Letters to My Grandchildren," p. 44, Davis Papers, OCA.

31. Henry S. Upson to Lydia Davis, Nov. 17, 1899, Davis Papers, OCA.

32. Eva Price to Lydia Davis, Dec. 20, 1899, Davis Papers, OCA.

33. Francis Davis to Lydia Davis, Feb. 19, 1900, Davis Papers, OCA.

34. Francis Davis to Judson Smith, Mar. 13, 1900, ABCFM, reel 323.

35. Francis Davis to Judson Smith, Apr. 28, 1900, ABCFM, reel 323.

36. Francis Davis to Lydia Davis, Mar. 19, 1900, Davis Papers, OCA.

8. "PARADISE COTTAGE"

1. Charles Price to C. O. Hale, Jan. 5, 1899 [1900], Hale Papers, WRHS.

2. Commencement programme, May 31, 1889, College General, Commencement Files, OCA.

3. Telephone conversation with author, Lucille Wilson, Eva Price's grandniece, Jan. 17, 1992.

4. Eva Price, *China Journal,* 133. Both the Fenchow-fu and the Taiku stations were known as "Little America" to other missionaries.

5. "In Loving Remembrance," 442, Williams Papers, OCA.

6. Rowena Bird to Alice Williams, Apr. 9, 1900, OSMA, OCA.

7. Francis Davis to Lydia Davis, Dec. 4, 1899, Davis Papers, OCA.

8. George Williams to Alice Williams, Apr. 27, 1900, Williams Papers, OCA.

9. "History of Miss'ys," OSMA, OCA.

10. Charles Price to C. O. Hale, Jan. 5, 1899 [1900], Hale Papers, WRHS.

11. Eva Price, *China Journal,* 95.

12. Eva Price, *China Journal,* 104.

13. Eva Price to "My dear friend," Mar. 1, 1899, Williams Papers, OCA.

14. Charles Price to C. O. Hale, July 4, 1893, Hale Papers, WRHS.

15. "In Loving Remembrance," 437–438, Williams Papers, OCA. Iranaeus Atwood is quoted.

16. Eva Price to "Dear Friends, one and all in the Pond homestead," Jan. 4, 1899, Pond Papers, OCA.

17. Eva Price to "My dear friend," Mar. 26, 1900, Pond Papers, OCA.

18. Eva Price to "My dear friends," June 28, 1898, Hale Papers, WRHS.

19. Eva Price to "My dear friends," Dec. 30, 1899, Pond Papers, OCA.

20. Eva Price to "My dear friends," Apr. 7, 1899, Williams Papers, OCA.

21. Eva Price to Lydia Davis and Alice Williams, Apr. 24, 1900, Williams Papers, OCA.

22. Eva Price, *China Journal,* 240.

23. Eva Price to "Our dear friend," Mar. 27, 1900, Williams Papers, OCA.

24. Eva Price, *China Journal,* 95.

25. Charles Price to C. O. Hale, Apr. 16, 1896, Hale Papers, WRHS.

26. Eva Price to "My dear friends," June 28, 1898, Hale Papers, WRHS.

9. THE ASSOCIATE MISSIONARIES

1. Resolution, Annual Mission Meeting, June 25, 1884, typescript, OSMA, OCA.

2. Report, Annual Mission Meeting, May 10, 1887, OSMA, OCA.

3. Charles Price to C. O. Hale, July 4, 1893, Hale Papers, WRHS.

4. Louise Partridge to "Dear friends," June 19, 1900, Williams Papers, OCA.

5. Rowena Bird to Lydia Davis, Mar. 18, 1894, Davis Papers, OCA.

6. Eva Price, *China Journal,* 133.

7. Rowena Bird to Lydia Davis, Mar. 30, 1900, reprinted in unspecified Oberlin newspaper, Pond Papers, OCA.

8. Eva Price, *China Journal,* 65.

9. Rowena Bird to "My Dear Mother," Apr. 6, 1900, reprinted in *Mission Studies* 18: 11 (Nov. 1900), 344, Williams Papers, OCA.

10. K'ung Hsiang Hsi to Mrs. Susan Bird, typescript of undated letter, Williams Papers, OCA.

11. Mrs. Arthur H. Smith, *Mr. Fei's True Story* (Chicago: Woman's Board of Missions of the Interior, n.d.), 5, OCL.

12. Francis Davis to Lydia Davis, part of undated letter, apparently written in winter of 1899–1900, Davis Papers, OCA.

13. George Williams to Alice Williams, Dec. 9, 1899, Williams Papers, OCA.

14. Bird to "My Dear Mother," Apr. 6, 1900, *Mission Studies,* 343, Williams Papers, OCA.

15. Louise Partridge to Lydia Davis, Jan. 6, 1893 [1894], Davis Papers, OCA.

16. Partridge, "Memorial of Mary Louise Partridge," Williams Papers, OCA. Alice Williams is quoted.

17. Ibid.

18. Ibid. Louise Partridge is quoted in the last letter to her father, dated May 8, 1900.

19. Louise Partridge to Judson Smith, Sept. 29, 1897, ABCFM, reel 320.

20. Partridge, "Memorial of Mary Louise Partridge," Williams Papers, OCA. the letter of May 8, 1900, quoted again.

21. Louise Partridge to Judson Smith, Sept. 29, 1900, ABCFM, reel 320.

22. "Journal of Miss Susan Rowena Bird," typescript, p. 7, entry of July 5, 1900, Yale. Hereafter referred to as Bird Journal.

23. Louise Partridge to Judson Smith, Sept. 29, 1897, ABCFM, reel 320.

24. Eva Price, *China Journal,* 163–165.

25. Partridge, "Memorial of Mary Louise Partridge," Williams Papers, OCA.

26. Vinton Books, Compilation of Biographies of Missionaries, vol. 4, CL.

27. "Manual for Missionary Candidates" (Boston: Beacon Press), Corbin Papers, OCA.

28. Louise Partridge to "My dear friends," Nov. 1899 addition to Mar. 1899 excerpt, typescript, Pond Papers, OCA.

29. Louise Partridge to Alice Williams, May 29, 1900, Williams Papers, OCA.

30. Alice Williams to Paul Corbin, Nov. 20, 1932, OSMA, OCA.

31. Ibid.

32. Partridge, "Memorial of Mary Louise Partridge," Williams Papers, OCA.

33. Louise Partridge to Alice Williams, May 29, 1900, Williams Papers, OCA.

10. FRIENDSHIPS

1. Lydia Davis, "Letters to My Grandchildren," p. 79, Davis Papers, OCA.

2. Ibid., p. 79–80.

3. Commencement programme, May 21, 1891, College General, Commencement Files, OCA.

4. "History of Miss'ys," OSMA, OCA.

5. George Williams to Judson Smith, Nov. 23, 1892, ABCFM, reel 321.

6. Examination Report, Mar. 12, 1895, ABCFM, reel 321.

7. Jennie Clapp to Alice Williams, May 25, 1900, Williams Papers, OCA.

8. "In Loving Remembrance," 439–40, Williams Papers, OCA.

9. George Williams to Judson Smith, Jan. 4, 1894, ABCFM, reel 321.

10. The Williamses' other daughters were named Rhea Eloise and Helen Marie.

11. Lydia Davis to "Mr. Price," Nov. 27, 1894, ABCFM, reel 321.

12. "Three Thousand Dollars," Williams Papers, OCA. In a letter of May 10, 1900 (George Williams to Alice Williams, Williams Papers, OCA), Williams identifies the house as being in "Hua chua'n." But in a letter to her on May 28, 1900 (also Williams Papers, OCA), he calls the suburb "Hsi chuang." A hand-drawn map of Taiku and vicinity gives the name of the South Suburb as Le-yuan-tzu, ABCFM, reel 322.

13. Alice Williams to Paul Corbin, Nov. 20, 1932, OSMA, OCA.

14. George Williams to "Dear Ella," Oct. 27, 1899, Williams Papers, OCA.

15. Francis Davis to Lydia Davis, Feb. 19, 1900, Davis Papers, OCA.

16. Alice Williams to Judson Smith, Jan. 24, 1900, ABCFM, reel 323.

17. George Williams to "Dear Ella," Oct. 27, 1899, Williams Papers, OCA.

18. George Williams to Alice Williams, Feb. 19, 1900, Williams Papers, OCA.

19. Francis Davis to Lydia Davis, Dec. 20, 1899, Davis Papers, OCA.

20. George Williams to Alice Williams, Feb. 15, 1900, Williams Papers, OCA.

21. George Williams to Alice Williams, Dec. 29, 1899, Williams Papers, OCA.

22. George Williams to Alice Williams, Feb. 15, 1900, Williams Papers, OCA.

23. George Williams to Alice Williams, Mar. 30, 1900, Williams Papers, OCA.

24. George Williams to Alice Williams, Nov. 10, 1899, Williams Papers, OCA.

25. Francis Davis to Lydia Davis, Nov. 9, 1899, Davis Papers, OCA.

26. Francis Davis to Lydia Davis, part of undated letter, c. Jan. 1900, Davis Papers, OCA.

27. Francis Davis to Lydia Davis, undated letter written while in village of Chang Sheng K'ou during scouting tour for new station that began Mar. 19, 1900, Davis Papers, OCA.

28. George Williams to Alice Williams, Dec. 9, 1899, Williams Papers, OCA.

29. George Williams to Alice Williams, Nov. 19, 1899, Williams Papers, OCA.

30. George Williams to Alice Williams, Mar. 30, 1900, Williams Papers, OCA.

31. Charles Price to C. O. Hale, Dec. 3, 1895, Hale Papers, WRHS.

32. Francis Davis to Lydia Davis, Dec. 20, 1899, Davis Papers, OCA.

33. George Rippey Stewart, *Bret Harte: Argonaut and Exile* (New York: Houghton Mifflin, 1931), p. 178.

34. "In Loving Remembrance," 441, Williams Papers, OCA.

35. Jennie Atwater to "Dear Lura," Aug. 26, 1893, typescript, Ohio.

36. Jennie Atwater to "Father Pond," Oct. 23, 1893, typescript, Ohio.

37. Ernest Atwater to "My Dear Friend Breed," Feb. 17, 1893, typescript, Ohio.

38. Ernest Atwater to "Dear Father and Mother Pond," Nov. 22, 1896, OSMA, OCA.

39. Ernest Atwater, part of letter, typescript, apparently to the Ponds, Dec. 4, 1896, Pond Papers, OCA.

40. Ibid.

41. Ernest Atwater to "Dear Folks at Home," Aug. 23, 1897, Pond Papers, OCA.

42. "History of Miss'ys," OSMA, OCA.

43. Typescript, untitled reminiscences about and copies of letters from Ernestine Atwater, Pond Papers, OCA. Rowena Bird is quoted in excerpt from a letter of Nov. 30, 1896.

44. Eva Price to "My dear friend," Mar. 1, 1899, Williams Papers, OCA.

45. Typescript, untitled reminiscences about and copies of letters from Ernestine Atwater, Pond Papers, OCA.

46. Ernest Atwater to "Dear Ones at Home," Apr. 10, 1898, Pond Papers, OCA.
47. Ernest Atwater to "Dear Father and Mother Pond," Nov. 22, 1897, Pond Papers, OCA.
48. Ernest Atwater to "Dear Ones at Home," Apr. 10, 1898, Pond Papers, OCA.
49. Ernest Atwater to "Dear Father and Mother Pond," Nov. 22, 1897, Pond Papers, OCA.
50. Ernest Atwater to "Dear Ones at Home," Apr. 10, 1898, Pond Papers, OCA.
51. Eva Price, *China Journal,* 181.
52. Ibid., 178.
53. Ernest Atwater to "Dear Ones at Home," Apr. 10, 1898, Pond Papers, OCA.
54. "A Marriage in China," undated, unspecified newspaper clipping, Clippings, OCA.
55. Lizzie Atwater to "Dear Grandma Thompson," Mar. 15, 1899, Williams Papers, OCA.
56. Lizzie Atwater to "My dear Grandma Thompson," July 18, 1899, Williams Papers, OCA.
57. Lizzie Atwater to Alice Williams, Apr. 25, 1900, Williams Papers, OCA.
58. Eva Price to "My dear, one and all in the Pond homestead," Jan. 4, 1899, Pond Papers, OCA.
59. George Farthing to Dwight Howard Clapp, Feb. 13, 1900, Pond Papers, OCA.
60. Eva Price to "My dear friend," Sept. 12, 1898, Williams Papers, OCA.
61. Annual Report for the Fenchoufu Station for the year 1899, ABCFM Papers, Houghton.
62. Francis Davis to Lydia Davis, Dec. 20, 1899, Davis Papers, OCA.
63. Ibid.
64. Louise Partridge to Lydia Davis, Apr. 12, 1898, Williams Papers, OCA.
65. Lizzie Atwater to "Dear Grandma Thompson," Mar. 15, 1899, Williams Papers, OCA.
66. Lizzie Atwater to Alice Williams, Apr. 25, 1900, Davis Papers, OCA.

11. TRIUMPHS AND ADVERSITIES

1. Report of Boys' Boarding School and Academy Taiku for 1899, ABCFM Papers, Houghton.
2. Report of Woman's Work for Tai-Ku for 1899, ABCFM Papers, Houghton.
3. Fen Chow Fu Report, Dec. 31 1899, from "Copy of Reports," Williams Papers, OCA.
4. Table of Statistics for the Year ending Dec. 31, 1899, American Board Shansi Mission, ABCFM Papers, Houghton.
5. Annual Report for Fenchoufu Station for the year 1899, ABCFM Papers, Houghton.
6. Charles Price to C. O. Hale, Jan. 5, 1899 [1900], Hale Papers, WRHS.
7. Ernest Atwater to "Dear Uncle Fred," June 23, 1893, typescript, Ohio.
8. Ernest Atwater to "Dear Folks at Home," Oct. 23, 1893, typescript, Ohio.
9. Ibid.
10. Francis Price, Description of Mission work in Shansi, 1877–1889, OSMA, OCA.
11. Ibid.
12. Ibid.
13. Downs, "Oberlin in China, 1880–1900," 15.
14. Charles Price to C. O. Hale, Dec. 3, 1895, Hale Papers, WRHS.
15. George Williams to Judson Smith, Nov. 23, 1892, ABCFM, reel 321.
16. George Williams to Judson Smith, Feb. 14, 1893, ABCFM, reel 321.
17. Jennie Atwater to "Dear Ones at Home," Feb. 7, 1893, Williams Papers, OCA.

18. Depository's Report for Year ending Dec. 31, 1899, ABCFM Papers, Houghton.

19. Annual Report for Fenchoufu Station for the year 1899, ABCFM Papers, Houghton.

20. Report of Taiku Station Medical Work for year ending Dec. 31, 1899, ABCFM Papers, Houghton.

21. Table of Statistics for the Year ending Dec. 31, 1899, American Board Shansi Mission, ABCFM Papers, Houghton.

22. Report of the Treasurer of the Shansi Mission of the A.B.C.F.M. for 1899, ABCFM Papers, Houghton.

23 Report of Committee on Building 1899, ABCFM Papers, Houghton.

24. George Williams to Alice Williams, Dec. 9, 1899, Williams Papers, OCA.

25. George Williams to Alice Williams, Feb. 15, 1900, Williams Papers, OCA.

26. George Williams to Alice Williams, Feb. 19, 1900, Williams Papers, OCA.

27. George Williams to Alice Williams, Apr. 27, 1900, Williams Papers, OCA.

28. George Williams to Alice Williams, May 28, 1900, Williams Papers, OCA.

29. Jennie Clapp to Lydia Davis, Jan. 4, 1900, Davis Papers, OCA.

30. Eva Price to "My dear friends, one and all in the Pond homestead," Jan. 4, 1899, Pond Papers, OCA.

31. Eva Price to "My dear friends," Dec. 30, 1899, Pond Papers, OCA.

32. Unless otherwise noted, the story of the death of Hu'er and the subsequent Fei-Liu controversy is an amalgam taken from the following accounts: five letters, George Williams to Alice Williams, Feb. 2, 1899 (which, because of the subject matter, is obviously misdated; it should read 1900), Feb. 15, Feb. 19, Mar. 4, and Apr. 27, 1900, all Williams Papers, OCA; Jennie Clapp to Lydia Davis, Jan. 4, 1900, Davis Papers, OCA; Francis Davis to Lydia Davis, part of undated letter, c. Jan. 1900, Davis Papers, OCA; Eva Price to "My dear friend," Mar. 26, 1900, Pond Papers, OCA; and Dwight Howard Clapp to Judson Smith, Mar. 30, 1900, ABCFM, reel 323.

33. Alice Williams to Paul Corbin, Nov. 20, 1932, OSMA, OCA.

34. Jennie Clapp to "My dearest Mary Ella," Nov. 10, 1899, Pond Papers, OCA.

35. Eva Price, *China Journal*, 203.

36. Harold S. Matthews, *Seventy-five Years of the North China Mission* (Peking: Yenching University, 1942), 63.

37. Ibid.

12. THE VOLCANO

1. Pat Barr, *To China with Love: The Lives and Times of Protestant Missionaries in China 1860–1900* (London: Secker and Warburg, 1972), 154.

2. Geoffrey Barraclough, ed., *The Times Concise Atlas of World History* (Maplewood, N.J.: Hammond, 1982), 107.

3. Fairbank, *China*, 209.

4. Varg, *Missionaries, Chinese and Diplomats*, 11.

5. Charles Price to C. O. Hale, Jan. 1, 1895, Hale Papers, WRHS.

6. Peter Fleming, *The Siege at Peking: The Boxer Rebellion* (New York: Harper, 1959), 57.

7. Speer, *Memorial of Horace Tracy Pitkin*, 254.

8. Forsythe, *American Missionary Community*, 81.

9. Richard, *Forty-five Years in China*, 294–97.

13. THE BOXERS

1. Esherick, *The Origins of the Boxer Uprising,* 293.

2. Fleming, *Siege at Peking,* 35.

3. Ibid., 52–53.

4. Charles Price to C. O. Hale, Jan. 5, 1899 [1900], Hale Papers, WRHS.

5. Campfield, "Oberlin in China, 1881–1957," 32.

6. George Williams to Alice Williams, May 28, 1900, Williams Papers, OCA.

7. Louise Partridge to "My Dear Mother," Sept. 28, 1894, Pond Papers, OCA.

8. Louise Partridge to "Dear Friends," Mar. 1899, Pond Papers, OCA.

9. Lydia Davis, "Letters to My Grandchildren," p. 43.

10. Eva Price, *China Journal,* 105.

11. Ernest Atwater to "Dear Folks at Home," Aug. 23, 1897, Pond Papers, OCA.

12. Partridge, "Memorial of Mary Louise Partridge," Williams Papers, OCA.

13. Eva Price, *China Journal,* 169.

14. Rowena Bird, May 10, 1900, handwritten copy, "Miss Bird's letters to her Mother," Williams Papers, OCA.

15. Rowena Bird, possibly Mar. 21, 1892, "Miss Bird's letters," William Papers, OCA.

16. Rowena Bird to "My Dear Mrs. Pond," Oct. 21, 1899, Pond Papers, OCA.

17. Francis Davis to Rev. McInnes Neilson and Ravenna Congregational Christian Endeavor Society, Mar. 30, 1900, Davis Papers, OCA.

18. Francis Davis to Rev. McInnes Nielson [*sic*] and Christian Endeavors of Congregational Church, Ravenna, Ohio, U.S.A., Apr. 30, 1900, Davis Papers, OCA.

19. Francis Davis to Judson Smith, Apr. 28, 1900, ABCFM, reel 323.

20. Dwight Howard Clapp to Judson Smith, Mar. 30, 1900, ABCFM, reel 323.

21. Partridge, "Memorial of Mary Louise Partridge," Williams Papers, OCA.

22. Rowena Bird to "My Dear Mother," Apr. 6, 1900, reprinted in *Mission Studies,* 18:11 (Nov. 1900), 343–44, Williams Papers, OCA.

23. Ibid., 344.

24. Annual Report, Apr. 25, 1900, OSMA, OCA. The report apparently covered the operations of the entire Shansi Mission. It was signed Charles Price, S. Rowena Bird and G. L. Williams.

25. Francis Davis to Judson Smith, Apr. 28, 1900, ABCFM, reel 323.

26. George Williams to Alice Williams, May 10, 1900, Williams Papers, OCA.

27. Jennie Clapp to Alice Williams, May 25, 1900, Williams Papers, OCA.

14. COLLEAGUES

1. "In Loving Remembrance," 444, Williams Papers, OCA. E. Henry Ewing is quoted.

2. Ibid., 443, Ewing again quoted.

3. Kyle, *In Memory of Mary Morrill and Annie Gould,* 35, USMA.

4. Isaac Ketler, *The Tragedy at Paotingfu* (New York: Fleming H. Revell, 1902), 152.

5. Kyle, *In Memory of Mary Morrill and Annie Gould,* 111, USMA. Dr. Willis C. Noble is quoted.

6. Partridge, "Memorial of Mary Louise Partridge," Williams Papers, OCA.

7. Kyle, *In Memory of Mary Morrill and Annie Gould,* 25, USMA. Morrill letter of Jan. 24, 1890 is quoted.

8. "In Loving Remembrance," 444, Williams Papers, OCA. Ewing is quoted.

9. Tsuai Yu to Mrs. Gould, undated, USMA.

10. Ketler, *Tragedy at Paotingfu,* 151.

11. Partridge, "Memorial of Mary Louise Partridge," Williams Papers, OCA.

12. Kyle, *In Memory of Mary Morrill and Annie Gould,* 76, USMA.

13. Partridge, "Memorial of Mary Louise Partridge," Williams Papers, OCA.

14. Mary Morrill to Mrs. Gould, May 27, 1899, USMA.

15. Kyle, *In Memory of Mary Morrill and Annie Gould,* 87, USMA. Gould letter of May 1899 is quoted.

16. The section was formerly named Westbrook and subsequently called the Deering District.

17. Kyle, *In Memory of Mary Morrill and Annie Gould,* 10, USMA.

18. Ketler, *Tragedy at Paotingfu,* 140–41.

19. Kyle, *In Memory of Mary Morrill and Annie Gould,* 13, USMA.

20. Ketler, *Tragedy at Paotingfu,* 147.

21. Annie Gould to "Dear Ones," Feb. 16, 1899, USMA.

22. Kyle, *In Memory of Mary Morrill and Annie Gould,* 11, USMA.

23. Ibid., 78. Gould letter of June 1897 is quoted.

24. Ketler, *Tragedy at Paotingfu,* 241.

25. Eva Price, *China Journal,* 162.

26. Speer, *Memorial of Horace Tracy Pitkin,* 134, Yale.

27. Pitkin Genealogy, Leith Papers, OCA.

28. Ibid.

29. Speer, *Memorial of Horace Tracy Pitkin,* 30, Yale.

30. Ibid., 62.

31. Ibid., 62–64.

32. Clifton J. Phillips, "The Student Volunteer Movement and Its Role in China Missions, 1886–1920," in John K. Fairbank, ed., *The Missionary Enterprise in China and America* (Cambridge, Mass.: Harvard Univ. Press, 1974), 92.

33. Speer, *Memorial of Horace Tracy Pitkin,* 204, Yale.

34. Annie Gould to "Dear Ones," Mar. 23, 1899, USMA.

35. Speer, *Memorial of Horace Tracy Pitkin,* 202, Yale.

36. Kyle, *In Memory of Mary Morrill and Annie Gould,* 89, USMA. Morrill letter of Mar. 1900 is quoted.

37. The Nobles had left on furlough. S. Henry Ewing and his wife left in May.

38. Speer, *Memorial of Horace Tracy Pitkin,* 250, Yale.

39. Ibid., 267.

40. Kyle, *In Memory of Mary Morrill and Annie Gould,* 13, USMA. The visiting missionary wife was Mrs. Frances E. Clark.

41. Speer, *Memorial of Horace Tracy Pitkin,* 255, Yale.

42. Ibid., 271.

43. Ibid., 254.

44. Kyle, *In Memory of Mary Morrill and Annie Gould,* 100, USMA. Morrill letter of May 30, 1900 is quoted.

45. Ibid.

46. Ketler, *Tragedy at Paotingfu,* 340.

47. Ibid., 341–42.

48. Ibid.

49. The incident in Jan. 1895 is an amalgam of two sources: Kyle, *In Memory of Mary Morrill and Annie Gould,* 61–63, USMA, and Annie Gould to "Dear friends at home," Jan. 10, 1895, typescript, USMA.

50. Kyle, *In Memory of Mary Morrill and Annie Gould,* 103. The last letter from Annie Gould to her family, dated May 29, 1900, is quoted.

51. Ibid., 95.

15. UNDER SIEGE

1. Esherick, *Origins of the Boxer Uprising,* 287.

2. Barr, *To China with Love,* 176.

3. Fleming, *Siege at Peking,* 97.

4. Barr, *To China with Love,* 176.

5. *Ravenna Republican,* Aug. 15, 1901.

6. George Williams to Alice Williams, May 28, 1900, Williams Papers, OCA. This is the last letter that Alice received from him.

7. Eva Price, *China Journal,* 225.

8. Journal Letter of Rev. C. W. Price, 1900, typescript, OSMA, OCA. Hereafter referred to as C. W. Price Journal.

9. *Oberlin News,* July 29, 1902.

10. Ibid. The article, entitled "From the Dead," included a letter from Eva Price to "Dear News" dated June 4, 1900. It was dug up with other letters in the cellar of Dr. Willis Noble's house in Paotingfu, where Pitkin buried them. They were discovered when the cellar was being excavated.

11. Eva Price, *China Journal,* 221.

12. Ibid., 222.

13. *Oberlin News,* July 29, 1902.

14. Lizzie Atwater to Robert Graham, June 6, 1900, ABCFM, reel 322.

15. Ernest Atwater to "Dear Father and Mother, And all in the Old Home," June 6, 1900, Leith Papers, OCA.

16. Jennie Clapp to Alice Williams, May 25, 1900, Williams Papers, OCA.

17. Ibid.

18. Francis Davis to Lydia Davis, May 28, 1900, OSMA, OCA.

19. C. W. Price Journal, OSMA, OCA.

20. Campfield, "Oberlin in China, 1881–1951," 50–51.

21. Luella Miner, *Two Heroes of Cathay* (New York: Fleming H. Revell, 1903), 184.

22. Louise Partridge to "Dear friends," June 19, 1900, ABCFM, reel 323.

23. Ibid.

24. Ibid.

25. Ibid.

26. Ibid.

27. Ibid.

28. Louise Partridge to Alice Williams, Apr. 29, 1900, Williams Papers, OCA.

29. Louise Partridge to "Dear Edith & Nellie," June 23, 1900, Williams Papers, OCA.

30. Louise Partridge to Alice Williams, June 25, 1900, OSMA, OCA.

31. Bird Letter, Bird Papers, OCA.

32. George Williams to Alice Williams, May 28, 1900, Williams Papers, OCA.

33. Bird Journal, Yale.

34. Louise Partridge to "Dear Friend," July 2, 1900, ABCFM, reel 323.

35. Eva Price to "My dear friends," June 22, 1900, Williams Papers, OCA.

36. Eva Price, *China Journal,* 32.

37. Eva Price to "My dear friends," June 22, 1900, Williams Papers, OCA.

38. Ibid.

39. Ibid.

40. Eva Price, *China Journal,* 226.

41. C. W. Price Journal, OSMA, OCA.

42. Eva Price, a record of events, June 28, 1900, ABCFM, reel 323. Hereafter referred to as Eva Price Record. The entry is dated June 29.

43. Eva Price, *China Journal,* 120.

44. Marshall Broomhall, *Martyred Missionaries of the China Inland Mission* (London: Morgan and Scott, 1901), 156–57.

45. The episode is an amalgam of Eva Price Record, ABCFM, reel 323, entry of June 29, and Eva Price to "My dear Belle," June 26, 1900, Williams Papers, OCA. The latter is signed "Jean," and in the margin someone has scrawled "Jennie Price." But Jennie Price, wife of Francis Price, was then in Micronesia. The letter is datelined "Fen Chofu." It could only have been written by Eva Price, especially as the two letters are identical in many instances in describing the incident. Eva's middle name was Jane, and it is conceivable that she was known to "Belle" as Jennie. The only other possible author is Jennie Clapp, but she was in Taiku, under siege, at the time, and no one but couriers traveled between the two Shansi Mission stations.

46. Eva Price to "My dear Belle," June 26, 1900, Williams Papers, OCA.

47. Ibid.

48. Ibid.

49. "The Shansi Massacres," typescript, Williams Papers, OCA. Although someone has written in the margin, "Notes taken from Mr. Fu's [*sic*] verbal account . . . written out by H.D. Porter," this is actually an account by Fei Chi Hao. In a letter to Chauncy Pond on Dec. 17, 1900 (Pond Papers, OCA), Mrs. Arthur H. Smith, author of *Mr. Fei's True Story,* enclosed a separate note that she labeled "private": "Perhaps the ghastly fear that came to me has haunted you. For your sakes I forced myself to ask dear Mr. Fei the hard question. 'Tell me the bottom truth[,] my young brother [,]—did—the—worst come to any of our ladies?' He dropped his eyes a minute and then said, 'No, not any of these I believe but it came to two C.I.M. ladies in another place—after *they were dead.*'!!!"

50. Louise Partridge to "Dear Friend," July 2, 1900, ABCFM, reel 323.

51. Ibid.

52. "Er Wu's Story of the the Massacre of Chinese Christians at Ti Ku [*sic*]," typescript of story related in Peking, Apr. 26, 1901, by Er Wu to Iranaeus J. Atwood, Williams Papers, OCA.

53. Louise Partridge to "Dear Friend," July 2, 1900, ABCFM, reel 323.

16. PAOTINGFU: THE FIRST LOSSES

1. The story of the massacre is an amalgam of several sources, unless otherwise noted: Ketler, *Tragedy at Paotingfu,* 377–91; Matthews, *Seventy-five Years;* J. Walter Lowrie, "The Missionary Crisis in China: The Tragedy at Paotingfu," Leaflet No. 6, Board of Foreign Missions of the Presbyterian Church in the U.S.A., Pond Papers, OCA; Speer, *Memorial of Horace Tracy Pitkin,* 284–92, Yale; Kyle, *In Memory of Mary Morrill and Annie Gould,* USMA; Luella Miner, *China's Book of Martyrs* (New York: Pilgrim Press, 1903), 355–67, 372, 379–84; and Smith, *China in Convulsion* 2:683. Some writers sensationalized the terrible nature of the tragedy. According to George Lynch, *The War of the Civilisations* (London: Longmans, Green, 1901), 205, Mary Morrill's breasts were cut off and the two women were naked as they were taken through the streets of Paotingfu.

2. Harold S. Matthews, *Seventy-Five Years of the North China Mission* (Peking: Yenching Univ., 1942), 67.

17. THE FLIGHT FROM SHOU YANG

1. The story of the flight from Shou Yang is an amalgam of several sources: Broomhall, *Martyred Missionaries;* "The Sheo-Yang and Tai Yuen-fu Medical Mission: An attempt to reach the surviving native Christians," an article containing extracts from the diaries of Dr. E. H. Edwards published in magazine *Supplement to All Nations,* Feb. 1901, Clippings, OCA; E. H. Edwards, *Fire and Sword in Shansi: The Story of the Martyrdom of Foreigners and Chinese Christians* (New York: Fleming H. Revell Company, n.d.); Miner, *China's Book of Martyrs;* "The Martyrdom at T'aiYuen-fu on the 9th of July 1900. By an Eye-Witness," typescript of account of Yung Cheng copied from *Chinese Recorder* of Apr. 1901, published by American Presbyterian Press, Shanghai, Leith Papers, OCA; and the following documents, all in Williams Papers, OCA—P. C. H. Dreyer, *The Boxer Rising and Missionary Massacres* (Toronto: China Inland Mission, n.d.); "The Last Days of the Missionaries (mostly English)," reprinted from the *Shanghai Mercury,* n.d.; "The Story of the Persecution of the Church at Sheo-Yang-hien . . . by Li-Pai, the Shepherd," *Shanghai Mercury,* Jan. 14, 1901; the *Christian,* Nov. 29, 1900; "The Shansi Massacres" [title of article], unspecified, undated newspaper clipping; and "The Reign of Terror in the Western Hills," reprinted from *Shanghai Mercury,* n.d.

18. TAI YUAN: THE COURTYARD OF SLAUGHTER

1. The story of the massacre at Tai Yuan, like the story of the flight from Shou Yang, is an amalgam of the same sources, to wit: Broomhall, *Martyred Missionaries;* "The Sheo-Yang and Tai Yuen-fu Medical Mission: An attempt to reach the surviving native Christians," being extracts from the diaries of Dr. E. H. Edwards, *Supplement to All Nations,* Feb. 1901, Clippings, OCA; E. H. Edwards, *Fire and Sword in Shansi: The Story of the Martyrdom of Foreigners and Chinese Christians* (New York: Fleming H. Revell Company, n.d.); Miner, *China's Book of Martyrs;* "The Martyrdom at T'aiYuen-fu on the 9th of July 1900. By an Eye-Witness," typescript of account of Yung Cheng copied from *Chinese Recorder* of Apr. 1901, published by American Presbyterian Press, Shanghai, Leith Papers, OCA; and the following documents, all in Williams Papers, OCA—P. C. H. Dreyer, *The Boxer Rising and Missionary Massacres* (Toronto: China Inland Mission, n.d.); "The Last Days of the Missionaries (mostly English)," reprinted from the *Shanghai Mercury,* n.d.; "The Story of the Persecution of the Church at Sheo-Yang-hien...by Li-Pai, the

Shepherd," *Shanghai Mercury,* Jan. 14, 1901; the *Christian,* Nov. 29, 1900; "The Shansi Massacres" [title of article], unspecified, undated newspaper clipping; and "The Reign of Terror in the Western Hills," reprinted from *Shanghai Mercury,* n.d.

2. Bird Journal, Yale.

3. The Chinese helpers were Chang Ch'eng Sheng, Liu Hao, Liu P'ai Yuan and Wang Hsi Ho. The teenage student was Ch'ang An.

19. TAIKU: CORNERED

1. Louise Partridge to Alice Williams, June 25, 1900, OSMA.

2. Chang Chen[g] Fu [Er Wu] to Alice Williams, typescript, undated, Williams Papers, OCA.

3. Rowena Bird to "My Dear Friends," July 5, 1900, OSMA, OCA.

4. Diary of Louise Partridge, typescript, OSMA, OCA. Hereafter referred to as Partridge Diary.

5. Bird Letter, Bird Papers, OCA.

6. "The Story of TaiKu Told by Kung Shiang Hsi [K'ung Hsiang Hsi] and Chang Cheng Fu [Er Wu]," typescript, ABCFM, reel 323.

7. Louise Partridge to Alice Williams, June 25, 1900, OSMA, OCA.

8. Mr. Clapps [*sic*] Diary, addressed to "Dear ones at home," and dated "July 4, 12:30 a.m.," typescript, ABCFM, reel 323. Hereafter referred to as Clapp Diary.

9. Partridge Diary, OSMA, OCA.

10. Rowena Bird to "My Dear Friends," July 5, 1900, OSMA, OCA.

11. Bird Letter, Bird Papers, OCA.

12. Francis Davis to "Dear Bro. Pitkin," July 5, 1900, Davis Papers, OCA.

13. Bird Letter, Bird Papers, OCA.

14. Ibid.

15. Clapp Diary, ABCFM, reel 323.

16. Edwards, *Fire and Sword,* 301. Louise Partridge letter to Mrs. Edwards of July 14, 1900, is quoted.

17. Louise Partridge to "Dear friends," June 19, 1900, Williams Papers, OCA.

18. Louise Partridge to her parents, June 25, 1900, Williams Papers, OCA.

19. Partridge, "Memorial of Mary Louise Partridge," Williams Papers, OCA.

20. Chang Chen[g] Fu [Er Wu] to Alice Williams, typescript, undated, Williams Papers, OCA.

21. Ibid.

22. Partridge Diary, OSMA, OCA.

23. Bird Letter, Bird Papers, OCA.

24. Ibid.

25. Bird Journal, Yale.

26. Clapp Diary, ABCFM, reel 323.

27. "The Story of TaiKu," ABCFM, reel 323.

28. Partridge Diary, OSMA, OCA.

29. "The Story of TaiKu," ABCFM, reel 323.

30. Partridge Diary, OSMA, OCA.

31. Bird Journal, Yale.

32. Partridge Diary, OSMA, OCA.
33. Bird Journal, Yale.
34. Miner, *Two Heroes of Cathay,* 187.
35. Ibid., 189.
36. Ibid., 191–92.
37.. Ibid., 196.
38. Ibid., 197.
39. Ibid.
40. Ibid., 199–200.
41. Bird Journal, Yale.
42. Francis Davis to Lydia Davis, May 28, 1900, Davis Papers, OCA.
43. Bird Letter, Bird Papers, OCA.
44. Partridge Diary, OSMA, OCA.
45. Clapp Diary, ABCFM, reel 323.
46. Rowena Bird to Eva Price, July 27, 1900, OSMA, OCA.
47. Francis Davis to Charles Price, July 27, 1900, Davis Papers, OCA.
48. George Williams to Charles Price, July 27, 1900, Williams Papers, OCA.
49. "The Story of TaiKu," ABCFM, reel 323.
50. Miner, *China's Book of Martyrs,* 367.
51. Miner, *Two Heroes of Cathay,* 210.
52. The story of the massacre is an amalgam of several sources: *Peking and Tientsin Times,* Nov. 24, 1900, and Chang Chen[g] Fu [Er Wu] to Alice Williams, undated, typescript, Williams Papers, OCA.; *Ravenna Republican,* Aug. 15, 1901, and Sept. 18, 1902; *Oberlin Tribune,* Nov. 22, 1901; Alice Williams to Florence Fitch, Mar. 3, 1909, Fitch Papers, OCA; Miner, *China's Book of Martyrs,* 468; Dr. E. H. Edwards, "Translation of the two natives who escaped from Tai Ku," and "The Story of TaiKu," ABCFM, reel 323; and the following documents from Williams Papers, OCA—Iranaeus Atwood, Notes, Report of Shansi Mission for 1901, typescript; Iranaeus Atwood to Alice Williams, reprint of letter, undated, in undated, unspecified newspaper; and E. H. Edwards to Alice Williams, Mar. 16, 1901.

20. FENCHOW-FU: ESCAPE TO TRAGEDY

1. Lizzie Atwater to "Dear Ones at Taiku, Mrs. Clapp, Rowena, Louise," July 30, 1900, reprinted in *Oberlin News,* Dec. 25, 1900.
2. C. W. Price Journal, OSMA, OCA.
3. Ibid.
4. Ibid.
5. Atwater found and retrieved his valuables at a pawn shop the following month.
6. Eva Price, *China Journal,* 231.
7. C. W. Price Journal, OSMA, OCA.
8. Ibid.
9. Ibid.
10. Ibid.
11. Ibid.
12. Fei, OCL, 10.
13. Ibid., 11.

14. Ibid.

15. Ibid., 15.

16. C. W. Price Journal, OSMA, OCA.

17. Fei, OCL, 16.

18. Rev. Watts O. Pye, "Story of Lu Chen San, The Murderer of the Fenchow-fu Martyrs in 1900," Williams Papers, OCA. Iranaeus Atwood is quoted.

19. Eva Price, *China Journal,* 266.

20. Fei, OCL, 18–19.

21. Iranaeus Atwood to Alice Williams, Sept. 5, 1901, reprinted in *Oberlin Tribune,* Nov. 22, 1901.

22. Fei, OCL, 19.

23. Lizzie Atwater to "Dear, dear Ones," Aug. 3, 1900, reprinted in *Oberlin News,* Dec. 25, 1900.

21. AFTERMATH

1. Fleming, *Siege at Peking,* 211.

2. Latourette, *History of Christian Missionaries in China,* 511–17.

3. Fleming, *Siege at Peking,* 253.

4. Speer, *Memorial of Horace Tracy Pitkin,* 298.

5. Samuel Isett Woodbridge, *Fifty Years in China* (Richmond, Va.: Presbyterian Committee of Publication, n.d.), 99.

6. H. D. Porter to "Dear Friends," Nov. 4, 1900, Leith Papers, OCA.

7. Speer, *Memorial of Horace Tracy Pitkin,* 296.

8. Iranaeus Atwood to Alice Williams, July 10, 1901, Williams Papers, OCA.

9. Iranaeus Atwood to Alice Williams, July 25, 1901, reprinted in unspecified, undated newspaper, Williams Papers, OCA.

10. *Ravenna Republican,* Oct. 24, 1901, reprint of an undated letter from E. H. Edwards to *Shanghai Mercury.*

11. Iranaeus Atwood to Lydia Davis, Sept. 25, 1901, Davis Papers, OCA.

12. Fleming, *Siege at Peking,* 236.

13. Smith, *China in Convulsion,* 2:615.

14. Edwards, *Fire and Sword,* 49.

15. Chester C. Tan, *The Boxer Catastrophe* (New York: Octagon, 1967), 152.

16. E. Backhouse and J. O. P. Bland, *Annals and Memoirs of the Court of Peking* (Boston: Houghton Mifflin, 1914), 450–51.

17. Unspecified newspaper, Williams Papers, OCA. The article, datelined "Victoria, Apr. 24," carries the headline "Conger Defends the Missionaries."

18. Robert Bacon, Acting Secretary, State Department, to Rev. James L. Barton, Nov. 20, 1906, Davis Papers, OCA. Lydia received a total of $16,668.73, including $1,500 for property damage and $168.73 in interest. Alice received a total of $16,359.45, including $1,222 for property damage and $137.45 in interest. Both had asked for $20,000.

19. Stuart Creighton Miller, "Ends and Means," in Fairbank, *Missionary Enterprise,* 276.

20. Forsythe, *American Missionary Community,* 84.

21. Miller, "Ends and Means," in Fairbank, *Missionary Enterprise,* 280.

22. Page 6 of a scrap of letter, typescript, signed by I. J. Atwood, Davis Papers, OCA.

23. "Lu Chen San: The Murderer of the Fenchow-fu Martyrs in 1900." Title of typescript letter from Rev. Watts O. Pye, n.d., OSMA, OCA.

24. Lydia Davis to Francis Davis, July 18, 1900, part of letter, Davis Papers, OCA.

25. Lydia Davis to Francis Davis, Aug. 14, 1900, part of letter, Davis Papers, OCA.

26. Francis Davis to Lydia Davis, May 28, 1900, Davis Papers, OCA.

27. W. A. Hemingway to "Dear Father," Aug. 24, 1907, OSMA, OCA.

28. Henry D. Porter to Rev. C. N. Pond, Nov. 11, 1900, Pond Papers, OCA.

29. *Ravenna Republican,* Sept. 18, 1902, copy of report of Iranaeus Atwood to American Board that was sent to Lydia Davis, n.d., OSMA, OCA.

30. Iranaeus Atwood to Alice Williams, Sept. 5, 1901, OSMA, OCA.

31. "The Story of Ehr [*sic*] Wu's 'Blackmail,'" handwritten copy of letter from Iranaeus Atwood, OSMA, OCA.

32. Typewritten sentence, dated 10/1/38, on margin of clipping from *Shanghai Evening Post and Mercury,* July 23, 1943, Alumni Records, OCA.

33. W. F. Bohn to Chi-hao Fei, Nov. 11, 1941, Alumni Records, OCA.

34. "China, the Situation and the Outlook," address by Judson Smith, presented at Annual Meeting of American Board, St. Louis, Oct. 11, 1900 (Boston: Congregational House, 1900), Davis Papers, OCA.

35. Barr, *To China with Love,* 195.

36. Woodbridge, *Fifty Years in China,* 215.

37. Lutz, *Christian Missions in China,* xx. T'ang Liang-li is quoted.

EPILOGUE

1. The philanthropist, who gave $20,000, was D. Willis James.

2. *Oberlin Alumni Magazine* 87:2 (Spring 1991), 17.

3. "Around the Arch," *Student News and Views,* undated, first edition of the publication, OCA.

4. *Oberlin Alumni Magazine* 87:2 (Spring 1991), 17.

5. Unspecified clipping, dated 1958, OCA.

6. *Oberlin Review,* Nov. 12, 1993.

Bibliography

MANUSCRIPTS

The Congregational Library, Boston

Vinton Books, vols. 1–4 (Photocopy)

China: Authors (Pamphlets)

Houghton Library, Harvard University, Cambridge, Mass.

Papers, American Board of Commissioners for Foreign Missions to Asia, 1827–1919

Oberlin College Archives, Oberlin, Ohio

Alumni Records, 1836–1977

College General, 1834–1988

Files in the Office of the Archivist

Letters, Boxer Martyrs

Missionaries, 1888–1917

Oberlin Shansi Memorial Association, 1882–1983

Papers of George N. Allen, c. 1830–1895

Papers of Susan Rowena Bird, 1893–1898

Papers of Paul L. Corbin, 1904–1936

Papers of Lydia Lord Davis, 1862–1944

Papers of Florence M. Fitch, 1807–1951

Papers of J. C. Leith, 1851–1954

Papers of Chauncy N. Pond, 1892–1916

Papers of Mr. and Mrs. George L. Williams, 1883–1952

Papers of George Frederick Wright, 1911–1921

Registrar's Office: Student Grade Records

Oberlin College Library, Special Collections

Cochrane, Thomas. *Atlas of China in Provinces.* Shanghai: Christian Literature Society for China, 1913.

Smith, Mrs. Arthur H. *Mr. Fei's True Story.* Chicago: Women's Board of Missions of the Interior, n.d.

Woodbridge, Samuel Isett. *Fifty Years in China.* Richmond, Va.: Presbyterian Committee of Publications, n.d.
Special Collections, United States Military Academy Library, West Point, N.Y.
Papers of Annie Allender Gould, 1867–1900
Western Reserve Historical Society, Cleveland
Papers of Jonathan Hale Family, 1763–1950
Yale Divinity School Library, New Haven
General Holdings: Manuscripts/Pamphlets
China Records: Personal Papers

BOOKS, ARTICLES, DISSERTATIONS, THESES

Anderson, John A. *Autobiography of John A. Anderson, M.D., China Inland Mission.* Aberdeen, Scotland: Aberdeen Journals Ltd., 1948.

Backhouse, E., and J. O. P. Bland, *Annals and Memoirs of the Court of Peking.* Boston: Houghton Mifflin, 1914.

Barnard, John. *From Evangelicalism to Progressivism at Oberlin College, 1866–1917.* Columbus: Ohio State Univ. Press, 1969.

Barnett, Suzanne Wilson, and John King Fairbank, eds. *Christianity in China: Early Protestant Missionary Writings.* Cambridge, Mass.: Harvard Univ. Press, 1985.

Barr, Pat. *To China with Love: The Lives and Times of Protestant Missionaries in China 1860–1900.* London: Secker and Warburg, 1972.

Barraclough, Geoffrey, ed. *The Times Concise Atlas of World History.* Maplewood, N.J.: Hammond, 1982.

Barrows, John Henry. *The Christian Conquest of Asia.* New York: Charles Scribner, 1899.

Baumann, Roland, and Carol Jacobs. "The Memorial Arch: An Unfolding Story," *Oberlin Alumni Magazine* 87:2 (Spring 1991), 15–18.

_______ . "Memorial Arch: An unfinished Story," *Observer,* May 24, 1990, p. 8.

Bohr, Paul Richard. *Famine in China and the Missionary: Timothy Richard as Relief Administrator and Advocate of National Reform, 1876–1884.* Cambridge, Mass.: East Asian Research Center, Harvard University, 1972.

Broomhall, Marshall. *Martyred Missionaries of the China Inland Mission.* London: Morgan and Scott, 1901.

Campfield, Mary Tarpley. "Oberlin in China, 1881–1951." Ph.D. diss., University of Virginia, 1974.

Carlson, Ellsworth C. *Oberlin in Asia: The First Hundred Years, 1882–1982.* Oberlin, Ohio: Oberlin Shansi Memorial Association, 1982.

_______ . *The Foochow Missionaries,* 1847–1880. Cambridge, Mass.: Harvard Univ. Press, 1974.

Cohen, Paul A. "The Contested Past: The Boxers as History and Myth," *Journal of Asian Studies* 51:1 (Feb. 1992), 82–113.

Crawford, Elizabeth A. "The Experience of Dedication and Optimism in the Face of Adversity, the Account of Ming Hsien Academy, Oberlin-in-China, 1937–1950." Honors Thesis, Oberlin College, 1981.

Crouch, Archie R., et al, eds., *Christianity in China: A Scholars' Guide to Resources in the Libraries and Archives of the United States.* Armonk, N.Y.: M. E. Sharpe.

Cummings, Joe, and Richard Storey. *China.* Hawthorn, Australia: Lonely Planet Publications, 1991.

Downs, Ray F. "Oberlin in China, 1880–1900." Senior Thesis, Oberlin College, 1954.

Duiker, William J. *Cultures in Collision: The Boxer Rebellion.* San Rafael, Calif.: Presidio, 1978.

Esherick, Joseph W. *The Origins of the Boxer Uprising.* Berkeley: Univ. of California Press, 1987.

Edwards, E. H. *Fire and Sword in Shansi: The Story of the Martyrdom of Foreigners and Chinese Christians.* New York: Fleming H. Revell, n.d.

Fairbank, John K. *China: A New History.* Cambridge, Mass.: Harvard Univ. Press, 1992.

Fairbank, John K., ed. *The Missionary Enterprise in China and America.* Cambridge, Mass.: Harvard Univ. Press, 1974.

Fairchild, James H. *Oberlin: The Colony and the College.* Oberlin, Ohio: E. J. Goodrich, 1883.

Fleming, Peter. *The Siege at Peking: The Boxer Rebellion.* New York: Harper, 1959.

Forsyth, Robert Coventry. *The China Martyrs of 1900.* London: Religious Tract Society, 1904.

Forsythe, Sidney A. *An American Missionary Community in China, 1895–1905.* Cambridge, Mass.: East Asian Research Center, Harvard University, 1971.

General Catalogue of Oberlin College, 1833–1908. Oberlin, Ohio: Oberlin College, 1909.

Gillin, Donald G. *Warlord: Yen Hsi-shan in Shansi Province, 1911–1949.* Princeton, N.J.: Princeton Univ. Press, 1967.

Glover, Archibald E. *A Thousand Miles of Miracle in China.* London: Hodder and Stoughton, 1908.

Green, Elizabeth Alden. *Mary Lyon and Mount Holyoke: Opening the Gates.* Hanover, N.H.: Univ. Press of New England, 1979.

Hand, Alexa. "Oberlin Reformers and China's Quest for National Sal- vation, 1927–1937." East Asian Studies Honors Thesis, Oberlin College, 1976.

Hersey, John. *The Call.* New York: Penguin, 1985.

Hinman, Susan F. *Ming Hsien: Memorial to Heroes of Three Nations.* New York: n.p., 1958.

Horizon Book of the Arts of China. New York: American Heritage, 1969.

Hsu, Immanuel C. Y. *China Without Mao.* New York: Oxford Univ. Press, 1990.

———. *The Rise of Modern China.* New York: Oxford Univ. Press, 1970.

Hummel, Arthur W. *Eminent Chinese of the Ch'ing Period (1644–1912).* 2 vols. Washington: GPO, 1943–44.

Hunter, Jane. *The Gospel of Gentility: American Women Missionaries in Turn-of-the-Century China.* New Haven, Conn.: Yale Univ. Press, 1984.

Hyatt, Irwin T. Jr. *Our Ordered Lives Confess: Three Nineteenth-Century American Missionaries in East Shantung.* Cambridge, Mass.: Harvard Univ. Press, 1976.

Ketler, Isaac. *The Tragedy at Paotingfu.* New York: Fleming H. Revell, 1902.

Latourette, Kenneth Scott. *A History of Christian Missions in China.* New York: Macmillan, 1929.

Legge, James. *Confucius: Confucian Analects, The Great Learning and the Doctrine of the Mean.* Oxford: Clarendon Press, 1893. Reprint, New York: Dover Publications, 1971.

Lodwick, Kathleen, ed. *The Chinese Recorder Index: A Guide to Christian Missions in Asia, 1867–1941,* vol. 2. Wilmington, Del.: Scholarly Resources,1986.

Lutz, Jessie G., ed. *Christian Missions in China: Evangelists of What?* Lexington, Mass.: Heath, 1965.

Lynch, George. *The War of the Civilisations.* London: Longmans, Green, 1901.

Matthews, Harold S. *Seventy-five Years of the North China Mission.* Peking: Yenching University, 1942.

Miner, Luella. *China's Book of Martyrs.* New York: Pilgrim Press, 1903.

———. *Two Heroes of Cathay.* New York: Fleming H. Revell, 1903.

Phillips, Clifton Jackson. *Protestant America and the Pagan World: The First Half Century of the American Board of Commissioners for Foreign Missions, 1810–1860.* Cambridge, Mass.: East Asian Research Center, Harvard University, 1969.

Poetical Works of Bret Harte. Cambridge, Mass.: Riverside Press, 1874.

Price, Eva Jane. *China Journal 1889–1900: An American Missionary Family During the Boxer Rebellion.* New York: Collier, 1989.

Richard, Timothy. *Forty-five Years in China.* London: Unwin, 1916.

Ruoff, E. G., ed. *Death Throes of a Dynasty: Letters and Diaries of Charles and Bessie Ewing, Missionaries to China.* Kent, Ohio: Kent State Univ. Press, 1990.

Seagrave, Sterling. *Dragon Lady: The Life and Legend of the Last Empress of China.* New York: Knopf, 1992.

Smith, A. H. *China in Convulsion.* 2 vols. Edinburgh: Oliphant, Anderson and Ferrier, 1901.

Smith, Mrs. Arthur H. *Mr. Fei's True Story.* Chicago: Woman's Board of Missions of the Interior, n.d.

Spence, Jonathan. *To Change China: Western Advisers in China, 1620–1960.* New York: Penguin, 1980.

———. *The Memory Palace of Matteo Ricci.* New York: Viking/Penguin, 1984.

_______ . *The Search for Modern China.* New York: Norton, 1990.

Stewart, George Rippey. *Bret Harte, Argonaut and Exile.* New York: Houghton Mifflin, 1931.

Tan, Chester C. *The Boxer Catastrophe.* New York: Octagon, 1967.

Varg, Paul A. *Missionaries, Chinese, and Diplomats: The American Protestant Missionary Movement in China, 1890–1952.* Princeton, N.J.: Princeton Univ. Press, 1958.

Weinstock, Frank J. *Management and Care of the Cataract Patient.* Boston: Blackwell, 1992.

Weisberger, Bernard A. *The American People.* New York: American Heritage, 1971.

Woodbridge, Samuel Isett. *Fifty Years in China.* Richmond, Va.: Presbyterian Committee of Publication, n.d.

❁ Index

Massacre in Shansi was composed in 11.75/13.75 Centaur MT in Quark Express 3.2 on a Macintosh by Kachergis Book Design; printed by sheet-fed offset on 60-pound, acid-free Glatfelter Natural Smooth, and Smyth-sewn and bound over binder's boards in Arrestox B-grade cloth with dust jackets printed in 4 colors and laminated by Braun-Brumfield, designed by Kachergis Book Design of Pittsboro, North Carolina; and published by Syracuse University Press, Syracuse, New York 13244-5160